THE KING'S BENCH

Changing Perspectives on Early Modern Europe

James B. Collins, Professor of History, Georgetown University
Mack P. Holt, Professor of History, George Mason University

(ISSN 1542–3905)

Changing Perspectives on Early Modern Europe brings forward the latest research on Europe during the transformation from the medieval to the modern world. The series publishes innovative scholarship on the full range of topical and geographic fields and includes works on cultural, economic, intellectual, political, religious, and social history.

Private Ambition and Political Alliances:
The Phélypeaux de Pontchartrain Family and Louis XIV's Government, 1650–1715
Sara E. Chapman

The Politics of Piety: Franciscan Preachers During the Wars of Religion, 1560–1600
Megan C. Armstrong

"By My Absolute Royal Authority":
Justice and the Castilian Commonwealth at the Beginning of the First Global Age
J. B. Owens

Meat Matters: Butchers, Politics, and Market Culture in Eighteenth-Century Paris
Sydney Watts

Civic Christianity in Renaissance Italy: The Hospital of Treviso, 1400–1530
David M. D'Andrea

Law, City, and King Legal Culture, Municipal Politics,
and State Formation in Early Modern Dijon
Michael P. Breen

Transforming the Republic of Letters:
Pierre-Daniel Huet and European Intellectual Life, 1650–1720
April G. Shelford

Reformation and the German Territorial State: Upper Franconia, 1300–1630
William Bradford Smith

Jenatsch's Axe: Social Boundaries, Identity, and Myth in the Era of the Thirty Years' War
Randolph C. Head

Enlightened Feudalism:
Seigneurial Justice and Village Society in Eighteenth-Century Northern Burgundy
Jeremy Hayhoe

The King's Bench:
Bailiwick Magistrates and Local Governance in Normandy, 1670–1740
Zoë A. Schneider

THE KING'S BENCH

Bailiwick Magistrates and
Local Governance in Normandy, 1670–1740

Zoë A. Schneider

UNIVERSITY OF ROCHESTER PRESS

First published 2008
University of Rochester Press
668 Mt. Hope Avenue, Rochester, NY 14620, USA
www.urpress.com
and Boydell & Brewer Limited
PO Box 9, Woodbridge, Suffolk IP12 3DF, UK
www.boydellandbrewer.com

ISBN-13: 978–1–58046–292–1
ISBN-10: 1–58046–292–8
ISSN: 1542–3905

Library of Congress Cataloging-in-Publication Data

Schneider, Zoë A., 1961–
    The king's bench : bailiwick magistrates and local governance in Normandy, 1670–1740 / Zoë A. Schneider.
        p. cm. – (Changing perspectives on early modern Europe, ISSN 1542–3905; v. 11)
    Includes bibliographical references and index.
    ISBN-13: 978–1–58046–292–1 (hardcover : alk. paper)
    ISBN-10: 1–58046–292–8 (hardcover : alk. paper) 1. Courts–France– Normandy–History. 2. Bailiffs–France–Normandy–History. 3. Justice, Administration of–France–History. I. Title.
    KJW3183.43.S36 2008
    347.44'201–dc22
                                                                    2008034069

A catalogue record for this title is available from the British Library.
This publication is printed on acid-free paper.
Printed in the United States of America.

To the three boys, Phillip, Ari, and Liam,
and to my parents

CONTENTS

List of Illustrations   ix

Acknowledgments   xi

Chapter 1
Rex and Lex: The Problem of Legislative Sovereignty   1

Chapter 2
Howling with the Wolves: The Normans and Their Courts   29

Chapter 3
Officers and Gentlemen: The Local Judiciary   47

Chapter 4
Law and Lawyers in the "Empire of Custom"   95

Chapter 5
The Red Robe and the Black: Common Courts and the State   124

Chapter 6
Villagers and Townspeople: Civil Litigants   159

Chapter 7
Uncivil Acts: Crime and Punishment   190

Chapter 8
Unruly Governors: Functions and Dysfunctions of the
Common Courts   213

Appendix A: Courts of the Généralité of Rouen   229

Appendix B: Jurisdictions of the Ordinary Courts   230

Appendix C: Criminal Trial Procedure   231

Contents

Notes   233

Glossary of Legal Terms   279

Bibliography   285

Index   315

ILLUSTRATIONS

Maps

1   Map of upper Normandy   xiii

2   Map of the upper pays de Caux, west   xiv

3   Map of the upper pays de Caux, east   xv

Tables

2.1   Local judicial officers of the pays de Caux, 1670–1745   41

3.1   *Qualité* of lower court offices, Normandy, 1702–46   64

3.2   Qualifications of high justice *baillis,* 1692–1740   72

5.1   Office prices and *gages,* royal bailliage of Cany, 1665   134

5.2   High justice appellate cases, Parlement of Rouen, Tournelle Chamber   145

6.1   Civil and criminal litigation with *qualité* of litigants, 1670–1745   163

ACKNOWLEDGMENTS

It takes a village to write a book. The particular village it took to write this one is as diverse and wonderful as any in seventeenth-century France; it includes colleagues, friends, collaborators, several institutions, and two children. As with any early modern community, many of those categories overlap serendipitously with each other. First among them is Jim Collins, whose intellectual range, boundless enthusiasm, and astounding patience lured me away from modern history and made this book thinkable. There are few terroirs that make wines good enough to thank you with. Jonathan Dewald and Bob Schwartz offered invaluable comments when this was still an unwieldy work in progress, and their thoughts stayed with me through many revisions. I am especially indebted to the reviewers whose thoughtful insights made this a far better book than it could have been without them. All of the remaining defects, it goes without saying, are mine.

Institutions are collections of people; but in many cases I can only thank the anonymous committees who make it possible for most of us to do our work. I would particularly like to thank the Fulbright Program, for a memorable and productive year in France; the National Endowment for the Humanities, for a year-long writing grant; and Georgetown University for both grants and fellowships over the years. I owe much to the Smithsonian Institution and its intellectually inquisitive audience for allowing me to present parts of this work over several years of lectures, and to students at Georgetown who challenged me to make history live and breathe. The archivists at the Archives Nationales, and at the departmental archives in Normandy, Brittany, and Burgundy worked a kind of magic bordering on sorcery to locate materials. Parts of this work were also presented at conferences of the Society for French Historical Studies and the American Society for Legal History. The comments of colleagues there allowed me to draw deeply on the communal well of their understanding. The editors at the University of Rochester Press, especially Suzanne Guiod and Katie Hurley, were generous with their advice and their expertise.

There are also personal connections that make a village a place of memory, as well as a place of productive work. I often think of the Norman farmer, on the heights above Grainville-la-Teinturière, who stopped me on a walk through the woods to complain about the state. Paris seemed not much less distant to him than it did to his ancestors, and he gave me confidence that I was on the right track. My grandfather, the poet, is still here somewhere, reciting on the village green; and my parents, Richard and Doris, are exactly what home means. To my children, I can only say that the noise and laughter made it all worthwhile, and reminded me that taking the longer road is often the better path. Phillip has been on the journey from first to last, a lifelong companion in adventure and politics, and a more patient editor of both daily life and manuscripts than I deserved. If the book is finished, the community is still there; thank you each and all.

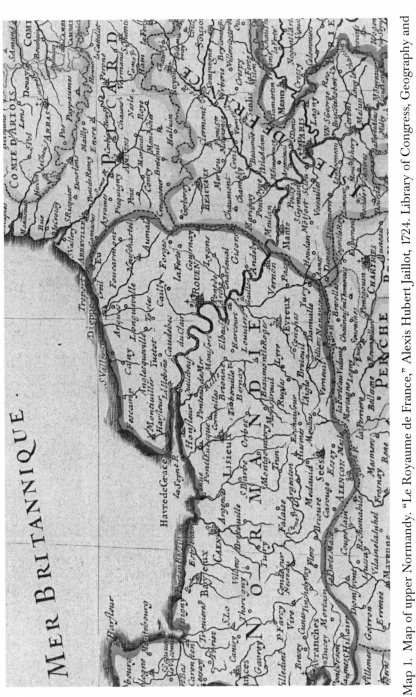

Map 1. Map of upper Normandy. "Le Royaume de France," Alexis Hubert Jaillot, 1724. Library of Congress, Geography and Map Division.

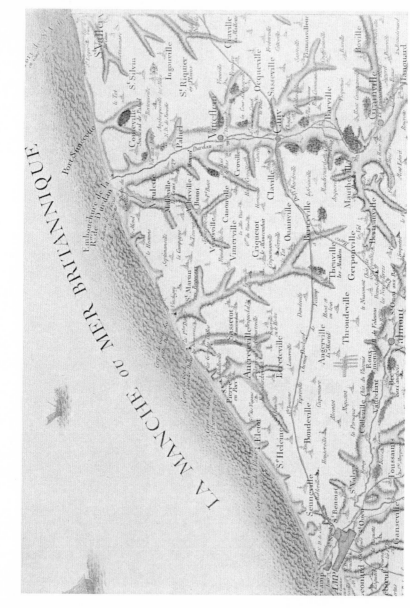

Map 2. Map of the upper pays de Caux, west. "Carte de France," César-François Cassini, 1756. Library of Congress, Geography and Map Division.

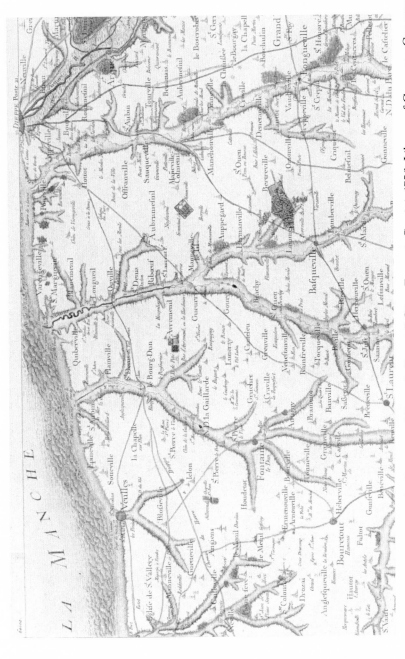

Map 3. Map of the upper pays de Caux, east. "Carte de France," César-François Cassini, 1756. Library of Congress, Geography and Map Division.

Chapter 1

REX AND LEX

THE PROBLEM OF LEGISLATIVE SOVEREIGNTY

Nestled densely in the countryside of seventeenth- and eighteenth-century France lay the largest permanent bureaucracy in Europe: twenty to thirty thousand royal bailiwick and seigneurial benches, dispensing justice to more than 85 percent of the French population.[1] The ordinary crown courts and lords' courts were far more than arenas of litigation in the modern sense. They had gradually become the nexus of local governance by the middle of the seventeenth century, a rich breeding ground for men who both administered and governed the villages and towns. The judges of the common courts were the front line of the French state. They kept the king's peace in thousands of parishes, on that vital border where the public commonwealth met the private realm of families. Yet from their court benches, these same magistrates and officers confidently controlled the law in ways which often expressed a startling independence from royal aims. The baron de Montesquieu put his finger on the central paradox of the French tribunals in his Persian Letters. They were "the sacred treasure of the Nation," he wrote, "and the sole one of which the sovereign is not the master."[2]

To understand this paradox of sovereignty, we need to look in a place that had long lain neglected: the bailiwicks of France, with their local worlds of judges and lawyers, jailers and clerks, and the ordinary men and women who daily beat a path to the assize courts. There we find a world that is both like, and strangely unlike, the state that we have come to know from studies of elites. Far from daily contact with the parlements, intendants, and power brokers that helped to shape urban politics, the bailiwick officers of village and town developed their own brand of governance. In the midst of an apparently centralizing state, they created an increasingly autonomous administration. Here was a judicial world where custom and equity, not the king's law, dominated the law courts; where the king's own officers grew increasingly detached from both the upper magistracy and the crown; and where men who had once been integrated into the governance of province and kingdom were cut adrift from the central state. Local judges grew more

1

socially and politically isolated from the centers of provincial and national power in the last century of the *ancien régime,* even as they accumulated power and wealth in their own districts.

The men who governed the bailiwicks–principally judges, lawyers, and petty court officials–formed a dense network of authority in the countryside by the late seventeenth century. Their focal points were the local courts: royal *bailliages* and *vicomtés* (in the north), *sénéchaussées* and *prévôtés* (in the south), and seigneurial high justices. But through widespread and often illegal accumulation of royal offices, their tentacles spread outward to embrace the fiscal, municipal, parish, and *subdélégué* posts in the countryside. These officers wore the long black robes of judges when they presided over the local assizes; but they also wore hats as mayors and syndics in the municipalities, *élus* and receivers in the tax *élections,* subdélégués in the intendancies, and lawyers and judges in the salt courts. Added to these were the hats they doffed as officials in the hospitals, poorhouses, and church vestries.[3] What made them formidable was not simply the scope of their judicial brief, but the fact that they monopolized so many of the key administrative positions outside of the judiciary.

These cumulative offices made them a far more compact governing class than has often been realized. Indeed, the profile of Norman chief justices of the ordinary courts is strikingly similar to those of English justices of the peace (J. P.s), about whom we have far more information. Like English J. P.s, French judges were typically in charge of police functions and administration,[4] as well as presiding as chief judges, making them rural governors par excellence.[5] French and English magistrates alike were accumulating powerful jurisdictions that had once been exercised by the church or by lesser courts, becoming the repositories of almost all justice that mattered in their bailiwicks. Despite their significantly different political roles on the national stage, both were propertied and privileged men who had assumed the natural leadership of their local communities. Like their gentry counterparts in Albion, French judges had inherited the mantle of order, absorbing much of the direct authority that had been vacated by the titled nobility of France by the late seventeenth century.

The local judiciary was both powerful and politically interesting in the ancien régime because of its unusual position. It straddled the crucial legal border between the public world of the state, and the private world of families. For the political theorist and judge Jean Bodin, the public realm of the commonwealth (*république*) and the private realm of families or households (*ménages*) were necessary corollaries, the front and back of the same political coin. Bodin, following Aristotle's *Politics,* argued that the commonwealth existed for no other reason than to protect the private world, especially property.[6] This vital dividing line between the public and private realms turned out to be one of the most contested borders in early modern French (and

English) politics, and it was a border increasingly policed by the judiciary. They held that border in the strictly legal sense, protecting the realm of *droit privé* (private or civil law) from the incursions of the *droit publique* (or public law) controlled by the king. But they also patrolled that border in a very practical sense, one that mattered deeply to the king's ordinary subjects. The men who sat on the royal bailiwick and seigneurial benches of France held first jurisdiction over the private domains of property and family in every parish. They were also the thin black line of magistrates charged with keeping the king's peace in the wider public commonwealth.

Because we still have much to learn about the daily functioning of the lower court system that served the vast majority of the French population, we have only very incomplete evidence about the practical limits of the crown's claim to legislative sovereignty: that is, the king's ability to make binding law on his subjects, and to dispense justice through the ordinary courts. Legislative sovereignty had meaning only if the king's laws had the power to directly affect his subjects' lives. Some royal laws certainly did, notably those that taxed his subjects; but the compass of the king's law was very circumscribed outside certain islands of competency. The droit publique had a limited writ in most of the kingdom. Administration, finances, crime, and foreign policy were accepted as legitimate fields of action for royal legislation; but their effect diminished quickly the farther one traveled from major urban centers. Custom, usage, and equity, all of which were locally derived, governed the vast majority of French law cases. Moreover, law and governance in the bailiwicks were controlled not so much by abstract codes as by a cohort of officers and gentlemen who had developed a very distinctive identity within the French state. Their interests and the king's coincided, but they were far from identical.

Legislative sovereignty has remained an enduring trope of the historiography of the ancien régime state, despite very incomplete evidence about how the king's law was applied to his subjects outside of criminal cases. "Absolute" power to make positive law defined the essence of "absolute monarchy." It also provided the basis for post-Bodinian theories of sovereignty in France, and by extension has underlain the western European model of modern state building. Yet the activities of the common courts demonstrate that in proclaiming the king's absolute authority to make and impose positive law, theorists often confused prescriptive hopes with political reality.

To a large extent, the wide acceptance of legislative sovereignty as a working description of the French state has simply reflected the nature of the evidence at hand. Until relatively recently, as many historians have noted, the local judicial archives were among the deepest and least explored records in France.[7] Civil cases, which made up the vast majority of the common courts' work, were particularly neglected in favor of criminal dockets. In recent years, some of that neglect has begun to be remedied. Studies of the functioning of urban sénéchaussées and *présidiaux* have begun to lift the curtain on lower jurisdictions in French cities.[8] The rehabilitation of seigneurial justice is also opening new perspectives on private jurisdictions, while historians of the family have profitably used testaments and contracts to understand private life.[9] For many decades, however, the main line of enquiry into local justice centered on the criminal dockets. A distinguished line of historians has mined the criminal records of the ordinary courts, opening perspectives on the history of crime (or more accurately, on the history of the criminalization of certain acts). Crime and punishment were indeed a part of the king's legislative sovereignty, especially over the poorest or unruliest of his subjects. They demonstrated the crown's power to decide who would be placed outside of civil society, and stripped of privileges, property, or life.[10]

But although colorful and interesting in their own right, crime and deviance were by their nature exceptional events in early modern courts. In the common courts of upper Normandy, more than 86 percent of the cases brought into the assizes were civil, not criminal. The lower judicial system can be fully understood only if we realize that its primary orientation was not toward punishing criminals, but toward ordering civil society. Indeed, civil cases had a far more permanent impact on ordinary people, and expressed the broad interests of the state far more articulately, than the punishment of exceptional crimes could do. As Steven G. Reinhardt has pointed out, what is needed is "a formidable task: to consider the relationship of royal justice to society as a whole."[11]

To bring to light this long-hidden world, then, we need to view local courts in the round, as their clients and officers must have seen them. And that requires us to begin to reconstruct the social and political context of the bailiwicks: the complicated networks of officers, the customary and royal legal codes that were their tools of the trade, and the ordinary clients who brought the community's business to their doors. Above all, it requires us to look at the civil dockets that were the focus of judicial activity. Perhaps the most unexpected influence on justice was hidden away here, in the quiet droning of daily litigation. The very nature of the lawsuits, and of the litigants who spun the wheels of justice as they passed through the assizes, sculpted the entire judicial system. In Normandy these were a true court of common pleas, in which over 94 percent of litigants were commoners, and in which the vast majority of both civil and criminal cases were brought to court by the king's subjects, not by the king's prosecutors. Villagers and townspeople used a full panoply of legal techniques, including witnessing, arbitration, composition, and raising the hue and cry (*clameur de haro*) to make the courts responsive to their needs. ("They are pretty well versed in the quirks of the law," wrote a surprised seventeenth-century English traveler through Normandy, "and have wit more than enough to wrangle.")[12]

Law and justice were not abstractions in early modern communities. They were vital forces, constantly mediated by human vectors, trimmed to fit the needs of local elites or communities, occasionally subverted, or merely ignored. Only by observing the bailiwicks in their daily functions can we begin to understand how legislative sovereignty was understood by early modern contemporaries, and especially by the officers who were charged with applying the laws to the king's subjects. It was here at the retail level, before thousands of benches in the common assize courts, that the public and private realms were joined.

The Public Realm: Bailiwick Administration and Governance

The judges and officers who ran the French common courts are doubly compelling subjects because much of the state administration in early modern France—and almost all provincial and local governance—was conducted through the judiciary. The same men who judged the law in the towns, villages, and bailiwicks of France were also the primary administrators of the local governments. As such, they were responsible for that consummate preoccupation of the early modern state, the maintenance of order. Jean Bodin, the founding theorist of legislative sovereignty, was very clear that sovereignty, in the legal sense, was quite a different power from day-to-day administration and governance. The administration of the kingdom rightly lay in the portfolio of magistrates and officers, he thought, and they should enjoy almost complete independence in those functions.[13]

The size of this judicial-legal class, which administered the countryside, was striking. France had approximately four hundred royal bailiwick and presidial courts by the late seventeenth century, with twenty to thirty thousand seigneurial justices practicing alongside them. The size of the judiciary can be placed within an order of magnitude, if still not precisely measured. In 1665, there were more than eighty-five hundred royal judges in France; when the seigneurial judges are added to the above figures, there was approximately one judge for every four hundred fifty to six hundred of the king's subjects.[14] The ancien régime judiciary was thus considerably larger than its modern analogues are. (Most Western nations, for example, have a ratio of approximately one judge per ten thousand inhabitants).[15] As one observer has pointed out, if France's judiciary had been "deployed on European battlefields, they would have made a considerable army by the standards of the time."[16]

A veritable army was needed, because the responsibilities of early modern judges went far beyond those of the modern judiciary. The separation of powers in modern states has trimmed away the executive functions that were naturally exercised by early modern courts. As Norma Landau has noted for English assize courts, to see these powers as purely administrative and bureaucratic is to miss the point of early modern governance.[17] Through seemingly routine administrative and executive decisions over common lands and parishes, markets, and seigneuries, people contested the power, reputation, and property of their neighbors (and often their governors). The magistrates' quotidian decisions, even on such simple matters as road repair, could incite riots in France, as they did in Brittany in 1701.[18] As Ralph E. Giesey has argued, Bodin's notion of legislative sovereignty was restrained not so much by abstract principles as by "the mundane force of administrative–can we not say 'bureaucratic'?–apparatus."[19]

Through their accumulation of powers, the common courts' reach stretched beyond simple administration to actual governance. Like the larger state, they had a wide-ranging political mandate to supervise social order, morality, and property in their communities. Their portfolio was the preservation of order itself, a function contemporaries called "*la police.*" Louis XIV had said as much in 1666, when he wrote to his heir that his "judges, in applying the laws, maintain security among men."[20] Chief among these functions were controlling or even distributing violence, and mobilizing the forces of order (if not relief) against the twin social threats of poverty and famine. Grain riots, subsistence crises, and poor relief (through their supervision of the parishes) ultimately ended up at the judges' doors. During weekly petty assizes, magistrates often found themselves weighing problems of order on a smaller scale. A parade of men and women who had been insulted at the church doors, assaulted at the King's Arms, or found drunk on the high road came before the ordinary courts to settle their affairs.

In wartime, all too frequent in this era, the local magistrates' mandate extended to France's foreign security. Many bailliage judges found that military responsibility for raising the king's *ban* and *arrière-ban* had fallen to them by default from the *bailli,* or sword noble in charge of raising the king's feudal levy.[21] The state's wars came home to magistrates a second time when deserting soldiers, fatherless children, and tax-exhausted parishes ended up at the doors of the bailiwick or occasionally the *maréchaussée* courts. At the end of these public crises, it was the judges' responsibility to reconstruct civil society and property, one case at a time, for their communities. They had few, if any, state resources at their command to fulfil these public functions. Law, custom, and their natural standing in the community were often the only tools available to judges in rural districts, and these were sometimes woefully inadequate. But magistrates were nevertheless the primary face of public order in their bailiwicks, in the midst of the environmental and human-caused disasters of the early modern world.

In quieter times, however, their mundane civil functions were the heart of the magistrates' governing power. Judges guaranteed civil society by mediating among the various corps, estates, and individuals who shared power and privileges in the community. As one historian has pointed out, it was the judiciary's broad authority to mediate in such a fractured polity that made them both powerful and unique.[22] There was almost no rural corporation, from the church vestry to the royal officer corps itself, that did not come to the bailiwick courts as the mediator of last resort. They were also empowered to mediate between individuals in a world of legal unequals where nearly every person was stamped with a unique set of privileges and obligations. Royal bailliage courts held first jurisdiction over all French men and women except only peers of France, state officers, or sovereign magistrates (with the privilege of *committimus au petit sceau* or *grand sceau*), and clerics accused of purely ecclesiastical delicts. From mendicant beggars marooned at the base of the third estate to landed lords and abbots enjoying an array of privileges in the second and first estates–all met together at a common bench before the bailiwick judge.

That this governing power was not always disinterested or benign should not surprise us. Local power, even more than state power, is likely to be personal and unmediated by other authorities. It was also the nature of the legal system to preserve and reproduce many of the unequal social and economic relationships of the early modern world, including (and perhaps especially) the status of its own judicial officers. Moreover, French assize court procedures set firm limits to the resolution of their clients' social or political discontents. The adversarial system of litigation gave individuals a field on which to maneuver against other individuals of different status; but it also confined their conflicts to a legalized form of personal combat. The bailiwick courts were not places to contest the wider system of classes, orders, or gender that underlay the French state. Yet the outcomes of these occasionally lopsided contests were not always so predictable as we might assume. If privileges, laws, and customs defined the place of individuals in early modern society, they also set limits to the rights of individuals that were often tested in court. Magistrates patrolled both of these borders: the border of law that upheld the privileged structures of society, and the border of justice that made those privileges more or less acceptable to the rest of the population.

French judges, like English J. P.s, ultimately wielded power in two kinds. They held public power that touched on the *polis* in its overlapping circles from the village community to the bailiwick to the central state.[23] But their offices were also a source of private power that radiated through family circles, a vocation that promoted social advancement for a kinship group. We cannot entirely unravel these two meanings from one another, as was altogether typical of public power in the ancien regime. This was, as James Farr has pointed out, the "core of the paradox of power" in France.[24] What makes the judiciary so intriguing is that their private and public powers, as individuals, so often intersected with their duty to patrol the public-private border within their communities, and across the realm.

The Private Realm: Property and Family

The nexus of the public and private realms across the kingdom was property. In France as in most early modern states, property issues were joined in two key places: in court, and in tax assessments. The orderly passage of property from one generation to the next, and the broader conservation of property within certain classes and estates, served a very public purpose. It preserved not only the security of the propertied classes, but also thereby the tax base of the French crown. John Locke could as easily have referred to France as England when he wrote, "The great and chief end, therefore, of men's uniting into commonwealths . . . is the preservation of their property." For early modern elites, the state preserved the "lives, liberties and estates" of the citizens, that is, of property holders.[25]

Local magistrates and lawyers controlled the flow of property in all its myriad forms, including land, offices, inheritances, dowries, leases, and rents. By stabilizing property relations, they stabilized families and communities throughout France. At the bailiwick level, this required judges and lawyers to have a working command of the bewilderingly diverse customs, usages, and privileges that overlay each piece of land or mobile property. This earthy preoccupation with the stuff of life meant that their portfolio was naturally human as well. Relations between husbands and wives, brothers and sisters, masters and servants, and the communal bonds of all in parish, market, guild, and bailiwick were their daily business.[26]

This commanding private brief flowed largely from French customary laws, which intently focused on the transmission of property. Each of the roughly six hundred provincial and local customary laws of Normandy was a flow chart of how land, cash, offices, and mobile goods might pass across generations, genders, and degrees of kinship. Through property laws, ordinary courts became natural trustees of the local economy. The assizes regulated land markets as well as the market in offices by supervising sales, leases, and contracts. They were no less active in early modern commodity markets. For rural merchants, guild masters, and artisans, the courts were a paternal presence supervising prices, weights, measures, coinage, markets, and fairs. The sworn masters of the guilds were required to appear at the court's assizes twice yearly to receive instructions from the bench. Disputes between masters or artisans not settled within the guilds would eventually wend their way to the royal judge. For towns and parishes, the judges supervised roads, bridges, and building regulations; parish accounts; and church land leases. They also ruled on those muddy bogs of property rights, the common lands. Local judges even influenced communal patterns of landholding and land use by defining customary grazing and gleaning rights as well as inheritance rights.[27]

Not only property, but consciences and bodies were part of these judges' spacious private jurisdiction. Concupiscent priests, slanderers, sorcerers, blasphemers, and unmarried pregnant women all found themselves in front of the assize bench, when two centuries earlier they might have been called up before church courts. As sins were gradually redefined as crimes, the men on the benches of the ordinary courts were left to regulate the morals and the religious conformity of the king's subjects (albeit with varying degrees of enthusiasm and rigor). By the seventeenth century, they did so with far greater reach and independence than they had ever done before, poaching the jurisdictions of the *officialités* (church courts) and minor civil courts alike.[28]

The courts' concern with moral order and property made them natural guardians of the private realm of family. Like their counterparts in late seventeenth-century Germany, French bailiwick judges found their family jurisdictions greatly enlarged by society's rising concern with the orderly passage of property and wealth.[29] In France, as Sarah Hanley has pointed out, the private behavior of women and of families was progressively "defined as public conduct," in part because of concern about inheritances and family property.[30] Wardship of orphans, inheritances, dowries, marriages, the upkeep of illegitimate children, marital separations and widow's dowers (and the immense amount of property that flowed through these family legal acts) were under the assizes' almost exclusive jurisdiction by this time. Town and village clients flocked to the common courts to resolve precisely these issues. Property disputes were also the proximate cause of many criminal suits, thus further blurring historians' traditional distinction between crimes against property and crimes against persons.[31]

The court records attest that the bailiwick's inhabitants had a deeply ingrained sense of order, too. It was based on local usages and customs, on community traditions, on religious sources (which strongly paralleled French customary laws, both in language and content),[32] and on a strong sense of social hierarchy. As in early modern England, ordinary people acted "with due respect for legitimate authority, but also with the expectation of proper behavior by their governors, which in turn meant due respect for law, natural justice, and custom."[33] The king's order in France largely operated through these preexisting mechanisms. But conflicts arose when royal priorities clashed with the community's traditional sense of order and justice.[34]

The kaleidoscope of litigants who came before the town and village benches—wealthy laboureurs and sieurs, to be sure, but also day laborers, widows, weavers, artisans, and orphans—had a determinative influence on the courts. What occupied them was seldom crime or the king's concerns, but most often the pressing civil matters of inheritance and property, family and community. Their disputes over pilfered burial plots and underweight pigs, their intricate maneuvering for court offices, land, titles, and inheritances were the daily coin of abstract justice. If the king's image was on one side of that coin, their own face was on the other. The ordinary acts of men

and women in the village courts thus helped to shape, define, and sometimes even subvert the course of royal justice.

Magistrates in Action: Power and Isolation

Bailiwick judges shared many of their private and public powers with magistrates of the sovereign courts. These powers were integral to the meaning of
early modern magistracy itself. But bailiwick officers also used their offices
in ways that sometimes defy what we know about how the state functioned
at higher levels. In short, they had developed a remarkable local autonomy
in their functions by the late seventeenth century.

Judges, king's prosecutors, and other officers drew particularly on three
sources of power and independence in governing their bailiwicks. The first
of these tools was the oldest, the law. Contrary to royal rhetoric, the king's
magistrates practiced little royal law at the king's bench. No more than
2 percent of civil cases brought before the Norman rural benches can be
definitively identified as falling under royal statutes; the vast majority were
judged by Norman customary laws, by local usages, and by equity. The
right to practice the Custom of Normandy as the provincial law code was an
ancient privilege, one granted under the Norman Charter (Charte aux Normands) by Louis X in 1315 and later reconfirmed by every king of France.[35]
Although French kings often violated other clauses in the charter (above all
those on taxation), the Custom remained remarkably impermeable to royal
alterations until the Revolution.[36] The same held true of the customary laws
of Burgundy, Brittany, and other French provinces.

Apart from law and custom, officers of the ordinary courts were independent of the crown in more material ways. Venal ownership of crown offices
presented well-known difficulties for state control of the judiciary; it had often
been cited by contemporaries as the greatest impediment to royal administration and justice. Chancellor Michel de L'Hôpital and Armand du Plessis,
Cardinal Richelieu had each in turn denounced the evils of venality, only to
accept the system reluctantly as a fait accompli and a financial necessity.[37] The
system of selling posts in the administration turned crown offices into partially
private property, thus giving their owners private ownership of the *chose publique* and, from the state's perspective, a regrettable measure of independence.
The work of Roland Mousnier, and more recently of William Doyle, has done
an immense amount to lay bare the machinations of venality in the higher
crown offices, but there is much left to learn about how venality functioned in
the thousands of ordinary offices at the town and village levels.[38]

The records of the local French courts reveal that venality worked quite
differently for judicial officers once one dropped below the level of the sovereign courts, and in ways that were fatally straining officers' attachment to

the state. The burden of royal exactions from officers, including *dédoublements* and *prêts,* was falling disproportionately on the lower officer corps, who typically had far less leverage for defending themselves from royal borrowing than the parlements did.[39] While personal and corporate debt mounted for officers in the ordinary courts, these men continued to be excluded from numerous privileges awarded to higher-ranking officers, both honorary and pecuniary. The crown gave them little more for their money than a license to practice while denying them access to the most coveted privilege, hereditary nobility through judicial office. Normandy was far from unique in these developments. As Séverine Debordes-Lissillour has argued, the rising independence of local sénéchaussée officers in Brittany was also based on the dominance of customary law, the crown's relentless erosion of the value of their offices, and a kind of benign neglect by provincial authorities.[40]

In response to these factors, the men of the common courts organized their offices into a well-oiled mechanism for acquiring land, cash, titles, and authority in the countryside. Far from practicing for honor or leisure, as has long been thought, they were instead carefully calculating about the economic and political advantages of office. Indeed, this fundamental misconception about the fruits of local office has long made local officers a cipher to historians. They practiced not simply for the *épices* (spices, or fees) that were legally allowed to them; rather, spiders at the center of the web of property in their communities, they were part of a rich economy of land transactions, leases, wardships, bribery, and other vital sources of income. A variety of opportunities presented themselves to any enterprising judge or lawyer who was shrewd enough to understand their value. We cannot understand these judges' professional or private involvement in the judicial system by thinking of them merely as leisured amateurs. We can only understand them as a governing class if we see them in the round: propertied, often ennobled men whose sources of wealth sprang from the careful exercise of their offices and who wielded levers of local governance that were infinitely varied.

If customary laws and the distinctive nature of bailiwick offices gave the men in the common courts both power and independence, their third source of local authority was the result of historical changes in the French state. Over the course of the seventeenth century, ordinary court judges and officers became the political beneficiaries of two large shifts in provincial governance. First among these was the disappearance of the higher nobility from the countryside as active governors. Second was the consolidation of provincial power in the hands of the judicial branch of government, including the concentration of bailiwick governance in the hands of local judges. The combined change was so profound that by the middle of the eighteenth century, as James B. Collins has pointed out, the king in conflict with his parlements "no longer faced royal judges against whom he could play off the local nobility; he faced royal judges who had displaced that nobility at the pinnacle of provincial political, social, and cultural life."[41]

This shift in provincial governance had profound consequences in the bailiwicks. The highest titled and robe nobility retained ample importance in the countryside as landlords, employers, and holders of privileges. But their direct involvement in local governance had receded significantly over time. They were legally barred from judging in their own seigneurial courts, and they ceased to recruit private armies from their dependencies after the Wars of Religion and the Fronde. Their estate stewards, bailiffs, and seigneurial judges also became noticeably more professionalized during the seventeenth century, leaving nobles free to pursue more urban and urbane lifestyles. By this period, as Jonathan Dewald has pointed out, "nobles typically defined retreat from public life—retreat to a country home—as a mark of incapacity, as morally shameful."[42]

By the later seventeenth century, too, the higher nobility enjoyed more satisfying fields in which to exercise their influence, develop clients and networks, and pursue family advancement than within the borders of their estates. Those who could afford the expense (and a good many who could not) resided in provincial capitals, at court, or in Paris for much of the year. In Normandy, the robe nobles of Rouen dwelled in the city roughly ten months a year, holidays aside, from the official opening of court in November (after Saint Martin's Day) to the end of August. Other high nobles who wished to be seen by the king, and to receive valuable commissions, pensions, and transfers from the crown, had no choice but to spend significant time at court under Louis XIV.[43] Changes in rural governance allowed them to do so. As in England, the "presence in the county of some men willing to govern allowed for the absence of those who were more inclined to rule."[44]

Those who were inclined to rule increasingly did so from the dais of the sovereign courts in the provincial capitals. Below them, in the bailiwick courts, those who were inclined to govern presided over their own concentration of power. Not only was the judiciary absorbing more governing authority in the countryside, but it was also consolidating its own sprawling network of courts by following economies of scale. Royal bailiwick courts and large high justices were an increasingly potent river of local authority, draining the smaller royal jurisdictions as well as seigneurial middling and low justices of their powers. Royal bailliage courts and seigneurial high justices in Normandy, often seen as competing sources of authority, had largely become a complementary system of justice by this period. Both courts practiced the same laws, with the exception of seigneurial privileges, and were typically run by the same small group of men, who moonlighted in each others' courts through multiple officeholding.

This devolution of local and provincial governance onto the judicial branch followed a multistage process whose origins went back into the mid-sixteenth century. The Estates General had recognized the rising importance of local and provincial courts to the proper functioning of the realm in a series of ordinances, especially those of Orléans (1561), Moulins (1566) and Blois (1579). In these omnibus codes, they reformed and reorganized judicial institutions to make them a stable platform for the growing state. The Estates also removed much of the jurisdiction of the ecclesiastical courts, the officialités, and transferred it to royal courts between 1539 and 1576. They thereby virtually eliminated one of the two main competitors for judicial control of French subjects, leaving only the private jurisdictions of nobles still on the field with the royal courts.[45]

Jurisdictional reforms were closely accompanied by legal reorganization. During the great century and a half of customary law redactions begun in 1453 and completed between the reigns of Charles IX and Henri IV, most of the provincial customs of France were put in their final form and confirmed by the crown. In 1583 and 1586, the Estates of Normandy published the newly redacted Custom of Normandy (along with its local usages) that would remain the centerpiece of Norman law until the French revolution. With this legal and institutional framework firmly in place, local courts were perfectly positioned by the mid-seventeenth century to assume a routine governing role in the countryside.

The final piece of the political puzzle was the development of the bailliage as the key unit of local governance. The bailliage, as Gerard Hurpin has suggested, has been one of the most neglected units of governance during the ancien régime. Unlike the province or the parish, it has received relatively little attention until recently, in part no doubt because of its bewildering jurisdictions and often haphazard records. Rather, there has been a tendency to treat the bailliage as an unchanging unit, making the term "one of the worst employed in the vocabulary of the ancien régime."[46] Dating from at least the thirteenth century, bailliages were conceived as broad units of royal administration from their beginning. Under the Valois and Bourbon kings they came to be associated more closely with court jurisdictions; the Edict of Crémieu in 1536 firmly established bailliages and sénéchaussées as the essential unit of justice.[47] But they remained important political units as well. In Normandy (as in most northern provinces), the bailliage was the consultative level at which the customary law codes were collected, including the Custom of Normandy in 1583–87. Deputies from the third estate to the provincial Estates of Normandy were elected and seated by bailliage, and typically included a strong contingent of bailiwick judges. The district was also the key unit for raising the local military from the feudal host, through the *ban* and *arrière-ban* overseen by the bailli. The French had strong vestigial memories of these legal and political functions. In 1789, the bailliage naturally became the principal unit for collecting parish *cahiers* and for electing deputies to the Estates General of France. Over the centuries, the bailliage had proved itself a fluid, adaptive, and powerful arena of local authority, and it remained so until the end of the ancien régime.[48]

The sovereign Parlement of Normandy gave substantial aid from above to the bailiwicks in their consolidation of local power. The magistrates fiercely protected the ordinary courts from interference by the intendants, and used *arrêts* (administrative laws) and appellate cases to reinforce the authority of the common courts. The *parlementaires'* personal, as well as professional, interests were deeply engaged in supporting the authority of royal baillage courts and high justices. The sovereign magistrates, who were almost universally landed justiciars on their Norman estates, had every motive to promote the security of property in the countryside. Local judges and attorneys, thus bolstered from above, reached out to monopolize the other local organs of parish, town, and fiscal governance as their courts rose in stature. The local state in Normandy was consolidating and redefining itself at the bailiwick level: a state where royal authority was translated by, and expressed through, magistrates in the common courts.

Yet this strengthening of the judicial branch in the provinces was paradoxically accompanied by a growing social and political distance between local bailiwick judges and the sovereign parlementaires. By the middle of the seventeenth century, the normal uptake mechanism of bailliage judges into the sovereign court of Parlement had stopped abruptly. Recruitment into the sovereign courts was restricted to stratospherically wealthy nobles, who had become an increasingly endogamous and closed elite. Local bailiwick judges (and their sons) could no longer aspire to rise to higher state positions through the ordinary courts. In Normandy this social barrier was only exacerbated by the demise of the Norman Estates, after their last sitting in 1655. The Estates were the only forum where bailiwick officers met and deliberated with sovereign court magistrates. Through the Estates, local judges had also participated in redacting the customary law codes and had negotiated with the central government over judicial grievances. When the Norman Estates were officially disbanded in 1657, a few decades after the last sitting of the Estates General of France in 1614, the last threads that bound bailiwick officers to national political involvement were severed.

The ensuing isolation of bailiwick officers from wider provincial and state governance would have long coattails. By the later eighteenth century, many of these legal men would decisively conclude that they could do better without the old state. Their rising professional status, legal skills, and propertied background gave them the confidence that they could continue to hold the levers of local administration and justice, even without the king's license. Their decisive role in the local bailiwick assemblies that drew up the cahiers in 1789, and later as deputies to the Estates General and the National Assembly, gave them the opportunity.[49] Their overwhelming success in being elected J. P.s for the new cantonal justices of the peace, and in staffing the more formal district courts established by the Assembly in 1790, proved them right.[50]

The growing independence of the ordinary courts from the central state during the seventeenth century was often overlooked at the time, except by a few acute observers. English contemporaries were likely to see French judges and lawyers as corrupt and even sinister agents of a centralized police state.[51] Contemporary French observers viewed the lower court officers more benignly, as the local eyes and arms of the king, but still saw them as mere dependencies of the crown. Theirs was a powerfully persuasive view, and one that makes a good deal of sense if seen from above and at a distance. But viewed up close, through the lens of their daily activities, the men of the common courts showed themselves to be marvelously complex and often refractory subjects. Their broad portfolios gave them independent political authority undreamed of by modern Western judiciaries. They judged the law, to be sure; but they were magistrates in the Roman sense, men occupied with the *chose publique*.[52] The preservation of property and order, police and morals, bailiwick administration—and that elusive pursuit, politics—were all in their professional compass.

Legislative Sovereignty and the Lower Judiciary

That the French state had turned bailiwicks into more or less free-standing units of local governance by the late seventeenth century seems fairly straightforward. But we also ought to ask the opposite, and perhaps more interesting, question: how did the local bailiwicks affect the French state? The answer to that question brings us back to the problem of legislative sovereignty, an idea with a long pedigree. Political theorists since at least the later sixteenth century have seen the king's ability to make unrestricted positive law as the essence of his sovereignty. Many have also assumed that royal laws were in fact applied and obeyed in the tens of thousands of ordinary courts that were the front line of French administration. As one historian put it, the absolutist state asserted itself through "the Law of the sovereign, imposed on everyone."[53]

But in a pioneering article, David Parker noted his "growing unease" with the notion of legislative sovereignty. Not only were we lacking good empirical studies of the legal system, he argued, but we had perhaps exaggerated the reliance of early modern political theorists on the concept as well. "Religious teleology," he pointed out, was still the real font of royal legitimacy and action.[54] Indeed, we need look no further than Bishop Bossuet's *Politics* to remind us that the king's role as a judge, not a lawmaker, was still a pillar of royal legitimacy. (The bishop, we should note, was also ridiculed for his antique ideas by some of his own contemporaries). Yet Bossuet did more than simply resurrect the biblical notion of the sovereign as a judge, rather than simply a legislator, in his instructions to the royal heir. He argued forcefully (as had many early sixteenth-century theorists such as Claude de Seyssel) that princes should submit "as much as others, or more than others," to the laws of the kingdom.[55]

Yet setting aside for the moment new questions about whether legislative sovereignty was really as pervasive an orthodoxy among early modern theorists as has been thought, the concept is still urgent for us on a more practical level. As a description of how political authority might be exercised, the sovereign's control of law raises vitally important questions about the exercise of power in the ancien régime.[56] If the king could establish the institutional framework for justice, but could neither write nor enforce royal statutes covering much of the kingdom's private law and some of its public law, then his powers need to be redefined. To begin do so, however, we need to understand how early modern theorists really understood the notion of legislative sovereignty.

The transition to the idea of lawmaking as the defining mark of sovereignty is often situated in the late sixteenth century.[57] The jurist Claude de Seyssel could still write in 1519 that the power of the sovereign was "not totally absolute . . . but regulated and bridled by good laws, ordinances, and customs."[58] By 1576, however, Jean Bodin had published the central treatise of a new generation of theorists. "The defining mark of a sovereign prince is the ability to give law to all in general, and to each in particular," he stated. "But this is not enough, for we must add: without the consent of one greater to, equal to, or below him."[59]

Bodin had boldly concluded that Aristotle had been wrong to think that sovereignty resided in the powers of rendering justice, appointing officers, and taking counsel on affairs of state.[60] These were merely derivative powers that flowed from a higher font, the right to make law. "Under this same power of giving and repealing law," he explained, "are all other marks and rights of sovereignty: so much so that one can properly say that there is only this one mark of sovereignty, since all other rights are comprised in it." Those derivative powers included the rights to tax, to make war, to install officers, and to oversee justice.[61] It was the first fully developed theory of unified sovereignty to emerge in France.

Yet Bodin's ideas on sovereignty were far more nuanced than his general theory appeared, and his subordinate arguments are essential to understanding his real sense of what constituted sovereign power. He was well aware of his contemporaries' arguments about the natural limits to the king's lawmaking power, including natural law and the fundamental laws of the kingdom.[62] As a practicing seigneurial judge, he was also acutely conscious of the practical limits of the king's legislative power. The thicket of competing customs, usages, and privileges that were the workaday reality of local magistrates and lawyers were an obvious prior restraint on the king's law-making powers. Bodin clearly understood that his colleagues on the bench were dualists, men who believed that there were two masters of the law. They held that "customs have no less power than the law: and if the sovereign prince is master of the law, private persons are masters of the customs." The king, in essence, was the master of public law; but not of those laws that touched on property and families.

In response to this dualism, Bodin pointed out that customs did not necessarily bridle or dilute the king's sovereignty, as Seyssel had argued, since customs were still executed under the sovereign's sufferance. The king can "repeal the customs; and the customs cannot derogate from the law."[63] Bodin freely conceded to his colleagues that magistrates wrote laws on their own authority, and that they naturally interpreted and bent royal laws to meet the circumstances of the case. But a magistrate's actions did not impair the sovereign's authority, he explained, since the king could repeal such local edicts at will, dismiss his judges, or require individual cases to be heard before him. This was a considerably more sophisticated argument in favor of the king's ultimate sovereignty over public law and his conditional sovereignty over private law.

Yet the weakness of Bodin's argument lies in his assumption that customs, privileges, and magisterial independence were freely granted by the king—that is, that he could have ruled without them. The reality was considerably more complicated. The crown granted customary law codes across France as part of an explicit contract through which royal sovereignty over certain state matters was confirmed in exchange for provincial sovereignty over much of the law. These contracts, as Bodin elsewhere acknowledged, were a mutual obligation, in which the "prince is not above his subject."[64] The sovereign's successors were moreover bound in perpetuity to honor such contracts in Bodin's view, particularly where the contracting parties were parlements, Estates, towns or communities.[65]

In the case of Normandy, the powerful Norman Charter guaranteeing the province the right to practice its Custom of Normandy dated back to 1315, an age of notably weaker central power. Kings of the seventeenth and eighteenth centuries had significant incentives to reform or alter many of those laws, not least because they interfered with the king's control of his own officer corps and administration. Later kings were able to violate the condition of the Charter that provided that no tax could be levied without the consent of the Norman Estates. (Indeed, the Estates had ceased to exist by the mid-seventeenth century.) But the customary laws held up with remarkably few royal incursions until they were swept away by the French Revolution. The crown decided to fight its battles with the province over money rather than law, given its limited resources to compel obedience over both. The same held true for all the provincial customs of France.

The French sovereign did not repeal these customs and privileges in part because self-governance in certain provincial matters was largely in the interest of the crown. But the king also did not repeal them, because he could not. Like all contracts, the Norman Charter reflected the strengths and weaknesses of both parties and their differing interests at the time it was negotiated. Despite Bodin's presumptions, it was virtually impossible for the crown to override customary laws, or to interfere in the judges' running of local bailiwick courts. Revoking the offices of rebellious or stiff-necked magistrates proved almost equally impossible, except in state emergencies, because these offices were private property. The expenditure of political capital (not to mention financial capital) required to deprive magistrates of their offices was something the crown could only rarely afford, and never without deep resistance. Nor did the crown evoke many cases out of the ordinary courts into the jurisdiction of the *conseil privé,* despite Louis XIV's advice to the Dauphin that it was a useful display of power to judge ordinary cases in person.[66]

In short, the presumption of royal sovereignty over the law was a polite fiction that served both sides reasonably well through the seventeenth century, until new developments in the eighteenth century made it seem an intolerable contradiction. As Parker has rightly noted, the transition from judicial sovereignty to legislative sovereignty had never been absolute, even in French theory.[67] But the idea became an irresistibly convenient political shorthand for contemporaries who were engaged in the discussion about the state. Seventeenth-century royal supporters found in legislative sovereignty an extraordinarily useful notion of the locus of the king's power, although their conceptual understanding had scarcely evolved beyond that of the late sixteenth century. For the last two centuries of the monarchy, "absolutism was the belief that the king had absolute ability to make *positive* law."[68] Even Richelieu, whose writings display little interest in abstract theory, assumed a largely Bodinesque position on unified legislative sovereignty as the basis for state action.[69] By the time Jean-Baptiste Colbert took the stage in the later seventeenth century, this notion was so thoroughly embedded in the background of royal action that it was scarcely ever talked about. Yet this polite fiction papered over a yawning divide between two different conceptions of the judiciary, and of the French state, that made it fatally easy for the crown's largest bureaucracy to walk away from the central government in 1789.

The Commonwealth of Magistrates

The limits of the king's sovereignty bumped up against the extensive rights of magistrates in the minds of early modern judges. For Jean Bodin, the bright dividing line between public and private spheres was essential, not incidental, to the state. The public realm overseen by magistrates existed in order to protect the private realm; there was no other justification for the creation of a state. Plato's Republic was a nonsensical polity from Bodin's perspective, because without private property there could be no purpose in establishing a state, whose primary function was to protect and maintain a private sphere based on private property.[70] Indeed, this public/private distinction was so central to the definition of the state that he seized on the first line of his masterwork to establish that border. A commonwealth was the "right government (droit gouvernement) of many households, and of that which belongs to them in common, with a sovereign power."[71] The sovereign, through the law, was naturally the master of those things held in common. This did not, however, make the king the master of the things households or families held in private, and as such, his sovereignty was limited where their property and persons began.

As Nannerl Keohane astutely pointed out, this apparent contradiction between limited sovereignty (over the private sphere) and absolute sovereignty (over the public sphere) was in fact entirely consistent (although it would make Bodin seem a rather "imperfect Hobbes" to later generations of thinkers). "It seemed obvious to him that the commonwealth must be composed of elements that have a definite structure and sphere of action apart from that of the commonwealth, so that the public realm can be distinguished from what it is not–the private."[72] It was also axiomatic to Bodin that this was precisely the border that magistrates were made to govern. They were not merely judges, but as the Latin root *magistratus* firmly implied, men who had the "public power to command."[73] Justice was designed to provide good order in the public sphere, and to protect the interests of property and households in the private sphere. Chancellor de L'Hôpital too had recognized justice as the key axis that linked the private realm of individuals and families to the kingdom as a whole. "The greatest plague and most pernicious contagion that can strike republics, cities, states and monarchies," he argued, "is undoubtedly injustice, because not only does it destroy individuals, but generally draws after it the ruin of the state."[74] Justice and law were the bonds that tied the body politic to its individual members. Indeed, apart from pure force, no other institution could do so.

French magistrates had a long and rich history of viewing themselves in precisely this role, as guardians of both the public commonwealth and the private realm. Every young barrister who had plowed through the *collège* curriculum had been schooled in Cicero's *De officiis* and Aristotle's *Ethics*. Aristotle described justice as nothing less than the "exercise of complete virtue," that is, private virtue translated onto the public plane through an active life.[75] For Cicero too, justice was the perfect virtue, "the means by which men gain the title of *boni*." It was a perfect virtue only if it was used in the service of the community, however, and one of its chief functions was to ensure that "communal property should serve communal interests, and private property private interests."[76]

A distinguished line of French political theory, eloquently developed in the sixteenth century, expanded on the magistracy's independent role within the state. Again it was Bodin who most clearly framed the crucial question: did the French magistracy answer to the sovereign, to the commonwealth, or to the public at large? He argued decisively that judicial offices belonged to the commonwealth, and that "the provision only belongs to the sovereign."[77] This distinction was of fundamental importance throughout the ancien régime. It was expressed in near identical language by the French Protestants Theodore Beza and Philippe du Plessis-Mornay, who were naturally concerned with developing theories of resistance to tyranny in the sixteenth century. Mornay called magistrates "officers, not of the king, but of the kingdom."[78] These men were not subordinates of the crown, he insisted, but "associates in the royal power . . . bound, just like the king, to look after the welfare of the commonwealth." Beza had used almost identical language five years before, when he wrote that officers held office "not of the sovereign, but of the sovereignty."[79] The independence of the officer corps was so essential to the constitution of the French state that François Hotman included it in his *Francogallia* as one of the seven fundamental laws of the kingdom.[80] Yet these startling ideas were not the exclusive province of would-be rebels, as Bodin illustrated. As a Catholic and a jurist he shared several of them, although he put them to use to show the legitimate spheres of action of the king as well as of the magistracy.

Though constitutionalist language vanished from political writing in the seventeenth century, the notion that magistrates were guardians of the *bien publique,* and as such were responsible to the commonwealth and the law, endured. It found a literary outlet in seventeenth-century drama, many of whose authors, such as Corneille, were lawyers or judges by training. The ideal of the bien publique was eloquently revived by one of the outstanding legal figures of the age, Chancellor Henri d'Aguesseau. In 1698, addressing the Parlement of Paris as its procurator general, he reminded the judges that "the perfect magistrate lives only for the republic. . . . [A]11 in him is consecrated to the public good."[81] The rapidity with which constitutionalist arguments were revived in the later eighteenth century showed their enduring hold on the moral and political imagination of magistrates. The king was allowed to create the office and to set certain standards of admission to office, but once accepted, the magistrate functioned as a guardian of the commonwealth. This was a practical, as well as theoretical, duty. To most magistrates it meant protecting the traditional customs, usages, and privileges that bound the community together and that gave the private realm its structure and independence.

For two hundred years, judges often defined themselves politically by protecting those customs and privileges against all royal incursions. Magistrates continued to assert their independence by "delaying, appealing and refusing royal legislation, reinterpreting the laws or enforcing them selectively."[82] Many of the seventeenth-century royal encroachments on their authority, as when Louis XIV stripped the Parlements of their right to preregistration remonstrances in 1667 and of their titles as "sovereign" courts, injured the magistrates' dignity more than their actual rights.[83] As William Beik has pointed out for Languedoc, Louis XIV in fact gave the parlement "a legitimate and satisfying role to play in the managing of the province."[84] John Hurt's recent work has argued that the parlements had already entered into a confrontational relationship with the crown by the later reign of Louis XIV, contesting genuine constitutional issues as well as protesting royal affronts to their private interests.[85] These were precisely the same tactics followed by lower court magistrates, at times with even more liberty and élan, in the village and town tribunals.

These contradictions lead us directly into the enigma of the local state by the middle of the seventeenth century. The local courts were essential to royal order; they stabilized property, family, and community across France. Moreover, as Roger Mettam has observed, the crown was not interested in controlling the day-to-day minutiae of local government, only in its efficient functioning.[86] But the local state also operated in ways that effectively deprived the French crown of both legislative and administrative sovereignty. The state's hands were bound in coping with some of France's most pressing problems at the highest levels, precisely because of its inability to revise the dense forest of local contracts, privileges, and laws that underwrote local administration. Chief among these limitations was the king's inability to touch property law, which was controlled by local custom and local magistrates, and thus his inability to expand control over property itself.[87] Perhaps equally frustrating, the king was denied real control over a significant amount of public law and administrative procedure by the provinces and localities. Any sovereign attempting to reform the state at higher levels would have found himself significantly burdened by the collective weight of local courts.

The Ordinary Courts of Normandy and the Pays de Caux

On the chalky downs of the pays de Caux, just north of Rouen, lay a group of towns and villages whose royal and seigneurial courts open a window onto the crowded stages of the common courts. A network of eight local courts— three royal bailliage courts, four seigneurial high justices, and the présidial court of Caudebec-en-Caux—were the loci of local governance. They spread their jurisdiction over more than 280 parishes, from administrative towns such as Cany to mid-sized villages and tiny hamlets. Between 1670 and

1745, we can trace across these courtrooms the careers of 357 of the magistrates, lawyers, and functionaries of the king's and lords' benches. Spanning the social registers from royal lieutenants general to sergeants at arms, royal measurers of weights, and jailers, they deeply grounded the king's and lords' courts in local society. The cases they heard and adjudicated tell us even more about the men and women they governed in the bailiwicks. This was not a simple system of elite rule and commoner acquiescence; it was a dynamic system where justice and law were constantly calibrated and negotiated to keep Cauchois communities and families functioning.

The courts of Normandy provide particularly rich material about the officers, clients, customs, and laws that were so central to local governance. In the *généralité* of Rouen alone, which covered only a third of the Norman province, there were at a bare minimum three hundred active crown courts and lords' high justices. They employed roughly two thousand officers in the royal and seigneurial jurisdictions, not including most of the attorneys, solicitors, and myriad functionaries who roamed the assizes. But it was Normandy's political history, as well as its judicial activity, that make it a particularly interesting corner of the realm for looking at the problems of sovereignty.

Normandy was perhaps the province that was best integrated into the French state system. Wealthy and close to Paris, the region provided an enormous percentage of the *taille* collected in France each year. That administrative closeness was reflected in a dense royal officer corps in the généralité of Rouen, which according to Intendant Voysin de la Noiraye's 1665 inventory numbered more than twelve hundred upper-ranking civil officials.[88] The vast majority of these officials were part of the royal court systems, above all the sovereign courts of the Parlement, Chamber of Accounts and Court of Aids in Rouen, and the regular lower courts of the présidials, bailliages, and vicomtés. Those listed in the inventory were only the cream at the top of the judicial system. The royal state was never far from Normandy, either fiscally or physically.

Yet Normandy also had a serious history of rebellion and revolt behind it by the mid-seventeenth century. Judicial officers played significant roles in all of them. The Parlement had entered into armed opposition against the crown during the Wars of Religion, a troubled relationship that endured to the end of the ancien régime.[89] In 1617 the Assembly of Notables met with the young Louis XIII in Rouen and secured the king's promise that he would stop using royal councils to intervene in the affairs of the regular courts.[90] Thirty years later, the province and many Norman parlementaires declared for the revolt of the *frondeurs* against Mazarin and the regent, Anne of Austria. This near calamity for the crown came on the heels of a popular and elite uprising over taxes in 1639–40, the revolt of the *nu-pieds*. After sending in Chancellor Pierre de Séguier and royal troops to pacify the province, the crown had seen fit to hang at least one royal bailliage judge and harshly punished the Norman Parlement by having it filled with a fresh-man class of more tractable magistrates. Séguier was not entirely mistaken in assuming that magisterial involvement, or at least silent encouragement, formed part of the volatile amalgam of angry salt panners, peasants, and urban artisans.[91]

This counterpoint of proximity and rebellion makes Normandy an ideal province in which to look for the myth and reality of advancing royal jus-tice. Of all the French provinces, Normandy—with its dense royal bureau-cracy, dominated by legal officials and capped by the Parlement—should have been the most fertile ground in France for establishing the royal judi-cial system. Yet at the same time the province proudly defended its particu-larism. Paradoxically, its independence was achieved primarily through the king's royal court system and the law. Normans used the weapons of the Norman Charter, a vigorous customary law code, and the provincial leader-ship of the Parlement and the lower bailiwick courts. As Sharon Kettering has pointed out for the south of France, provincial liberties were made more elastic by "the interpretations of local institutions, in particular provincial law courts and law codes."[92]

For compelling political and social reasons, this study is set between 1670 and 1745. The period between Louis XIV's assumption of personal rule to approximately the middle of the eighteenth century has long been suggested as a crucial period in the transition from seigneurial to royal justice in the countryside. It also closely coincides with an era of intense judicial activism at the top of the state. The formation of the royal Council of Justice (1665) under the stewardship of Jean-Baptiste Colbert and his uncle Henri Pussort produced the largely administrative (rather than legal) reforms of the Civil Code (1667) and the Criminal Code (1670). These were joined to signifi-cant reforms of the forest code (1669), commercial code (1673), marine code (1681), and colonial code or *Code Noir* (1685), marking the boundaries of expanding state ambitions in those areas of public law not monopolized by custom. The epoch of activism was bookended in the 1730s by Chancellor d'Aguesseau's last attempts to enact significant judicial and legal reforms. By 1745, too, the ancien régime had already come to a close in economic and demographic terms in the pays de Caux. Intensifying protoindustrialization, monetarization, and mobility had transformed local society several decades before the political events of the Revolution formally announced the death of the political ancien régime. This study thus stretches from the birth of the political ancien régime to the death of the social ancien régime.

To understand the judicial dynamics of Normandy between 1670 and 1745, the method chosen here has been to take a vertical slice of the court system from bottom to top. The records of eight lower tribunals, capped by the sov-ereign Parlement of Normandy, provide a composite picture of justice at four key levels in the French provincial administration: seigneurial high justice, bailliage, présidial, and Parlement. The présidial of Caudebec-en-Caux; the royal bailliages of Cany, Grainville-la-Teinturière, and Longueville; and the high justices of Valmont, Vittefleur, Cany-Caniel, and Eu create a broad profile of local courts across the Cauchois plain.[93] Above them, the Parlement of Normandy provides a useful gauge of the relationship between provincial and bailiwick courts through their appellate decisions from the lower jurisdictions, judicial investigations of abuse, and administrative arrêts. The Parlement's records help to express the interests (and at times lack of interest) of the higher magistracy in local governance. The use of a network of courts also helps to correct the court documents' individual defects and lacunae, which are many at the local level.[94]

Radiating out from the local records, sources from the central and provincial administration help to fill in the complex dynamics between center and periphery. The intendants of the generality of Rouen, the Council of Justice, Colbert, Pussort, and chancellors Louis Phélypeaux de Pontchartrain and Henri François d'Aguesseau give evidence here of the intentions of royal reformers and judicial administrators. The relationship between state and subjects also leads us out of administrative documents and toward a constellation of sources from those who had a far different relationship to justice than royal commissaires or sovereign magistrates. Popular plays and tales about justice; artisans' guild statutes; lawyers' manuals; and the musings of village arbiters, rural clerks, attorneys, weavers, and peasants all had a surprising amount to say about the mask and the reality of justice in the ancien régime.

Because of the bewildering number of lesser jurisdictions in France, and the fact that their formal titles often obscure their underlying connections, I have adopted several umbrella terms here for the sake of clarity. The terms *ordinary courts* or *common courts* have been used to designate the main line of the court system beneath the sovereign courts. This includes the présidial, bailliage, and vicomté courts of northern France (called sénéchaussées, prévotés, vigueries, and châtellenies elsewhere) and the highest rung of the lords' seigneurial courts, the high justices. They were called ordinary courts (*tribunaux ordinaires*) to distinguish them from the exceptional tribunals (*tribunaux d'exception*), which had narrow jurisdictions; Louis XIV used the phrase to describe them in his instructions to the Dauphin.[95] The term *bailiwick* has been used here as a territorial designation. It corresponds to the geographic territory of a royal bailliage court but includes other jurisdictions, both royal and seigneurial, that were active in that territory. (A typical northern bailiwick covered about a hundred parishes, although bailiwicks could vary dramatically in size. Numerous other royal and seigneurial jurisdictions cohabited any given bailiwick). I have also chosen to translate the offices of *procureur du roi* and *avocat du roi* as "king's prosecutor" and "king's advocate," respectively. Because the office of royal procureur was a public ministry that required lawyers to serve the interests of the king (and some-times of the public), the term *prosecutor* is the closest American translation.

Within each bailiwick might also be anywhere from one to several dozen seigneurial courts, along with the usual direct-tax courts (*élections*), salt-tax courts (*greniers à sel*), waters and forests courts (*eaux et forêts*), consular courts for merchants (*juridictions consulaires*), and other specialized jurisdictions. The tax courts in particular were a vital part of the public sphere, but I have eschewed them here in favor of courts that dealt more broadly with public and private matters and that heard cases beyond the very narrow jurisdic-tion of the tax courts. Other special royal jurisdictions, such as waters and forests, tended to dry up in the seventeenth century as their cases were pur-sued in the bailiwicks. The lowest seigneurial courts, known as low and mid-dling (*basses et moyennes*) justices, have been excluded here too because their jurisdiction was largely limited to rents, tenurial disputes, and seigneurial privileges on their estates. Many of them have unfortunately left no records behind. Among those that have, their records testify to the continuing pri-vate and partially public powers of seigneuries, but those abilities were far more powerfully expressed by their larger cousins, the high justices. I have tried to choose here, among an embarrassment of riches, the institutions that had the broadest public and private jurisdictions, and that served the largest number of the king's subjects in the towns and countryside. Both private and royal jurisdictions continued to fill those functions through the eighteenth century, despite premature announcements of seigneurial justice's demise.

The role of the high justices was one of many surprises to emerge from the bailiwick records. It has very naturally been assumed that royal and seigneurial courts in the countryside were opposing factions, one standing for the advance of royal power, the other clinging to noble privileges. This opposition makes sense if we assume that these courts were run by different people with different objectives. But that was not the case in upper Nor-mandy. The attorneys and judges of the district served in both courts simul-taneously, or sometimes at different stages in their careers. Over the course of the seventeenth century, high justices were increasingly owned by royal judges in the sovereign courts, who were committed to the same govern-ing values of order and protection of property in their seigneurial courts as they were in their royal offices. Moreover, in Normandy (as in many other regions), the important seigneurial high justices were almost universally stand-alone jurisdictions whose cases could be appealed only to the Par-lement. High justices enjoyed broad public powers that were often equiva-lent to those of royal bailiwick courts, and their public jurisdiction was often only distinguished from royal courts by their inability to try rare *cas royaux,* or cases deemed threatening to royal authority. Although privately owned and therefore serving private and fiscal functions for the seigneurie, they were also a royally sanctioned part of state authority in France. The high justices cannot be separated from the state judicial system. As will be seen, they were in fact deeply integrated into that system through their many parlementaire owners, their shared court personnel, and the Custom of Normandy. The two systems, private and public, together constituted the French judicial state.

But was upper Normandy an anomaly? To see whether these trends would hold true in other regions and provinces, it seemed useful to compare the Norman records with those of ordinary courts in Brittany, Burgundy, and the jurisdiction of the Parlement of Paris. Although most of that material has been eliminated from the narrative for simplicity, the main lines of evidence were consistent elsewhere. Whether we turn to the royal bailliage and sénéchaussée courts of Beaune and Nuits-Saint-Georges in Burgundy; or to those of Hédé, Rennes, and Fougères in Brittany; or even to high justices such as those of Chateauneuf, Nuits-Saint-Georges, and the comté d'Eu, dominant common themes still rise above the inevitable local variations. The use of customary law and local usage as the foundation of judicial proceedings, the remarkable independence and sometimes alienation of local officers from royal policies, and the determination of clients and communities to use the courts for private, not public, ends were common to all. The exact combination of local authorities who made up the state in the bailiwick varied, but their essential powers did not.

The final body of scholarship that forms a touchstone here is that on the nature of the French state. The underlying premise of this work builds frankly on a thesis put forward by Willaim Beik, James Collins, Roger Mettam, and others about the problematics of the term *absolutism,* at least in its nineteenth-century sense, as a description of French governance. In a series of groundbreaking studies, Collins has shown the profound limitations on the crown's ability to tax at will and has underlined the continuing strength of provincial power brokers in Brittany and in other provinces. Beik has shown how Languedoc's provincial Estates and local authorities continued to mediate royal power despite the rhetoric of central control. Mettam's synthesis on Louis XIV's administration has brought together much of the recent scholarship on this topic.[96] But one leg of the horse of absolutism is still an open question: the problem of legislative sovereignty.

The chapters here each focus thematically on a key aspect of the common courts and local governance. Chapter 2 sets the common courts in their broad social and economic framework and takes a bird's eye view of the villages and towns where magistrates, lawyers, officers and functionaries of the courts lived and worked. Chapter 3 examines the officers and gentlemen who governed as well as judged in the bailiwicks and whose complex economic and social identities were often radically different from those of magistrates in the higher courts. Chapter 4 analyzes the thick layers of usage, custom, equity and law that informed the daily practice of lawyers and clients and made up the legal foundation of the local state. It also appraises the extent to which the king's legislative sovereignty, his ability to make binding law on his subjects, actually obtained in the French courts. Chapter 5 examines shifting power relationships in this period between the common courts and provincial or national institutions, particularly the Parlement of Normandy, the Estates of Normandy, and the intendants.

The next two chapters bring us down to street level, in the villages and towns of the Caux. The civil and criminal dockets of the Norman bailiwick courts ground the abstractions of law in the daily round of cases before the king's bench. Chapter 6 looks at the deep influence that ordinary clients of the courts exercised over the judicial system by using it for their own civil purposes to regulate property, family, and community. Chapter 7 explores the criminal cases heard before the benches and analyzes the ways in which local communities also drove the prosecution and punishment of crime through the traditional tools of witnessing, hue and cry, and community decisions about whom to prosecute and for which delicts.

Chapter 8 brings the kaleidoscope of officers, clients, laws, and local institutions back into focus in order to pose larger questions about the functions and dysfunctions of the local state. Against the traditional interpretation, in fact the French ordinary courts and their style of local governance had profound analogs to their English counterparts, the county quarter sessions and local petty sessions. English contemporaries (and most historians after them) drew sharp contrasts between two styles of local governance, one under a despotic monarchy on the French side of the Channel, the other under a constitutional commonwealth on the English side. The assumption—and it has been a powerful and understandably persuasive one—is that venality and absolutism in France created fundamental differences in local governance, especially when contrasted with an English local state based on constitutional government and a largely volunteer magistracy. ("The Sale of Offices," asserted the English observer John Northleigh about the French judiciary, "excuses, almost necessitates, their Knavery.")[97] As will be seen, however, there were in fact surprisingly deep similarities in the ways these institutions governed the towns and countryside in both France and England. Propertied landowners, these judges held nearly all the levers of local administration in their hands and rose to the occasion that political opportunity had offered them.

Ultimately, the emergence of a class of propertied men who governed as well as judged in the countryside made it possible for the traditional noble governing classes to focus their attention elsewhere. Magistrates and officers, they maintained order, managed property, and negotiated the slippery and contentious relations of classes, orders, estates, and individuals across the parishes of France. No piece of business, from grain riots to collapsing chimneys, was beneath their adjudication; no transaction, from the inheritance of enormous estates to the willing of a tin spoon, was outside their jurisdiction. It was both ridiculous and sublime, and it kept the king's peace in ways that often owed remarkably little to the king's law.

Yet the many useful functions the common courts performed also concealed deep dysfunctions. Those dysfunctions would be exacerbated by the shifting social and political ground of the eighteenth century. Chief among them were hidebound customary codes that the crown could not revise because of the parlements, and that the parlements would not be allowed to revise by the crown. Added to this were the changing nature of property and of family relations that the courts had to mediate with increasingly petrified legal codes; and the deep, hidden fissures that were developing between the crown and its largest permanent bureaucracy, the courts. This was obvious by the end of the ancien régime to Alexis de Tocqueville, who famously mused that "in no other European country were the ordinary courts as independent of the government as in France."[98] But the conditions of that alienation had been laid down more than a century before, in the ordinary bailiwick courts that governed most of the population.

The common courts shared with the rest of the French legal elite the increasingly acute awareness that they controlled many of the day-to-day executive and judicial functions of the state, but had virtually no control over legislative functions, as did their analogs in England. Through it all, local magistrates and officers maintained an ideal of the bien public, and of their natural place in the commonwealth, that carried them through decades of declining access to the higher magistracy and over a rising tide of corporate and personal debt foisted on them by the king. In the end, the border of public and private that they defended, across hundreds of French bailiwicks, remained crucial to the stability of the state. When these men finally shifted their allegiance from the forces of order to the forces of change, the French state shifted with them. After all, they had placed their bets on the right horse: consolidating their power, property, and influence as local governors of the towns and villages of France, they rode the Revolution into the nineteenth century.[99]

Chapter 2

HOWLING WITH THE WOLVES

THE NORMANS AND THEIR COURTS

All these Normans would amuse themselves with us;
We have to learn to howl, said the other, with the wolves.

Racine, *Les plaideurs*

To a visitor in 1670, riding north across the great sweep of plains that angled down to the Atlantic Ocean in Normandy, the pays de Caux would have looked aptly like a golden loaf of bread rising out of the English Channel. Cut across the crown with deep river valleys that drained into the ports of Rouen, Dieppe, and a half dozen other towns, the district looked like the rich, rural cereal producer that it was. But the countryside surrounding the old Roman towns hid myriad complexities by the late seventeenth century. Fields of blue flax now covered the downs in spring, making it one of the most intensively protoindustrialized regions of France. Weavers, spinners, dyers, and cloth merchants were almost as common a sight in town and countryside as those farming wheat and rye.[1] For a close observer, change would have been just as marked in the streets of the towns and villages. The crown of the loaf had become the administrative center of gravity for the central and northern Caux, a place where local self-governance had firmly taken root (see map 1).

This vibrant Cauchois economy and its social life formed the subsoil for its judicial institutions. The villages and towns of the district were governed through several hundred king's and lords' offices, most in the ordinary royal bailiwick and seigneurial courts. From their benches at weekly petty assizes, judges and lawyers supervised the parishes, towns, guilds, and families that bound the Cauchois together. On other days of the week, they helped run many of those local institutions personally. They presided over parish vestries, town councils, hospitals, tax bureaus, and subdelegacies. Even when they were not in robes, their public roles encircled them; court officers willingly stood as godparents and tutors for their neighbors and kin. They had

29

long been an intimate presence in daily life for those in the community. But increasingly they also had to govern, keeping the district upright through the swells of famine, war, and social change that swept through every part of France during the late seventeenth and early eighteenth centuries.

The horizons of their small empire could be clearly mapped from one of the hills overlooking the central assize and market town of Cany (see maps 2 and 3). The greater Caux spread across roughly 5,000 square kilometers of upper Normandy, north from Rouen to Dieppe, and east from Le Havre to Neufchâtel.[2] Strewn across the central plain were 816 parishes within the bounds of the presidial court district of Caudebec, which excluded the capital at Rouen.[3] At the geographical heart of the district, surrounding the town of Cany, lay about 280 parishes under the direct jurisdiction of seven local bailiwick and seigneurial courts. The men and women who populated the chalky downs near Cany were precisely the kind of village, bourg, and small-town dwellers who made up perhaps 85 percent of the French population during the ancien régime. Like the rest of the king's subjects, the Cauchois brought virtually all of their lawsuits to the doors of the ordinary courts, which heard most cases in the first instance. Their cases began, and almost invariably ended, within the tribunals of the main royal bailiwick courts (bailliages in the north of France, sénéchaussées in the south), the lower tier of royal courts (vicomtés, prévotés, and *châtellenies),* or the lord's seigneurial courts (high, middle, and low justices). But the local courts themselves were embedded in a larger field of jurisdiction, one that spread far beyond the daily circuits of most inhabitants.

Town and Gown: Assize Towns of the Caux

Laid across the Cauchois landscape were invisible filaments of jurisdiction, overlapping in layers that radiated from cities as far as 50 kilometers away, including the Norman capital of Rouen. A bailiwick judge looking out from the wooded heights above the town of Cany would have been able see these filaments in his mind's eye, stretching far beyond the horizon in every direction. Yet the gravitational pull of Norman judicial centers on the towns of the Caux varied greatly. The presidial towns, though sometimes close by, had little influence outside of their immediate bailliage jurisdiction. Few cases went there on original jurisdiction, and even fewer on appeal. The province's sovereign courts, though more powerful, attracted only very specialized cases and clients from the countryside. Those included highly privileged individuals with the right to be heard in higher courts in the first instance, cases involving large sums of money (typically greater than 500 livres) or expensive tax disputes, and capital convictions, which came under mandatory review. The bailiwick towns, though smaller, enjoyed the power of proximity. They exerted by far the greatest pull on local clients and their cases.

The largest of these judicial centers, and the farthest away, was Rouen to the southeast. In 1670 it was the second largest city in France, a cosmopolitan port on the river Seine, and a hub for French, Italian, Spanish, and Dutch merchants.[4] More vital for the Cauchois countryside, Rouen was the judicial and administrative nerve center of the province. The capital housed the sovereign Parlement of Normandy, the sovereign financial courts of aids, accounts, and monies, a royal presidial and bailiwick court, a merchant's consular court, and a direct-tax court (élection). It was also home to many lesser royal jurisdictions, including those of the admiralty, customs, waters and forests, and salt taxes. Rouen was thus the final (and usually only) destination for most cases appealed out of the Caux. Despite its distance, nearly two days' ride on rural roads, the king's officers in the district were hardly strangers to the streets of the Norman capital. Many local judges had kinship ties to attorneys and judges in the financial courts in the city (though few had family ties to the sovereign judges of the Parlement), and many more had practiced as attorneys in Rouen before buying local judgeships or king's prosecutors' posts. Moreover, bailliage judges from the central Caux were required to ride into Rouen each winter by January 7, the day after Epiphany, for their annual harangue by the Parlement of Normandy[5] (see appendix A).

Due south, and closer to hand, was the administrative town of Caudebec-en-Caux. Enclosed by the steeply forested banks of the Seine, the town was only 30 kilometers across the plains from Cany. But its royal courts were far less significant for the central Caux than those of more distant Rouen. It housed the presidial court for the central Caux region, along with a baillage and vicomté, and the direct-tax élection for the entire district. The minor jurisdictions included the usual complement of courts for salt taxes, waters and forests, and the admiralty. It also housed a *maréchaussée,* or mounted constabulary court, with approximately nine archers, who served as the only armed constabulary for most of the central Caux. The presidial court of Caudebec in theory was the doyenne of seven bailliage courts spreading over most of the Cauchois plateau. The court was supposed to be the sovereign appellate jurisdiction for all cases involving sums from 250 to 500 livres and could judge cases between 250 and 500 livres with appeal to the Parlement. But its close proximity to the Parlement of Rouen robbed it of much original or appellate jurisdiction.[6]

In the midst of the wide plain north of Caudebec lay a series of judicial villages and towns, strung along the placid rivers of the Durdent, Scie, and Arques as they flowed down to the Atlantic Ocean. Near the center of these, straddling the Durdent, was Cany. In size it was not much more than a bourg, with around three hundred taxable and non-taxable hearths, and perhaps twelve hundred inhabitants.[7] But it functioned as a vibrant small city, serving a large rural hinterland with its royal and seigneurial courts, weekly markets, and quarterly fairs. Scattered to the four compass points around it were other rural court communities: to the south the prosperous textile-dying bourg of Grainville-la-Teinturière; to the east the ancient ducal seat and town of Longueville; to the northeast the seat of the comté d'Eu; to the north the farming and weaving village of Vittefleur; and to the southwest Valmont, the seat of the duchy of Estouteville. Their jurisdictions overlapped bewilderingly with each other, sometimes skipping over parishes to connect a far-flung village with invisible lines of jurisdiction to the home seat. What held these diverse communities in common, besides the broad plain of the pays de Caux, was that all were nodes of royal or seigneurial justice in the ancien régime (see appendix B).

A visitor arriving in the royal bailliage town of Cany on the old Roman road would first see the slate roofs of the houses and the spire of St. Martin's Church, clustered below in the valley of the green Durdent river. Once the visitor descended into the town, however, the most impressive structure was the old medieval chateau, not far from the river. It cast its shadow over the market halls, which the seigneurs of Cany would shortly rebuild in grand style. But the old chateau, imposing though it seemed, was an empty monument by 1670. The baron (later marquis) of Cany had decamped with his family to their striking new brick chateau outside the town, designed in 1640, it was said, by François Mansart, uncle of the king's future architect. It was a building that announced the modernity of its owners: a rising judicial family, steeped in the urbane culture of Rouen. They patronized the town from a distance now, far from the seigneurial law courts and market lanes that the old seigneurs of Cany had commanded for centuries. The assize courts and the public market, surrounded by artisanal quarters and parish churches, had become the real centers of civic life.

Cany's small size was deceptive. The town looked like a floating, gray-roofed island adrift in a sea of yellow cereal plains and blue flax fields. The rural horizon's only limit seemed to be the Atlantic Ocean 8 kilometers north, at Veulettes-sur-Mer. Yet in the fields and river valleys of the pays de Caux, the population of a middling-sized, early modern city practiced open-field agriculture on the chalky downs and ran a thriving international export industry in woven and dyed cloth. Small though it was, Cany performed the services of an urban center for perhaps twenty to thirty thousand Cauchois inhabitants, a number that would grow to more than forty thousand over the course of the century.[8] As the royal assize seat as well as seigneurial high justice for the district, Cany held invisible bonds of legal jurisdiction over more than ninety parishes. It was the center of a noble sergeantry covering thirty-one parishes, and the country seat of a wealthy marquisate stretching expansively over more than 1,200 hectares.

A visitor entering Cany would be naturally drawn down the high street toward the royal and seigneurial courts, occupying the center of town, directly across from the market halls and near the chateau. The seigneurial court of Cany-Caniel was a heavily trafficked jurisdiction, even well into the eighteenth century. It held sway over fifty-two to fifty-seven parishes, and by royal privilege its decisions could only be appealed to the Parlement in Rouen.[9] The royal bailiwick court of Cany held jurisdiction over ninety-one parishes, but nearly half of these were also under the jurisdiction of the high justice of Cany-Caniel. The royal court also occasionally served as an appellate court for five other high justices in its embrace.[10]

Yet the presence of two jurisdictions in Cany, royal and seigneurial, was more than a little deceptive. Not only did the officers share the same bench, they were in fact often the same men, simply changing hats from one sitting to the next. Both the royal and lord's courts occupied a house leased out from the seigneur of Cany, taking sittings on alternate mornings and afternoons. The royal bailiwick court of Cany held forth on Mondays, and the lord's high justice of Cany-Caniel took the bench on Mondays, Wednesdays, and Fridays. A rump seigneurial court then moved across the river to administer low and middling justice in their other chambers at Canville on Tuesdays, and in Doudeville on Saturdays.[11]

Close by their courthouse stood the rather flimsy jail, whose windows were often unbarred. Like most early modern prisons, the Cany jail served more as a lockup for vagrants, drunks, and disorderly revelers than as a penal institution. Its aged jailer, Jacques Badou, would eventually be arrested by the presidial court of Caudebec for giving his prisoners French leave on Sundays, while he went out to visit his grandson.[12] The permeable nature of jails was one of the more revealing reflections of the courts' powers and limitations in the early modern world. Judges had a far greater range of punishments available for miscreants than closed prison. Moreover, the community's sense of justice, as well as the urgent need for able-bodied villagers to be at work, usually demanded that judges apply those alternatives.

A visitor to Cany in 1670 could scarcely avoid contact with royal officials in the streets and taverns. As an assize town, it had an unusually large contingent of judges, lawyers, councillors, surgeons, notaries, sergeants, bailiffs, jailers, and other minor functionaries of the courts. Seventy-five officers and functionaries made their required appearance before the twice-yearly mercurial assizes, or grand assizes, in the fall of 1671.[13] These officers' relationships to the town and countryside, as well as their more distant ties to urban administrative centers such as Rouen, were crucial to the way justice and the royal state functioned in the district. Less noticeable on the streets of the town were the crown's fiscal officers. The élus of the tax district were based in the presidial town of Caudebec-en-Caux, and the closest royal salt warehouse (grenier à sel) was on the coast in Saint-Valéry-en-Caux (although it was staffed by a Cany attorney). Among the elites of the community, there were also eight privileged households of nobles living in the town and outlying parishes. But the town's nobles closely overlapped with the court officers. Two of them, Jacques and Jean Tallebot, were respectively the chief judge and the king's prosecutor in the royal court at Cany. A third, Jean Baptiste de Meville, was the son of the chief judge of the high justice of Cany-Caniel in 1659 and the grandson of a Rouennaise judge.[14]

As a royal assize town, Cany aspired to being a provincial cultural center, albeit on a modest scale. Touring theater troupes entertained the town during markets and fairs.[15] Magistrates from the parlements of Paris and Rouen had country seats and estates in the neighborhood, bringing stylish servants and noble guests in their train for visits. Cany was also a stop on the official royal post road that linked Dieppe, Fécamp, and Rouen, thereby spreading royal and official news. The assize courts, especially, functioned as the newspaper of record for the district, making announcements from Paris, Versailles, and Rouen to the assembled community. At the royal grand assizes twice yearly, the judge or his clerk announced the news of the realm, registered and read out new royal edicts to the audience, and admonished the community to keep good moral and social order. The magistrates' harangues from the bench must also have provided fuel for local gossip. At the royal assizes in Cany in December 1720, the judge revealed that a scandalous libel on the bishop of Bayeaux had been published at the University of Caen, announced that the crown was issuing 8 million livres in new rentes, and reminded the audience anew that the king forbade holding fairs on feast days and Sundays.[16] A mere dot on royal maps, Cany was a beacon of urbanity to the surrounding countryside.

During the late seventeenth century, Cany's thriving markets were a source of substantial profit (and frequent lawsuits) for the assize courts, the town, and the seigneur.[17] Regular markets were held every Monday, with four annual fairs on Quasimodo's, Saint Barnabas,' Saint Gilles', and Saint Simon–Saint Jude's days. The neighboring parish of Canville held Tuesday markets, with three more fairs on the Feast of the Innocents, Tuesday of Holy Week, and Saint John the Baptist's Day. More than fifty types of merchants paid customary duties on their wares at these events, including those in the luxury trades, such as goldsmiths. The ordinary provisioning and building trades of any early modern town were all resident here: the butchers, bakers, chandlers, coopers, and carpenters had their shops along the central lanes. But the streets in town were also crowded with the shops of arquebus masters, cabinetmakers, parchment pressers, leather tanners, glassblowers, drapers, and tailors.[18] The textile industry was especially prominent in the artisans' quarters of the town and in the outlying parishes. A few years later, thirty-nine master drapers of serge fabrics alone would appear at the assizes to register the guards of their trade.[19] The drapers' shops were merely the tip of the rural textile iceberg: the spinners, weavers, and dyers who kept the draper's workshops busy provided its vast, often hidden base.

Not coincidentally, market Monday was often the busiest petty assize session of the week for the high justice and royal court. The two events were held together not only for the convenience of those traveling in from the hinterlands, but also because the two institutions were in fact closely related. One of the courts' most important function was regulating property in the district, and many market disputes and contractual agreements simply crossed the street to the assizes to be notarized or adjudicated the same day.[20]

Like any early modern town, Cany was held together by overlapping circles of authority. The parish, the craft guilds, the community of inhabitants (*communauté*), the mayor and syndics, the seigneury, and the crown courts all shared in the maintenance of order and the distribution of wealth and power. Through these institutions, an interlocking directorate of judges and royal officers, sieurs and seigneurs, masters of the trades and merchants, priests, and laboureurs coalesced. But the circle was much smaller than the list of titles would have it appear: many of these posts were filled by the same people, either in rotation or cumulatively. Despite royal edicts, the mayors, élus, and treasurers were often the judges, councillors, or public prosecutors of the assize court. In turn, these judges and king's prosecutors, such as the Tallebots above, were almost invariably landowning sieurs or seigneurs. By 1670, these men already controlled the countryside with very little direct interference from great landed nobles, the provincial government in Rouen, or the crown at Versailles and Paris. The crown wanted two things from them: order and tax revenue. So long as they provided both, the crown had no reason to interfere in local governance.

If the traveler were to return south, 2 kilometers' walk out of town from St. Martin's Church would bring him or her to the magnificent gardens and chateau of the baron de Cany, Balthasar la Marinière. Built in 1640–46 around a *cour d'honneur,* the three red-brick wings of the chateau framed terraces, gardens, and pools surrounded by hunting woods and the river. Claude Saugrain described it in 1726 as "well-built, ornamented with great gardens and beautiful avenues."[21] Even that consummate snob, the duke de Saint-Simon, was delighted by the estate and its owners during his visit.[22] But la Marinière was forced to sell the chateau and seigneury to stave off bankruptcy, to his brother-in-law Pierre de Becdelièvre. Thereafter it was the country seat of the marquesses de Cany, a line of venerable and increasingly wealthy robe nobles who were judges in all three superior courts in Rouen. Henceforth, the family often spent only court vacations from late August to Saint Martin's Day in the Caux. Their new chateau reflected a new sensibility among elites: the growing emphasis on privacy and detachment from the common life of the countryside that can be seen in noble architecture throughout the period.

Following the wooded Durdent valley upstream another 3 kilometers
from the chateau would shortly bring a traveler to the bourg of Grainville-la-
Teinturière. This was a solidly prosperous, nucleated settlement, dotted with
about two hundred slate- and thatch-roofed houses. The dyers, or *teinturières,*
who lent their craft's name to the town in the Middle Ages claimed to trace
their roots back to the age of the Neustrian kings. The banks of the stream
were still lined with dyers' workshops, linseed oil mills, and grain mills that
lay along one of the high roads. The town's largest guilds were housed along
the river, using the Durdent's waters to turn linen and cotton from the Cauchois countryside into brilliant and highly exportable wares. The river ran
with dye pollutants, however, an unintended export that flowed downstream
into Cany and Vittefleur on the way to the Atlantic. Trade followed production in the town. Three fairs a year drew in textiles, livestock, and manufac-
tures on the day after Ascension Day in spring, the twenty-fifth of July, and
the third of February. Despite the fairs and the significant artisanal quarters
along the waterway, the name *bourg* might still be the first to a visitor's lips.
By 1713 the community would have around 780 solvent souls, with 173 taxable hearths and four privileged noble hearths. Again, one of these noble
houses belonged to the judge of the assize court.[23]

Apart from its natural complement of textile workers and rural artisans, an
observant visitor in Grainville-la-Teinturière would see lawyers, judges, notaries,
surgeons, and sergeants in the streets and buildings of the town. Like Cany,
Grainville-la-Teinturière was a small administrative center, with law courts
and a hospital. Close by the river was the seigneurial and later the royal assize
court, with jurisdiction over approximately thirty parishes, and the seat of a
noble sergeantry extending over thirty-nine parishes.[24] The high justice was a
ducal seat, one of seven high justices under the jurisdiction of the vast duchy of
Longueville. The community sheltered the nearby hospital and lazar house of
St. Jacques, dating back to 1292. By order of the king in 1695, St. Jacques gathered in the residents of eleven other lazar houses, and the Religieux de Charité
were brought in to care for the occupants of its twelve beds.[25]

The inhabitants of Grainville-la-Teinturière took civic pride in their
ancient institutions. They had been governed far longer by the Romans and
the Normans than by the French, a fact that was reinforced by their dependence on a customary code and usages whose core dated back to Norman
times and by their use of the local patois. The bourg was built over the ruins
of the Roman town of Gravinium, and the Ruelle de Rome that ran through
the center of town was the old Roman road that stretched from the Seine to
Boulogne. In the later Middle Ages, the village's lord had been the explorer
Jean de Béthencourt, who in 1402 added the rather more impressive title
king of the Canary Islands to that of seigneur of Grainville-la-Teinturière.

Despite the diversity of social strata, this was also a town whose judges
and officers still participated in the common life of the community. The

magistrates and attorneys were above all a familiar presence in the taverns. The old ducal courtroom flooded frequently when the Durdent overran its banks, and in the early eighteenth century Judge Jean Rousselet threw in the towel. He began holding itinerant court in three of the larger taverns in Grainville-la-Teinturiére: the Croix Rouge, the Trois Marchands, and the Image Saint-François.[26] Each year, on a Sunday in July, the entire community gathered after mass for the "white procession" in honor of the town's escape from the plague in 1610. Those who had been cured of an illness draped themselves in white cloth and led the procession from the church to the feast. On ordinary Sundays, officers and parishioners met together on the high street at Ste. Vièrge (or Notre Dame) Church, where they confronted a terrifying sequence of religious paintings at mass, beginning with the fall of Babylon and ending in the Apocalypse.[27] By the custom of the seigneurie, the judge enjoyed the place of the seigneur at mass when the lord was out of town.

After nearly two centuries in the hands of the ancient Longueville family of dukes and peers, the duchy escheated to the crown in 1694, dramatically affecting the town. The family's rule ended with the redoubtable Anne-Geneviève de Bourbon. The mother of the final duke, she had been a famous frondeur and the mother of one of the duc de la Rochefoucauld's sons. The last duke, mentally ill since childhood and genteelly imprisoned as an abbot in his own monastery, left no heirs.[28] Through both sale and inheritance, the seigneury of Grainville-la-Teinturière passed from the dukes of Longueville into the hands of the neighboring marquis de Cany. The new connection brought a surge of civic patronage to the town. The de Becdelièvre family, who spent Parlement recesses in their chateau downstream, rebuilt the hospital, church, and market, giving new life to the town's center.[29] By the ancient law of escheat, though, Grainville's high justice reverted to the crown in 1694 as a royal bailiwick court. The transfer was largely cosmetic, however. The court performed many of the same functions, and with much the same personnel, as the old high justice.

Thirty kilometers east across the wheatfields lay the the principal seat of the duchy of Longueville (and the appellate court for Grainville-la-Teinturière), at Longueville-sur-Scie. The Scie River was another water route down to the sea, running parallel to the Arques River, which passed through the royal bailiwick town of Arques and the port city of Dieppe. The town was still dominated by the rather brooding medieval chateau and priory on the hill above it. But the impressive ducal superior court was entirely separate from the chateau. It was inside the town proper, and the royal judge from Arques who came to look over the domain on the last duke's demise described the imposing six columns standing along the length of the courtroom. Its geographic scale was grand as well. The high justice had appellate jurisdiction over six inferior ducal courts and approximately 105 parishes spread across the central Caux, of which Grainville-la-Teinturière was one.[30] Longueville was, in fact, larger than most royal jurisdictions in the province. As in Cany-Caniel, the court enjoyed appellate oversight from the Parlement alone. Many of Longueville's records, sadly, vanished in the neglect of Duke Jean's long twilight years. Judge François Boneventure Quilleboeuf de Blosville described his consternation on opening the charter room of the chateau in the summer of 1694 to find three wagonloads of papers strewn about.[31] Enough survived to indicate the large scale of the duchy as a judicial and economic enterprise, however, and to shed some light on its functioning as a superior court.

Numerous other lords' courts dotted the plains and coastal districts of the Caux, three of which appear in the story as representatives of village high justices. Ten kilometers southwest of Cany, a traveler in a small river valley would find Valmont, the principal seat of three high justices in the sprawling duchy of Estouteville. Atop a rocky outcropping above the village were the medieval donjon and the delicate Renaissance wing of the chateau, attesting to the longevity of the duchy. Valmont's noble jurisdiction over more than sixty parishes was thoroughly enmeshed with the marquis de Cany's noble jurisdiction at Cany-Caniel, spawning court battles into the 1780s over which portions of the parishes of Cany and Barville belonged to which seigneur's court.[32] Three kilometers' walk north of Cany towards the Atlantic coast was the small high justice of Vittefleur, overlooking the Durdent as it meandered down to the sea. And far across the flax fields and cereal plains to the northeast was the high justice of the comté d'Eu. A sprawling, fragmented court with at least twenty-three parishes cut adrift from its main jurisdiction, the county of Eu had two parishes within the bailliage of Cany.

Thoroughly intertwined with each other, these eight royal and seigneurial jurisdictions in the central Caux were broadly representative of provincial justice in France. From ancient manorial courts deep in the countryside to royal bailiwicks seated in bourgs and towns, these were the assizes that served most of the French population. They were very far from the specialized law practice of the superior courts of Parlement or of the king's councils at Versailles. But they were very near to the problems of property, family, and local order that absorbed early modern villagers and townspeople. Increasingly, they became the real locus of order and authority across much of the Caux countryside.

Dramatis Personae: Officers of the Ordinary Courts

The pays de Caux provides a useful profile of the men who crowded the stage of the king's ordinary courts (see table 2.1). Between the years 1670 and 1745, the central Cauchois courts examined here employed 357 officers for whom identities can be found. Thirty-six of these men were the highest rank-ing judges in their courts, twelve of them seated in the royal courts (known as lieutenants general) and another twenty-four occupying the seigneurial court benches (baillis).[33] Below them served four lesser judges with criminal or civil specialities; their most important function was replacing the presiding judge in his absence (lieutenants civil, criminal, and particular in the royal courts, and the confusingly named lieutenants general in the seigneurial seats). These forty men completed the top echelon of offices, whose functions were primar-ily judging and overseeing la police in their jurisdictions.

Practicing before them on the parquet were 161 barristers, solicitors, and councillors in the courts. First among them, and often far more influential than the lower-ranking judges, were the twenty-three king's prosecutors (*pro-cureurs du roi*), who served only in royal jurisdictions. Their formal function was to defend the interests of the king, and by extension the public, a role in certain ways equivalent to that of a modern public prosecutor. As the legist Daniel Jousse described their broad mandate, it was to "watch over the interests of the king, the public, minors, and others persons who cannot defend their rights by themselves."[34] In the conclusion phase of a case, the prosecutor recommended both a verdict and a sentence to the judge and his councillors before their deliberations. Paralleling the king's prosecutors in the lords' jurisdictions were the fiscal prosecutors (*procureurs fiscal),* who were employed to represent the interests of the seigneur in his or her court, prosecute public crimes in the jurisdiction, and as the name implies, to pur-sue the lord's financial interests and revenues in court. Most lower royal courts also had *avocats du roi,* or king's advocates. These were lower-ranking public posts and were sometimes held cumulatively by the king's prosecu-tor. In many rural jurisdictions, they performed few if any functions.

Beneath the king's or seigneurs' prosecutors ranked the thirty-four coun-cillors of the courts, who counseled the judge in making his decisions from the bench. Councillors were required to have legal training, since their brief during the trial was to help conduct inquests and examinations and report the facts of the case to the judge. In the final deliberations in a case, they took a majority vote with the judge on the verdict and sentence. By the late seventeenth century, the offices of the councillors had been split into a half dozen subspecialities and sold off as a royal fund-raising measure. Need-less to say, the same councillors frequently bought up the functions that had been alienated from their original offices.

The councillors were joined by seventy-seven barristers (*avocats*) and twenty-three solicitors (*procureurs)* to make up the solid core of the middle ranks. Barristers, or attorneys, were required to have a law license from one of the French law faculties, and they alone were allowed to submit oral or written arguments to the court. Solicitors, trained by apprenticeship, were allowed to prepare the written facts of the case. Plaintiffs in royal courts were legally required to use a solicitor, and they were often the only quasi-legal services used by plaintiffs or defendants in simple cases.

Supporting the professional cast of solicitors, lawyers, councillors, and judges was a company of characters whose social origins reached deeply into local society. One hundred fifty-six sworn surgeons, notaries, clerks, sergeants, ushers, jailers, guards, adjudicators, royal measurers of weights and land, and receivers of goods worked the eight courtrooms in central Caux. They were almost invariably local sons, most from peasant or weaver backgrounds, and their family networks firmly grounded the king's and lords' courts in local society. Indeed, it would be hard to walk through any good-sized village in the Caux that did not have an extended family member working in the courts in some capacity. Because these lesser functionaries were not required to be received formally in the court and often did not appear in court records, their numbers were surely much higher than the actual records allow us to document. Together, these men formed a distinctive hierarchy in the French countryside. They were a vertical cross section of tax-paying families who worked together in the assize courts, forming the thin black line of daily governance in their bailiwicks. (See Glossary for further definitions of officers.)

The Pyramid of Ranks: Cauchois Society

The economy of the Caux, like its political institutions, was undergoing major change. Our astute observer riding along the Roman roads would have recognized it in the waving fields of flax that now covered the Caux, announcing the proto-industrialization of the region.[35] Weavers, drapers, dyers, and spinners were as much a part of the landscape as rural cultivators and rich landlords. With such an intensive economy, nearly a quarter of a million people were hidden in the folds of the rural Caux. Roughly eighty thousand of them were dispersed across the the élection of Caudebec alone, almost equivalent to the total population of Rouen.[36] In the later eighteenth century, the peripatetic Englishman Arthur Young remarked that the pays de Caux was "a district more of manufacturing than agriculture; in the resources of its inhabitants, the farm only comes after the factory."[37] The Caux was also wealthy, exporting not only linen and (after 1700) cotton, but brilliantly dyed cloth, glass, paper, playing cards, and lace as far as the West Indies and Guinea.[38] "From the twelfth century onwards," wrote Marc Bloch, "there was no countryside richer than that of the Caux and lower Normandy."[39]

By 1670, a traveler through the pays de Caux would find a markedly different social structure than had existed at the beginning of the century. Alongside the explosion of spinners, weavers, and textile workers in the

Table 2.1. Local judicial officers of the pays de Caux, 1670–1745

Royal baillages of Longueville, Grainville-la-Teinturière, Cany; high justices of Cany-Caniel, Grainville-la-Teinturière, Valmont, Vittefleur, Eu, and Longueville

Office	Number
Highest ranking officers: judges	
Lieutenants general (royal)	12
Baillis (seigneurial)	24
Lieutenants civil, criminal, particulier (royal) and lieutenants général (seigneurial)	4
SUBTOTAL	40
Middle-ranking officers and legal practitioners	
Procureurs du roi (royal)	23
Procureurs fiscal (seigneurial)	4
Conseillers, conseillers-assesseurs, et al.	34
Avocats	77
Procureurs	23
Controlleurs	8
Receveurs des consignations, commissaires aux saisies réeles	3
Adjudicateurs	1
Chirurgien juré	2
Notaires	20
SUBTOTAL	195
Lower-ranking offices	
Greffes	17
Huissiers	14
Sergeants	65
Gardes	6
Arpenteurs (surveyors)	11
Jaugers (measurers)	9
SUBTOTAL	122
TOTAL OFFICES	357

countryside came an increasingly sharp differentiation between wealthy peasant land exploiters and the nearly landless peasants beneath them. Change had been just as dramatic at the summit of the social pyramid. The district was effectively emptied of resident titled nobles much of the year, except of the impoverished variety. Local power devolved ever more on the rural property exploiters who held both land and administrative authority in their hands. The dominance of that group one historian has called "les ruraux aisés,"[40] a loose oligarchy headed up by the gentry (both sieurs and lesser seigneurs), wealthy laboureurs, and rural merchants, was perhaps the salient political and social feature of the pays de Caux.

At the top of the social pyramid, we can see a transformation much like that observed in England in the same period, the "abdication of local government responsibility by country-house owners."[41] Three prominent aristocratic families had held sway in the bailiwicks of the central Caux before the later seventeenth century. The dukes of Longueville had been governors of Normandy and sword *baillis* of the Caux, and under the leadership of their last duchess, first-class rebels in the Fronde. But the duke, Henri d'Orleans, died at Rouen in 1662.[42] The duchess, Anne-Geneviève de Bourbon, left the French court for Normandy in 1655. She found a new political outlet there for several years, protecting her subjects through court cases in Parlement and exercising direct patronage on the estates, even hand picking the judges for their ducal courts. (A vivacious extrovert, she remarked that she always loved being acclaimed by a crowd of "gens sans condition."[43] Another contemporary explained that she was always searching for something to "console herself for the disgust" that she felt for her husband.)[44] But she surprised everyone by withdrawing from provincial politics to the convent of Port-Royal in her later years and died in 1679. The estate was then managed in absentia by her brother, the prince de Condé, before it escheated to the crown in 1694.[45]

The Longueville family had also held the duchy of Estouteville since 1563, when Marie de Bourbon brought it into the family as a generous dowry. After Anne-Geneviève's death, however, the duchy and the high justice at Valmont were run by remote control for more than thirty years by her stepdaughter, the duchesse de Nemours (yet another absentee landlord), until her death in 1707. The new eighteenth-century dukes of Estouteville focused their attention on their Mediterranean principality, where they were the Grimaldi princes of Monaco, and at court, where they also held the title of dukes of Valentinois.[46] As with the grands elsewhere in France, the dukes and duchesses of Etouteville's orientation towards the court and urban centers had long drawn them out of direct contact with the Cauchois countryside.

The same noble absenteeism held true in Cany under the parlementaire family that acquired lordship and the high justice of Cany-Caniel over the surrounding community. Balthasar la Marinière, whose line had been ennobled by Charles VIII in the fifteenth century, had been a largely resident seigneur as baron of Cany. But his brother-in-law Pierre de Becdelièvre, the new marquis of Cany, lived most of the year in his elegant Rouen townhouse in St. Godard Parish, attending his judicial duties. The marquises occasionally spent more time in the countryside than their husbands, and at least one was notable for her charitable patronage in the town seats of their seigneuries. But it was a newer patronage that focused on civic building, patronage both less personal and less political than that of the old seigneurs of Cany and Grainville-la-Teinturière.

A new category of Caux landowners was perceptibly replacing part of the old resident nobility. Seigneuries vacated by older noble families, some of the middling sort such as Balthasar la Marinière's, were increasingly snapped up by absentee magistrates and financiers who inhabited upscale quarters of Paris and Rouen most of the year. Their judges (baillis), stewards, and wealthier tenants kept order on their estates. Cany had a growing list of urban officers who exercised lordship in the surrounding countryside. Among these was a Parisian master of requests, two Parisian parlementaires, at least three Rouennaise parlementaires (including the first president of the Parlement of Normandy) and the first presidents of both the Court of Aids and Chamber of Accounts in Rouen.[47] Several of these high royal officers were also seigneurs of high justice on their own estates in the Caux, thus thoroughly mixing both private and public forms of justice in their portfolios. As will be seen, they were hardly royal enemies of seigneurial justice or of local courts more broadly; their private and public interests were equally engaged in having local courts function as independently and as well as possible.

The most prominent Cauchois seigneurs were increasingly distant from local governance, despite their continuing charitable patronage. As in England in the period 1670–1700, they built new country seats, enjoying more privacy and detachment from the towns and villages.[48] At least thirty new chateaux were built in the Caux in the seventeenth century, including that of the barony of Cany, which was moved out of the center of town and into the countryside.[49] Much as with English nobles, their charity too became "less personal and more institutional."[50] As one historian of the European nobility has shown, the traditions of patronage and open hospitality in the great houses was declining as privacy and new norms of civility took hold.[51]

In France as in England, the governing void was filled by men from similar social stations. On private estates in both countries, management was left to a group of increasingly efficient stewards. In France, estate stewards were usually drawn from the ranks of substantial laboureurs: men who were by and large literate, numerate, and expert at managing tenants, livestock, and money.[52] In England, the middling and lesser gentry rose to dominate public governance and law, swiftly replacing elites as active justices of the peace and as tax commissioners. With a few adjustments, the same generalizations held true across the Channel in the Caux; the officers of the bailiwick and tax courts assumed those public functions. As one historian has noted, the most prominent families could comfortably withdraw from local government by the late seventeenth century. They did so because of their "confidence in the stability and durability of local government without their participation."[53]

By the late seventeenth century, the Caux countryside was run on a daily basis by a network composed of three key units: landowning sieurs and (lesser) resident seigneurs; laboureurs and merchants (who were often indistinguishable from sieurs in the extent of their property exploitation and the amount of their taille assessment); and royal and seigneurial officers, who were normally drawn from one of the above two groups. These men, and occasionally women, found the court system an enormously useful arena for pursuing their family interests in land, market commodities, and offices. As the governors of local society, they also pursued their public duty in the courts: the obligation to keep good social order in the pays de Caux.

That local social order had sharply defined borders by the late seventeenth century, even below the level of sieurs and seigneurs. The village of Aubermesnil, in upper Normandy, provides a useful snapshot of rural Cauchois social structure. In 1695, the village had twenty-four taxpaying households. Eight percent of the taxpayers were notables, while another 8 percent were very substantial laboureurs who resembled sieurs and dames in the size of their exploitations. Next came the 21 percent of taxpayers, who were small but self-sufficient farmers, and the bottom 63 percent, who were petty farmers or exercised other occupations to survive. Below that, of course, came those too poor to appear in the tax rolls. Virtually all of the land exploited by villagers was rented, even that of the wealthiest laboureurs.[54] The vast economic gulf between neighboring peasants is starkly apparent from the tax records, even in a very small Norman village. Between the laboureur Terrien, who worked 64 hectares with a large herd of livestock, and the valet Testelin, who rented his small *masure* (farmstead) and less than a hectare of land, lay a world of difference.[55]

Guy Lemarchand found comparably large class differences in other Cauchois villages. At the bottom of the heap were the 5 to 20 percent of households that were considered *feux inutiles,* too poor to pay taxes. Just above them lived a class of *journaliers,* or day laborers, who worked fewer than 5 hectares of land, forming a population bulge of 30 to 39 percent of the parish. At the top were laboureurs, whose households numbered as little as 5 to 15 percent of the village, and who typically had an annual income that was twenty to twenty-five times greater than that of a day laborer.[56]

This social pyramid in upper Normandy—a few wealthy nobles, gentry, and laboureurs, set off against the mass of nearly landless agricultural and textile workers—was hardly unique within France. Many other French provinces achieved a similar profile through different combinations of customary laws and social mechanisms. Not unexpectedly, England too saw a similar shift in rural social structure in the seventeenth century.[57] For our purposes, the tax-paying threshold in the Caux can be regarded as a rough litigation threshold—that is, the population of those who had sufficient property to fight over or adjudicate. Those in the higher tax-paying brackets—the laboureurs, sieurs, merchants, and officers of the Caux—were naturally the litigating class par excellence. Those at or just below the tax threshold appeared in court more often than their status might suggest, but still considerably less frequently than their wealthier neighbors. The Caux's social structure was thus continually reenacted and reinforced in the royal and seigneurial courtrooms.

The intricate social hierarchies and institutions that made up the Caux were much like those in villages and towns everywhere in France. They were knit together by invisible filaments of law, custom, privilege, and usage that lay over the bailiwick like a fine mesh. These social structures were also constantly being tested by that motley crew that tested every early modern community: the young, the poor, the ambitious, and the nonconformist, especially the drinkers, Sabbath breakers, and rebels. Royal justice owed many of its successes, as well as its limitations, to these underlying contours. Understanding this social subsoil is essential to understanding the daily functioning of justice, because the real goal of the judicial system was the regulation of civil society, above all cases involving family, property, and social order. It was precisely through this useful regulation in the countryside that justice emerged as such a powerful force for shaping both the village and the state in the Norman province.

Crown and Gown: The King's Commissioners in the Caux

In fact, observant visitors did ride through the Cauchois countryside in the late seventeenth century, some of them the king's commissioners. They remarked on the district's local governors and inhabitants in their official memoirs, as well as surveying its economy and resources. The intendant of Rouen, Jean-Baptiste Desmarets de Vaubourg, toured the pays de Caux in 1698, apparently in gloomy weather. He found it "abundant in all sorts of grains which make up its principal resource," but "very high and cold, [and] inconvenienced by the extreme dearth of good water." Vaubourg reflected wryly on the people he met with during his official visit, presumably the officers who governed the district in the king's name. "One has to be accustomed to their manners," he mused, in order to advance the king's business with them. "But if they are more attached to their interests [than others are], this attachment can become useful to His Majesty when one knows how to use it."[58]

Exploiting the Normans' self-interest for the good of the king was a delicate art, however, even for a seasoned courtier. As Vaubourg journeyed deeper into the pays de Caux, he found himself tangling with local worthies whom he icily marked down as "ill-mannered and difficult."[59] They were not readily impressed, nor easily intimidated, by the king's envoy. Nearly a century later his successor, an infuriated Intendant Etienne-Thomas de Maussion, received the same treatment at the hands of local lawyers and judges. Maussion galloped into Cany in May 1788, summoned the bailiwick's royal officers, and delivered them a scalding rebuke for their refusal to register the Brienne edicts. The Cauchois officers' long habit of independence in local governance helped them weather both threats and bribery for eight days. They at last registered the acts (although "we cannot dissimulate our repugnance," said the king's prosecutor), then went out on strike for four months until the Parlement of Normandy was restored. The intendant of Rouen and the local Cauchois officers were fated to remain on different paths. Maussion would die on the scaffold in 1794, whereas one of his most vocal opponents in Cany went on to become a deputy to the Estates General. The local Cauchois courts were hardly unique in opposing king and chancellor. Lower courts had already done the same in Brittany and Dauphiné.[60]

Yet in 1698 Vaubourg firmly believed that the province was a royal success story, despite his annoyance with the king's local officers. Quite apart from the substantial tax revenues that flowed to the crown from Normandy, the region was in many ways an administrative showcase. "Justice has not flourished less in this province than arms," he noted with satisfaction.[61] He was not deceived in this belief. Normandy and the pays de Caux had, in fact, proved fertile ground for rooting the French judicial system. The province supported a complex structure of crown and seigneurial courts that was ultimately tied to royal administration in Rouen, Versailles, and Paris. Vaubourg had discovered a functional paradox. The Normans were rich in royal judicial institutions but preferred to use them for private or local ends. They were still amusing themselves, as the judge's porter grumbled in Racine, with their independence.[62] Yet the independence of the officers and gentlemen of the Caux was maturing and changing under the social conditions of the late seventeenth century, making them the obvious heirs to local governance. Such were the conditions of the Caux and the larger world when they stepped into that inheritance.

Chapter 3

Officers and Gentlemen

The Local Judiciary

These officers, having dearly bought their offices wholesale, must avariciously sell them again retail.

Charles Loyseau, Offices

Sieur Pierre Doré rode into the town of Grainville-la-Teinturière in late December 1699 to hold his first assizes as chief judge of the royal bailiwick. No one in the community would have been surprised to see him don the long black robe as a royal justice in court that day; he was already a prominent figure in local circles. Doré had been a practicing barrister before the bar of Grainville for at least five years, and before that an avocat au Parlement in Rouen. He held a parish office in his home village as treasurer of Bosville, a twenty-minute walk through the woods from the court. Three years earlier, in 1696, the rising lawyer had bought the judicial post of councillor-inquestor-examiner in the tax élection of Caudebec, the principal tax court for the entire pays de Caux. His banner year would be 1699, though. In the space of a few months he took over from the late sieur de Mongrime as the chief bailiwick judge of civil, criminal, and police affairs and ascended yet a third royal bench as president and councillor of the salt tax court (grenier à sel) in the port of Saint-Valèry.[1] To the parishioners in Bosville, Doré was omnipresent: dispensing poor relief and leasing church lands for the parish, sitting in judgment on their direct tax and salt tax disputes, policing the bailiwick as the lieutenant general of the assize court, and for a luckless few, being their landlord into the bargain.

"These men's places are not very considerable," thought John Locke, when he observed French ordinary judges during his travels in 1676.[2] He was both right and wrong. Comparing them, as he was, with the judges of the Parlements, he perceived that they had indeed fallen into the penumbra of the increasingly brilliant, wealthy, and closed society of the superior courts. Yet within their districts, the same legal elite was growing richer and more influential by the year. Their contradictory fates make them challenging political subjects. Unlike the judges of superior courts, whose world has been intimately analyzed in recent decades, the judiciary of the ordinary have only recently become objects of interest. For want of detailed evidence, they have often been portrayed as men who practiced merely for honor, in the absence of apparent income from their work.[3] But these men were far more economically calculating and politically powerful than Locke's remarks imply. It is not too much to suggest that they had concentrated much of the local administration of France into their hands by the late seventeenth century, enjoying a deep, hidden reservoir of both profits and power.

The singular nature of local governance becomes apparent when we look at the officers of the ordinary courts in the round, as their neighbors must have seen them. The most distinctive feature of their power was the possession of cumulative offices, held simultaneously or in rotation with their colleagues in the district. It was usual for men of the king's bench or lords' courts in Normandy to command cumulative posts as mayors and échevins of towns, élus, judges, and receivers in the tax élections, lieutenants of police, subdelegates of intendants, presidents of salt warehouses, business managers of titled nobles, treasurers of parish churches, and overseers of hospitals.[4] Through these *cumuls,* or accumulated offices, a small coterie of legal men often monopolized posts at every level of local administration: the parish, the bailiwick, the élection, and even the généralité. The bailiwick court provided the natural locus of their authority. It was the institution with the broadest jurisdiction, the highest prestige, and the busiest clientele.

The activities of men such as Doré throughout the civic institutions of the Caux invite us to rethink local governance. It was carried out not so much by a set of discrete institutions as by a traveling nucleus of men who fluidly handled taxes, crime, poor relief, property law, communal disputes, and dozens of public matters from the stirrup. They functioned in a way that was deeply analogous to the way English J. P.s did, even though the J. P.s have long been supposed to be an utterly different kind of local governor. Despite important formal differences in the provision of their offices and in their national roles, both types of judges performed work that was essential to the stability of early modern communities. Judge Doré had much in common with such men as Edmund Tew, an English J. P. in Durham who was also a governor of Newcastle Infirmary, the rector of Boldon parish, and a middling landowner.[5] English J. P.s were the usual commissioners of the window and land taxes, arbitrators, and judges with extensive civil and criminal jurisdiction. They were also in charge of the equivalent of *la police* (including markets, roads, poor relief, and grain supplies).[6] With some variations, their French counterparts across the Channel in the Caux performed the same functions, buttressed by their natural authority as landholding sieurs and seigneurs.

The purely local powers of these legal elites in France would translate itself onto the national level only in 1789. Recent studies of the Revolutionary period and the early nineteenth century have emphasized precisely the critical role of the legal notability, who dominated the third estate in elections to the Estates General of 1789 and went on to become part of the backbone of provincial governance.[7] But the century and a half before the Revolution was their true formative period, one that forged an educational, political, and administrative elite in the French countryside. Their revolutionary role was in some ways an unlikely journey for men who had enjoyed none of the national outlets that English J. P.s could take for granted by the late seventeenth century: influence and "interest" in local elections, seats in a lawmaking Parliament, and a working relationship with the crown courts in London.[8] Only by understanding the French legal elites' local powers can we see how they stepped so confidently into the breach in 1789.

To reconstruct their political trajectory, we must also attempt to pull back the curtain on their mysterious economic underpinnings. Historians have long shared a widespread misconception that lower judicial offices were not *rentable,* or profitable enough to justify the capital investment, except in the coin of prestige and dignity.[9] Their offices, concluded one scholar, were a "means for the intelligent and dignified use of their leisure, because the real thing for them was the administration of their fortune, daily life, or even the life of the cabinet."[10] William Doyle has recently challenged the notion that there was a uniform decline in the desirability of ordinary court offices over the eighteenth century. But he too has concluded with Phillip Dawson that these offices "could not have been bought for financial gain," the profits being "notoriously slender and erratic."[11]

Yet it is increasingly difficult to reconcile this theory with the almost meteoric careers (in early modern terms) of many local court families, who accumulated capital at a pace unmatched by any other group in the countryside. The legal class of the Caux can give us some insight, however tantalizing, into their admittedly murky finances. They indicate that the economic value of local judicial offices has long been underestimated, on the assumption that the king's insufficient and often unpaid *gages* (or interest on the office) and official *épices* (fees or emoluments) were the principal sources of judicial income. Although many officers earned substantially more in fees than had previously been thought, those fees would scarcely seem enough to raise middling officers such as king's advocates and councillors into the company of king's judges and noblemen. But this ignores the key economic incentives for judicial offices: preferential access to local land and loan markets and a panoptic view of the entire economy of their distict.[12] The focus on formal payments obscures the fact that judicial offices tended to draw other kinds of wealth in their train, above all land and other offices. Many years ago, Victor Tapié fruitfully speculated that these offices might be "an observation post and a defense, a means of influence and a source of indirect advantages from which an entire family group would profit."[13]

From their perch high above the parquet, officers and attorneys were at the epicenter of the rich land market in the Caux. Debtors' auctions, sales by decree, curatorships of minors, and secured loans (preferably by seigneuries) all passed through their hands, and not a few properties remained in their hands at the end of the day. They were also at the epicenter of a hidden treasury of fees, collateral offices, and yet higher titles. The courtroom provided the nexus of their varied investments, allowing them to wade deeply in the revenue stream. With the profits from these investments, they could pursue, either for themselves or for their children, the property, titles, and education so necessary for a person of culture in the late seventeenth century. The misjudgment of earlier observers was to separate the public performance of the officers' duties from the private stewardship of their property. The effective and careful use of office was, for many judges, the most important element in the stewardship of their private fortunes. We need to look at both the public and private sides of magistracy to understand these men's place in local society.

Bailiwick Governance and Administration

Historians of early modern courts across Europe have long been fascinated with the powers judges held over the least members of their jurisdictions, especially criminals and the poor. These were indeed great powers. But as a recent study of English J. P.s astutely noted, the judges themselves were surely more gratified by the influence they had over people who really mattered in their jurisdictions: the gens de bien. These were the powers that allowed a magistrate to assume the "leadership of his neighborhood," not merely the domination of those almost helplessly beneath him in the social scale. "Because he wielded power over both the poor and the taxpayer, a justice could regard himself as the leader of an entire community."[14] This complete identity, as both leader of his peers and paternalist to his inferiors, is what helped transform French local judges into administrators and governors.

The functions of the chief judges were both broad and deep. Quite apart from holding original or appellate jurisdiction over all but a minority of law cases in the kingdom, they were local administrators par excellence. Their most vital administrative function, from the crown's perspective, was *la police:* the moral, political, and economic regulation of their districts. It was so central to a local magistrate's identity that Intendant Michel Chamillart wrote Colbert in 1689, worried that the establishment of the new office of lieutenant of police in Rouen would ruin the chief judge of the bailiwick court, "whose principal functions are policing."[15] (Many royal judges simply did the obvious and bought the post of lieutenant of police). When the crown announced the creation of lieutenants of police in every town with a lower royal jurisdiction in the Edict of October 1699, the posts were usually either bought by local magistrates or bought out and suppressed by the communauté of the town.[16]

Local military functions also flowed to the king's bench during the seventeenth century. Under Louis XIV, who reinvoked the arrière-ban, responsibility for raising the feudal levy or the payments that replaced military service often fell to the lieutenant general of the bailliage in default of the bailli, or sword noble.[17] Around these three poles of their identity—as magistrates, keepers of public order, and quasi-military figures—they attracted a large set of civil responsibilities. Their tools of the trade were not only court judgments and mercurial assizes (which brought together all the notable corps of the district for mandatory instruction from the judges), but also regulatory sentences issued from the bench that were the local equivalent of parlementary *arrêts de règlement.*

We can see the judges' public functions best as a series of concentric circles spreading outward from the parish to the central state. Within the district's parishes, those duties included auditing the accounts of parish treasurers; settling disputes over church leases; supervising the village communities (where villages were functional legal corporations); and attempting to keep unwed mothers, the poor, and vagabonds from becoming a charge on the parish. Since the Ordinance of 1539, all disputes between parishioners and their curés, or priests, except for purely spiritual matters, came into the bailiwick courts. The Ordinance of Blois in 1579 required curés to turn over each year the parish registers of births, marriages, and deaths to the royal bailiwick courts, where they were kept. Magistrates were also kept busy at the parish level enforcing employment terms between masters and servants, supervising taverns, and upholding moral order at the retail level.

The parish was the most intimate level of their public jurisdiction. Much as with English J. P.s, a magistrate's parish duties were at bottom about ensuring the "customary social behavior on which communal life depended."[18] Judges took calumny, slander, and verbal abuse seriously, particularly if an affront to the reputation of the more propertied villagers was involved. A noble seigneur appeared in the audience of Cany-Caniel in 1730 to complain that he had been a victim of "profane insults" by another parishioner on the street next to the church, a man who had also spread calumnies about his wife. In a rather unusual move, Judge Bréard had the defendant confined in jail to prevent his flight from the jurisdiction.[19]

Much of the moral jurisdiction that had once belonged to the church and the officialité courts were now by law brought to the bailiwick benches. Almost every act, civil or criminal, that could be considered a sin had gradually been poached from the church. Sins were redefined as crimes: usury, perjury, sorcery, and blasphemy, to name only a few. The border between church and state justice was finally stabilized by an edict of April 1695 that reserved some jurisdiction to ecclesiastical courts. The church retained its jurisdiction over spiritual matters and over the internal discipline of its own clergy, but the nonspiritual behavior of either clergy or lay people was now in the hands of a secular judge. Dancing, gaming, and drinking were the most common moral behaviors that taxed bailiwick magistrates, judging by their administrative orders from the bench. Taverns were natural sites of moral disorder, and magistrates often had to send out sergeants to police the taverns on Sundays and feast days.[20] These were common issues for early modern communities. English single justices (acting alone out of sessions) or double justices (in petty sessions) spent significant time licensing alehouses and punishing minor offenders for verbal abuse and drunkenness.[21]

French magistrates took particularly seriously cases of unwed mothers and their infants in the parishes of the jurisdiction. Their concern was not only to uphold the religious and moral fabric of the community but also to prevent mothers and children from falling into poverty and requiring poor relief from the parish. Not merely young women, but older women and widows also appeared in the courts to pursue paternity cases. The chief judge of Grainville-la-Teinturière, Jean Rousselet, firmly enforced the paternity claims of a thirty-one-year-old widow against the illiterate man she had been living with for more than a year and a half.[22] On becoming pregnant, women were required by royal law to file *déclarations de grossesse* with the courts, the better to police infanticide in the parish. But such cases were exceedingly rare, and the few infanticide prosecutions in the Cauchois records were mostly prosecuted against men, not women.[23]

The constant preoccupation with preventing the poor from becoming settled in the parish or a drain on local charity was just as pressing in other early modern states. It was exactly these sorts of cases that occupied Richard Gough, the seventeenth-century Shropshire diarist, who often brought poor-law cases before the English county quarter sessions.[24] Poor relief to illegitimate children and the indigent from parish funds was one area where French magistrates enjoyed less direct authority than English justices, who administered the poor rates as part of their duties.[25] But as Judge Doré reminds us, judges often performed those functions as treasurers of their own parish churches.

Overseeing the accounts of the *fabrique* (church vestry) and keeping an eye on the important arable land leased out by the vestry were sometimes vexing judicial responsibilities. A rash of cases in the early eighteenth century saturated the Cauchois courts as curés, parishioners, and treasurers engaged in increasingly frenzied suits and countersuits. Within two weeks in the royal court at Cany, three men had sued the curé for mismanagement of funds, and the treasurer of the church at Clasville had sued four other sieurs for mismanagement of their church funds.[26] A month later, the surgeon and treasurer of

Ancourtville parish sued the priest to force him to return the church coffer and its documents to their accustomed place and to restore the cemetery. The judge ordered that the communauté be called to hear the matter before issuing a final ruling on the case, a very rare instance of the community's being acknowledged in the Cauchois records.[27] The parish cases reveal a very tight world of sieurs and seigneurs, dames and demoiselles, some of them charged with "borrowing" parish funds or renting church properties amongst themselves or to relatives at strongly favorable rates. The overlap of court officers with treasurers was so common (and abuses so troublesome) that the Norman Parlement issued an arrêt in 1736 forbidding chief judges, lawyers, and king's prosecutors to act as treasurers of the fabrique.[28] The directive, like so many others, was a dead letter on arrival.

Within the circle of the communauté, the corps of propertied inhabitants who controlled the common lands, apportioned taxes, set dates for harvesting and planting, and made other communal decisions, the bailiwick courts had also absorbed some of the functions of adjudication and decision making. In Normandy, the community of inhabitants had only a weak legal presence.[29] One historian has attributed the frailty of the village community in part to the dispersed habitat in the Caux but even more to a social structure that allowed a small group of exceedingly wealthy land exploiters to reserve the use of the common lands to themselves, where such plots still existed.[30] The community was legally nonexistent in another sense as well. Neither the Custom of Normandy nor the Custom of the pays de Caux mentioned it as an institution, leaving it almost destitute of legal status in the local courts. Without juridical or village support, the community rarely appeared as a presence in the courts of the Caux, although it appeared regularly in Burgundian courts.[31] Disputes over communal issues were brought to court by individuals, not by the community of inhabitants. The community appears to have been replaced for tax-assessment purposes by an irregular village assembly, an assembly that also elected churchwardens and village syndics after 1680 but almost never engaged in other financial or land-use decisions.[32]

As they stepped outward into the larger circle of the bailiwick, judges were required to enforce the upkeep of roads and bridges by an often unwilling populace, police the markets and fairs, oversee the craft guilds and swear in their guards, and supervise royal and seigneurial officers practicing in the jurisdiction. Perhaps their most challenging, and sometimes impossible, charge was executing new economic and political orders that emanated from the royal councils or the king. Magistrates had to enforce (or choose not to enforce) in their bailiwicks major royal policies, such as those on Protestants, dueling, and coinage. These public matters of police and administration naturally often overlapped their court jurisdiction over the private matters of individuals and families. But the magistrates' civil and criminal jurisdictions were more properly judicial functions and are treated separately in chapters 6 and 7.

The judges' powers of economic regulation over markets, guilds, grain prices, fairs, and taverns gave them broad discretion to intervene in the daily economy of their bailiwicks. Most crucial was their control over bread and alcohol, the vital life forces in any early modern community. Bread was so central to public order and private life that bailiwick judges, usually in consultation with the bakers and grain merchants of the jurisdiction, were allowed to set prices. The king's prosecutors were required to pass along the prices of grain and bread in their jurisdiction to the parlement once or twice a month in most provinces, one of the few communications that central authorities required from the localities. Alcohol had the added importance of being one of the principal sources of indirect taxes, or *aides,* for the French state. The court of Cany-Caniel's royal charter gave magistrates control over "bread, wine, cider, and other items in all villages and bourgs," as well as supervisory rights over the guards of the crafts and control of weights and measures. In Brittany, as one historian noted, roughly 30 percent of regulatory orders issued from the bench in some sénéchaussée jurisdictions involved foodstuffs and subsistence, especially fixing the prices of bread and grain.[33]

It was no coincidence that local courts usually held petty assizes on market days, as Cany-Caniel's judges did on market Mondays.[34] Magistrates did so not only for their clients' convenience, but also because the market halls fed them a steady stream of lucrative cases. It also gave judges an immediate opportunity to police the price of goods in the market and to ensure that bread and other essential commodities were not being sold on the black market, outside of the public market or customary shops. They seem to have exercised their economic powers with discretion, however. In most cases judges and public prosecutors appear to have waited for disputes to be brought to them from the market halls, rather than aggressively seeking out problems. Plaintiffs, for their part, were eager to bring cases across the street from the market to the assize sessions, making the system largely self-regulating.

Magistrates on local benches also exercised early modern versions of zoning and public safety authority, to the extent that they existed. They patrolled public fire hazards such as falling chimneys, insisted on rudimentary street cleaning as a sanitation measure, and ordered bridges and dikes to be rebuilt, the latter sometimes in tandem with other authorities. Magistrates also ruled on who had the right to construct and run profitable enterprises such as mills and taverns. The judge of Longueville was called to rule on a dispute between a titled noble and a noble sieur when the latter began building a new grain mill in the central parish of Longueville.[35] The rights of *banalité,* which allowed seigneurs to force their tenants to use grain mills, bread ovens, or wine presses belonging to the lordship, were frequently disputed by commoners in the courts. Both parishioners and mill owners came to the Cauchois assizes to make good their claims that their households were not under the ban of a particular seigneur. The king's prosecutor Charles de Lombard, a nobleman and sieur, sat in as judge on the royal bench of Cany during one such quarrel. The marquis de Cany's attorney arrived to complain of a repeat offender against the seigneury's *ban de moulin*. He was prosecuting the laboureur Charles Le Rouge for at least the third time for refusing to use his seigneur's grain mill, even after having 500 livres in amends judged against him the previous year.[36] Local sieurs, too, contested their "servitude" to a particular seigneur's ban at the royal assizes, using the courts to adjudicate both real financial exactions and pricklier honorary ones.[37]

Economic policing of their districts was a large charge for magistrates, one complicated by royal financial schemes such as the Law scandal. The syndicate of the Scottish banker John Law had issued nearly 2 billion livres of share certificates. They circulated as legal tender in France until the pyramid collapsed in 1720–21.[38] The circulation in the Caux of paper *billets,* which rural peasants used profitably to pay off debts, was rapidly followed by the billets' demotion to worthless paper. The collapse sent novel cases to attorneys and judges as creditors scrambled to refuse the worthless billets of debtors. As one historian has noted, Law's introduction of paper money had the happy effect of allowing many French villagers to repay creditors and get out of debt after 1719.[39] The Law cases provide striking evidence of the monetarization of the countryside and the speed with which new instruments of exchange or credit penetrated into rural communities. The parties to the cases were not only sieurs and seigneurs but also laboureurs, all of whom had been unwittingly caught in the net of international speculation.[40]

The bailiwick courts were no strangers to state financial schemes even before Law. Judges and notaries, who regulated markets and handled contracts, were left with the day-to-day responsibility for enforcing or ignoring the king's orders concerning exchange rates, foreign currency, and other commercial regulations. In early 1679, Intendant Louis Le Blanc began corresponding with the controller general about the crown's attempts to regulate foreign exchange rates. "Foreign monies, ducatons, patagons, and esqualins circulate throughout the généralité of Rouen," he explained, and royal attempts to fix the exchange rates "make the Normans cry out a great deal."[41] Nevertheless, on May 22 the king issued a royal declaration that no foreign coins would be accepted for payment. That order was unenforceable by local judges who supervised the markets and executed contracts, not least because the king's own officers paid their debts and did business in foreign specie. A few years later, Intendant de Vaubourg was remarking anew on the steady current of foreign coins entering Normandy through the Spanish trade.[42]

In the absence of merchants' consular courts in the countryside (they existed only in Rouen and, later, Dieppe and a few other port towns),[43] bailiwick courts exercised their functions in regulating mercantile matters. Judges were the court of last resort for most corporations in the Caux, too, which turned to local magistrates when self-regulation failed. The mayors and *échevins* of the municipal corps, the guilds, hospitals, and royal officers' corps all found their way to the king's bench, the one jurisdiction broad enough to resolve their differences. Early modern corporations collectively controlled cash, offices, wages, prices, apprenticeship terms, and craft production, so the residual authority granted to courts was significant. The corporations were a legal enclave unto themselves, governed by private statutes and therefore largely self-regulating. But the bailiwick courts had to administer the oaths of many of their members, including the sworn guards of the trades, who were required to attend twice-yearly mercurial assizes to hear the judges' harangue on local regulations. The inhabitants' complaints about prices, quality of goods, attempts to circumvent tariffs or market dues, and misappropriation of corporate funds crossed every magistrates' bench.

Many rural corporations were landlords as well, particularly churches and hospitals. In regulating the usage rights and privileges attached to virtually every piece of land in the bailiwick, magistrates exercised perhaps their broadest and most dramatic economic power. Because seigneurial fiefs were regularly subdivided, leased, and subleased throughout the Caux, determining which obligations were attached to any given field or orchard could be confounding. Seigneurs could not agree on which houses in a parish were in their jurisdiction; tenants fought to escape their seigneurs' monopolies on milling, baking, and wine pressing. Case documentation could span several centuries, including competing charters, conflicting witnesses, and appeals to traditional usages. One such contest, a struggle between a titled noble and an ecclesiastic over property rights, allows us to see the wide jurisdiction over both privileged persons and property enjoyed by judges. The marquis de Cany sued the sieur curé of Bosville for seigneurial dues owed on church lands, which had been donated to the parish in a notarial contract in 1673 by the previous lord, the almoner of the duchess of Longueville. The contestants brought in a sheaf of *aveux* from tenants dating back to the sixteenth century, to prove whether or not the disputed dues had ever been paid to the seigneur. The judge condemned the curé to pay back dues. More important, he had the authority to transfer responsibility for the church *terrier* (the record of lands and tenant obligations) from the curé to Bosville's treasurer.[44]

A judge's decision from the assize bench could mean substantial economic or property advantages to the winner and always involved the honor of the contestants. In these sorts of cases, judging the rights and privileges of their district's elites, Cauchois judges and attorneys were in their element. Their legal expertise and their power to uphold or undermine the property and honor of neighboring elites through judgment made them considerable in their own right. This was why, as will be seen, it was imperative for magistrates of bailiwicks and of important high justices to be men of property and substance, always sieurs and often nobles. It would have been unthinkable for noblemen and noblewomen to submit their claims to a judge who did not at least belong to a rough "gentry" class, if not already a nobleman himself.

Not least among the elites and corps they judged, royal magistrates supervised the king's officer corps in the district. Bailiwick judges were required to investigate the mores, religion, and professional capability of all men before receiving them into office in their jurisdictions. In 1680, seigneurial judges were also required to submit to examination and be received into royal courts, which then administered their oath of office.[45] For candidates well known in the district, these could be cursory inquiries, but they were often taken seriously. The royal bailiwick court at Grainville-la-Teinturière inquired into the characters of lawyers, clerks, and even inspectors of weights and measures. They called in attorneys and sergeants to testify that candidates had regularly attended divine service and to affirm that they were capable of fulfilling the office.[46] Judges and prosecutors were also called on to discipline royal and seigneurial officers for malversation, theft, and violence in the performance of their duties. The local powers of bailiwick officers were great, and the consequences of official corruption could be dire for the justiciables of their districts.

The right of magistrates and public prosecutors to police both individuals and corps throughout the parishes of the Caux was extensive, but officers typically exercised their powers with discretion. Judges of high justices, like that of Cany-Caniel, were explicitly granted rights of "police and visitation over all tenants" in their charters.[47] French judges, like their English counterparts, also exercised the right to summon parishioners to court with bench warrants to answer charges of disrupting the peace or violating the law.[48] The power of French courts to pursue and investigate suspected malfeasance even without a plaintiff, which makes up much of the work of the modern "police," gave magistrates and public prosecutors a large reserve authority over their neighbors. But contrary to the English stereotype of a French judiciary teeming with police spies and prosecutors, the rural bailiwick system tended to work much like the English county model. Court cases were largely plaintiff driven, and if no victim complained in civil or misdemeanor cases, the courts usually initiated no pursuit.

Beyond the horizon of the bailiwick, in their widest circle of responsibilities, magistrates found themselves facing the same issues that plagued officers of state on a national scale. The conditions of late seventeenth- and early-eighteenth-century life in the Caux increasingly required magistrates to cushion their districts from national and international turmoil. Warfare, famine, taxes, and that unofficial fifth horseman of the apocalypse, global markets, repeatedly threatened the stability of local Cauchois communities. The nobility no longer deployed their own private armies or arsenals to maintain local order in the breach, nor were the highest titled nobles more than an occasional presence in the district, unless they were financially ruined. As one historian of the European nobility has noted, by the middle of the seventeenth century the "community changed within the country . . . as gentlemen ceased to accept the natural leadership of the most eminent local landowners."[49] These gentlemen increasingly asserted their own leadership as officers and land exploiters.

Of all the challenges they faced during public crises, the judges' most onerous and sometimes dangerous duty was policing the grain and bread market during times of dearth. With only nine archers of the maréchaussée to act as armed backup for more than eight hundred parishes in the élection of Caudebec, magistrates had little ability to compel obedience when parishioners started a grain riot or sacked a bakery.[50] Particularly violent or threatening offenders during food disturbances might be disciplined in court later, but only after the whiff of popular violence had dissipated. Like the rest of France, and often more intensively than its urban centers, the Caux experienced successive waves of dearth and famine between 1670 and 1745. The worst local episodes, in 1685, 1693–94, and 1709–10, presented Cauchois magistrates with urgent cases. The sufferings of villagers and townspeople fetched up in the royal and lords' courts in the form of rising caseloads of game poaching, wheat theft, debt foreclosures, and wardship hearings for new orphans. The specter of rioting and disorder was never far from officers' thoughts. In January 1685, Intendant René de Marillac remarked on the enormous number of mendicants plying the parishes of the pays de Caux, adding that emergency grain was being imported from Holland and Danzig to attempt to head off the crisis.[51]

The grain shipment in 1685 was a relatively rare offer of rural assistance from the crown. Crisis imports usually went straight to cities such as Rouen, where the potential for disorder was highest. Bailiwick judges were charged with regulating the grain trade in the countryside, a duty they shared with town councils in larger towns (although again they often filled these municipal offices themselves). Little help was forthcoming in the next famine, infinitely worse, which brought devastating mortality to France in the winters of 1692–94. Four years later, the intendant could still clearly see the marks of demographic carnage written across the district. The Caux, he remarked, "had suffered more than the others in 1693 and 1694, and had lost a great number of inhabitants."[52] That was still a gross understatement; parishes such as Saint-Vaast-Dieppedalle buried nearly a tenth of their residents.[53] The great freeze and famine of 1709–10 were little kinder. As elsewhere in France, peasants lost their leases in waves of foreclosures, which had to be executed by the courts.[54] The hunt for surviving heirs and for orphans' curators was the grim task of lawyers and judges across every courtroom in the district.

In rioting and famine, we can most clearly see the disconnect between local magistrates' political responsibilities (to keep order) and the resources they were offered by the state to do so (none). Like urban magistrates, local judges often had only one recourse when confronted with subsistence riots: they simply negotiated the sale of grain or bread at more or less the price the crowd demanded.[55] The bulk of a magistrate's responsibilities in the somber aftermath of famine, pestilence, or war had to do with reconstructing families, inheritances, and communities, one case at a time. The assize records of Grainville-la-Teinturière during the famine of 1692–94 are littered with property seizures and wardship hearings, in which judges supervised the transfer of both children and goods into the hands of living inheritors.[56] Some of these transfers naturally underline the superior resources of those with landed wealth during economic crises. Judge Pierre Alexandre, the sieur de Mongrime, approved property seizures in at least six parishes during the famine, many of which reunited the property of commoners with the sieurs or seigneurs who had leased them out. His colleague downstream, Judge de Neville, entered a default judgment at the July 1694 Cany-Caniel assizes against a widow who had not paid her *fermages* since the last Saint Michael's day and who likely was unable to afford legal counsel either.[57]

More than cruelty on the part of landlords was involved in these property seizures, however. A number of Cauchois farms had been abandoned or vacated by death during the famine, and the courts needed to issue judgments voiding the leases in order to bring lands back under production. There were also cases of sieurs and dames appearing at the assizes to pay the debts of tenants during the famine, as a dame from Cany-Caniel did in 1694.[58] Here we can see the judges performing, on a crisis scale, their normal functions in the bailiwick: the orderly transfer of property and children from the dead to the living. But through such crises, we can see how quickly their functions crossed over from affecting the private sphere of families to the public sphere of the bailiwick. By establishing new tenancies, transferring property to new owners, distributing inheritances, and ensuring the care of children, judges helped restore the community's ability to reproduce itself.

Foreign wars were second only to famine in creating vexing problems of local governance in the Caux. Coastal areas became scenes of devastation during twenty-eight years of intermittent French warfare, leaving officers to cope with whole towns reduced to begging, homelessness, and hunger. During the Dutch War (1672–79), Intendant Louis le Blanc wrote to Colbert asking for urgent repairs to the jetties in Saint-Valéry-en-Caux and Fécamp and relayed a message from the towns that they lacked both powder and bullets to defend themselves with.[59] The War of the League of Augsburg (1689–97) added injury to insult during the harshest famine of the seventeenth century. Dieppe suffered a "disastrous bombardment" in 1694 that knocked down many houses in the port, while the hostilities cut off one of Saint-Valéry-en-Caux's principal fishing routes to Newfoundland for cod. Had the war not ended, Vaubourg recorded in his memoir, the Caux "would have lacked men for farming, [and] one can see even since that time that the people . . . have been reduced to letting part of the land lie uncultivated or ill cultivated."[60] The misery spread into the robust trade of Rouen, as merchants deserted the Seine River for the safer harbors of the Loire.[61]

The king's foreign wars were costly for French villagers and townspeople. The assize courts were where many of the bills came due for the king's subjects, long after the battles had ceased. Judges and lawyers coped with a steady stream of dismal cases: deserting infantrymen caught on the run, heads of household who had left for the king's service and not come home, peasant families tipped over the edge by escalating taxes, and creditors unable to collect debts or rents in the general chaos. In the royal court at Grainville-la-Teinturière, Anne Broux appeared before the king's bench one winter for permission to act as a free woman in her financial affairs. She had heard news that her husband had been "killed in the bloody battles at the siege of Mantua, during which there have been cruel and numerous defeats."[62] The judge agreed that her husband would likely never return home from the campaign and granted her request to become head of household so that she could settle their debts.

The war came home in other ways, too; the royal recruiting militia were almost as feared as the enemy in the Caux. They roamed the roads in the late seventeenth and early eighteenth centuries, drafting reluctant and often drunken soldiers for French campaigns. During the War of the Austrian Succession, two sabot makers from the village of Hocqueville fled from army recruiters, only to murder the cavalier from the mounted constabulary who captured them.[63] Three potential soldiers were lost to their Cauchois villages without having set foot on the battlefield. The courts were left to pick up the pieces, both dispensing punishment and redistributing property.

Wars and taxes were not the only state policies that magistrates grappled with in their parishes and bailiwicks. Religious edicts placed local judges and prosecutors in the position of enforcing religious conformity in their district or dealing with the extensive civil and family consequences of non-conformity. In 1669 the king eliminated the *chambre de l'édit* at Rouen, the parlementary chamber responsible for trying cases involving Protestants, which threw these matters back to the lesser jurisdictions.[64] The revocation of the Edict of Nantes (the Edict of Fontainebleu) in 1685 required Protestant churches to be razed, their ministers to leave the country, and property to be confiscated from Protestants who had previously left France and not returned within four months of the edict. Protestants still in France were forbidden to leave the country, and their children had to be brought into parish churches for baptism and Catholic instruction. "Local judges are to supervise this," the edict pointedly decreed, leaving bailiwick magistrates to police the consciences and property of their Protestant neighbors.[65]

With its close proximity to the Dutch Republic and England, Normandy had traditionally sheltered a large Protestant minority, so the religious edict was particularly burdensome to local bailiwick courts. Greedy kin who had remained Catholic or returned to the fold fought in court over the property of fleeing nonconformists. Those who stayed had to petition the courts for proper burial for their Protestant family members. In 1697, the royal bailiwick judge of Longueville was petitioned after religious conflict broke out in Dieppe, culminating in a deadly fire. The bourgeois plaintiff's brother, a lifelong Protestant, was killed in the conflagration, and the plaintiff needed permission to bury the cadaver. The judge gave the order for burial, but stiff fees were sometimes exacted for such permission.[66]

If the king's men in the bailiwick had long helped to articulate and order the local society around them, then, they were increasingly called on to buffer it from stresses above. The expanding Atlantic economy, foreign wars, and escalating royal demands for taxes drew the Cauchois ever deeper into world currents. French and international affairs became local problems that local officers had to remedy at the court bar. In small country towns across the Caux, events as diverse as the collapse of the Mississippi bubble, the Dutch War, and the international herring markets and cotton markets drove the wheels of local litigation. Judges and lawyers worked to restabilize families and villages one case at a time. They resolutely waded through successive tides of bankruptcies, orphans' wardship hearings, and the melancholy aftermath of wholesale deaths in their bailiwicks. The courts had insufficient tools to stave off human-caused catastrophes originating at Versailles, never mind natural catastrophes on the order of those that struck France in the seventeenth century. But the king's men did provide a way for communities to reorganize their property and families after each blow while restraining disorder and rioting.

Gentlemen and Gentry: Social Status of Bailiwick Officers

To exercise such wide governing responsibilities in the seventeenth and eighteenth centuries, a judge needed to occupy a social berth that would give him natural authority, not merely juridical authority, over his district. Ruling on the privileges, rights, and properties of nobles, clerics, officers, and seigneurs–that is, of the wealthiest and most influential members of his district–was a matter of great prestige and influence for a judge. The foundation of that authority was the personal jurisdiction enjoyed by bailiwick courts, which made them the first arbiter of every individual's dispute in the district, regardless of class, estate, or privileges. The only exceptions to a bailiwick court's personal jurisdiction were those enjoying the privilege of committimus au grande sceau (princes, peers of France, and high state officials) or au petit sceau (officers of the sovereign courts) and clergy accused of purely ecclesiastical crimes. The status of judges began to rise as early as the middle of the sixteenth century, as one observer noted, when courts replaced armed combat as the usual arena for property disputes. Nobles suddenly "found themselves waiting as humble petitioners before even minor judges and officials" who controlled litigation and therefore controlled their property outcomes.[67]

The judges who sat on the assize benches of the Caux occupied a social and economic plane that in England was largely covered by the term *gentry*. Sieurs and seigneurs, and in many districts often from the lower nobility, they were among the comfortable landowning classes of the countryside. (In smaller jurisdictions and in poorer districts, French judges were taken from a slightly deeper strata of the third estate than English justices of the peace would have been.) Judge Doré of the bench of Grainville-la-Teinturière was an exemplar: a holder of sieuries and multiple offices, he concentrated his investments in local land and royal posts. Yet despite his long local resumé, Judge Doré was merely an *arriviste* compared with his colleague Tallebot de Saint-Ouen. Holding court a few kilometers north down the Durdent River, Judge Saint-Ouen commanded the king's bench in Cany for at least twenty-five years, from 1691 until his death in about 1716.[68] Like the majority of Norman lieutenants' general, he was noble before buying his judgeship and the seigneur of a parish just outside the town.[69] Wealthy and well connected, his estate continued to generate lucrative fees for his old colleagues long after his death. For us, the court dossiers have a different payoff in helping form an idea of his family wealth and connections. Saint-Ouen's judgeship was worth 15,000 livres on the market; the buildings of his manor house at Saint-Ouen were rented out for 150 livres a year.[70] His minor children were granted annual funds sufficient to support a small parish. His widow, Dame Marguerite Claude De la Champagne, consoled herself with a new husband, the seigneur de Fremont, who sued the Saint-Ouen curators for 3,000 to 4,000 livres a year in upkeep for the six children. (The grant was apparently moderated to 1,000 livres a year.)

In royal bailiwick courts and important high justices alike, significant property was both an official and an unofficial qualification for acting as a local magistrate. Early modern magistrates were presumed to be the natural judges of their peers—that is, of other propertied men and women—as well as legally licensed judges. In England, that status was enforced by Parliament, which set a property qualification for magistrates as early as the fifteenth century.

English magistrates also had to pay the *dedimus* to the crown to qualify as active justices, fees which amounted to nearly one-fifth of their required 20 pounds' annual income from land. (The income threshold was later raised to 100 pounds.) The fees were steep enough that "justices developed scruples over the purchase of a judicial office," with a few unable or unwilling to pay to exercise their appointments.[71] In France, the propertied status of local magistrates was essentially ensured by the price of the office. Cardinal Richelieu had finally resigned himself to venality by seeing it in precisely those terms: the cost of ensuring that disinterested and economically independent men would serve on the bench, instead of men avid for money. Venality, he concluded, "excludes from charges and offices many people of low condition," a feature that made the practice of selling offices "more tolerable."[72]

One observer has aptly characterized the local French jurisdictions as "the antechamber of the petty nobility," at first glance a curious observation about offices that were not ennobling per se. Yet they were not merely an antechamber but a manufactory of new nobles. Despite the speculation of earlier historians that the number of nobles was actually declining in the ranks of local officers in the seventeenth century, and that these officers were separated from the nobility by a "sensible barrier,"[73] the Norman records tell a surprising story. The Parlement's receptions of 176 lower royal officers between 1702 and 1746 reveals that 61 percent of the highest-ranking judges (lieutenants general and presidents) were already noble before taking office, and 48 percent of the lower-ranking judges (lieutenants civil, criminal, and *ancien*) were also noble. In total, 30 percent of all officers accepted into the lower bailliwick and presidial jurisdictions were members of the second estate. Below the level of judges, however, the gulf of nobility widened abruptly; only 14.5 percent of officers below their rank were noble[74] (see table 3.1). The Cauchois records indicate that in titled high justices, the seigneurial judges were frequently noblemen as well. Moreover, few of those whose family histories can be traced in the Caux emerged from the old nobility. Rather, they came from families that had shrewdly used the advantages of legal offices to insinuate themselves into the nobility over several generations. The few detailed studies that have been done in other provinces indicate variations in the rate of heredity and the percentage of nobles among local officers, depending on the wealth and size of the jurisdiction. But even in Brittany, a significant number of noble judges remained after the crown purged the lists of the nobility in 1668–71.[75]

The Saint-Ouens, like other elite Cauchois court families, were intimately connected with the middling nobility of their district as well as with royal financial court families as far away as Rouen. When twelve tutors were elected from the late Judge Saint-Ouen's and Dame Marguerite's relatives before his old bench at Cany, they included nine seigneurs and sieurs, at least five of them noblemen.[76] The noble judge Alexander Baudry, who

Table 3.1. *Qualité* of lower court officers, Normandy, 1702–46 (présidials, bailliages, vicomtés)

Officers received	Years	Total no. of officers received	No. of écuyer	Percent of écuyer
Lieutenants general and presidents	1705–46	41	25	61.0%
Lesser judges and officers	1702–18	135	28	20.7%
All officers	1702–46	176	53	30.1%

Breakdown of lesser judges and officers received

Officers received, by category	Total no. of officers received	No. of écuyer	Percent of écuyer
Lieutenants particulier (civil, criminal, ancien)	25	12	48.0%
Lieutenants assesseurs	2	1	50.0%
Conseilleurs also holding office as procureurs du roi or avocats du roi	9	2	22.2%
Procureurs du roi	27	4	14.8%
Conseillers and conseillers assesseurs	48	5	10.4%
Avocats du roi	20	3	15.0%
Enquêteurs	1	1	100.0%
Assesseurs certificateurs	1	0	0.0%
Unknown	2	0	0.0%
TOTALS	135	28	20.7%

Source: ADSM 1 B 3654, Parlement, réceptions des lieutenants générals, 1705–46; réceptions des officiers, 1702–18.

Sword nobles confirmed as vicomtes and baillis of lower royal courts have been subtracted from this list, as have the lieutenants general of the admiralities.

The list of *Réceptions des Officiers* included several lieutenants general of the lower courts, who for some reason were not recorded in their own list of *Réceptions des Lieutenants Général*. Since this first list ends in 1718, it is probable that additional lieutenants général were received between 1718 and 1745 who were also mistakenly recorded on a general list of officers.

shared a courtroom with Saint-Ouen as the judge of the high justice of Cany-Caniel, together with his wife, Barbe de Miot, were also closely related to four nobles in Rouen. It is interesting to note that two of her noble relatives in Rouen were the king's general advocate and one of the councillors of the Court of Aids and Accounts, to which local Cauchois officers had far closer connections than to the Parlement.[77]

In one of the few personal letters remaining in the judicial records, Barbe de Miot's kinsman, M. D'Angouville, wrote to her eloquently as well as calculatingly less than two weeks before the curatorship hearing for her children. "I don't doubt that you will be a good mother," he reassured her, and he was confident that she would never "leave the management of [the children's] property to another who will not manage it like we will." He explained how he would use the court's controller to help secure his own election, or that of his alternate choice, as principal cocurator with Madame Baudry. "The judges will make no difficulty," he reassured her, "the same thing being practiced in the tutelle" of another family. The close familiarity of court families with each other, and with the procedures, customs, and precedents of the courts, gave them considerable property advantages.[78]

Kinship relations were found everywhere among Cauchois lawyering and judging families. Tallebot de Saint-Ouen had for many years shared his courtroom in Cany with the judge of the high justice of Cany-Caniel, Jean-Baptiste de Neville, seigneur of Rommanville. Neville was in turn a tutor of the children of his kinsman the prominent Grainville lawyer and sieur Jacques Ozment, who perished during the famine of 1693–94.[79] In 1704, Neville was succeeded on the Cany-Caniel bench by the above-mentioned seigneur Alexandre Baudry, whose own children came under the tutorship of both the court officers also noted above and of his kinsman, the judge of the high justice of Valmont.[80] These families were linked together by marriage and godparentage, as well as by vocation and education. The families were not endogamous in the strict sense of parlementaires; their wives came from a broader rural social spectrum than only judicial families.[81] But their fictive and real kinship bonds made them a visible and distinctive elite within the small world of the bailiwick.

As with the English justices of the peace, it can be difficult to assess precisely the level of landholding or land exploitation among assize court and high justice judges.[82] Their status as sieurs and seigneurs is suggestive within an order of magnitude, certainly placing them in the top 10 percent of local inhabitants. Unfortunately, not enough notarial records or testaments remain from the Caux with which to fully reconstruct their landed wealth. But the circumstantial evidence suggests that significant landholding was a prerequisite to the highest local judgeships, ensuring that a judge had the leisure to pursue public duties and the excess capital to invest in the office.

One of the most magnificent magistrates in the pays de Caux was not a royal judge, but the last seigneurial judge of the ducal house of Longueville, the noble seigneur Jacob Bontemps. His stature is not surprising, since Bontemps in effect served the same functions as a royal judge in the duchy of Longueville, overseeing 108 parishes. He supervised a half dozen lower courts and took appellate cases from them, which made him the head of one of the largest jurisdictions in Normandy outside the city of Rouen. All civil and most criminal cases in the district were heard by his high justices. All appeals from his central court at Longueville went directly to the Parlement of Rouen, just as a royal bailiwick's appeals would have.[83]

Bontemps also held an estate equivalent to that of a lieutenant general of a bailiwick court. First President Claude Pellot noted that he bought his office for 34,000 livres, although the office "wasn't worth 1,500 to 2,000 livres of rentes to him."[84] Pellot's statement not only gives us an index of his wealth; it also acknowledges that magistrates at all levels thought seriously and with calculation about the financial returns from their royal or noble offices, far beyond the honors and privileges attached to them. The cost of a lieutenant general's office in the royal courts of upper Normandy ranged from about 15,000 to 60,000 livres, which placed Bontemps well within this rank.[85] He could, in fact, have bought a royal judgeship instead. Although royal edicts and ordinances, including those of Blois and Orléans, explicitly forbade the sale of judgeships in high justices, Bontemps' case illustrates the actual state of affairs.[86] Offices at all levels in noble courts were purchased. Seigneurial venality was not unique to Normandy, either. Victor Tapie noted that the office of bailli for the barony of Craon in Anjou sold for 13,000 livres in the mid-seventeenth century, and most interesting, that the officer paid an additional 8,000 livres to the seigneur for the right of survivance.[87]

This right of survivance gave the seigneurial judge the same hereditary rights and conditional property rights in office as most royal officers acquired through the paulette (an annual fee guaranteeing hereditary office), creating yet another parallelism between these offices. Not only judgeships, but the offices of fiscal prosecutor, lieutenant, clerk, and others in high justices were sold or leased like royal offices, although the seigneur had considerably more control over who the purchaser would be than the king did.[88] The rationale behind seigneurial venality and heredity was simple. As Tapié pointed out, "the monarchy engaging in commerce with its judicial offices, the seigneurs also sold theirs."[89]

Despite the internal social split in the local chambers between noble magistrates and their usually nonnoble subordinate colleagues, they often shared an important underlying social and economic orientation. Both middling and upper court officers had a strong class identity with propertied sieurs and seigneurs in the countryside. Local capitation (direct tax) records and ordinary court records indicate that many of the nonnoble officers were sieurs, that is, men who held sieuries (lands without feudal rights) but not seigneuries (lands with feudal rights).[90] As a group they were strongly entrenched in property in their districts, as landlords, land exploiters, and holders of local *rentes.*[91] This judicial profile corresponds rather closely to that observed in England. J. A. Sharpe has remarked on the "close correspondance of the hierarchy of officers and the social hierarchy" in the English courts, noting that judges were typically country gentry, and that constables and other low-ranking officers were normally drawn from the ranks of substantial villagers.[92]

The capitation records for court officers in the Caux tell a useful story about their berth in the rural and bourg hierarchy. In 1701, for example, the king's prosecutor for the royal court of Cany paid 45 livres in capitation, while the clerk of the court paid 30 livres; both men were sieurs.[93] In 1713, the bailli of the high justice of Cany-Caniel, the noble seigneur Baudry, paid 25 livres. The king's prosecutor, the sieur Fauconnet, paid even more: 46 livres, 10 sols. In contrast, the three highest-assessed nobles in the bailiwick district were the Dame de Cany, the widowed mother of the current marquis de Cany, at 40 livres; the widow and inheritor of the marquis de Houdetot, who paid her capitation in Rouen at 86 livres; and the seigneur de Criquetot, at 68 livres. The twelve other nobles who can be definitely identified as inhabitants of the bailliage were all assessed at under 40 livres, and three of them paid 5 livres or less. Both royal and seigneurial officers paid capitations that placed their fortunes well within the middling ranks of nobles in the district, and some officers were considerably wealthier than many resident nobles. Surprisingly, that ranking included the clerk of the court, whose capitation was higher than those of approximately half the nobles of the bailiwick.[94]

The social and professional status of magistrates was reflected in the mirror of local standing. The judges of the pays de Caux, like those elsewhere in Normandy, were men who took their places high above their fellows, whether their bench was in court or in church. One observer described the judiciary as a corps "installed at the summit of the provincial third estate, above the rentiers and the merchants."[95] Quite apart from their property and offices, they also enjoyed educations and local privileges that ranked them above even much of the old nobility of the plateau. If the lord and his family were absent, chief judges of high justices took their seigneur's place in the parish church. As one historian has remarked, they enjoyed "bread blessed by distinction and *préséance,* during processions and the divine office, before the other gentlemen inhabitants."[96] If the lord's judge was also absent, the honorary distinctions fell to his fiscal prosecutor or lieutenant judge. Symbolically and physically, the judge took the place of the noble seigneur in the rural pecking order.

The Power Grid: Local Governors and Their Networks

When Judge Doré surveyed his colleagues and subordinates across the chalk downs of the Caux, he saw a local governing class finely fused together by cumulative offices, marriages, and education. At least two of the practicing attorneys before his own bench were judges (baillis and lieutenants general) of high justices in the district. The attorney George Sausse was a sieur and a judge for the high justice of Ourville, 3 kilometers from Grainville. Sausse was also an élu, or financial overseer, for the tax élection of Caudebec, 14 kilometers south along the high road, where Judge Doré regularly met him again wearing his hat as a tax councillor.[97] Judge Doré's fellow attorney at Grainville during his lawyering years, and now his right hand on the bench, was the king's prosecutor for the bailiwick, Robert Maribrasse. Robert's father and brother, the attorneys Nicolas Maribrasse père et fils, practiced in the royal bailiwick court downstream at Cany.[98] Nicolas the younger also worked with Doré, though, as the fiscal and then as the king's prosecutor in the tax élection at Caudebec, just as his brother Robert filled those functions for him in the ordinary bailiwick court of Grainville.

The amicable relationships among Judge Doré and the Maribrasse brothers extended well beyond the courtroom doors. Their collaboration included circulating royal offices among themselves in the tight world of legally trained sieurs and seigneurs in the district. Nicolas the younger soon rotated one of his tax offices to Doré: he sold him his post as president of the salt tax court and put the capital into new offices and land for himself as he carefully maneuvered his family into the gentry. Indeed, Nicolas' ascent through the social and governing class of the bailiwick is a highly instructive one for us. Starting with a law degree in 1657, he bought the office of business solicitor (*soliciteur des affaires*) from the prince de Condé, brother of Duchess Anne-Geneviève de Bourbon de Longueville, in 1667. He simultaneously practiced as a lawyer in the royal bailiwick of Cany and in the high justice of Cany-Caniel, became the chief judge of the high justice of Epréville by 1689, and became the fiscal prosecutor for the royal tax élection in Caudebec.[99] His four-court straight ultimately depended on his lawyering skills: it required him to be proficient in Norman customary law, tax law, civil and criminal law, seigneurial privileges, and estate management.

By 1698, Nicolas Maribrasse had become sufficiently wealthy to add the presidency of the salt warehouse in Saint-Valèry-en-Caux to his portfolio, an office that had been worth 4,000 livres on the market in 1665.[100] By 1704 he had converted his local successes into the title of king's councillor (*conseiller du roi*), and had moved up to the post of king's prosecutor in the tax élection. The golden seal of the family's success was achieved in 1694. The attorney-brothers were reunited at the parish church in Saint-Vaast-Dieppedale for the summer wedding of the daughter of one of them, Françoise. Scions of a local legal dynasty, they were marrying the following generation into the Cauchois nobility. The groom was the son of the seigneur and patron of Grainville-la-Teinturière, who at that time may have been the insolvent parlementaire Jacques Le Roux.[101]

Over the course of their long careers, the attorney Nicolas Maribrasse and the judge Pierre Doré held multiple offices at every level of local governance: seigneury, parish, bailiwick, and élection. Their circuit of influence ran the length of the central Caux, from Saint-Valèry-en-Caux on the Atlantic coast to Caudebec on the Seine River. Nicolas' various jurisdictions were more than 40 kilometers apart as the crow flies. But he chose to remain domiciled in the parish of Saint-Vaast-Dieppdalle, a fifteen-minute horseback ride east through the woods from Grainville, where his land and family connections were centered. There he happily acquired a new style, perhaps the most coveted of all: the sieur of Dieppedalle.[102]

Ladders of Ascent: Cumulative Offices

On any given day of the week, men such as George Sausse, Nicolas Maribrasse, and Pierre Doré could be found at the center of every public body in the Caux. Their authority in each institution was enhanced by their membership in the others. If we look closely at the way cases were distributed in bailiwick chambers across the Caux, moreover, we can see how that power tended to become concentrated in the hands of an even smaller legal elite. Hundreds of men were either licensed as lawyers or held offices in the local Cauchois courts; up to seventy-nine of them regularly appeared at the royal grand assizes of Cany alone.[103] But a much smaller coterie really mattered. In the bailiwick courts, it was the chief judge, the king's prosecutor, the three to six attorneys who dominated most cases, and occasionally the lieutenant judge for civil or criminal affairs or the councillors.[104] These were the men most likely to hold other offices across the district, especially in the royal administration. Other provinces followed similar patterns with different offices. In Burgundy, for example, nineteen of the twenty-eight "Notables de la Ville de Beaune" who met to deliberate town matters were current or former judicial officers. The chief judge of the bailiwick court was the mayor, and several other court officers were current or former mayors and échevins of the town.[105] The creation of venal municipal offices by the Edict of August 1692 simply formalized this state of affairs.[106] The usual suspects bought the offices, despite the crown's intention of forbidding them to hold judicial and municipal offices cumulatively.

Cumulative offices were a financial strategy as well as a social one. As the judges and attorneys of Grainville-la-Teinturière demonstrate, lesser offices were sold and rotated among the legal class, sometimes over periods as short as a year. Although we cannot be certain, such practices suggest that officers might temporarily "park" capital in lower royal or seigneurial offices while waiting for land parcels or higher offices to become available. These practices would also suggest that the officers were getting sufficient short-term returns on these investments to make them attractive, without the longer terms of investment implied by rentes on the hôtel de ville, for example. Those who diversified their investments over several types of royal offices appear to have risen fastest, both in property acquisition and in the judicial hierarchy.[107]

Three main types of cumuls were practiced by men who served the king's bench in the Caux. Most common among young practitioners or new legal families was the simultaneous exercise of royal and seigneurial court offices. Those who were already rising in the ranks combined royal bailiwick posts with royal tax or municipal offices. Those who had truly arrived combined royal judgeships or councillors' offices with service as subdélégues to the intendants.[108] Multiple officeholding flowed in strong geographic patterns bound together by roads and trade. The royal administrative centers of Cany, Grainville-la-Teinturière, and Saint-Valèry-en-Caux formed one of these circuits. Longueville, Arques, and Dieppe formed a second circuit, with little exchange of officers between the two.

The latter type of cumul, with magistrates in the ordinary or tax courts acting as subdelegates to the intendant, is particularly interesting. It explicitly ties the local judiciary to another center of administration in the province, the intendancies, from which the courts were otherwise careful to protect their jurisdiction. In the 1690s, for example, the intendant's subdelegate at Arques was the chief judge of the royal bailliage court. He was a natural choice to carry out the commissaire's requests, since he already sat atop the local administration. He performed various commissions for the intendant, conducting local enquiries and collecting information on the district for the central administration.[109]

The intendants also tapped middling court officers for duty. In 1678 Intendant Louis Le Blanc authorized 2,101 livres to be paid to Aveline, a councillor in the bailliage of Rouen, and Le Page, president of the tax election, for expenses incurred as his subdelegates. In 1685, Councillor Aveline was still working for one of Le Blanc's successors, Intendant René de Marillac, receiving a 500 livre gratification for having "often aided him in his task, during his frequent absences from Rouen."[110] This service was more than a temporary necessity for the intendants of the district. Between 1672 and 1715, the intendancy of Rouen passed through the hands of no fewer than nineteen men, each on average serving a little more than 2.2 years.[111] With revolving-door intendancies such as this, it was necessary for the commissioners to rely on permanent local officers, preferably those in the courts or tax élections. In Brittany too, as one historian discovered, there was a "quasi-monopolization" of subdelegate posts by judicial officials, who were naturally placed to survey their jurisdictions and convey information to the intendants.[112]

The most lucrative cumul, one favored by those well up in the ranks in the ordinary courts, was the combination of royal judiciary posts with tax and municipal offices. These types of cumuls were explicitly forbidden by the crown–and everywhere practiced in the Caux.[113] Among the most common were the combination of chief judgeships with the office of mayor or lieutenant of police, both created as venal royal offices during and after the war exigencies of the 1690s. Posts as élus, tax judges, treasurers, and hospital administrators were avidly sought after as well. Cases of fiscal cumuls reached down into very small jurisdictions; the king's councillor for the élection at Arques, for example, was the fiscal prosecutor for the tiny high justice of Bacqueville in 1721.[114] Nor were such cumuls unique to Normandy. The chief judge of the royal sénéchaussée of Rennes was also the lieutenant of police, as well as the son-in-law of the king's master of accounts in the Chambre des Comptes.[115] The chief judge of rural Gueronde served repeatedly as the mayor of the town; both the chief judge and lieutenant judge of Dinan were administrators of the hospital.[116]

The practice of cumuls allows us to look more deeply into the social hierarchy of the courts, showing us the anatomy of a successful career that might eventually catapult a family into both judgeship and nobility. By far the most common cumul among the up-and-coming staff of the assize courts (and one not formally prohibited by the crown) was the exercise of judicial offices in both royal and seigneurial court jurisdictions. By the late seventeenth century, these two types of courts formed part of a single system, operated mainly by the same group of families in the Caux. The hypothesis that seigneurial and royal courts were engaged in a death struggle with one another, a struggle in which the state was destroying the power of noble jurisdictions, no longer makes sense when we look at the real individuals who held these offices. Largely the same officers and staff occupied both benches, although sometimes at different stages in their career cycles. Of the twenty-nine baillis who were accepted into office as judges in high justices between 1692 and 1740, eight had practiced as *avocats au grand conseil, au Parlement,* or *en Parlement* (see table 3.2).

The career of Simon Villedieu reveals how a savvy lawyer could braid together multiple royal and seigneurial offices into a sturdy ladder of social ascent. Villedieu first appeared as the marquis de Cany's fiscal prosecutor in the mercurial assizes of November 1700. By 1707, he was presiding over many of the high justice's sessions in the absence of the chief judge, Lanfran Hue. Over the next three years Villedieu pursued a successful strategy of clambering up through the royal court ranks at Cany while retaining his post in the high justice. In October 1708, he appeared at the mercurial assizes in

Table 3.2. Qualifications of high justice *baillis,* 1692–1740

Legal backgrounds of seigneurial baillis, 1692–1740	Number	Percentage	Percentage of avocats vs. nonavocats or unknown
Avocats au grand conseil	1	3.4%	
Avocats au Parlement	4	13.8%	93.1%
Avocats en Parlement	3	10.3%	
Simple avocats	19	65.5%	
Unknown or nonavocats	2	6.9%	6.9%
TOTAL	29	100.0%	100.0%

Source: ADSM 1 B 3646–3649.

the royal bailliage at Cany as an attorney for the court. By April 1709 he had bought the office of councillor-assessor in the royal court; in January 1710 he had risen to the post of lieutenant general of the vicomté (which was in effect the second judge of the bailiwick, since the bailiwick and vicomtal jurisdictions met as one court in Cany). Meanwhile, Villedieu continued in active practice as fiscal prosecutor in the high justice of the marquis until 1714. (He also apparently kept his post of councillor-assessor in the bailliage, which put him in the enviable position of giving counsel to himself on days when he substituted on the bench for the chief judge).[117] Villedieu simply changed hats when he arrived in the council chambers of the court in Cany each week, according to whether the king's bench or the lord's bench was in session.[118]

These patterns of royal-seigneurial inbreeding grow increasingly pronounced as we look down the social scale in the courtroom. Royal notaries, sergeants, ushers, clerks, and solicitors were the foot soldiers of the local courts, sometimes working as family clans in four or five courts simultaneously.[119] Rising clerks, notaries, and solicitors trained and lived as apprentices in the houses of current practitioners, strengthening the ties between them.[120] The unsung heroes of the Cauchois courts in this period were the sturdy Beuzebosc dynasty from the bourg of Cany. For more than thirty years, they made the rounds in a slow social ascent as clerks, notaries, and then solicitors in at least four courts.

Adrien and François Beuzebosc, father and son, were the scions of the family over the late seventeenth and early eighteenth centuries. Between 1689 and 1710, Adrien simultaneously practiced as the clerk, or *commis au greffe,* in the high justice of Grainville-la-Teinturière, the bailliage of Grainville-la-Teinturière, and the high justice of Cany; it is likely his practice actually began before 1689. François moved one step up the ladder from his father and practiced simultaneously as a royal notary and solicitor in the bailliages of Cany and Grainville-la-Teinturière and in the high justice of Cany from 1689 to 1723. François' son, Adrien François, became a fully fledged barrister in the royal court of Grainville-la-Teinturière.[121]

The strongest pattern of multiple practice was among the eight sergeants at the bottom of the tree of offices, who by law served both royal and seigneurial jurisdiction in the three sergeanteries of Cany, Canville, and Grainville-la-Teinturière. The royal sergeantries were owned by the marquis of Cany as a noble fief, but their holders performed the same functions for the royal courts as well. The tenures of sergeants who practiced in family dynasties were usually long: men such as Robert and Charles Auray, Pierre and Jean-Baptiste Hertel, Jacques and Pierre Le François, and Jean Huezé and Jean-Baptiste Cherfils I (whose families moved up in the court), served for twenty to forty years in their Cauchois posts. They often served concurrently with their sons or brothers, sometimes splitting up each sergeantry between them. In the late seventeenth century the Aurays took the sergeantry of Cany and the Le François family the sergeantry of Grainville-la-Teinturière. Those who practiced individually tended to have far shorter tenures, often fewer than five years, perhaps because they were squeezed out of exploits by established families.

The longevity of sergeant dynasties testifies to the educational barriers that stood between them and higher offices such as those of clerks, notaries, and solicitors. This was perhaps the longest and most difficult step of all up into officialdom. Nevertheless, Jean Huezé's son Pierre Huezé rose further in the royal courts, becoming both a solicitor and notary in the royal bailliage of Grainville in the 1720s.[122] Sergeant Jean-Baptiste Cherfils' son would become a seigneurial judge and a king's prosecutor for a royal court. These small dynasties at the lowest rung of the rural courts were thus one of the feeder schools for the next generation of legally trained men in the countryside: the notaries, solicitors, and lawyers, men who would in turn begin the difficult rise into the world of sieurs and judges.

A very different category of court cumuls were those bought out of necessity rather than for profit. The extraordinary multiplication of offices for revenue during the reign of Louis XIV fell most heavily on the local jurisdictions, which had few means of resistance other than to buy up superfluous offices either as syndicates or as individuals. The Parlement's records confirm the well-known collapse of some judicial offices into a few hands in each jurisdiction, a process that local records indicate intensified over the eighteenth century.

The most common of these "collapsed" cumuls recorded were those of the lieutenants general or presidents of presidials (appellate courts above the level of bailliages), who also held the chief judgeships of their bailliage courts (11 of 12, or 91.6 percent). They were followed by lieutenants general or presidents of bailliages and presidials who were also lieutenants civil, criminal, or particular, or in other posts (14 of 41, or 34.1 percent); and by king's prosecutors and advocates who were also councillors in the same court (7 of 36 king's prosecutors, or 19.4 percent; 2 of 20 king's advocates, or 10 percent).[123]

Since the Parlement did not formally receive most officers ranking lower than councillor or king's advocate, numerous categories of local office are not recorded. The Cauchois court records show, however, that these lower offices were particularly likely to be owned as individual cumuls or by syndicates of officers. The offices of receivers of consignations, assessors, reporters, inquestors, and examiners were often merely the second or third hats worn by councillors, king's prosecutors, and others in the middling echelons of local office. Royal notaries often practiced as solicitors in the royal court, more rarely as king's advocates. The joint effect of cumuls, whether voluntary or necessary, was to create a relatively compact administrative and governing class in the Caux.

Culture, Education, and the Ideal of the *Bien Publique*

An English visitor and justice of the peace, John Evelyn, was pleasantly surprised by the courtesy shown him by a local French judge. During one of his seventeenth-century journeys in France, Evelyn was falsely accused by his valet, served with a summons, and hauled into ordinary court the next day. "Both our advocates pleaded before the Lieutenant Civil," he recounted,

> but it was so unreasonable a pretense, that the judge had not patience to hear it out, but immediately acquitting me, was so civil . . . he rose from the Bench, and making a courteous excuse to me, that being a stranger I should be so barbarously used, conducted me through the court to the very street door.[124]

In short, the bailiwick judge behaved like an English gentleman, one of the highest compliments the English were wont to pay foreigners in their travels abroad. What passed between the two judges was not merely professional courtesy but a kind of social recognition as well.

The ordinary judge's level of civility should not be surprising. By the late seventeenth century, the judge of an important high justice or royal bailiwick court had a formal education that was nearly identical to that of a parlementaire. Both the sons of rural lawyers and the sons of noble urban magistrates were expected to pass out of the collège curriculum before matriculating in a law school, although wealthier families tended to patronize a select group of schools. As Richard Mowery Andrews has pointed out, this was a "total immersion" approach to the Latin language and the classics, requiring six to eight years of study in the humanities and philosophy. The content of their studies was so rigorously focused on the literature of ancient Greece and Rome and the seventeenth-century French classics that the next generation of elites emerged with an intellectual formation that set them apart from any other social group.[125]

Once they reached the law faculty, a two-year course (for the *gradué*) or a three-year course (for the *license*) was required. Many Cauchois practitioners graduated from the university in Caen, but a few had been to Paris or to other provincial faculties. There students got a sweeping (if often haphazard) introduction to the vast fields of Roman law, canon law, royal ordinances, parliamentary arrêts, and provincial customs. Roman law, with its standard texts, tended to be covered more thoroughly. The *droit français* was subject to rather idiosyncratic choices by different faculty, so unorganized and overwhelming were the various sources. But then, "formal education," Andrews reminds us, "was meant to shape the mind, not fill it with facts."[126]

The content of their education did shape minds, at least for those who were paying attention. Cicero's *De oficiis* ("On Duties") was standard collège fare, with its strong emphasis on public service as the centerpiece of a good life. For Cicero, justice was the highest form of public service and conferred the highest personal honor on those who exercised it. He particularly stressed the two cardinal duties of every magistrate: protecting individuals from injustice and protecting the boundary between the private and public spheres. "The primary function of justice is to ensure that no one harms his neighbor," he wrote. "Its second concern is that communal property should serve communal interests, and private property private interests."[127] The emphasis on a magistrate's obligation to protect private property (even against the state itself) is noteworthy here. As we have seen, the French jurist Jean Bodin, among others, elaborated on the same themes in his sixteenth-century *Six livres de la République*.[128]

French judges at all levels took these duties seriously, despite the inevitable lapses of some individual magistrates. As James Farr has pointed out, judges had a strong social motivation to take their magisterial duties seriously, since "their social persona was legitimated by the impartiality of their task, and their claim to high social status in turn rested upon this legitimacy."[129] Many internalized their vocational duties at a deeper level, too. Judging was considered a complete vocation—moral, ethical, and political all at once. The act of judging served the bien publique by preserving communal harmony, the foundation of a civilization.[130] Serving the bien publique was considered a higher magisterial duty than serving a particular ruler; it was a duty that magistrates performed *qua* magistrates, and not merely as the licensees of the king. Cicero's twin emphases on public duty and justice were widely reinforced in the judges' professional milieu, as well as in the collège curriculum. He was, of course, consciously evoking Aristotle, and especially Plato: "We are not born for ourselves alone (*non nobis solum nati sumis*)."[131]

The personal honor attached to skillful judging and lawyering was also brought home to collège students as they ground away at their Latin. "Justice," wrote Cicero, is "that brightest adornment of virtue, the means by which men gain the title *boni*." The boni were understood to be "the politically sound elements in the state"[132] as well as the morally good. To gain these honors, he explained, required practical skills, particularly in oratory and in mastery of civil law.[133] Magistrates also needed considerable private judgment to acquire a reputation for being just. In Rome, as in France, "we do not possess . . . a substantial, fully fashioned model of true law and genuine justice; we make do with its outline and hazy appearances."[134] Those who used their judicial gifts for the benefit of the greatest number would surely gain public glory, Cicero stated, no matter their station. He must have greatly reassured the many destined for provincial careers, too. "A reputation for justice is vital," he wrote, "even for the isolated country dweller."[135]

The education of lawyers and lower-court judges had experienced a rapid evolution by the later seventeenth century, enhancing exposure to both theory and practice. Since the Ordinance of Blois, the license from a law faculty had been required for all bailiwick judges as well as for all barristers. In a flurry of judicial reform measures enacted before the war years descended, Louis XIV required the law faculties to resume teaching civil law in 1679. As the edict regretfully noted, the study of civil law had been "almost entirely neglected for a century throughout France." (The king graciously omitted to mention that one of his predecessors had forbidden the teaching of Roman law.) Louis XIV also affirmed that the faculties should teach customary law alongside royal ordinances as an integral part of the droit français taught in the third-year curriculum.[136] In the Déclaration of January 12, 1680, the crown extended the requirement for the license in law to all seigneurial judges whose appeals went directly to the Parlement.[137]

As with any educational system, there were naturally wide variations among those who took the license: the students who cleverly managed to evade the attendance and examination requirements, those who chose less rigorous faculties, and those who graduated at the bottom of their class. It was not even unheard of for law licenses to be bought outright. ("The faculty of Reims," writes one legal historian, "was a veritable 'bridge of donkeys,'" much sought after by those with little time or aptitude.)[138] But the gradual enforcement of new educational requirements made legal men the most rigorously educated group in the French countryside, even surpassing the clergy.[139] In this area, French magistrates excelled their counterparts in Albion. Fewer than 45 percent of English justices of the peace had attended university, and fewer than 40 percent had attended the Inns of Court in London for legal education and apprenticeship.[140]

Although the effects of any one reform measure were dilute in the extreme, the local court records document that local justice had attained a noticeably higher standard by the early decades of the eighteenth century. The results were strikingly evident in the rural pays de Caux by mid-century. In the audience chamber of the small high justice of Valmont, two attorneys met to argue the case of a unmarried, pregnant linen worker who was claiming 1,500 livres from the estate of her child's father. The ambitious young attorney for the prosecution, Jean-Baptiste Cherfils, cited Latin law texts, Rousseau's commentary on the Criminal Ordinance of 1670, precedents from other Norman jurisdictions, and customary law in his client's suit. The opposing counsel, Christophe Viellot, matched him in Latin oratory. Not surprisingly, Cherfils would later become a deputy for the third estate in the Estates General of 1789.[141] Far from being the refuge of unskilled and ignorant practitioners, the high justices and royal ordinary courts in the countryside provided a debating ground for rising young men, who honed their skills on homespun cases.

The level of provincial legal culture was thus not nearly so primitive as literary wags liked to jest. Molière's *Comtesse d'Escarbagnas*, Racine's *Plaideurs*, La Bruyère's *Caractères* and La Fontaine's *Fables* all entertained readers with caricatures of the judiciary. They drew on stock figures going back at least to the sixteenth century, embellishing them with modern details. Rabelais was an inspiration; in his tale of Judge Bridlegoose, a royal magistrate was tried and acquitted for deciding his cases by rolling dice. "But, my friend," inquired the appellate judge, "how do you become familiar with the obscure points of law brought up by the two parties to the proceedings?" "Why, just as you do, gentlemen," answered Bridlegoose. "I push all the defendant's sacks of paper off to one end of the bench, and assign him the first throw of the dice."[142] *Gargantua and Pantagruel* was a brilliant lampoon of the king's ordinary courts. They were a carnival of chicanery, a mecca for ignorant and avaricious lawyers—and there they remained in the literary imagination.

But satire can be a backhanded compliment. Judges and lawyers were stock figures of fun in the theater, like clerics and doctors, because they were so ubiquitous in daily life. They also reflected a milieu that writers knew all too well. A remarkable constellation of French literary figures and philosophers sprang from legal and judicial backgrounds and often mined mined their rich material for satire. Pascal, Racine, and Rabelais were all the sons of legal men; Corneille and La Fontaine were practicing judges; and even Molière had studied law.[143] For the eighteenth century, of course, the connection scarcely needs to be reprised: the parlementaire Montesquieu, Voltaire, d'Alembert, and a host of lesser figures came from families of royal court officers. These same legal elites naturally formed the core of the audience for this intellectual output during the seventeenth and eighteenth centuries. "From the sixteenth century to the Revolution," wrote one observer, "magistrates and other royal civil officers formed much of polite and cultivated society in Paris and the provinces."[144]

The level of general culture among local judges was rising rapidly, thanks in part to their ascending professional and economic status. When Pierre Goubert analyzed the death inventories of local judges and officers, including their libraries and paintings, he found a remarkable key to judicial *mentalités*. They were "the cultivated element *par excellence*" in the provinces by the late eighteenth century. Prior to 1680, their libraries were dominated by law texts, Bibles, Latin and Greek from school, and a great number of Jansenist works. Their household furnishings inclined to family portraits, religious paintings, and tapestries.[145]

After 1680, their horizons broadened notably; books on the Indies, England, and Holland appeared in their homes, alongside the dramas of Racine, Corneille, and Molière. More suggestive yet, Goubert found Bayle's dictionary, Bacon, Erasmus, Calvin, Descartes, Hobbes, and Machiavelli in provincial libraries, signs of an intellectual and critical watershed. This cosmopolitan outlook could be plainly seen on local legal officers' walls: secular and classical paintings, landscapes and still lifes replaced austere religious and family portraits in the inventories.[146] The combination of collège and legal education enabled them to continue their self-education in fairly deep political and theological waters. During the eighteenth century, men from the bench and the bar made up an important core of local lending libraries and philosophical societies.[147] The grounds for their entry into revolutionary politics through local clubs, bailliage assemblies, and the Estates General were already being prepared by the late seventeenth century.

Moreover, legal officers' educations equipped them with three fundamental tools that made them increasingly dominant and wealthy in rural jurisdictions. They held the formal qualifications necessary for all of the top judicial and many financial posts in the countryside; they thoroughly understood property law and contracts; and their family portfolios were widely diversified through the acquisition of legal offices. They were also open to diverse intellectual influences through their education, from English treatises on scientific agriculture to Montesquieu's ideal state in *L'esprit des lois*. In this rural world of increasingly transitive property and ideas, the legal men were the best poised to take the leadership of both in the countryside.

Buying Wholesale, Selling Retail: Methods of Capital Acquisition

Turning a lawyer's sheepskin into more than 50,000 livres cash and a sieurie in a rural jurisdiction was akin to spinning straw into gold, and yet Nicolas Maribrasse's was by no means an isolated career trajectory. Where, indeed, did the cash and land come from that were so necessary to the acquisition of higher offices, titles, and desirable marriage partners? Calculating the fees and property advantages of legal elites brings us into the murkiest part of an officer's professional life, a part often intentionally cloaked by the men who ran the courts.[148] But the role of capital in producing new rural nobles and royal judges cannot be overlooked. Significant capital or credit accumulation was a prerequisite for the purchase of a local judgeship; buying a seat on the bench of a lieutenant general of a royal bailliage in Normandy required an outlay of some 15,000 to 60,000 livres, which at the upper registers was almost enough to secure a low-ranking judgeship in the Parlement at Rouen.[149] The short answer is that the courts themselves were the main avenue for acquiring the land, cash, and connections necessary to continue rising in the ranks of the landlords and local governors of the Caux.

The first piece of the puzzle comes from legal or quasi-legal épices (emoluments) and procedural fees, often underestimated as a revenue source. Although it is extremely difficult to calculate annual épices from the court records, since rural officers routinely ignored royal laws requiring them to list the court fees at the bottom of each case, some suggestive fragments remain. In July 1694, for example, probably during the annual *gages-plèges* (payment of rents, fees, and dues) of the seigneurie, the high justice of Cany-Caniel paid out 223 livres to the attorney Maribrasse, 130 and 45 livres respectively to two other attorneys, and 100 livres to the clerk of the court. Although the period of service is unknown, it would certainly have been no more than a year and perhaps less. A simple scrivener in the seigneurial court was thus earning twice as much in client fees as the noble judge of the king's bailliage was collecting in royal gages in a year's time.[150]

Fees charged for civil matters such as tutelles (see below) and *curatelles* (which involved the election of a curator to oversee the property of minor children) can also provide a rough index of fee incomes. Registering acts of tutorship and curatorship was a common function of local courts and must have been a fairly steady source of moderate income for officers and attorneys. Acts of tutorship recorded for the high justice of Cany-Caniel from 1726 to 1747 note that the judges Cabot and Bréard charged from 4 to 18 livres for each act. It is interesting to note that the fees responded quite flexibly to the social status of the clients in the case, rather than being fixed at the same rate for all clients as the crown and Parlement had seemed to order in their arrêts on fees. The least expensive tutelle—which produced 4 livres for the judge, 2 livres 5 sols for the clerk, and 1 livre for the solicitor—was to settle the tutorship of five minor children of the cabaret keeper Jean Hauthorne. The most expensive fees, at 18 livres to the presiding judge and 12 livres to the fiscal prosecutor, were for the fifteen-year-old daughter of a nobleman.[151]

We can cobble together an extremely rough estimate out of these and other standard fees remaining in the court records, on the basis of court caseloads from 1670 to 1745. A judge in a Cauchois royal bailliage who held the lieutenants general, civil, and criminal posts cumulatively could expect to bring in from 750 to 2,000 livres in legitimate fees annually. For the royal lieutenant general of Cany, this would place his legitimate income from a 15,000-livre office at about 5 to 7.5 percent annually, not a bad rate of return for the times. This is also significantly higher than Droualt's estimate that a lieutenant general in a vicomté might take in 200 to 300 livres per year in épices.[152] More recently, Séverine Debordes-Lissillour found that assiduous local lawyers and judges in Brittany earned enough from épices to live at a level commensurate with the dignity of their offices, and that a simple king's advocate could earn about 2 percent of the value of his office from fees annually, roughly twenty times the return paid by the king's gages.[153] Although then as now, court fees were collectible only in a percentage of cases, early modern courts had a formidable array of techniques for compelling payment in a small jurisdiction. These did not exclude property seizure, violence, and threats by roving court sergeants.

Part of the disparity in older estimations of épices may have arisen from using a more limited list of acts for which procedural fees were allowed. Mousnier noted that officers were allowed to take épices only for extraordinary acts, those concluded outside of the regular audience such as inquests, interrogations, accounts, and studies of case dossiers.[154] But officers were legally allowed to take standard fees for a broad range of acts in their normal course of business. An arrêt of 1671 passed by the Parlement allowed judges and their clerks, for example, to take fees for their signatures on every act, sentence, mandement, commission, exploit, adjudication by decree, seizure, or cry made in their parishes. Clerks and other officers were further allowed to take fees for examining the accounts of minors and for dealing with estates, inventories, defaults of debtors, acts of marital separation, and other daily business of the courts that were often conducted during the regular audience. Clerks and notaries were paid by the page for their work, apart from their signatures and other fees. Any work requiring officers to leave the courtroom, including judges and clerks traveling to hear witnesses or court surveyors examining land boundaries, netted them fairly handsome épices. Lieutenants general of the bailliage were allowed to charge 16 livres per day away from home and court; baillis of high justices were allowed 8 livres per day.[155]

Moreover, it should be noted that this fairly extensive list of chargeable acts was imposed by the Parlement because officers regularly exceeded them.

Many local courts in France refused even to register the act or post the official list of fees in their jurisdictions, a clear signal that they had no intention of obeying it. The magistrates passed the arrêt of 1671 in order to execute Article 22 of the new Civil Ordinance and to "remedy the abuses that have slipped into the fees of judges, clerks, ushers, sergeants, and other ministers of justice." Over the course of the seventeenth century, they argued, officers had abandoned the modest sums specified in a règlement of 1612,[156] "under the pretext of the rising cost of everything since that time . . . and to the oppression of the king's subjects of the jurisdiction."[157] If the Norman bailliage of Pont-Audemer is any indication, these new specifications largely fell on deaf ears. Indeed, the potentially enormous black budget hidden by the blanks in the records leaves serious questions. Were the court officers overcharging 95 percent of the time and thus reluctant to state their fees in the court registers? If so, their illicit income from fees alone may have inflated their legal income substantially.

What could successful clerks or lawyers do with a few hundred livres a year in cash income? Lease land. And they did: the 1691 gages-plèges for just one of the marquis de Cany's fiefs, that of Barville, listed four lawyers and judges owing dues for their landholdings. They included the chief judge of the Cany assizes, Saint-Ouen, with "numerous pieces of land," and the lawyer D'Aubrey, with land in two parishes, some of it subleased to another tenant.[158] Acquisition of land and the honorary titles that were so intimately bound up with the land were fundamental to an ambitious officer. Indeed, historians have speculated that royal offices made up a tertiary or even an insignificant part of the fortunes of local officers, which were primarily invested in rentes and land. Mousnier found that among the officers of the bailliages, vicomtés, and élections, almost all had more than half their fortunes invested in land alone.[159]

Legal office gave members of the courts preferential knowledge about and access to property in the first instance. With land strategies, we are again left with many suggestive tracks, although tracks that are difficult to precisely quantify in a rural jurisdiction. All land leases, auctions, curatorships, *hypothèques* (mortgages), and sales passed through the notaries, attorneys, or judges of the courts. Among these, the most frequent and worrisome sources of abuse were curatorship (typically involving the collusion of judge and curator in exploiting a minor's property) and abuse of judical leases and auctions. As the case study below demonstrates, it was possible for an officer to bid on properties being auctioned or leased before his own bench, frequently under the guise of a third party in the audience.

Another artful technique for land acquisition was taking advantage of nobles who were in arrears paying the annuities on their rentes. As their seigneuries or other properties were sold off by judicial decree to satisfy debts, judges and middling officers were often the beneficiaries.[160] Tapié uncovered an even more subtle approach. Using their court knowledge to identify land-lords charged with debt, officers would loan funds to insolvent nobles and sieurs, securing the loans with noble fiefs, seigneuries, or sieuries certain to default to them. Such acquisitions were one of the most important roads to nobility in the countryside, allowing a careful family to insinuate itself into the nobility in three or four generations without resorting to the expensive expedient of buying patents of nobility from the crown.[161] Pierre Goubert once fruitfully hypothesized that land sales by decree and other property transactions were probably "one of the greatest sources of profit conferred by judicial and financial offices."[162] As rentes from local loans became an increasingly important source of income for court officers, the pace of both judicial loans to nobles and land defaults from them no doubt intensified.

Land and office were thus mutually reinforcing strategies. The cash, connections, and access to information about land markets and loans that came with judicial offices probably enabled officers to acquire more local property and rentes through debtors' auctions, defaults, purchases, and marriage. The income from property in turn would allow them to acquire successively higher offices in the local royal administration. The courts in Normandy were thus a fountain of youth and of fees for the rising legal classes. As John Morrill has noted for the same period in Stuart England, these lawyers and officers prospered because they "serviced an increasingly complex and uncertain market in lands and goods."[163] But new clouds had gathered on their professional horizon, as careers in the sovereign courts of Normandy and in the Estates General were closed off to them and to their progeny by the middle of the seventeenth century. The consequences of this separation between local and provincial powers would be large.

Les Chicanneurs: Judicial Corruption in the Bailliage of Pont-Audemer

On a cold February day in 1692, the Parlement of Normandy issued a lengthy monitoire throughout the royal bailliage and vicomté of Pont-Audemer. The order, read out by curés at mass in dozens of parishes, demanded that witnesses step forward with information about twenty-six crimes allegedly committed by officers of the king's ordinary court. The charges against the king's men were grave: menacing and intimidating witnesses, demanding silver plate in exchange for permission to bury the bodies of Protestants, and using false names to acquire property adjudicated before their benches. Along with the clerks and sergeants of the court, they were also charged with theft of seized property, falsification of court papers, bribery, and overcharging.[164] As the investigation unfolded, far more serious allegations surfaced. Inventing a phony royal office and later selling it, winking at dueling, and flagrantly ignoring the king's law were acts that stepped across the line of simple concussion and teetered on the brink of lèse-majesté. The monitoire brought forth so much testimony from witnesses that the king's procurator general and the Parlement required four years, and some one thousand pages of documents, to wade through it.

The investigation was exceptional on one level: it was the only parlementary or royal investigation of local justice undertaken in Normandy during the last two centuries of the ancien régime. Like the Grand Jours of Auvergne, this was an unusual occurrence. But the records from the criminal investigation are really most valuable for what they unintentionally reveal to us about civil life. They dredge up a microcosm of local authority that is so often submerged in silence in the countryside and inaccessible through other sources. Pont-Audemer was unusual in the ferocity of its abuse.[165] But the court was not particularly exceptional in the independence of its judicial corps or in the composition of its local power networks. These facts were what made serious public corruption possible on occasion and were also what made royal offices *rentable* and desirable on a regular basis. The records reveal a great deal about the daily and unexceptional practice of justice in the bailiwicks.

The bailliage and vicomté of Pont-Audemer, although technically under the présidial jurisdiction of Rouen, was situated less than 25 kilometers from the présidial court of Caudebec. Built along the banks of the river Risle, Pont-Audemer had a long established dyers' and drapers' trade. (Claude Pellot, first president of the Parlement of Normandy, was more impressed with its "exceptionally good sausages, sold everywhere") The taille rolls of 1665 indicate that there were perhaps ten thousand inhabitants in the town and outlying faubourgs, but its role as the administrative heart of an overwhelmingly rural jurisdiction was becoming increasingly important.[166] The royal bailliage was geographically sprawling, with jurisdiction over at least 147 parishes, three smaller royal vicomtés, and a number of seigneurial high justices.[167] The landscape concealed a highly populated jurisdiction, with perhaps eighty thousand inhabitants, dispersed in hamlets and villages.[168]

The patterns of official inbreeding in the bailliage conformed closely to those displayed in the bailliages of Cany and Grainville-le-Teinturière. There were approximately thirty-six crown offices in the bailliage and vicomté, a figure that does not include attorneys, solicitors, or notaries. As the crown's local node, Pont-Audemer also had a full complement of specialized jurisdictions that each performed some judicial functions. Eight king's prosecutors and king's advocates practiced in these specialized courts, and almost all of the men simultaneously practiced in or owned judicial posts in the bailliage and vicomté.[169] The royal tax election was by far the most important of these specialized jurisdictions. Again the usual suspects were in office: the chief judge of the king's bailliage court, Jean Le Grix, was a receiver of the taille under his other hat.[170]

Holding simultaneous posts in the direct tax bureau and the royal court was a particularly prohibited type of cumul, but temptingly lucrative. The taille collected in 1698 was 222,522 livres, significantly more than the contribution of the urban election of Rouen or of any other tax district in the province.[171] His office in the tax election made up a substantial portion of Judge Le Grix's personal fortune (or of his personal debt). In 1665, the two offices of receiver had last been sold on the market for 30,000 and 32,000 livres respectively, or approximately half the value of his judge's post of lieutenant general in the bailliage.[172] This was not his only foray into double dipping; Le Grix was eventually called before the Chambre des Comptes in Rouen to account for irregularities in several other minor financial offices that he had bought along with his receiver's post.[173] The ties between tax court and ordinary court officers were social, too. The judge of the vicomté, or lower royal court, Sieur de Formeville, was a commensal of the president of the tax election, Sieur Pierre Dupuys. In one deposition, Dupuys was seated at the judge's table enjoying an amicable dinner when de Formeville dispatched his court sergeant on an illegal errand, seizing and liquidating the property of the magistrate's neighbor.[174]

Within its stone walls, Pont-Audemer was governed by the municipal corps, headed by the mayor and the échevins. The two centers of civic power in Pont-Audemer, the king's court and the *hôtel de ville,* were naturally both in the hands of the same magistrate. Pierre de Formeville, a judge of the lower king's bench, quickly bought the office of perpetual mayor of Pont-Audemer in 1692, when Louis XIV created royal municipal offices by edict.[175] This post gave de Formville close ties to the échevins, and thus to the hospital administrators, who were often drawn from the échevins. (De Formeville also held three other judicial offices as the *tiers referendaire,* the *premier assesseur,* and the *vérificateur des défauts*). In theory, the *échevinage* was an elective office in most of France. The electorate was variously composed of inhabitants, notables, or corps and corporations, depending on the locality. But as one observer has pointed out, "the election was nothing more than a simulacrum, and always ended, in the last analysis, with having the corps de ville nominated by the corps de ville itself,"or at least by a very narrow electorate firmly under their influence.[176]

Not surprisingly, this same small group of judges, attorneys, and town officers also had its fingers deep into the pie of the local hospital, as its administrators and receivers.[177] In November 1691, the procurator general of the Parlement, Antoine De Marest, expanded the investigation of abuse beyond the king's ordinary courts into their broader circles of influence. He immediately put his finger on the property and revenues of the hospital in Pont-Audemer, calling the hospital's administrators to his bench and demanding the accounts and land titles. With remarkable sang froid, the sieurs échevins of the town replied that the key to the coffer in the town hall had been stolen.

They regretted that they could not oblige the magistrate. Commissioner De Marest, however, was unlikely to be taken in by this dodge. Two of the hospital administrators had already filed suit against one another before the bench, and we can assume with fair confidence that their suit was over mismanagement of the hospital's accounts and leases.[178]

This inbreeding between court and hôtel de ville in the towns of France was a particular hobbyhorse of Colbert, a great enemy of the municipal corporations. He wrote indignantly to the intendant of Dauphiné in 1679 that local magistrates who controlled the village communities and town halls tried to "pillage them by every means they can imagine." The crown tried to rein in the municipal corps through edicts in 1692 and 1693, which created the offices of royal mayors and assessors in every town except Lyon and Paris. As Marcel Marion has noted, the crown hoped that the edicts would prevent the election of cabals of magistrates, "since it almost always happened that the officers thus elected . . . surcharged the inhabitants of the towns who refused them their votes."[179] The effect of the edicts in Pont-Audemer was to raise the king much-needed cash, but not to clean house. Instead, it merely further institutionalized cumulative officeholding by the judiciary.

The vertical pressures that the crown exerted on the value of offices in lower jurisdictions, combined with the enormous independence that bailiwick judges enjoyed, were bound to create temptations for some officers. The most frequent and obvious abuses were those involving exchange of money or goods for consideration in court. These always straddled the border of legality, since it was perfectly legal for judges, lawyers, notaries, and clerks of the courts to receive set fees, variously called épices, *salaires,* or *taxes,* from parties to a case after the judgment had been handed down. These fees were set out in minute detail by arrêts issued by the Parlement of Normandy and by royal edicts.[180] In Pont-Audemer, however, the most common charge against the officers was for clear solicitation of bribes, including demands for "money, presents, wheat, oats, cider, wood, gleanings, and days of horse and harness work" before judging trials. Judges had also demanded "grand sums" from the guild masters and guards of the town in exchange for allowing price fixing and in payment for regulating the guilds as part of their police duties in the bailliage.

The minor officers of the court—the clerks, ushers, and sergeants—were also impeached for running their own lucrative businesses in petty abuse. Court clerks commanded immense sums for preparing documents, forcing litigants to pay for a "multiplicity of useless acts" before performing the necessary acts, and illegally withholding litigants' documents after their trials in exchange for money. They backed up their demands with intimidation. With the complicity of the judges, they kept the proceeds of seizures and sales of mobile property, "and by this means rendered themselves the masters of seized goods by taking them home." Virtually all of these violations had been explicitly forbidden in repeated edicts dating back to at least the late fifteenth century. Perhaps the broadest charge leveled against the officers was that of "aggravation of the public."

One of the worst offenders was Louis de Villecoq, sieur de Freteuil, the thirty-eight-year-old lieutenant particular, civil, and criminal of the bailliage. Villecoq was an outsider to the jurisdiction who had bought one of the offices of new creation, and then found himself obliged to sign a private contract with the chief judge limiting his exercise of an already meager office. The head of the accusation against him ran to twenty-three pages of testimony. The majority of offenses were overcharging, acceptance of bribes, or demands for money before giving his conclusions in a case. All three of these categories were acts of *concussion* that were strictly forbidden by royal and parlementary laws.

Villecoq had taken little care to conceal his illicit income from his colleagues. One evening Thomas Cousins, the clerk in the admiralty court of Honfleur, sent six bottles of Spanish wine to him. Villecoq was responsible for reporting the facts of the case to the court in a lawsuit Cousins was embroiled in. Cousins passed the wine to an usher of Pont-Audemer's court, Coustain, who promptly delivered it to Villecoq's house for a repast on the feast of Saint Yves, the patron saint of French judges and lawyers.[181] Villecoq would thus almost certainly have had a house full of judicial colleagues when the prized wine was presented at their confrerie's feast.

His colleagues at the dinner had equally good taste and may have brought a number of illicit items to the table to complement the Spanish wine. Sieur Pierre Le Bourg, for example, was both a councillor-assessor and a king's advocate of the court. Le Bourg took full gastronomic advantage of his powers. Early in his interrogation, he was questioned by the parlementaire Hervé de Crosseville about his appetite for Honfleur salmon. Crossville ordered, "Ask him if he had not made one named Herault of Honfleur win his case . . . in consideration of a Salmon that the said Herault had presented to him, which obliged the said Herault to say that the Salmon had its effect."

Le Bourg acknowledged that Herault had perhaps made him a "petit présent" after the trial. He might have washed it down with the tonneau of small cider that he was accused of receiving from the curé of Sellée while considering his case, followed up by the four chickens sent by the miller of the sieur de Saint-Hilaire before judgment of a summary matter. All this, while sitting comfortably in front of a fire lit by a load of wood delivered by the sieur de Marie, at a table illuminated by a hundredweight of candles he had extorted from a candlemaker in town, during their respective trials. The dinner would have been nicely concluded by a quantity of fruits delivered to him by the sieur de Saint-Maclou and *pain sucré* from the dame du Four, for similar legal considerations. Le Bourg's Rabelaisian delight in the fruits of office might have made him a charming man to sit at table with, but it must have been much less pleasant to approach his bench.[182]

Not all of the abuses were small. Le Bourg was accused of taking 8 louis d'or from a sieur in a landed-property case. Other judges in the court were accused of taking bribes ranging from 60 to 680 livres in criminal cases, depending on the status of the criminal and the severity of the crime involved.[183] The value of their illegal traffic in goods and cash may have well exceeded the value of their annual gages and épices taken together. Their motivations were quite transparent on one level. Bribery and over-charging were lucrative and were even to a certain extent quite accepted parts of the judicial system. But these abuses should alert us to more serious financial problems with local royal offices in the ancien régime. Le Grix, Villecoq said, had "made him hope for an advantageous establishment" in the bailliage, but Villecoq noted that he had come to regret the move within the year. Villecoq's office of lieutenant particular was not always filled in royal bailliages and vicomtés, since his functions were merely the crumbs left over from those already filled by the four principal judges of the court, the lieutenant general, the lieutenants civil and criminal, and the vicomte. According to documents filed in a separate case, his office was evaluated at 6,000 livres by the *parties casuels*, but Le Grix sold it to him for 1,665 livres less than its official value on the books. The qualifier *ancien* in Villecoq's title indicates that the office was in fact the original office of the lieutenant particular, which had since been dismembered into other offices, account-ing for some of its loss of value. There were in fact three other lieutenants particular in the jurisdiction, each with a fragment of the original functions of a royal lieutenant particular. Worse, when Le Grix sold him the office, he had Villecoq sign a contract allowing him to sit beside the principal judge but forbidding him to judge any cases except during the absence or recusal of the principal judge. Villecoq was thus squeezed out of the most lucrative fees he could have expected from his office.

Villecoq's predicament is a textbook case of the pressures facing local judicial officers by the late seventeenth century. These pressures came from three directions: the king's creation of thousands of new royal judicial offices at the local level, which reduced the income of old offices; the decades-long inflation of many office prices, which was out of alignment with general eco-nomic trends and was only officially (but not always actually) halted by the reevaluation of royal offices in 1665; and the waves of *augmentations des gages* and prêts imposed by the king. Taken together, they significantly increased the temptations of officers in the countryside to indulge in illegal practices. The crown was thus favored with its left hand the very abuses it tried to rein in with its right hand. Court officers were pressed toward illicit gain to recover their investments in office or merely to stay afloat.

But did the royal court's clients view illicit fees and acts as abuses? Petty exactions by court officers were certainly well known in the community. Le Bourg, for example, was already seventy years old when he was called to account for his malversations. He was charged with forty-five counts of bribery and case fixing. These probably were only a fraction of his actual abuses on the bench, since he had been received into office in the bailliage forty-six years earlier, in 1647. Many of the potential plaintiffs were either dead or well satisfied with their investment. A few of his accusers were upset not so much that bribes were expected as that they hadn't worked. The miller complained that he had paid 6 livres and several chickens to have the councillor act as reporter in his case but hadn't gotten his money's worth. Le Bourg never reported the facts of the miller's case to the judges out of consideration for the sieur de Neuville, who also had an interest in the matter. The case never came to trial. Nor did Le Bourg practice discrimination in his choice of victims: they included sieurs and dames, artisan tailors, candlemakers, and peasants. It seems he often scaled his exactions fairly carefully to match the financial resources of his victims. There was even a certain poetic, if not formal, justice to some of his abuses. The farmer Auber had beaten out his employer and social superior the dame de Campigny in court simply by proffering a larger bribe.

Other inhabitants of the jurisdiction, however, were angry. A peasant came forward to complain that he had been compelled to plow Le Bourg's fields for several days. Boursy, the jailer of the prisons, complained that he was charged a louis d'or by Le Bourg before the councillor would discharge prisoners from the jail. This was a substantial sum for a jailer, and Boursy may well have been motivated to pay up by the fact that jailers were responsible for providing bread, straw, and water to prisoners at their own expense. They had to recover the expenses as best they could from their captives and from the intendant.[184] Councillor Le Bourg later had the effrontery to demand grain from Boursy, worth more than the original louis d'or. Both the peasant and the jailer were under the compulsion of Le Bourg and were in no position to refuse his illegal requests.

On the whole of course, the poor of the jurisdiction suffered more from their inability to compete in the judicial market. The majority of the forty-five plaintiffs who came forward to testify against Le Bourg in response to the parish monitoire were not identified as either sieurs or dames; at least 73 percent came from the ranks of the commoners. Among them were small craftsmen, peasants, and widows for whom 2- to 10-livre bribes were a difficult, if not impossible, sum to come by. Vauban estimated that 12 sous was the mean daily income for an artisan in a French town at the end of the seventeenth century.[185] Undoubtedly, more remained silent. To testify against the king's officers, these individuals had to cross the boundaries of illiteracy, deference, and the parish. Several came from a considerable distance outside the town to be deposed before the magistrates in the Hostellerie du Louvre or in the audience chamber of the Pont-Audemer court. They also had to run what turned out to be a very real risk of retaliation from judges who were reinstalled in their offices.

Spanish wine and salmon were really only minor stakes in judicial abuse in Normandy. The real focus of judicial activity, like the focus of the Norman Custom, was property. Three brief examples of abuse, involving misuse of curatelles, *héritages,* and judicial leases and rents, illuminate the field of possibilities. Curatelles, which involved the election of a curator to oversee the property of minor children, were one of the more frequent sources of complaint in royal bailliages. They presented obvious opportunities for the curator, in tandem with the judges or attorneys charged with overseeing the accounts or cases, to profit from the inheritances of children whose tutors were less than vigilant. In 1693, the king's attorney in Pont-Audemer, Nicolas de Buisson, was called to account in the Parlement for skimming funds from minors, together with the chevalier de Saint-Maclou. Saint-Maclou was the tutor and curator of his eldest brother's children, and their property was entangled in a case against the sieur le Bras. De Buisson drew up the conclusions of the case, which favored Saint-Maclou, and took 34 livres from the children's inheritance as a fee. The court remonstrated him for not telling the truth. They had evidence that Saint-Maclou was acting for his own profit, not as a disinterested tutor, and that de Buisson had used this illegality as a pretext to demand an exhorbitant fee. The Parlement was not moved by the lawyer's protestation that he would "rather die than to have not told the truth."[186]

Villecoq had more lucrative property rackets afoot, too. He was accused of seizing a third of the héritages, or property income, of Pierre le Vavasseur, whose father had died in debt to Villecoq for the sum of 214 livres, 5 sols. The investigators claimed that Villecoq had learned by means of the court usher L'Espard that le Vavasseur had the means to pay the debt, and had the man's inheritance seized by court decree. He then leased the property out under the terms of judicial lease, a method by which all seized properties were administered until final adjudication. The lease was awarded to a third party "for a very modest price," that is, evidently under the going market price. The officer then set terms that made it impossible for le Vavasseur to resume control of his property, with the officer retaining control of the income. At about the same time, le Vavasseur had agreed in court to pay his sister Elizabeth le Vavasseur the arrears on her *dot* (dowry) from the same héritages. But as she approached the clerk of the court with her papers in hand, Villecoq snatched them from her hand and refused to return them, despite her supplications. Pierre Le Vavasseur finally had the temerity to take Villecoq to the Parlement for redress in 1686. Villecoq was ordered to return the house that had been part of the inheritance, but he evidently ignored this order and continued to pocket the income from the lease.[187]

By far the most tangled of these examples combined abuse of curatelle, abuse of judicial auction, and capital stripping of land. According to Hervé de Crosville's investigation, Judge Le Grix had conspired with the sieur L'Eschelard, a curator of minor children, to lease out the children's property at below market value and to strip it of its capital assets. The swindle began when Le Grix corrupted the course of a judicial auction that was intended to lease properties fairly under curatelle. With the curator's complicity, he ignored fair bids on the property in the court audience. Instead, Le Grix had his valet La Forest bid on the wooded lands and grain fields at far below the market value of 1,000 to 1,200 livres, with Le Grix as his silent backer. La Forest had later been seen splitting the fruits and grains of the property with the curator L'Eschelard. Le Grix, fronted by his valet, enjoyed the property for six years. His other valet Pierre de la Rue and his domestics had frequently been seen carrying wood and grain into the judge's house from the property; the degradations to the woods alone had considerably lowered the property's value. The judge was also accused of letting his chickens run wild on the *prairies* of the children's property to fatten up. After stripping it of assets and enjoying the fruit of the land at reduced rates, Le Grix then laundered the property by passing it on to the sieur de Lisle, the king's *commis des aides,* who remitted it to the curator.[188]

Perhaps the most interesting and suggestive class of offenses committed by the king's bench were those that affronted the interests of the crown. These were qualitatively different kinds of charges; they could no longer be classed as administrative offenses or even as ordinary misdemeanors. Several were categories of cas royaux, crimes that involved the sovereignty and majesty of the king.[189] Perhaps the most audacious of these acts was the invention and sale of a royal office that had not been created by the king. Abusing a royal office was one thing; inventing one was quite another. This appropriated one of the most sovereign prerogatives of the king. In late July 1693 Le Grix, the chief judge of the upper king's bench, was ordered by the investigating magistrate to appear for interrogation in the Hostellerie du Louvre. On the same day, Sergeant Champaigne was given two weeks' notice to appear in court with the documents proving his reception into office. Champaigne deposed that he had leased the office of sergeant from Judge Le Grix but confessed that he had neither an act of reception nor the provisions of office. During his most gruelling interrogation, beginning on August 8 and lasting for several days, Le Grix gave a confused and tangled response to the accusation. He finally claimed that the sergeantry he had leased out was a "branch" of the sergeantry of Saint-Croix, which was still in the legal possession of the widow of the previous owner. This was a daring crime.[190] Not even the most independent of parlementaires had ever claimed that the magistracy had the right to create its own judicial offices.

On the same day, Le Grix was questioned about a gunfight among several sieurs on the high road to Caen in August 1681. Judicial combat, above all dueling, was a particularly serious royal offense. He remembered it well, he replied. Four sieurs and at least one of their valets had been in a dispute in Honfleur. They had run across each other again on the way home where the great roads to Caen and Honfleur met. Across from the mill, on a busy market day, they battled with firearms. When Le Grix arrived on the scene with the king's prosecutor, he found the culprits wounded with shot, but alive. He did his duty at the trial, he stated, but "no one having been killed and not having found anything else to impute against their conduct, he did not find in the trial that it was a duel, but only an encounter."[191]

The officers' defense before the parlement's commission tells us a great deal about their view of the magistracy and of their responsibilities to the crown. We cannot ascribe the judges' actions to simple ignorance or to lack of contact with the norms of the sovereign courts. The bailiwick judges were surprisingly informed and forthcoming in their views about judicial regulations and norms of behavior. In the winter of 1691, De Marest accused Judge Pierre de Formeville of overcharging against the regulations of the Parlement. Formeville told the magistrate that he made a clear distinction between the letter and the spirit of the law. His fees were not against "the spirit of the ordinances, and the *règlements,* although it seems as if there is some contravention of the letter," and after all, "the spirit ought to bring to life that which the letter kills."[192] This was a bold claim: the right freely to interpret the laws of the king and of the sovereign court of Normandy. But as we will see in later chapters, it expressed a normative view among local judges.

Lieutenant General Le Grix, too, believed that he had a serious public function as a magistrate. His duty was to "render justice to everyone equally, and to reestablish good order." This two-sided sense of duty, to equity (the equal distribution of justice) in the bailiwick, and to good order in the state, had clearly penetrated the minds of bailiwick judges. Whether there was even the ghost of sincerity in these self-serving arguments is beside the point. What matters is that the judges knew enough to make these arguments. Vicomte de Formeville claimed that his conduct toward his clients had always been regular; he had "never enriched himself in the seventeen years he had held the office, and on the contrary had performed [his office] with all possible disinterest."[193]

Judges and lower functionaries of the court also argued for the legitimacy of local custom in setting fees. They used the informal yardstick of tradition or the practices of other royal bailiwick courts, not arrêts handed down from the crown, to establish their fees. The clerk of the court, Jean l'Enseigneur, argued that he charged his fees according to "ancient usage," not the regulations. He added pertinently that the vicomte of the court had never corrected him, although he knew perfectly well what l'Enseigneur charged.[194] Lieutenant General Le Grix stated that he "was always accustomed to take a great deal less than any jurisdiction in Normandy." His illegal charges, he insinuated, were rather a bargain in the province, although it is difficult to determine whether they were or not.[195]

Pont-Audemer's judges revealed an important fact about the exercise of justice in the king's lower courts. Their judgments, they argued, were ultimately founded on three legs: local custom, their own interpretation of the *"esprit"* of the laws, and equity. It should not seem surprising that royal judges generously interpreted the laws governing their offices too, since they had powerful financial incentives to do so. Royal laws and provincial customs were melted down into what we can reasonably call a local common law in the lower courts. Judges defended the use of that common law, even against the explicit laws of the king and Parlement.

The Pont-Audemer officers' insouciant denials in the face of overwhelming evidence, and their frank reinterpretation of royal law, are perhaps an index of their invulnerability. Although most of the final judgments in the case have disappeared, the story is told well enough by the tax and court records of Pont-Audemer over the succeeding years. The capitation rolls of the officers in 1703, a decade later, included Lieutenant General Le Grix (assessed at 62 livres), the king's advocate Pierre le Bourg (at 46 livres 10 sols),[196] the king's advocate Nicolas du Buisson, and the widow of Councillor-Assessor Nicolas Cauvin. Jean Le Grix's younger son or nephew, Gaspard Le Grix, was now the lieutenant general of the vicomté. By 1713, three members of his family would hold judgeships in the court: both he and his eldest son Jean Le Grix fils were listed as judges in the bailliage, while Gaspard continued as the lieutenant general of the vicomté.[197] The vicious usher Charles Le Maistre had moved up the ranks to the post of commis au greffe. Not surprisingly, the malcontent lieutenant particular Louis de Villecoq was missing from the tax roll, having likely sold his office.[198] A few petty officers and functionaries of the court were evidently dismissed from their posts. They were considerably easier to get rid of. Indeed, since the public often suffered physically more at the hands of roving sergeants and ushers than from judges, their absence probably brought some relief to the community.

The strange conclusion of the Pont-Audemer case is particularly troubling because of the officers' dual affront to crown and community. The Parlement and the king's procurator general in Normandy verified that royal officers had violated the letter and spirit of the law, the authority of crown and parlement, and the moral standards of the community. Yet nearly all were restored to their offices in the jurisdiction. The simple answer is that private ownership of public offices tied the crown's hands. Claude Seyssel, Michel de L'Hôpital, and Cardinal

Richelieu had predicted as much decades earlier. But in fact the king's hands were not entirely tied. Royal judges still held their offices through mandatory *lettres de provision* from the king. There were legal mechanisms, though rarely invoked, by which the crown could buy judges out of office or revoke their letters. A more common procedure, used with some success with aging parlementaires, was privately to persuade judges to resign their offices in favor of their successors. Chancellor Pontchartrain used the simple mechanism of a private letter to convince a senile and peevish *président à mortier* in Rouen to resign his office and stop sitting at the audiences in the Palais de Justice.[199]

We need to look deeper than venality of office as an obstacle to removal of judges, given the extraordinary time and energy invested by the Parlement and the crown in this highly public trial. Unfortunately, the remaining documents in the case hold few clues about the *raisonnement* of the Parlement and the king's procurator general in sending these legal wolves back into the sheepfold. We can advance two tentative hypotheses, however. The first is rooted in the community of the jurisdiction. Because nine of the principal judges, councillors, and attorneys of the court were implicated in abuse, rooting out the abuse would have required a near decapitation of the court. Consequently, the leadership of the local community would also have been decapitated. The judges and councillors held so many cumulative offices in the municipal and tax administration of the district that something very like administrative collapse would have occurred. Moreover, they were allied to or related to many of the other principal landlords in the bailliage, who were the only feasible replacements for the existing officers. The royal court had the virtue of promoting order in the countryside, if not especially virtuous in itself.

This question of public order was particularly pressing to the parlementaires in the spring of 1693 as the Pont-Audemer case was entering its final months. Order writ large was now their bigger concern, and all hands, even tainted ones, were needed on deck. Famine and grain shortages had ravaged the Norman province, and the worst was not over. On the 17th of April, a "considerable horde of people, in consequence of the little bread that could be found in the town," collected outside the Palais de Justice in Rouen. From their windows in the elegant Renaissance parlement building, the judges looked down on three hundred women crying out for bread and demanding to be let into the courtyard of the palais. Only after the first president charged that they were "rendering themselves guilty of sedition" did they disperse. Not reassured by this temporary retreat, the first president ordered the bourgeois of the town to arm themselves, called out two companies of the *cinquantaine* and *arquebusiers,* and instructed the bakers' guild to bake bread or give alms. The Ascension repast of the Parlement was converted into money, and the lawyers of the court did the same, "all for the poor." Until the end of that year and the beginning of the next, the judicial officers of the province engaged in a series of stopgap measures and almsgiving, to feed the hungry and prevent riots. The crown did little to help. "The king, on his side," they noted acerbically, "created offices and imposed taxes."[200]

Chapter 4

LAW AND LAWYERS IN THE "EMPIRE OF CUSTOM"

Whoever would abolish an old law or establish a new one should present himself to the people with a rope around his neck, so that if the novelty is not approved by all, he can be forthwith strangled.
Michel de Montaigne, *Essais,* "De la Coutume"

To a young lawyer such as François Papillon, just beginning his practice at the king's bench in the Caux, the problem of applying the king's law to the countryside might seem a formidable task.[1] French royal law was a vast filing cabinet of disorganized directives, many unheeded or even contradictory. These positive laws of the French crown were impressive in their volume, if not in their congruity. By the late seventeenth century, royal law amounted to a collection of well over a million ordinances, edicts, arrêts, and declarations that had never aspired to the coherence of English common law. Astoundingly, the crown issued more than eight hundred thousand royal arrêts alone in the 119 years separating the reigns of Henri IV and Louis XIV.[2]

By contrast, the provincial *Custom of Normandy,* a compact book of six-hundred-odd customary laws, was almost Lilliputian in size.[3] Yet the more closely we examine provincial court dockets, the more the king's law begins to resemble a French Gulliver, tied down by a thousand tiny threads of customary law. Distilled into this ancient provincial code were a few concise rules that laid out the jurisdictions of the royal and seigneurial courts and governed the actions of families, communities, markets and seigneuries. Most important, it governed how almost every piece of property in the province could be transmitted from one generation to the next. First committed to parchment by 1200, during the High Middle Ages, and formally redacted in 1583, the Custom of Normandy remained the keystone of legal practice in the province until the French Revolution. This was equally the case in such provinces as Brittany and Burgundy.[4]

For a new young attorney such as François Papillon, then, who was admitted to the bar at the king's bench of Grainville-la-Tenturière in 1729, ideas about applying the king's law might quickly evaporate into more practical legal questions.[5] His clients in the villages and towns of the district expected him to resolve their everyday problems with property and family by mastering a pastiche of laws, only some of which were actually taught in the law schools. Papillon would practice at least eight principal types of law in the common courts over his long career in the district–the general Custom of Normandy, the local Custom of the Caux, seigneurial privileges (a kind of microcustom practiced on each estate), royal laws, case precedents, and equity–in addition to navigating around several surviving islands of Roman and canon law. Worse, a good number of these competing codes and practices claimed to regulate the same matters. It seems untidy to us, and it seemed so to many lawyers at the time. But law, like property, admitted multiple owners in the ancien régime.

Perhaps the most important distinction to make among these many codes was that between the droit privé and the droit public.[6] The droit privé was civil law, and it was virtually synonymous with customary law in France. But as the word *privé* suggests, it was also understood as private law. Private law affected families and property, those things which made up the commonwealth but were not owned by the king. The droit public, however, was more properly in the portfolio of the sovereign or the state. Administration, state finances, foreign policy, and religious conformity were all legitimate spheres of public law and could be made either by the king or (in certain matters) by the parlements.[7] The king was relatively uncontested in his right to make laws affecting the droit public in some arenas by the later seventeenth century, but he was deeply restrained in his ability to make private or civil law.

The boundary between the droit privé and the droit public was by no means clear, however. Public and private overlapped in countless ways in the ancien régime, most contentiously in the possession of state offices (which were also private property) and in taxation (which enabled the king to tap private property for state purposes). The crown often wished to invade the realm of private law for public purposes, as will be seen below in the case of legislation on marriages, but the crown was often stymied in many areas. Nor was the king's monopoly of public law anywhere near absolute. As Denis Richet has pointed out, the French customs not only dominated civil law, but much of public law as well.[8]

The border between droit privé and droit public was therefore far more than a legal distinction. It was a constantly negotiated political border whose line was held by the judiciary. The magistrates of the parlements were the first and most determined line of defense. Although the right to preregistration remonstrances was denied to the parlements between 1673 and 1715, several historians have pointed out that this only limited, not eliminated, the magistrates' right to remonstrate against unpopular laws.[9] They also maintained the right to pass binding laws and administrative decisions within their own provinces, usually in the form of arrêts or judgments on individual cases.[10] The lower courts, in turn, retained the right to issue regulatory sentences for their jurisdictions, which were sometimes confirmed (*homologued*) by the parlements and turned into provincewide laws.[11] But if the parlements were the first line of defense against royal incursions into droit privé, bailiwick judges (and even lawyers such as François Papillon) were the last line of execution. They determined how, or even if, royal laws on public and private matters were applied in villages and towns. Bailiwick magistrates did not enjoy the right of formal remonstrance, but they held wide latitude in making judgments in equity rather than in law. Far from the daily supervision of the crown, they had surprisingly broad powers to interpret or even ignore royal laws, within the context of their local society.

The Cauchois lawyers charged with mastering this imbroglio of royal, customary, and equity law were therefore a perhaps surprisingly convivial lot. They formed a close-knit fraternity, bound by their common education and formation and further united by socializing, godparentage, and marriage. In court records we find Norman attorneys drinking together in taverns (where one was handily assaulted by an opposing client), enjoying wine-drenched feasts at their confrérie of Saint Yves (patron saint of lawyers), and playing the violin at dances in private homes.[12] In a large seigneurial jurisdiction, a band of seven merry (and very young) lawyers took advantage of the judge's absence to dress up the lord's personal chef as the clerk of court. They then ordered the sergeant at arms to arrest a detested fellow attorney and deposited him in the prison of the high justice.[13] Most of their relations were more collegial, however. When François Papillon approached the bar at Grainville to be accepted into practice in 1729, his former fellow law student Adrien François Beuzebosc stepped forward to testify in favor of his mores and religion.[14] The two litigated together in the Cauchois courts for many years, engaging in a friendly rivalry through their clients.

What made the lawyers a distinctive brotherhood, though, was a community of the mind. Among a tiny elite of university-trained men in the countryside, whose educations often surpassed those of many local nobles, they could see all around them in the rural landscape what few others saw: the invisible filaments of law that spread over every field, from horizon to horizon, and over every Cauchois inhabitant, from birth to death. Understanding how these laws functioned in a rural corner of the kingdom requires us to follow in the footsteps of men such as Papillon, the living human vectors through which law was practiced. And that requires following them, at least briefly, through the sometimes torturous meanderings of French law codes.

The "Empire of Custom"

Papillon's and his colleagues' most indispensable field tool was usually a leather-bound pocket edition of the Custom of Normandy, such as the one put out by the Rouen printer Jean Besonge in 1697. The diminutive volume, not much larger than a deck of cards, was the lawyer's almanac. It contained not only the Custom of Normandy, but also listed the sixty-six feast days and holidays observed by the courts, the annual dates at which bailliage judges had to present themselves in Parlement, rules for trial procedure, and a list of approved fees. The bible of provincial practice, it was carried by rural Cauchois attorneys and cosmopolitan Rouennais prosecutors alike.[15] It not only encapsulated local and provincial law, it also came from the localities: it had been collected and written down within the bailiwicks by local officers and notables, during the formal codification of the Custom of Normandy in 1583–87.

A Burgundian jurist complained in the mid-eighteenth century that customary law consumed so much of the attention of young law students that they labored under a "general innundation" of customary classes at the expense of other law studies.[16] The Edict of Saint-Germain in 1679, which allowed university masters to resume teaching civil law in Paris, had also mandated the teaching of customary law in French. Although some faculties failed to hire professors to do so for many years, others quickly realized the utility of teaching practical jurisprudence. A new-minted attorney from law school may have been educated in the kingdom of France, but in the countryside and urban capitals alike he would quickly find himself practicing law in what Montaigne called the "empire of custom."[17]

The study of customary law was more than practical training for barristers and judges; it was an education in political philosophy. Customary law occupied a central space in jurists' arguments about the constitution of the French state and the role of the magistracy right up to 1789. As J. H. M. Salmon has argued, magistrates were politically inspired by the mass of commentaries, glosses, and treatises on custom that had poured forth since the early sixteenth century. In "the belief that they somehow defined a constitutional relationship between king and people of which they, the judges, were the proper guardians," the Customs came to embody a "doctrine of natural rights much older than that presented by the Enlightenment." Theorists disagreed about whether the crown simply ratified the laws of the people, which had been made in essentially legislative assemblies, or whether the king's decision to treat customs as law was an act of sovereign legislative authority. But "the point remained that a substantial body of juristic opinion agreed on its popular origin." This long-flowing current of thought rose to the surface quickly in political crises, and it was never entirely absent from a magistrate's idea of himself, the magistracy, or the state.[18]

Montaigne's image of the "people" standing firm against legal meddlers also reminds us how invested in customary law ordinary commoners could be. Law was more than an abstract expression of royal sovereignty, or even of class rule, imposed from on high. It was an expression of complex property and social relations that extended through every parish and household in the Caux. Customary law was a social creation, one that was constantly being contested and negotiated in the assize courts. It expressed not one power, but many powers; not one definition of property, but multiple definitions.[19] Thus it was a useful tool for villagers and townspeople negotiating their own struggles over property, family, and order, far from the calculations of kings and ministers.

Throughout France, both customs and royal statutes enjoyed equal status as written laws. "What is sure, and essential," remarked one jurist, "is that one and the other have equal power over the people." The Norman and Cauchois emphasis on customary law was a normative one. Like most northern French provinces, Normandy was ruled by a unique set of customs that long antedated the annexation of the province by the French crown, and whose practice was an inviolable privilege granted by the king. (In southern provinces, as will be seen, an adapted version of Roman law became in essence the customary law.) Montaigne exaggerated little in calling it a hanging offense to interfere in these laws. The provincial parlements were the first line of defense against royal incursion into the domain of custom. In Normandy, parlementaires invoked the Charte aux Normands, the king's contract with the province first issued in 1315, at every whiff of interference in customary matters. In Burgundy, as elsewhere, the judges delayed, diluted, and evaded on the rare occasions when the crown insisted on registering such a law.[20]

Ironically, this customary restraint on royal legal activism developed out of one of the crown's greatest sources of power and success since the High Middle Ages. Over the centuries, the royal state had grown by leaps and bounds, in part because of its willingness to endorse and guarantee the privileges, or private laws, of thousands of individuals, corps, towns, and provinces. Yet because the crown had become the guarantor of provincial law codes and private contracts, its ability to make broad public laws, or to respond to changing social conditions with new private laws, was deeply compromised. What had been a pragmatic solution in medieval conditions became an entanglement in the early modern context, as the king began to wish to assert his sovereignty, as well as his suzerainty, over his realm.

Since the thirteenth century, the crown's attempts to intervene in private or civil law had borne only intermittent fruit. Phillipe Auguste promulgated new laws on widows' dowers to protect patrimonial property in 1204–14, but his successors largely left the field of private law alone. When Charles IX attempted to interfere in inheritances in 1567, every parlement but one in the south of France refused to register the edict.[21] The most successful interventions in civil or private law were accomplished with the aid of the Estates General. They collaborated in the publication of several omnibus ordinances in the sixteenth century, especially those of

Villers-Côtterêt (1539), Moulins (1566), and Blois (1579). The three matters of clandestine marriage, clandestine pregnancy, and male household authority were at the center of these royal initiatives in the ancien régime. As Sarah Hanley has argued, the state was increasingly concerned about the flow of wealth and offices through patrimonial lines.[22] Jean Bart has also noted that only in the realm of marriage and paternal authority was the crown notably successful in legislating new droit privé in the years between 1579 and 1730, and then only because it had the support of the parlements and the propertied classes. Especially after the demise of the Estates in 1614, the crown accomplished little in the field of civil law. With only rare exceptions, the crown ceased to interfere in private law and custom, choosing instead to place the parlements in control of customary law in exchange for royal control over other matters.[23]

During the fifteenth and sixteenth centuries, kings clearly understood that customary law had become the crux of provincial practice. A "vast crusade of redactions and reformations"[24] was begun under Charles VII in 1454, with the goal of creating a standard, written body of customary laws. The newly reformed customs of France admirably suited the crown's purposes in certain respects. The customs gave the crown a formal counterweight to the waning force of canon law, and to Roman law in the south of France. The written customs also provided the king with his first clear map of the secular legal territory he was free to conquer. The crown considered any subject not treated in the customary laws as fair game for royal edicts and ordinances.

This open territory for royal legal conquest was both more and less than it appeared. The Custom of Normandy, in common with the other provincial customs of France, nearly monopolized private law, especially the transmission and ownership of property. This focus left potentially enormous tracts open to the crown for shaping both criminal law and large bodies of public law, including commercial, financial, forest, and royal domainal law. The field was less large than it seemed, however, because the majority of cases heard in the lower courts of the pays de Caux in Normandy were in fact heard under customary law. Nor was Normandy alone in this state of affairs. The Estates of Brittany had written Charles IX in the sixteenth century, asking permission to redact the provincial Custom on the grounds that the majority of trials in Brittany stemmed from inheritance issues and other matters governed by local usages and customs.[25] As one legal historian has noted, the realm's "juridical space was fixed and congealed" by the formal redaction of the customs.[26]

But the crown, at the time it ordered the sixteenth-century reformation of the customs, was not in fact aiming at the creation of a single legal code for France under royal direction. Rather, it viewed the local customs as a source of strength and even of native genius, permitting the localities to remain largely self-governing in matters that were of direct interest to the crown but could be better managed locally. Henri III charged the parlementaires of Normandy to "guard and observe, as perpetual and irrevocable law," their native customs.[27] He was of course obliged to allow them to keep their customs under the Charte aux Normands, which he confirmed in 1579. According to this provincial charter, the French crown could not amend the customs and usages of Normandy for any reason. Even in the later eighteenth century, the king felt it necessary to tag the bottom of his more controversial acts in Normandy with the disclaimer "nonobstant clameur de haro ou Charte Normande."[28] The customs were an efficient, not to say necessary, solution to the problem of provincial governance in the ancien régime.

The defects of this solution only became more apparent and acute during the seventeenth and eighteenth centuries, as the expansion of public law and the state's desire to revise private contracts and privileges bumped up against the empire of custom. The sheer fragmentation of customary law was a great source of power and independence for the provincial parlements, which had long defended their right to sole control of the provincial law codes. Since most private law and some public law was fragmented into sixty general customs and roughly three hundred usages in the provinces and bailiwicks, the crown faced almost insuperable obstacles in trying to force each parlement in turn to accept new provisions or alterations in even minor matters. Localism was also the hobgoblin that prevented French jurists from emulsifying customary law into a single code, though many died trying. Such eminent jurists as Charles Dumoulin and Guy Coquille in the late sixteenth century, and Antoine Loisel and Pierre de L'Hommeau in the early seventeenth century, were among the early pioneers who tried to reduce the provincial customs to their underlying principles, to no avail.[29] In 1689, the great jurist Jean Domat issued his *Lois civiles dans leur ordre naturel,* a heroic attempt to synthesize a *coutumier français* based partly on the Custom of Paris.[30] Eighteenth-century jurists such as Robert-Joseph Pothier searched for natural law or Roman-law principles to undergird a common *droit coutumier* with no better success, although Pothier's treatises on civil law were taken up in Napoleon's Code.[31] The result was that France had no unified droit privé, or private law, to strengthen the hand of the sovereign.

By the seventeenth and eighteenth centuries, customary laws across France had a mixed reputation among jurists. Sometimes derided for having taken root among the uncivilized bands of Normans, Burgundians, and other medieval peoples, customs were thought to lack both consistency and legal principles. Monsieur du Bois complained that customary laws had been imposed by local lords, "dictated by caprice, and [whose] numerous articles, as odious as they are bizarre, demonstrate that they could not have been accepted except by force."[32] He was echoed by jurists such as Guiné, who charged that the laws had suffered undue corruption at the hands of sixteenth-century commissioners, whose private interests were reflected in the texts. None have equalled Denis Diderot, however, in his critique in the *Encyclopédie,* where he argued for the absurdity of laws "whose authority is bordered now by a mountain, now by a stream" and which evaporates as soon as a subject passes out of range.[33]

The hazards of war and political upheaval had also taken their toll. The jurist Argentre noted that the customs of Brittany had been hastily written up during the Wars of Religion by reformers "who had one foot in the stirrup."[34] Like several French customs, that of Brittany had the misfortune of undergoing its final redaction during some of the worst disorders of the ancien régime. In Brittany, only ten of the twenty-nine deputies assigned to compile the Custom of Brittany in Rennes in 1580 ever arrived in the city. Bourdot de Richebourg complained that the renewal of civil war toward the end of that year made it impossible to get Bretons to pay attention to the task. As a result, the Breton Custom failed to include large numbers of local usages that nevertheless continued in practice, including crucial tenurial arrangements such as the *domaine congéable* in lower Brittany.[35]

Yet French magistrates also had a certain pride in the adaptability of customary laws to regional conditions. For many parlements, as for that of Normandy, it was the true *droit commun,* or common law, that bound the province together.[36] Both Auguste-Marie Poullain du Parc in Brittany and Jean Bouhier in Burgundy saw numerous expressions of the will of the people written into the customs alongside those imposed by force.[37] Bouhier used the language of Montesquieu, eight years before his more famous colleague did, in describing the genius of law codes that were tempered for the humors and climates of their residents. Customs, he argued, perfected Roman law by bending it to local peculiarities—except when they corrupted it by being written down by ignorant practitioners. As he expressively phrased it, in the relationship between the customs of France and Roman law, "the daughters have supplanted the fathers."[38]

Roman Law: Equity and *Raison Écrit*

What was in that small volume of customs had taken well over seven hundred years to form, and it can be understood only in the context of two other broad legal streams that flowed around and through it as it wound its way down to the seventeenth century. Traditionally, secular jurisprudence in the ancien régime has been divided into three isolated currents: Roman law (drawn principally from the emperor Justinian's *Corpus iuris civilis* as well as from medieval glosses), tribal customs handed down from the medieval period, and the more recent laws of the French crown.[39] Maps of France have traditionally bisected the country into a customary-law region in the north, contrasted with a Roman-law region in the south.[40] Yet the relationship of Roman, royal, and customary law was far more dynamic than that suggested by these geographical or even temporal divisions. The roots of these three vines had in fact become so intertwined that each province or local pays produced a distinctive varietal, resulting in well over three hundred sixty local and provincial law codes.

Roman law in the south had been so altered and permeated with local custom over more than a millennium that it had become, in effect, the customary law of the south. Even in the late empire, Roman jurists had recognized that written law in the West had devolved into local customs and usages that were impossible to root out. Emperor Constantine acknowledged custom's legitimacy in 319 C.E., as long as it did not contradict the written Roman law.[41] Over the centuries, Roman law in what had been Gaul continued to absorb local influences and shed outworn provisions. By the seventeenth century, there had long been strong regional or provincial differences in the Roman-law derivatives practiced in the south, just as there were in northern provinces. The eighteenth-century jurist Jean Bouhier, who practiced in the Burgundian region of mixed Roman and customary law, asserted that Roman-law regions should more usefully be described as *pays coutumiers*.[42]

The transformation of Roman codes into local customs was also a natural outcome of the texts in use. Justinian's Code, Digests, and Institutes (revised in 533–34), and his later Novels, formed the core of the Roman *Corpus iurus civilis* (civil law). But waves of glossators during the High Middle Ages and Renaissance had substantially altered, edited, and reinterpreted many of the original commentaries and laws. Moreover, the church, as the primary repository of Roman law during the Middle Ages, had selectively chosen those principles and texts that would be later mined by secular jurists.[43] Even the line of Roman influence was by no means an impassable border. Just as Roman law had devolved toward custom in the south, customary law in the north had collected important features of Roman law over the centuries. Roman laws tended to fill in the interstices between royal and customary law in both regions. In Burgundy and Franche-Comté, it was explicitly stated during the redaction of the customs that Roman law would play a default role when other laws were silent.[44]

Roman law was the oldest of the three root stocks that made up French jurisprudence, and it had contributed both broad legal principles and specific provisions to legal practice. From the king's point of view, the most important concept was that of *imperium*, the broad powers of the prince as sovereign. As the Roman jurist Ulpian elaborated, "quod principi placuit legis vigorum habet" (what pleases the prince has the force of law). Historians now, like legists then, are still divided on the importance of the concept of imperium in legitimizing the legislative sovereignty of French kings.[45] For that matter, French constitutionalists had their own motto from the Digest: "quod omnes tangit, ab omnibus approbatur" (what touches all must be approved by all).[46]

But perhaps the most powerful of the classical legal principles in daily practice was not imperium, but *equitas* (equity), which was applied alongside both customary and royal laws to make judgments. Indeed, many court cases during the ancien régime were settled by no written law at all, but rather by this ancient Greek and Roman legal precept. In simplest terms, equity allowed judges to bring informed reason to bear on a case in default of (or even in spite of) the written law. Aristotle, in the *Nicomachean Ethics,* explained that "what is equitable is just, but not what is legally just–rather, a correction of it."[47] The ability of equity to correct for the situational defects of general laws made it a crucial tool for judges. According to the Roman law glossators, there were in fact two levels of equity. The simplest was *equitas rudis,* which was a natural sense of what was fair or just; the higher level was *equitas constituta,* which required judges to consider what was just in the whole context of the law.[48] Early modern jurists believed that the ability to judge in equity came from a rare combination of skill, legal education, and a natural gift for reason.[49] They enjoyed wide liberties in using both forms of equity rather than the written law as their guide, so much so that it was considered a French magistrate's absolute prerogative. As one legal commentator noted, if a judge could find no written law that perfectly applied to the case, "reason and equity ought to be the rule of his decision, and of his judgement."[50]

In England, the crown was able to use the classical prestige of equity law to its own advantage, setting up royal equity courts that bypassed the common-law courts. The Court of Chancery, which developed out of the king's secretariat, was hearing roughly ten thousand cases a year by 1700 and developing equity law into a set of written principles. In France as in England, the sovereign was the foremost practitioner of equity law. He or she reserved the right to judge any case in the last resort and was not bound by written law in doing so. By the privilege of *évocation,* the French king could evoke a case from any jurisdiction and hear it in royal council or in person. In practice, however, the king could only use évocations for a tiny fraction of the kingdom's law cases every year, usually in matters involving particularly important individuals or principles. As one historian has noted, the conseil privé used great circumspection in evoking cases and heard few in number every year, although it regularly dealt with jurisdictional disputes among the regular courts.[51] The royal councils were occupied with too much other state business to sit as permanent law courts. Apart from the regular judicial system, there were no royal equity courts in France that could handle large volumes of business as did the Court of Chancery in England.

Equity law in France was, however, a prized tool of judges sitting in the ordinary courts. It was practiced not only in formal court cases, but also in informal and binding arbitration alike. Equity was all the more essential in bailiwick courts because local jurisdictions did not compile books of case law or case precedents, although they did issue regulatory orders for their jurisdictions. Lawyers and judges invoked precedents from memory, and those precedents became part of the collective memory of many communities. Court records sometimes indicate that the judges had reached a particular decision, as "the court had rendered a similar judgement" in other situations.[52] But many judgments had to be constructed from the individual circumstances of the case, and equity was critical to this process. Both of these practices, equity and arbitration, are treated more fully in chapter 6, because they exist in that gray area where written law melded into community traditions.

Numerous axioms of Roman property law also had wended their way into French customary laws over the centuries, most notably the ancestral forms of marital community property; the *douaire,* or widow's portion; and *retrait linéagère,* or the principle of lineage property. *Garde noble* (noble wardship), *censives* (annual dues owed by vassels on seigneurial lands), and the distinction between maternal and paternal property were Roman-law derivatives, although the latter had actually faded in regions of Roman law and become more firmly rooted in customary regions.[53] The responsibilities of tutelle, or tutorship of minors, were also elaborately defined in Roman codes.[54] As legal historians have pointed out, these were seldom pure contributions. Some Roman laws came from glosses of glosses; some were altered as they metamorphosed into customs; and virtually all were changed through practice.[55]

Perhaps most suggestively, the Roman principle of "the dead seize the living" was passed down through the customary law of Normandy and other provinces.[56] The phrase refers to the automatic succession of the nearest (usually male) relative to the property of the defunct, and the beginning of a new property life cycle. Although a seemingly self-evident principle of law in Western culture, it separates the Roman-influenced world from those cultures in which property is viewed as the collective possession of an entire kin group or tribe. In law as in life, seventeenth-century men and women in the French provinces were metaphorically seized by their ancestors, who passed on to them Roman and customary law codes along with their material inheritances.

Roman law did retain two special and universal functions, even in the northern provinces. As the jurist Poullain du Parc noted in Brittany, most provinces that were governed by customary law used Roman law as their fallback position, filling in where custom, usage, or royal legislation were silent.[57] Bouhier went so far as to call it the only real common law in France, an underlying source of unity that far exceeded royal legislation in that capacity even into the late eighteenth century.[58] Roman law also held a near mythical intellectual status among French jurists. They crowned it with the title of *raison écrit,* that is, reason itself distilled into written law. Their admiration stemmed from the belief that the Roman code was founded on abstract principles of natural law and equity. Claude de Ferrière, in his preface to the Custom of Paris, called the *Code Justinian* "a ray of divinity" because of its logical and universal character.[59] Many jurists further believed that its abstract principles had been spun into a coherent fabric of statutes, the holy grail of legal codification. Although Roman law was not so internally consistent as its admirers imagined, the codes did support a complex structure of both public and private laws from which a coherent state philosophy could be derived.

This lingering admiration among French practitioners had powerful consequences. Royal law in France, despite its increasing range, was never able to lay full claim to the Roman intellectual territory of reason and natural law. More a compendium of state decisions than a true code, royal legislation was ever forced to dance with its elder sisters, customary and Roman law, in the courtrooms of France. As a consequence, eighteenth-century jurists were intellectually seduced by the prospect of discovering a new set of natural law principles on which to found a more universal law code. The classical ideals of natural law and reason continued to tantalize French magistrates as far flung as the baron de Montesquieu in Bordeaux and Jean Bouhier in Burgundy.[60] It is not difficult to see how Revolutionary models of natural law might spring from a legal class so steeped in admiration for these principles.

Royal Law: Practice and Theory

For attorneys in the bailiwicks of the Caux, royal law proper was a rather specialized practice that took them far afield from their ordinary round of cases. These laws most often touched on the chose publique: a handful of crimes deemed cas royaux that attacked the dignity of the crown, and in civil matters, the duties and privileges of royal officers, the royal domaines, taxes, the church, and the military. Some of these matters were heard in specialized jurisdictions such as the tax courts (élections and greniers à sel) or the mounted constabulary courts (maréchaussées), which further reduced the number of royal cases in the ordinary jurisdictions. Two of these matters of public law, however, were routinely heard in the bailiwick courts. The first were matters regarding the church (including benefices, the fabrique, and parish management). The second set of royal laws that absorbed officers' attention were the règlements and arrêts affecting their own profession, especially forced loans and office creations, which were a source of constant worry for officers.

The commentator Houard mapped out the territory of royal law in Normandy that was legitimately recognized by the eighteenth century. The province, he noted, accepted the droit public regarding the succession of kings, immunities of ecclesiastics, punishment of crimes, distribution of justice, administration of state finances and the royal domain, navigation, commerce, and the arts and crafts.[61] These were truly important administrative areas, above all control over financial administration and the distribution of justice. They indeed were an advance over prior centuries, establishing the administrative and executive framework for the state and laying out clear islands of state sovereignty. The practical effects of royal law on daily life outside of these two large areas were small however, and diminished rapidly the farther one traveled from major administrative centers such as Rouen or Paris.

French crown laws, unlike Roman and customary laws, resisted all attempts at codification. Collectively, and rather optimistically, these laws were simply called the "droit français."[62] Colbert's celebrated attempt to reform French justice did little to alter the law. The work of the Council of Justice, headed up by his redoubtable uncle, the councillor of state Henri Pussort, resulted in the *Ordonnance civile* (1667) and the *Ordonnance criminelle* (1670). But the commission's long labors produced an administrative manual, not a law code. Both were books of uniform procedure in their fields, intended to expedite trials, reduce costs for litigants, and in some cases lessen reliance on written documents in favor of oral proceedings.[63] The crown's more specialized codes–those on forests (1669), commerce (1673), and maritime commerce (1681)–effectively established the rules of engagement in their respective domains. But as Peter Stein has pointed out, they "did not significantly affect the core civil law . . . and left the customs largely intact."[64]

Finding the underlying principles in the droit français was an even more daunting task. The Burgundian magistrate Jean Bouhier dismissed the pretension of some jurists that French laws could be emulsified together into a set of common principles. He did not even know of a single work, he admitted, "where all the parts of this Law have been assembled into one body."[65] The volume of laws alone was daunting; during the reign of Louis XV, the crown was churning out nearly four thousand arrêts du conseil annually.[66] Bouhier, president à mortier of the Parlement of Burgundy, particularly criticized Pierre de L'Hommeau's *Maximes générales du droit français* (1614), one of the best-known synthetic works on French law for his contemporaries. He noted that even L'Hommeau had confused droit français with droit roman and droit coutumière and mixed them all together.[67]

In the early eighteenth century, Chancellor Henri-François d'Aguesseau made a valiant new assault on royal and customary law, an effort that was cut short by both death and futility. He compiled ordinances on very narrowly defined matters, including donations (1731) and testaments (1735), that sought to iron out provincial differences.[68] The jurist Poullain du Parc praised him for his attempt to establish a uniform jurisprudence but warned that "if one continued this project, so vast and so usefully begun, it would never touch upon feudal matters . . . nor (matters) in each Custom, which ought to be regarded as the result of the genius of each nation." In 1783, Poullain du Parc himself turned to what he thought a more useful task: organizing the customary law of Brittany.[69] His effort too was cut short by events, but it is remarkable that he and his contemporaries still recognized medieval and Renaissance customs as the foundation of most legal practice just six years before the French Revolution. The inability of the most celebrated jurists of the age to arrive at a compendium (much less the common principles) of the droit français gives us some idea of the obstacles facing a king intent on legislative sovereignty.

In contrast with the natural law principles of Roman law, then, French royal law was often understood as a collection of ad hoc responses to the conditions of the moment. This did not prevent it from expressing a certain vision of the state or the monarchy over time, or from asserting the field of action of the crown. But royal law seldom reached beyond *raison d'état* or religious sanction for its power or justification. The standard flourish at the bottom of many royal laws read, "for such is our pleasure," and this neatly summed up French law as an expression of the monarch's personal will *tout court*.

The Creation of Royal Laws

Royal laws went under several names that can be sketched out for clarity. Most common were the arrêts and déclarations du roi, both of which treated matters that were specific but important. Declarations of the king were the narrowest in scope, and the crown typically issued them to alter existing laws. Arrêts or decrees, however, came in several kinds. The most prestigious decrees were those issued by the king's council (arrêts du conseil). Other decrees were issued by the parlements on provincial matters (arrêts du Parlement) and regulatory matters (arrêts de règlements). Arrêts de règlements typically dealt with administrative issues and were often dispatched by the parlements in response to problems in a particular locale. Broader in scope than the arrêts and declarations, and much rarer, were the royal edicts. These treated matters both general in scope and important in nature.[70] The infamous Edict of Fontainebleau of 1685, which revoked the Edict of Nantes, established a major state policy banning Protestantism. But edicts could also overlap more hazily with rule-making arrêts, such as the Edict on Spices of 1673, which attempted to reform the abuse of fees or épices collected by judicial officials.[71]

Larger still were the omnibus law codes, the *ordonnances,* which were intended to apply to the entire kingdom and made a broad statement of royal policy. Yet until the late seventeenth century, these were almost universally focused on laws affecting the administration of the state itself: justice, police, the army, finances, or the royal domain.[72] Like the Ordonnance of Villers-Cotterêt of 1539, the Ordonnance civile of 1667, and the Ordonnance criminelle of 1670, these were collective projects of many years' gestation. They were often drawn up in conjunction with the Estates General until the Estates' demise, and were always supervised by the chancellor of France or by a minister of Colbert's or Henri Pussort's stature.[73]

What is most notable about this royal classification system for laws is that it was largely based on the source of the law rather than its subject matter: what mattered was whether it had been issued by king, council, parlement, or royal commission. Colbert's smaller ordinances, such as those on commerce (1673) and forests (1669), were among the first substantive attempts to codify law in a modern sense. They brought together relevant laws from different sources in a single work, where they could be compared and consulted. This was, in its way, almost as dramatic a development as Diderot's *Encyclopédie* in changing the way legal knowledge was classified. Unfortunately, the effort had few successors in France.

Royal laws were also manufactured far from the king's councils or chambers. Hundreds of thousands of arrêts were issued by the twelve (later thirteen) provincial parlements, each having the force of law in its jurisdiction. Many were issued in the form of a judgment on a particular case, but they usually established provincial precedent on the matter. First among equals were those decreed by the Parlement of Paris, the *arrêts de la cour;* but they served only as a general guide for emulation by the provincial sovereign courts. The Parlement of Normandy issued many thousands of arrêts du Parlement before the end of the ancien régime, as well as churning out administrative *règlements du Parlement.* Lower présidial and bailliage courts asked the sovereign courts for rulings or règlements, too. The judges of the bailliage of Pontchartrain, for example, successfully petitioned the Parlement for an arrêt allowing them to charge 7 sols, 6 déniers for hearing criminal witnesses, among other favors.[74] This gave bailiwick courts a share in local rule-making authority. Unless later overturned by the sovereign parlement or the king, they stood as local law.

Some of these these provincial arrêts were certainly prompted by the crown, as when the king sent secret *lettres de cachet* to the Parlement of Normandy in 1666, forcing them to deliberate on several articles of local usage. The alterations themselves were slight, however, and were produced after numerous sittings of the court to debate the substance and language of the changes.[75] Indeed, the parlements were usually slow to respond or even disobedient when faced with orders to alter provincial usage. After a Burgundian noble complained to the king in 1643 about the number of witnesses necessary for a property division (*partage de biens*) under the Custom of Burgundy, the king declared that the royal Ordonnance of Blois should be followed instead of the custom. In 1662 the king sent the refractory Parlement in Dijon letters of *jussion,* and they registered the declaration in 1666, twenty-three years after the original complaint.[76]

The first president (*premier président*) of the parlement could strong-arm his colleagues into issuing unpopular arrêts from time to time on behalf of the crown as well. First presidents of the sovereign courts were venal but nonhereditary officers hand picked by the crown and frequently outsiders to the province. In Normandy, for example, first president of the Parlement Claude Pellot was an intimate of Colbert, married to his niece Madeleine, and the former intendant of Guyenne. Pellot's iron will never faltered when it came to imposing the unpopular arrêt that halted an outbreak of sorcery trials in the Norman courts. These tactics were not the general rule, however, and the parlements enjoyed a subordinate but quite real legislative power in their jurisdictions.

"A Dialogue with the Masters": The Creation of Norman and Cauchois Customary Laws

In the autumn of 1586, two magistrates and a lawyer from the Parlement of Normandy made their entry into the remote Caux villages of Gournay, in the jurisdiction of the duc de Longueville, a peer from an illegitimate stem of the Valois dynasty and one of the largest property-holders in the province. These jurists had been dispatched into the countryside to collect and reform hundreds of distinct legal usages and customs that had settled into the province over the course of centuries, taking root along river valleys and in village clusters as luxuriant varietals of law. The noble magistrates from Rouen were openly exasperated by their task. Arrayed along the banks of the river Epte they found a tiny legal enclave of twenty-four villages and hamlets, practicing among themselves twenty-three separate customs on property and succession.

Henri III had chosen the bailiwicks and their officers as the key instruments for compiling the Custom of Normandy and local usages, and they vigorously defended the local character of law. The bailli or sénéchal was in charge of assembling deputies from the three estates, some chosen from among the bailliage and high justice officers, to consult on which customs were still in force and to homologize them. The record of the gathering at Gournay notes that it was attended by all the seigneurs' agents, including the duc de Longueville's fiscal solicitor and his lieutenant bailli. The Parlement of Normandy reserved the right of final approval, but the initiative lay with the bailiwicks.[77]

The involvement of local judges, officers, and notables was a key feature of the redactions. Jean Yver called the participation of more than thirty Norman jurisdictions in the project a "veritable referendum" that required the active assent of the rural governing strata of propertied men and officers. But as he also pointed out, they were under considerable influence from the commissaires sent out from the Parlement of Normandy to each of the bailliage assemblies.[78] The only remaining documents of this far-flung deliberation across rural Normandy are the *procès verbaux* (official reports) of the local customs written down by the parlementaires, undoubtedly condensed from much more extensive notes. Within the laconic notes, only a single sentence of comment on their experiences in the hamlets of Gournay allows us to see beneath the surface. It provides a tantalizing glimpse of the struggle between judicial center and periphery in the pays de Caux, and into the tenacity of local men on behalf of local custom.[79]

As the magisterial parlementaires faced the black-robed local judges, who were flanked by the lawyers, seigneurial officers, and substantial inhabitants of the district, they deposited a rare comment into the record of the proceedings. "We have remonstrated," they wrote, "that there are numerous local usages in these twenty-four parishes, some of which have led to great trouble and confusion, like the division of fiefs."[80] After heated deliberations the commissaires decided to annul the Gournay usages on the king's authority, citing the confusion they created in property matters in the riverine villages. But on October 22, the Parlement without comment approved the usages and added them to the Custom of Normandy.[81] The magistrates may have been dispatched from the sovereign courts of Rouen, but their sovereignty began to unravel as they traveled into the hinterlands.

There is no indication of why the judges, officers, and inhabitants of the Caux won out in preserving their local usages against parliamentary impatience. But the possible mechanisms are not difficult to imagine. The villages of Gournay were in the sphere of the powerful duc de Longueville. Moreover, the parlementaires heading the two commissions that redacted the customs were both sons of the Caux, first presidents Jacques de Bacquemare and later Claude Groulart. Bacquemare was the first Norman to be appointed to the highest judicial post in the province since the Exchiquier had become a sovereign court in 1499. (It was chartered and reorganized as a parlement in 1515.) Groulart had been born in Dieppe, well within the magic circle of Longueville patronage and influence, which may partly account for his decision to relent.[82] Bacquemare and Groulart's benign outlook on local practices may have been largely responsible for the pays de Caux's becoming the most tangled and idiosyncratic legal enclave in all Normandy.

The extreme fragmentation of local usage that the Parlement's magistrates found on the banks of the Epte existed in lesser degree everywhere in the province, and it was cemented into provincial law for the next two centuries. The reformed *Custom of Normandy* allowed twenty-seven royal vicomtés and seigneurial châtellenies to remain partial legal enclaves, each retaining several unique articles governing crucial matters of property.[83] Nevertheless, the editing of the customs had the virtue of putting a halt to any further legal fragmentation. Localities were henceforth forbidden to practice any usage not offered for inclusion during the official redaction, although minor usages almost certainly continued in force.[84]

The province itself had taken the initiative in asking for an official revision of the custom in 1576. Representatives to the Estates General from Normandy requested the king's permission to reform the *Très Ancien Coutumier,* which had partly fallen into desuetude. Henri III responded with letters patent from Blois the following year, and the ten-year project produced a new customary code that would last to the end of the ancien régime.[85] The general *Custom of Normandy* appeared in 1583; in 1586–87 the local pays-coutumiers and usages were reformed and appended to the general custom. Its most salient feature, according to Jean Yver, was its deep conservatism.[86] Unlike the customs of Paris, Burgundy, Brittany, Orleans, and other regions, the Custom of Normandy had never undergone intermediate revisions. It retained much of its full late-medieval flavor in the hands of a cautious commission of magistrates, lawyers, and deputies. The archaic and rigid nature of many of its prescriptions would become a source of legal criticism and popular resistance, affecting the daily lives and court activities of the Normans for the next two centuries.

But to what extent can the usages enshrined in the reformed Custom of Normandy be identified as popular in origin as apart from simply local? Were they a distant echo of a once truly popular local law, or had the customs merely been imposed by more ancient rulers, in a time out of mind? Georges Duby has argued that at least during the High Middle Ages, villagers strongly defended the local customs as their own. "The power of the subjects resided there," he explained. "[T]he custom found a depot in their memory and the custom was imposed on the masters, as powerful as they were." But the medieval custom had also been fluid in its oral state, requiring what Duby called "a permanent dialogue" for the exercise of power.[87] The redaction of the customs in the fifteenth and sixteenth centuries both hardened them into semipermanence and tended to preserve their more archaic qualities, in keeping with the legal thought of the age.

The balking of royal parlementaires in the villages of Gournay clearly demonstrates that the political dialogue of the villagers with the "maîtres" had not entirely worn itself out. But the defenders of the local custom were now new men whose existence was only just being sketched in during the Middle Ages. Those who sat on the bench across from the red-robed parlementaires on the banks of the Epte river were not only villagers, but men of the black robe: royal and seigneurial judges and their legal brethren the barristers, solicitors, and petty functionaries. A few seigneurs attended the session at Gournay, but the real daily power in these villages increasingly wore the robe. They spoke the language of the law. They were the king's men and the seigneurs' agents, and often landlords and sieurs in their own right. The written custom that they inscribed on the Norman landscape and social structure strongly reflected their landed interests, interests that the three estates charged with the redaction largely shared. Its dominant feature was not popular control of village institutions but an insistence on property, order, and family.

This local tenacity in keeping local usages in the face of the parlement's and the Estates' envoys alerts us to the high stakes that every Norman had in the legal order. Law and custom were animate forces in ancien régime Normandy, not unlike powerful rivers molding the landscape and communities around them. Far from being a foreign language spoken only at the king's bench, the language of customary law helped govern a Norman villager's life chances from cradle to grave. Whether a man or woman inherited a house and fields, or nothing more than a spinning wheel; whether he or she was able to marry or consigned to solitude; even whether in his or her dying hours he or she could dictate a last testament were fixed to a large extent by a powerful and local set of written codes.

And yet Normans were equally tenacious in attempting to assert their independence from the custom when their families, property, and lives hinged on its terse formulations. Customary law in Normandy, as elsewhere in France, was almost synonymous with property law. Property was not an abstract concept but the stuff of daily survival, of family prosperity over generations, and of village structures. Ordinary men and women in the village courtrooms of the pays de Caux manipulated and skirted, outfoxed, and even permanently altered the uses and meanings of Norman property law. Their close engagement with the law and the court system was not exceptional but rather normative. By the late seventeenth and early eighteenth centuries, however, they found themselves struggling against a custom that was an increasingly poor mirror of real property arrangements. There is evidence that Normans both engaged in a de facto revision of some customary legal practices on property during the late seventeenth century and gradually abandoned the court system during the eighteenth century, partly as a response to the inflexibility of a custom that was never again officially revised.[88]

In the end there was a certain consistent blindness to the customs of the Caux and of Normandy. The law saw no individual but recognized only the rights of the institution: the family, the seigneurie, and the law court. The court records of Normandy are full of a kind of fifth-column rebellion against these tight restrictions of custom. Village men and women asserted themselves around the margins of the custom, resorting to courtroom trickery, hiding wealth, creatively adjudicating matters outside of the courtroom, and committing seemingly inexplicable acts of vengeance that had their tortured roots in these family and legal rigidities. The victims of these legal wrangles were almost invariably the families themselves: pitting brother against sister, mother against son, uncle against nephew, Normans fought for the remains of generations past. The notorious litigiousness of the Norman peasant, the dozens of *contes* and tales that displayed his penchant for trickery and cleverness in the courts, may well have been the creative response to the apparently iron law of the Custom.

Despite these dominant characteristics, it is important not to overlook the function of customs in granting very limited kinds of rights to even the poorest villagers, including the right to due process before landlords and creditors could seize their property. A few customary provisions even allowed villagers a proactive role in the court system. The court records of the Caux reveal that the genuinely popular articles on the clameur de haro were widely and inventively used by villagers as a citizen's arrest mechanism. Normans cried haro to halt illegal property seizures, improper marriages, violence, and even the abuses of royal officers.[89] Court records provide glimpses through a narrow door that reveals villagers using customs in a non-literal way, to advance their own unwritten concepts of justice. Cases brought under customary law in Normandy were often about quite different breaches of justice by the parties from those charges that were actually being litigated. Hugues Neveux has rightly pointed out that written laws had an "exterior function" for peasants. They used them to legitimize their griefs in the eyes of authorities, authorities who only partially participated in their value system.[90]

The General Custom of Normandy

The Norman Custom was perhaps the most important privilege ever granted to the province. Ultimately this small text formed a significant brake on the extension of royal law into the region, and thus over the vast majority of Normans. The oldest written customary law in France, Normandy's Très Ancien Coustumier's first known edition appeared at the end of the twelfth century.[91] But as medieval legal historians point out, it had been gestating for at least three hundred years before its appearance in manuscript form, creating insoluble arguments over the respective contributions of the Normans, the English, and even earlier influences.[92] It was a remarkably succinct handbook that mixed both public and private law. Distilled into this ancient provincial code were a few concise rules that laid out the jurisdictions of the royal and seigneurial courts, provided for the administration of families and seigneuries, and most important, governed how almost every piece of property in the province could be transmitted from one generation to the next.

Yet the text was also full of gaping lacunae and perplexing definitions of property. On the day of its appearance, the *Très Ancien Coustumier* was already a historical monument to an older society, displaying little interest in commerce or cities or new social categories, forces that had already emerged by the late twelfth century, when the *Très Ancien Coutumier* was written down. At the same moment, the Norman custom was surprisingly modern in its approach to certain property issues. As Emily Tabuteau has demonstrated in her work on eleventh-century Norman property law, by the high medieval period its focus was already far more tenurial than feudal, a transitive feature that was captured in the written customs and remained there until 1790.[93]

The Paris-trained magistrates and lawyers who prepared most of the legal commentaries on the Norman Custom down to the Revolution were quick to criticize the code's harsh and inflexible character. They found it inequitable, even in a legal world built on acceptable privileges and inequalities.[94] But it had at least the virtue of an iron-clad consistency. The customary articles were almost exclusively concerned with matters of property, a feature that allied them to most of the customary law codes of northern Europe, including the Teuto-Gothic laws. Custom focused like a laser on the problem of preserving property in the male line of succession, seemingly allowing almost no alienation of the patrimony away from the eldest male.

The two famous features of the Norman custom were its successoral and matrimonial régimes, which sharply curbed the freedom of Normans to dispose of inheritance property and strictly controlled female access to property. In 1698 Intendant de Vaubourg remarked on the stringency of Norman inheritance law, noting that "this province is ruled by a custom that one honors with the name of wise, favorable to males, to husbands and to the eldest, and leaving almost no liberty to dispose of one's property."[95] These régimes applied, quite unusually among the French customs, to nobles and commoners alike. In Brittany, for example, noble succession favored the eldest, but commoner inheritances were shared equally among the siblings.[96] The Norman custom thus distinguished itself both by its stranglehold over the movement of inheritance property and by its application of these inheritance rules to every stratum of society.

The foundation of the inheritance regime was the concept of male *preciput*. A feature of Norman law that has been often overlooked, it had profound implications for Norman villagers and townspeople. Preciput was the right of the eldest son to claim an unusually large portion of the family's *immeubles* (immovables), or real property, on the death of the parents, and under many circumstances to claim the entire inheritance of real property. His advantages actually began before taking his share of the succession. From the moment of the death of the parents in a Norman family, the custom stated, "the eldest son, whether noble or commoner, seizes the succession of the father and mother" with the authority to settle the inheritance.[97] As David Sabean recognized, the age differences among children alone gave a substantial advantage to the eldest son from the moment of the parents' death, since he could manage the full inheritance until his younger brothers and sisters came of age.[98]

Once the succession was settled, the eldest son's share of the *propres,* or lineage property, varied slightly according to whether he was noble or commoner. Both noble and commoner preciput, however, gave him his most significant advantages over his siblings, male and female. Under the rules of noble preciput laid down in Articles 335–367, the eldest was entitled to the principal fief in the countryside. By definition the noble fief encompassed the manor or house and its income-producing properties, including land that provided seigneurial income or ground rents.[99] He was further entitled to choose the noble fief he desired in both successions, paternal and maternal.[100] The fiefs he chose were outside and above his interest in the remaining property. If there was only one noble fief in the succession, it was indivisible and belonged to him alone; he owed no recompense to younger brothers for the property value.[101] He did owe all his brothers together one-third of the value of rents or income from the fief during their lifetimes.[102]

Commoner preciput followed similar lines of division. The eldest son was entitled to the rural manor or house, with its court, enclosures, and gardens.[103] If this was the sole inheritance, he was also not required to compensate younger brothers for the value of the property but only to give them a share of the income for life. Additional manors or houses went to remaining sons in birth order. Under both commoner and noble succession, the youngest brother drew up the remainder of the lineage property into lots, which the eldest was entitled to share in beyond his preciput.[104] But the custom strongly discouraged the dismembering of properties during the drawing up of lots, insisting that as much as possible each piece of property should remain integrally attached to its sources of income and should remain self-supporting.[105] The Custom thus did grant some property and independence to younger male siblings in cases where the inheritance was unusually large and where it was also divided into legally and economically distinct pieces of property with sufficient sources of income. As a matter of practice, however, relatively few rural families held more than one noble fief or principal farm with income-producing dependencies to be divided among the younger male siblings.

As a result, as Joan Thirsk has pointed out, Normandy was a region of virtual primogeniture. Its customs on inheritance were comparable to those practiced in Scandinavia, England, and certain German states, though not quite so harsh or exclusive as some customs and common laws.[106] A number of general historical works describing Norman inheritance customs have unfortunately relied on erroneous maps of European customary regions that were produced in the nineteenth and early twentieth centuries, such as those found in Wilhelm Abel's *Agrarpolitik*. These atlases erroneously grouped Normandy into the western customary region of partible inheritance laws, a region that included the province of Brittany.[107]

The mischaracterization of Normandy as a region of partible inheritance has in turn led to misunderstandings about the traditions of Norman society and its economic structures. Emmanuel Le Roy Ladurie, followed by Jack Goody and others, has praised the "formidable egalitarian traditions" of Normandy,[108] crediting its partible inheritance customs with creating the independent bocage system of agriculture and the individualistic spirit and celebrated egotism of the Normans.[109] Outside of the pays de Caux, Ladurie argued that "popular law knows no right of primogeniture as a 'general custom'; it has equality between male heirs quite unequivocally as its first provision."[110] From a small mischaracterization, he came to an interesting but unfortunately untenable theory about the origins of Norman individualism and economic behavior. The question is still compelling, even if one has to look elsewhere for the answer.[111]

The Norman customs on succession, daunting as they were for younger sons, turned a far more severe gaze on the succession of daughters. Article 248 set the tonic note for female succession with the axiom that "as long as there are males or descendants of males, the females or descendants of females cannot succeed." Norman fathers had no obligation either to dower or to set aside an inheritance for their daughters. If they did so voluntarily, strict limits were placed on their freedom to dispose of family property to daughters. All daughters together could inherit only one-third of the lineage property that remained after the preciput had been taken by the eldest son, and no daughter could inherit more than a younger son.[112]

The sole, and extraordinarily important, exception to the rule applied to families with daughters but no sons. Unlike in many customary regions where male heirs would be sought outside the immediate family, Norman daughters inherited as if they were male in this circumstance.[113] This exception allowed a significant minority of Norman women to inherit lineage property. For women in the highest nobility and among families of royal officers, this opened the door to their inheritance of seigneuries, high justices, and the monetary value of royal offices.

These restraints on female control of property were followed consistently throughout the Custom, above all in its unusual marital régime. Unlike most of the provincial customs of France and Roman law, the Custom of Normandy denied community property between husband and wife.[114] All property acquired during the marriage was the sole property of the husband. During his life, he was presumed to hold full rights to sell, alienate, or donate the property of the couple without the signature or agreement of the wife. The sole exception was alienation of the principal of the wife's *dot* (dowry), which required her assent. As a widow the woman held only the usufruct of a portion of the marital conquests, usually one-third, which she held in trust for the male heir. The customs thus rigorously restrained women from disposing of their own *dots, douaires* (widow's dowers),[115] inheritances, or earnings, or from making wills or *donations entre vifs* (gifts between the living), without their husbands' or other male heirs' consent. The Norman customs lastly closed the box by curbing the use of marriage contracts to circumvent these rules.[116] Successoral laws, combined with extensive restrictions on women's acquisition or control of property throughout their life cycles as daughters, sisters, wives, widows, and tutors of minor children, imposed the most rigorous regime on women's property in France.[117]

The severity of these controls on women's property struck even seventeenth- and eighteenth-century jurists as extreme. They described them as "hard," "rigorous," and "inequitable."[118] The commentator Berault even stoutly defended the right of women to marital separation in Normandy, since "the license to divorce being abolished, it would be just to give some help to unhappy women, and to deliver them in some way from the captivity of their husbands, when their bad conduct, their violence, their angry or strange humors render their condition miserable."[119] Modern legal historians have agreed with the Norman jurisconsults. "The Norman regime," stated Yver, "constituted the most severe situation of inferiority for women under the French customs."[120]

And yet the de jure rigor of Norman customary law was bent in practice by Norman women and their families. The larger social interests of protecting families and lineage property often mandated that women be left in control of both as widows, tuteurs, or separated wives. The amount of both cash and land that was left under female control, though significantly smaller than that left under male control, still required that women be recognized as landlords, lenders, owners (though not exercisers) of offices, and as contracting parties in the courts. Moreover, Norman women were inventive and active litigators on their own behalf, often seizing from the courts and from open practice what the law sought to deny. They are the best gauges of how far all Norman villagers, however legally disadvantaged, could bend the custom and the judicial system to their private advantage.[121]

The intended purpose of the Norman successoral and marital régimes was simple: preserving large and coherent property holdings in the male line of descent against the natural tendency of families to fragment and divide them at every generation. As the legal historian B. E. J. Rathery summed it up, the custom "rigorously maintained the transmission of goods from male to male by order of primogeniture, the constant preeminence of man over woman, and of the eldest child over the other children."[122] As has been seen, there were significant exceptions in practice to this seemingly iron-clad rule. Nevertheless, the Norman custom remained one of the most prescriptive in all of French law.

The Custom of the Pays de Caux

The population that fell under the local Custom of the pays de Caux was considerable. The pays encompassed much of upper Normandy, from the outskirts of Rouen and the Seine river in the south to the Atlantic coast in the west and north. Its eastern boundary was roughly fixed on a line running from the Bresle river at Eu down to Gournay.[123] For these purposes, the Caux can most usefully be thought of as covering the jurisdiction of the présidial of Caudebec-en-Caux, which encompassed 816 parishes but excluded Rouen and its environs.[124]

The pays de Caux had the distinction of remaining the most complicated legal enclave in Normandy. Appended to the general custom as a separate chapter under Articles 279–303, the Custom of the pays de Caux granted even more extensive rights to the eldest over his succession to the preciput than did the general Custom of Normandy. The preciput was here defined in all cases, even in the case of commoner property, as if it were a fief: it included not only the principal house with its *clos* and gardens, but also included the *pourpris*, that is, the outbuildings, plantations, ponds, dovecotes, and mills dependent on the house. Noble property was indivisible here as in the general custom. If a noble fief was the entire inheritance, it went solely to the eldest; he owed his younger brothers nothing except a one-third life interest in the income of the estate or to teach them a *métier*, so that they might subsist.[125]

The eldest son in this region held the right to two-thirds of the entire succession, including property outside of the Caux or *en bourgage* (in town). Parents could voluntarily donate up to one-third of the immeubles or héritages to one or all of their younger sons after the preciput had been taken out, but in that case they had to include a life provision for other sons not included in the disposition.[126] If the younger brothers renounced their share in the succession, they could demand only a life provision equal to no more than one-third of the income of the succession. That usufruct returned to their brother's estate on his death, not to their own heirs.[127] All daughters together were still restrained to no more than one-third of the succession, and there was no obligation to set anything aside for younger daughters: the succession could be exhausted in favor of the eldest daughter if so desired. Again, the only exception was made for daughters without brothers. They inherited as if male, in preference to the collateral male heirs. Even more than the general custom, the local custom circumscribed the right of fathers to determine their children's inheritance or to favor children other than the oldest male. As Jean Yver has noted, the Custom of the pays de Caux marked "an extreme point in the protection of lineage against acts of individual will."[128]

Local Usages of the Pays de Caux

Apart from retaining the right to practice its regional Custom of the pays de Caux, the district also surrounded several smaller seigneurial and royal enclaves, hidden like matriushka dolls inside the pays. Among the most important of these enclaves were two noble seigneurial jurisdictions. The first was a sizeable section of the eastern Caux belonging to the comté d'Eu. The count's judges successfully defended their right to appeal to the Parlement of Paris instead of the Parlement of Normandy. The seigneurial high justice also asserted its right to practice the phantom Usage de la comté d'Eu, a legal custom whose very existence was a subject of some debate among eighteenth-century magistrates.[129]

In eastern and central Caux, the duc de Longueville held several micro-enclaves of law within his vast duchy, including the troublesome villages of Gournay that formed a part of his domain. The twenty-four parishes around Gournay held onto their twenty-three local usages. Of these, twenty-one affected wills, heritages, widows' douaires, the seigneurial *relief* owed on the death of a tenant, and similar inheritance issues. Fifteen of the twenty-three articles addressed the property of women. A few of them liberalized articles of the general custom regarding women's property, but others further stripped women of any property rights. The héritages (generally rent income) from commoner property could be shared equally by brothers and sisters in Gournay. On the other hand, a widow had no absolute right to the usufruct of the *acquêts* of the marriage if there were no children. "The husband can use a testament to dispose of their acquisitions and conquests to whomever seems good to him," the usage crisply stated. Apart from the duchy of Longueville and the comté d'Eu, several smaller noble châtellenies were also given official blessing to practice their ancient usages in the Caux.[130]

Not to be outdone, the three royal vicomtal courts of Caudebec, Neufchâtel, and Arques (within the présidial jurisdiction of Caudebec-en-Caux) each practiced several distinct articles of law. The most novel were the seven articles of Caudebec, of which five involved the inheritance rights of sisters. Unusually, they allowed four parishes to practice partible inheritance between brothers and sisters, and two more parishes to do the same unless the sister had been married off with a dowry. Seven parishes allowed partible inheritance among brothers, with complete exclusion of sisters; three parishes and hamlets restricted all sisters together to one-third of the inheritance (as did the general custom). The bourg of Bans le Conte, with wonderful specificity, allowed equal inheritance of brothers and sisters of the houses and héritages that were inside the streets on which processions were held on Ascension Day. One can imagine residents petitioning the bourg to change the procession route as a short cut to inheritance.[131]

The patterns of the other Cauchois vicomtés were slightly less idiosyncratic. Like Caudebec's however, their usages focused almost exclusively on inheritance, and the majority were intently centered on the question of female control of property. All five of Arques' usages were partly or entirely about the inheritances of sisters and wives. Houses and gardens within the walls of Longueville and a few surrounding parishes, for example, could be shared equally with wives; "during their marriage the women here have half in property."[132]

Lastly, despite stern injunctions from the Parlement of Normandy forbidding the practice of any local usages not written into the final reformation of the Custom, reality dictated otherwise. Each high justice in effect practiced what could be called its own microcoutumier, in reality simply the rules of the manor. In the courts of the marquis de Cany, for example, there is no discoverable record of some customary laws having been enforced, whereas they were enforced in neighboring seigneurial jurisdictions. Moreover, each high justice was legally allowed to enforce its own unique pattern of seigneurial privileges or private laws. These could change from house to house or street to street in the parish as one seigneur's jurisdiction ended and another's began. Houard notes that in cases of jurisdictional doubt a Norman householder was presumed to live in the jurisdiction onto which his front door opened.[133]

Unwritten usages stubbornly persisted on the margins of written law everywhere in France. As President Bouhier willingly acknowledged in eighteenth-century Burgundy, "it is nevertheless certain that the non-written usages have remained in vigor, and are still punctually observed."[134] Although he does not indicate whether he thought these were legitimate local regulations or merely abuses, Bouhier's tone suggests that these were long-standing and legally accepted variations on provincial laws.

The immediate purpose of these local and microcustoms concerning property and women was to prevent the fragmentation of property in the pays de Caux. They were designed first to ensure the passage of a coherent and self-sufficient holding to the eldest male heir, and as much as possible to preserve property in the family lineage in which it originated. But the customs worked only imperfectly in this second goal of keeping property in the original line of succession. The vicissitudes of male heirs and intensive wrangling in the law courts meant that a substantial percentage of property continued to pass through the female line. Aveux and gages-plèges held by the high justice of Cany-Caniel indicate that 20 to 25 percent of *roturier* parcels were normally held through the wife's rights or through absolute inheritance.[135]

One of the most illustrative property issues that permeated the court dockets and law codes of the seventeenth and eighteenth centuries was therefore the issue of women. Despite their presumed disabilities in property ownership in Normandy, women were the vortex of furious legal activity in property cases. Perhaps the most unremarked feature of the local common law of the Caux, which was faithfully reflected in the other pays-coutumiers in the province, was that the majority of these laws were devoted to the problem of women. Sixty-four percent (fifty-one of eighty) of the local customs in force across Normandy were about the imperative problem of what to do with the property of wives, widows, sisters, and daughters.[136] Their rights over inheritances, douaires, *dots,* and marital property, and the conditions under which they could transmit that property by sale, alienation, testament or donation, are the principal concern of the local customs. The family, and above all women within the family, were a constant source of conflict and negotiation as property conduits in the Custom of Normandy.

But we should not rely entirely on the letter of customary law, any more than on that of royal law, in understanding the full social consequences of property law on women or other Norman villagers. The court records amply document that Norman women, for example, found a variety of ways to assume control over property despite their presumptive exclusion. Some of these loopholes were provided in law itself. A wife could regain substantial control of her property through a formal *séparation des biens* (property separation), a surprisingly common tactic in Normandy. Women also used curatelles (curatorships) granted over their children's property, contracts guaranteed by third parties, and other legal instruments to enter into effective possession of property ranging from noble duchies to royal offices. Here women provide the strongest evidence that villagers and townspeople of all types found ways to manipulate or evade provincial law and authority, not to mention evading the authority of the king.[137]

Despite the potential for a legal Tower of Babel, a remarkable theoretical unity runs through the microcustoms or usages of the pays de Caux. The local usages of Normandy were everywhere different, and everywhere the same thing: determining the proportion of property that could go to the eldest as opposed to the youngest, to sisters as opposed to brothers, to wives as opposed to husbands, to widows as opposed to their children or heirs, and under what conditions. They shared an utterly singleminded interest in the transmission of property, and an unswerving interest in regulating female property.

The complexity of the customary law was a great stimulus to even more court cases. The laws governing succession to property in the Caux were at times so torturously complicated that they required several steps of mathematical equations, including double fractions, to fulfill them correctly.[138] This presupposed a high degree of mathematical literacy among those laboureurs and villagers of the Caux who held enough property to be passed down to more than one child. More to the point, it also left a wide-open door to chicanery and creative distribution of inheritances, not to mention simple mistakes, for those involved in these crucial village decisions. The real windfall, of course, went to the lawyers and to the historians. The *sacs de procès* of the Cauchois courts were stuffed with lawsuits that provide a remarkable picture of village society.

The Caux's harsh inheritance laws also created strong tensions at the village level. The property laws split individuals within families and between families, setting brother against brother and wife against father-in-law, and were thus a frequent source of court cases. Parisian and Norman jurists, playwrights and poets, lawyers and intendants all shook their heads over the litigiousness of the Normans, who appeared to be addicted to court cases. But we would do well to look at the law itself as a source of conflict in Norman society. Those conflicts were destined to become even sharper as individuals gradually emerged from the background of the family, pushed by rising literacy and mobility. Villagers were less resigned to the will of the customs and more willing to contest their lot in life in a court of law or through extra-legal arrangements.

Dry and inert as they might appear on the surface, customary laws and usages exerted a vigorous influence on daily life. In Norman villages, one can partially trace wealth distribution in families, rural landholding patterns, royal and seigneurial court use, and the rising power of the legal class back to a few hundred articles of legal custom. The reason was simply that custom controlled property. And property in the village was not an abstract concept, but the very stuff of life, as it has always been. Grain fields and apple orchards, thread and cloth, cows and chickens, bread and peas, were the immediate stakes in the customary battles in the village. But property was also the currency of local power and position in the Caux. Those who controlled property (in the private and family realm) and property law (in the public realm) were at the vital center of public authority in the Caux.

Chapter 5

THE RED ROBE AND THE BLACK

COMMON COURTS AND THE STATE

One of the least-known aspects of governance during the ancien régime is how the lower-court system was integrated with the sovereign courts, Estates, and intendants at the pinnacle of provincial administration to provide order and authority in the countryside.[1] In Normandy, this relationship changed dramatically after the mid-seventeenth century. With the demise of the Norman Estates after 1665, and the only very specialized interests of the intendants in provincial matters, the Parlement and the bailiwick courts were perfectly poised to inherit the mantle of power. By 1665, over 90 percent of the 1,219 principal royal officers of the généralité of Rouen served in the judicial administration.[2] Yet this concentration of power in the judiciary was paradoxically accompanied by the growing isolation of bailiwicks from provincial and even national politics. Excluded from ascension into the closed elite of the Parlement and no longer seated in either the defunct national or provincial Estates, bailiwick officers were increasingly sealed into the world of local governance.

The loss of the Estates of Normandy, which had traditionally seated a large contingent of bailiwick officers in the third estate, was especially acute for the lower judiciary. Through the Estates, bailiwick officers had enjoyed not only a deliberative role in provincial affairs but a vital lawmaking role as well. The bailiwick was the level at which the Custom of Normandy and the local customs of the province were collected and redacted in 1583–87 to form the province's primary law code. The Estates were also a key forum for negotiating royal judicial policies with the crown, especially the king's multiplication of lower judicial offices. In 1593 and again in 1605, the Norman Estates had sent remonstrances to the king on the subject of office creation. "After the inconveniences of wars," they explained, "that which most leads to the trampling, oppression and expense of his poor subjects . . . is the multitude of supernumerary offices."[3] The poor subjects the deputies had uppermost in mind were their own corps, whose functions and rewards were being diluted by new offices.

Besides the loss of a negotiating tool, the fall of the Norman Estates was also the loss of the only forum where the crown's ordinary and sovereign court officers met together as a body to conduct common business.[4] The demise of the Estates followed from their inability to maintain control of Normandy's tax-bargaining power with the king. The crown effectively bypassed the Estates as a revenue-raising instrument with a complete system of élus under the Bureaux des Finances, thereby undermining the Estates' negotiating position over other provincial matters, including justice. In its last sessions in 1655, the Estates defied the king by refusing to vote him the subsidies he had already imposed in fact. In 1657 a final Norman Estates was called, but it was never convened.[5] This growing disconnect between local and provincial institutions was equally apparent in Brittany, which retained its Estates. Despite the fact that some lower-court judges (who often held cumulative office as mayors of towns) continued to serve as deputies to the third estate, they had grown socially and politically more distant from the real power brokers of the province.[6]

A hazard of politics in Normandy thus came to reinforce the trend toward professional isolation between the two levels of the magistracy. Henceforth, the lower courts' contact with judges of the sovereign courts would be limited to their official reception into office, passive attendance at the annual harangues of the Parlement, and rare appellate cases. This was accentuated by a second development, both social and economic in nature. By the mid-seventeenth century, bailiwick officers experienced sharpening social distinctions between their own corps and the corps of sovereign magistrates in Rouen, whose brilliance, wealth, and endogamous habits made them an increasingly closed elite. The sealing off of nearly all upward professional mobility between lower courts and the Parlement was complete by 1670. The paulette had helped create a system whose end result was partly unforseen: the creation of a new governing and political dynamic within the provinces.

Despite the yawning social gulf that had opened between parlementaires and local judges, bailiwick judges were nevertheless firmly supported by the Parlement in consolidating local judicial power. The magistrates of the Norman Parlement, nobles who almost universally owned seigneurial justices and often leased out royal bailiwick sergeanties, had every reason to promote stable and competent governance in the countryside. They protected the bailiwicks from interference by the king's intendants and confirmed the common courts' local authority through parliamentary arrêts and by upholding the majority of appellate cases. The consequences of this localization of power, and the buffering of the common courts from the central state, were significant. As one observer of Brittany put it, the local courts "detached themselves from the monarchy to anchor themselves locally."[7]

Armed with this support, local judges and attorneys began to drain numerous specialized rural jurisdictions, such as the woods and waters courts (eaux et forêts), of their cases. The vicomté de l'eau in Rouen was still an active court for port cases in the provincial capital, but elsewhere in upper Normandy these courts have left only intermittent traces of their activities.[8] In 1664 Anne-Geneviève de Bourbon, duchess of Longueville, was forced to file suit in Parlement because the regular courts were taking jurisdiction over cases belonging to her family's vicomté de l'eau in the pays de Caux.[9] In tandem with the high justices, the bailliage courts absorbed much of the public business that had once gone to middling and low justices, gradually bringing most cases into the main watershed of the bailiwick courts. The local state in Normandy was consolidating and redefining itself at the bailiwick level: a state largely independent of direct royal or noble control and centered instead on the common courts.

An important and often unremarked part of this consolidation was the integration of royal bailliage courts and high justices into a single system of state justice. They shared not only officers and legal practices in the countryside, but were in fact treated equally by the sovereign courts as integral building blocks of royal justice. Only recently have scholars begun to rewrite much of the earlier scholarship on the decline of seigneurial justice, which often relied on French royal apologists. Before the sixteenth century was out, Guy Coquille wrote perhaps the most famous obituary for seigneurial courts, calling them "bodies without soul and without blood."[10] Despite the fierce rhetoric of political theorists and royal administrators, however, the largest of these lords' courts were neither dying nor especially corrupt. The real breaking point in the French judicial system was not between royal justice and seigneurial justice, but between high justice and the lesser forms of middling and low justice beneath it. For this reason, both high justices and royal bailiwick courts can be more usefully treated together as the ordinary courts or common courts.

This process of consolidation in the judiciary can be graphically traced across two royal maps. In 1569, Charles de Figon, a master in the Chamber of Accounts in Montpellier, drew up an elaborate *Tree of States and Officers of France*. He visualized the administration of the kingdom as an organic tree, emerging from the king's councils at the roots into a mass of branches. The lower trunk of the tree was formed by the chancellor of France, and well over half of the limbs were made up of judicial offices in the ordinary or fiscal courts. As one observer has noted, even many of the financial branches were dependent on the king's system of justice, "the most royal function of royal functions."[11] The drawing has a rough vitality that is accurate in spirit as well as in form. The main royal courts, which take up fully half the tree of state, had indeed grown out of the medieval king's curia into an organic wilderness of jurisdictions.[12]

In 1740, Chancellor D'Aguesseau and royal officials in Normandy undertook an entirely new mapping exercise.[13] For the first time, the crown made an attempt to draw detailed geographic maps of royal jurisdictions in the province and across France. The state hoped to impose a new sense of rational borders, of order, over the organic wilderness of centuries. But the king's skilled cartographers were unable to subdue the reality of jurisdiction in the ancien régime.[14] The fluidity of boundaries; the maddening fact that jurisdiction was often not geographic but legal, personal, or material; and the constant overlapping of jurisdictional authorities turned their careful maps into mere geometric abstractions.

And yet these two mapping exercises, separated by a little more than a century and a half, captured a fundamental transition in the judicial system of France. By the early eighteenth century, parts of Figon's baffling tree were withering at the expense of the growing ordinary courts. In Normandy, the main stem of the judicial system, which branched out from the Parlement and ran through the présidial, bailliage, and vicomté courts, had gradually sapped competing jurisdictions and was consolidating within itself. The same consolidation was occuring in the sovereign fiscal courts–the Court of Aids and Chamber of Accounts. The two jurisdictions were collapsed into one court through an edict of October 1705. Through a series of royal edicts during the 1740s, many Norman vicomtés were extinguished and united with their bailliages.[15] The remnants of the salt-tax courts were disbanded at the national level, and their cases granted to baillages and présidials, by the Edict of May 1788. Even the sovereign Court of Monies was stripped of its legal jurisdiction in Normandy, and most of its functions given to the ordinary courts. D'Aguesseau's maps, dominated by bailliage jurisdictions and acknowledging no others, traced the idealized outline of a more unified jurisdiction and authority, one that was just beginning to exist in fact.

Lines of Authority: Sovereign Courts and Local Bailiwicks

The heart of Normandy's judicial system was housed in a few square blocks in the center of Rouen. The Renaissance Palais de Justice, built around a large cour d'honneur, elegantly housed the Parlement of Normandy and the Table de Marbre. A few streets closer to the river, facing the parvis of the Cathedral of Rouen, stood the sovereign fiscal courts, the Chambre des Comptes and Cour des Aides. From these two squares, the lines of authority ran along the post roads and rivers throughout the province (see appendix A.) But the nature of that authority had gone through a quiet transformation over the seventeenth century, becoming both more routine and less directly involved in local governance.

The main body of the courts was in fact rather well defined: the Parlement of Normandy supervised seven présidial and forty bailliage and vicomtal courts, with jurisdiction over more than 4,200 parishes. Within the généralité of Rouen alone, which covered only a third of the province, there were four présidials and fifteen bailliage and vicomtal courts. But the Parlement shared sovereign jurisdiction with three other royal courts, the Cour des Aides, the Chambre des Comptes, and technically the Cour de la Monnaye, which gradually lost its jurisdiction and sovereignty to the other courts. Specializing in tax, accounting, and monetary cases, these jurisdictions formed a parallel court system that handled crown finances. They also formed the only truly widespread and powerful royal jurisdictions outside of the main stem of courts overseen by the Parlement.

The authority of the Court of Aids and Chamber of Accounts in particular had been greatly enhanced by the collapse of the Estates, and they remained vigorous and important jurisdictions throughout the period.[16] The vitality of these courts rested partly on Normandy's fiscal importance to the crown; it was assessed at just under 18 percent of the direct taxes collected in France through the taille in the *pays d'élections*. The province was also a major contributor to the actual bullion flow to Paris through a combination of tax collection, income from international exports, and its proximity to the capital. In addition, the province paid significant indirect taxes through aides on cider, wine, and other consumer goods, and through upper Normandy's classification as a region of *grande gabelle* for payment of the salt tax.[17] In part because of its fiscal value, the province enjoyed one of the most developed judicial systems to oversee tax and financial cases outside of the Paris basin.

The Chamber of Accounts and Court of Aids of Normandy were united into a single office after 1707. The Court of Aids was the sovereign court for cases involving the taille, aides, gabelles, and lesser taxes and customs in the province. It heard appellate cases arising from local courts under three Bureaux des Finances for Normandy, which supervised such direct and indirect tax-collection agencies as the élections, greniers à sel (salt warehouses),[18] and *traites foraines* (customs). The court's personal and property jurisdiction was wide: the élections could hear the cases of any person liable for taxation in its district. The local élections were also the courts of last appeal for all tax cases under 5 livres in value (although this amount was later raised), which made them in essence the sovereign courts for perhaps 60 to 70 percent of all taxpayers.[19] Norman vicomtés and bailliages left the élections uncontested in their right to hear local tax cases. Although the bureaus of finance undertook the repartition and collection of the tailles and supervised collection of other taxes, final resolution of these legal disputes was supposed to be the privilege of the Chamber of Accounts or the Court of Aids. The Chamber of Accounts audited the accounts of royal financial officials in the province, supervised the king's domain, received *aveux et dénombrement* from his vassals, and heard appeals on those domainal matters. There was no appeal from either financial court in civil matters, save direct royal intervention. The sovereign Court of Monies in Rouen supervised currency and the mint, but the court gradually lost most of its authority to the other sovereign and ordinary courts during this period.

Jurisdictions became considerably murkier once a litigant stepped out of the main body of ordinary courts. There were more than seventy exceptional jurisdictions in the généralité, handling everything from forest law and salt taxes to vagabonds on the high roads.[20] These coexisted with at least 218 high justices in the présidial districts of Rouen and Caudebec-en-Caux alone and dozens of ecclesiastical courts, without counting several hundred low and middle seigneurial justices as true jurisdictions. In the généralité of Rouen, then, a minimum of three hundred jurisdictions cohabited in a territory roughly the size of a county in Texas. In this, Normandy's judicial system was typical of that found in other French provinces. Indeed, the disorder was even worse in provinces such as Brittany.[21]

The extraordinary courts, sometimes called jurisdictions of attribution, administered and judged not so much a territory as particular kinds of cases or resources. The Table de Marbre de Rouen, seated in a wing of the palace of justice, supervised the port and coastal courts, or *admirautés*[22]; the mounted constabulary courts, or maréchaussées (also called *prévôtal* courts);[23] and the woods and waters courts, known as eaux et forêts jurisdictions.[24] A small set of urban courts, the popular juridictions consulaires, or merchants' courts, rendered final judgment in commercial cases involving amounts under 500 livres. The two consular courts in Rouen and Dieppe were expanded to a few other towns after 1710.[25] Alongside these courts practiced the local tax and customs courts, the élections, greniers à sel, and traites foraines.[26] Out in the countryside of the généralité of Rouen, offshoots of these extraordinary jurisdictions multiplied like runners: eighteen greniers à sel, eleven eaux et forêts, thirteen élections, seven maréchaussées, seven traites foraines, seven admirautés, and several juridictions consulaires spread over the généralité.[27] The vestiges of these jurisdictions created confusion for litigants, judicial competition, and lawsuits. Yet by the late seventeenth century many jurisdictional conflicts were more apparent than real. The main branches of the royal courts, and the largest high justices, were gradually absorbing the territory of their minor brethren.[28]

The Red Robe and the Black:
Distinctions between Sovereign and Local Magistrates

By the mid-seventeenth century, the sovereign courts floated above the lower jurisdictions on a sharply different social plane. These were the first level of judicial offices that ennobled some or all of their judges and conferred hereditary nobility on their families. By the later seventeenth century, the majority of these judgeships went in fact to men who were already noble before entering office. This meant that social mobility for magistrates between the lower and sovereign courts had been largely extinguished, particularly within the Parlement. In 1640, ten of the seventy-seven magistrates sitting in the Parlement of Normandy, or approximately 13 percent, had come from lower jurisdictions or families of échevins. In the sixty-six years between 1649 and 1715, only five of the 255 magistrates, or less than 2 percent (of those whose background is known) had ever practiced in a lower jurisdiction, and one of the five bought the lesser judgeship after becoming a parlementaire. Two hundred nine of these magistrates came from the city of Rouen alone.[29] This pattern conforms to that of Brittany and other provinces, where the introduction of the paulette created an increasingly closed elite within the parlements.[30]

Henceforth, the relationship of sovereign and lower courts would become one of rather distant stewardship on the part of the Parlement. The lower-court officers began to consolidate their position in the countryside through multiple officeholding and land strategies. The Parlement did not discourage this development. The lower judicial officers were both a bastion of local order in the province and an extension of the Parlement's own authority.

The fissures that separated the officers of the ordinary courts from the scarlet-robed magistrates in the sovereign courts of Rouen and from the king in Versailles were complex. They can be gauged by looking at the key markers that have been successfully used to understand the behavior of higher royal officers: venality, heredity, crown transfers such as gages and pensions, endogamy, and career cycles. Two of the most outstanding features of royal offices in France were heredity and venality, that is, the right to buy one's office from the king and the right to pass it down to one's heirs through payment of an annual tax known as the paulette, or *droit annuel.* Established as a royal fund-raising measure in 1604 by Henry IV, the edict authorizing the paulette had to be renewed by the king every nine years, establishing fresh grounds for extracting new loans in exchange for the privilege of full heredity.[31]

The paulette was quickly followed by another durable innovation, the augmentations des gages, in the regency following Henry IV's death. Augmentations required the individual officer or his corps to make additional capital investments in their offices; the new gages were then paid directly to the creditors who had provided the capital. Although augmentations were typically raised from various corps at the end of the nine-year cycle, they could be imposed at any time. During the wars of the late seventeenth century, augmentations became an increasingly frequent and onerous burden on the royal officer corps. In 1684, for example, the Parlement registered a declaration raising 500,000 livres in augmentations from the Norman officer corps.[32]

Despite these financial burdens, upper-ranking officers considered heredity of office to be one of their most inviolable and valuable privileges. The crown was never able to retract either venality or heredity, despite ambitious reform programs for judicial venality dating back to Chancellor Michel de L'Hôpital.[33] As James Farr has pointed out, the "conflicted relationship between patrimonial and public justice that resided at the heart of this system" quickly became second nature to judges.[34] Yet the divergent patterns of heredity that higher and lower magistrates followed are remarkable. Lower judicial offices were originally conceived as nonvenal, nonhereditary appointments, just as were the offices of procurators general or first presidents of the parlements. Well before the late seventeenth century, however, local judgeships were bought and sold at the *parties casuel* (office controlling sale of royal posts) by private individuals, subject to both gages and augmentations just as sovereign court offices were. Yet despite these hereditary rights, chief judgeships of Cauchois bailiwick courts seldom passed through direct succession. This places the local magistrates in a substantially different mold than officers who sat in the higher echelons of the royal judiciary.[35] With the exception of the neighboring Norman bailliage of Pont-Audemer (which appears to have been exceptional in judicial abuses as well), father-son, uncle-nephew, or even father-in-law–son-in-law transfers were strikingly rare.[36]

In the pays de Caux, of the thirty-six chief judges studied (twenty-four seigneurial baillis and twelve royal lieutenants general), only one seigneurial judge and no royal judges can be determined to have passed judgeships on to relatives, a heritability rate of 2.8 percent. Among the five adjunct judges in the local courts (lieutenants general in seigneurial courts and lieutenants civil, criminal, or particular in royal courts), again only one seigneurial and no royal judgeships were passed on to heirs. André Corvisier also found no heredity of office at work in his analysis of eight seigneurial justices in upper Normandy.[37] (This is despite the fact, as we will later see, that seigneurial judgeships were typically bought and sold on contracts with rights of survivance, just as royal offices were.) As Roland Mousnier has pointed out, these apparently unrelated transfers could mask an agreement to transfer an office outside of a family temporarily, during the minority of the heir. But in the Caux, there is no evidence that heirs later reclaimed judgeships; they were normally passed onto a third or even fourth unrelated or only very distantly related party.[38]

If we look at Normandy as a whole, a similar picture emerges. None of the forty-one royal bailliage judges accepted by the Parlement between 1705 and 1746 shared the same last name, title, or properties, even though the chief judgeship at Caen changed hands four times (in 1705, 1715, 1730 and 1731), that of Bayeaux changed hands three times (in 1705, 1710, 1712), that of Coutance three times (in 1713, 1718, and 1746), and four other bailliage and vicomtal courts changed hands twice each.[39] Although it is not possible to track down uncle-nephew or father-in-law–son-in-law relations between these men through the remaining court documents, those judges whose sieuries or seigneuries were listed do not correspond with lists of their predecessors' properties. (Typically, an office was passed along to heirs with a sufficient estate in property to support it.) This rate of heredity appears to have dropped even lower than that recorded in the early seventeenth century. Mousnier found that among forty-four sales of local offices in Normandy between 1604 and 1643, only slightly over 20 percent went to sons, nephews, or sons-in-law.[40]

In England, a rather higher percentage of justices of the peace had fathers, grandfathers, or paternal relatives on the bench, ranging from 23 to 46 percent between 1679 and 1761.[41] But there, too, the majority did not enter office on the heels of a direct ancestor. The recruitment of local magistrates in both English counties and French bailiwicks came from a relatively small elite of propertied men, but it was an open elite by early modern standards, one that regularly brought new families into public functions. The king's ordinary court judges in France took the fullest advantage of the upward mobility offered by offices, exchanging them far more fluidly as social and professional capital than their higher-ranking colleagues in urban Rouen.[42] Some sénéchaussées in Brittany exhibited higher rates of endogamy, and further investigation may bring to light other rural bailiwicks in France where offices were more often passed down to heirs.[43] But the Caux demonstrates that it was by no means the rule and did not constitute a significant part of a magistrate's considerations upon buying the office.

An officer's calculations about royal office in both higher and lower courts included direct or indirect transfers from the king: his interest rate or gages, pensions, tax exemptions, and other monetary privileges. Secure exemption from the direct tax (taille), often from the salt tax (sel d'impôt) and town excise taxes,[44] and usually from quartering soldiers or performing curatorship (curatelles) of minors, were strong financial and practical incentives for officeholding at the highest level.[45] Buying an exemption from the taille through office could also form part of the long-term strategy of an ambitious sieur who wished to begin living nobly. Although Rouennaise magistrates enjoyed relative confidence in these matters, however, local officers endured considerable insecurity. In April 1715, the crown suppressed all privileges of lower officers, and the officer corps resecured them only after considerable struggle (and undoubtedly after considerable cash payment to the crown).[46] Royal privileges acquired in the sovereign courts were more extensive, more lucrative, and more secure than those at the bailliage level. They ranged from substantial pensions for first presidents of the Parlement to the right to produce and sell wine without paying the aides. Direct or indirect transfers from the crown in the form of privileges, pensions, and gages were perhaps not large in comparison with parlementaire landed fortunes; nevertheless, they formed a significantly larger constellation of royal privilege than that enjoyed by local officers.

Gages are the most easily measured of these benefits. In the royal court at Cany in 1665, the gages of the lieutenant general were 50 livres for an office bought on the market for 15,000 livres; the gages of the lieutenant criminal were 30 livres. The gages were paid only on the official price of the office, however, which was often lower than the market price. The chief justice's return would therefore have been a rather contemptible .33 percent annually on the officer's real investment, had the king actually paid the gages; as it was, he had only paid one of the last four quarters of gages, making the actual rate of return .08 percent (see table 5.1). Moreover, neither in the présidial court of Caudebec, nor in any of the eighteen other bailliages and vicomtés in the province, had the king paid more than two of the quarterly officers' gages.[47] Court records from Brittany indicate that the augmentations des gages, the interest due on additional investments in the office demanded by the king, were paid at no better rate. Sixteen companies from the ordinary courts sent records to the intendant and Parlement of Rennes in 1717, documenting that the crown was as much as twelve years in arrears in payments.[48]

Moreover, the paulette that royal officers owed back to the crown each year was equal to or significantly more than their actual gages. The lieutenant general of Cany owed 111 livres annually on his droit (one-sixtieth of the official valuation of 8,666 livres); he actually received 12.5 livres back in gages. The lieutenant particular of the court owed 30 livres for his hereditary rights and received back 7.5 livres in gages.[49] Local officers ran a permanent deficit vis à vis the crown each year. Conditions were no better in Brittany. One historian has noted that middling royal officers in sénéchaussée courts saw annual returns of barely one-tenth of 1 percent in gages each year, compared to a nominal 6 percent for parlementaires.[50]

The sovereign magistrates of the Parlement of Rouen, too, saw to it that all 125 presidents, councillors, king's prosecutors and advocates, and the main ushers and secretaries of the court had been paid three-quarters of their gages. (Ironically, even the receivers, payers, and controllers of gages in the Parlement were given only one-quarter of their due). These were not contemptible sums, either, although they were indeed insignificant relative to the market value of the office. The first president of the Parlement was supposed to receive 4,125 livres from the king, or a nominal 1.6 percent rate of return on his 250,000-livre office; his actual return that year was 1.2 percent. Simple lay councillors did even less well; they were paid three-quarters of their 300-livre gages, and their actual rate of return on the market price of their offices was .25 percent.[51] The situation was no better in 1743, at the end of the period under consideration.[52] Nevertheless, sovereign magistrates had the honor of usually being paid the interest due on their investments, unlike the foot soldiers in rural jurisdictions.

Table 5.1. Office prices and *gages*, royal baillage of Cany, 1665

Title of office	Number of offices available	Gages attributed to each office, in livres	Number of quarters, out of four, that gages have been paid	Evaluation of each office by the parties casuels, in livres	Droit annuel of each office; equals 1/60 of the evaluation	Current market price of each office, in livres	Total value of current market price of offices, in livres
Lieutenant général et particular	1	50	1	8,666	111	15,000	15,000
Lieutenant criminel	1	30	1	1,333	30	3,000	3,000
Avocat du roi	1					2,000	2,000
Procureur du roi	1			2,666	44	4,000	4,000
Procureurs postulans	4			200	3	150	600
Total value of offices, in livres							24,600

Sources: BN Ms. 500 Colbert 260, fols. 180–205; Edmond Esmonin, *Voysin de la Noiraye: Mémoire sur la Généralité du Rouen en 1665.*

To add injury to insult, the sovereign courts were exempted from many of the crown's augmentations des gages, which were then passed down to the lower courts to shoulder. In 1665, for example, Colbert exempted the parlements from the nine-year augmentation, imposing the full burden on the subordinate courts instead. Exceptional augmentations for war expenses were levied on the whole judiciary in 1689; in 1693 they were levied on the lower tribunals alone, barely two years after they had paid their nine-year imposition. The 1700 renewal of the annual extracted a further 11 million livres from the judiciary of the whole kingdom.[53]

The multiplication of judicial offices as a royal fund-raising measure also accelerated at a far more breathtaking rate in the lower tribunals than in the sovereign courts, forcing officers to go to the well yet again for local credit to slake the thirst of the crown. In some Norman jurisdictions, the number of royal offices in the ordinary courts quintupled over the course of the seventeenth century.[54] The burden of both augmentations and office creations fell disproportionately on the lower courts for obvious reasons. Dispersed over the countryside, local officers were unable to organize effectively as a group to resist the crown's demands. Moreover, they were perfectly positioned to tap the enormous pool of small credit sources in the countryside, a source that could scarcely be reached more effectively and cheaply by the crown. (The crown was thereby transferring state borrowing to a group that local lenders also deemed more creditworthy than the crown.) As a result, by the first decades of the eighteenth century, many companies in the lower courts had exhausted their sources of local credit. Some were far enough underwater to begin declaring bankruptcy as a corps. Nor could they find new officeholders to buy into the corps as posts fell vacant, since they would thereby become liable for staggering corporate debt.[55]

The upshot of this net drain was considerable financial distress in the king's ordinary courts, above all in the lower offices below those of chief judge and king's prosecutor. In the bailliage of Cany, four of its eleven offices, including those of three councillors and the substitute king's advocate and prosecutor, had fallen vacant by the turn of the eighteenth century and were still vacant in 1777. Of the remaining seven offices, the five highest posts (those of the multiple lieutenants general, particular, and police) were gradually gathered into the hands of the chief judge by the early eighteenth century.[56] Three men were thus left to fill the functions of a court of eleven offices. In Brittany, where correspondence between the intendant and the ordinary court officers provides far more detail about financial distress, during the early eighteenth century officers and widows wrote imploring letters, complaining that their entire capital had been placed at risk, since their offices no longer brought in enough income to pay the paulette. The small royal sénéchaussée of Fougères, with forty-one parishes, hosted an incredible 103 royal court offices, of which fifty-five had fallen vacant at the parties casuel by 1741. These victims included the chief judge of the court and the king's prosecutor, who were declared "hors d'état" of paying the annual. The latter had frankly abandoned his office to take up a post with a seigneurie. Through the intervention of both Parlements and intendants, by this juncture the message had reached Chancellor d'Aguesseau that the well was dry.[57]

But the underlying story is that not all offices were suffering equally. Intendant Voysin de la Noiraye's survey of office prices and gages in the généralité of Rouen in 1665 tells the more nuanced story about the fiscal divide in the lower courts. In the royal bailliage of Cany, three of the highest royal offices were still selling on the market at prices significantly above their official price at the parts casual. The offices of lieutenant general, lieutenant particular, and king's prosecutor had last sold for 173 percent, 225 percent, and 150 percent of their official prices, respectively. But the offices of postulant solicitors (*procureurs postulans*) had declined in value to 75 percent of their official valuation. Despite the Edict of 1665, which (until its repeal in 1709) was supposed to set ceilings for royal offices, local offices continued to circulate at their real market value.[58]

The statistics on the bailliage of Cany did not include information on other middling officers, but in other vicomtés and bailliages in the same présidial district these men were clearly in distress. In the Cauchois courts of Arques, Neufchâtel, Havre-de-Grace, and Montvilliers, several middling and lower offices were selling below their official price: commissioned examiners, receivers of consignations, inquestors, some king's advocates, and a few ushers and sergeants. The reasons are obvious: the first three categories of office were relatively late creations and therefore consisted of limited functions alienated from other offices.[59] A king's advocate was a poor second cousin to a king's prosecutor, and in many local jurisdictions he was a portfolio without a brief. Like the new creations, king's advocates existed mainly to provide revenue to the crown, not to provide legal services to the courts.

Had these offices been desired for purely honorary or tax purposes, one would expect to see them still filled in the eighteenth century. These officers were avid for more than honor from their investments. Nonpayment of gages, forced loans, and falling office prices were more rents in the financial fabric that connected the local judiciary to the king's interest. The attention of town and village officers must have been even more firmly focused on their local clients, fees, and land markets as sources of income. By the late eighteenth century, the fragility of this arrangement at the village level would become starkly clear. If officers' ownership of property or security in office could be secured by new political arrangements, without the inconveniences and expenses of royal patronage, local officers would be net gainers.

The men who presided over the local bench were distinguished from their parliamentary colleagues by their professional life cycle as much as by finances. Their career trajectories reinforce André Corvisier's observation that rural chief judges were typically mature men with a long career already behind them before acquiring their judgeships.[60] Prior records of their legal practices in the local courts of the Caux suggest that most were at least in their thirties, and many considerably older, before they reached the pinnacle of their judicial careers. Lower court judges were legally required to be thirty years of age, but there were routine procedures for waiving age requirements had they been necessary. In the forty-one receptions of local chief judges in Normandy, no age dispensations were noted down by the examining magistrates.[61]

In contrast, age dispensations had become routine in the sovereign courts of Parlement, where the average age of magistrates was actually falling during the late seventeenth and early eighteenth centuries. François Bluche's study of the Parlement of Paris found that the average age of councillors received into the Parlement was below the minimum age from 1659 through the end of Louis XVI's reign. (In 1665, the legal age for a simple councillor in the Parlement was raised from twenty-five to twenty-seven).[62] As Albert N. Hamscher discovered, the average age of new parlementaires fell further during Louis's later reign, dropping to just below twenty-three for lay councillors in the early eighteenth century.[63] Richard Mowery Andrews noted that even at the Châtelet, the présidial court of Paris, the average age of new judges in the eighteenth century was twenty-three.[64] By implication, few of these parlementaires or urban lower-court judges were self-made men who had acquired the bulk of their property during their own lifetimes. Indeed, some of them were still teenagers.

Taken together, these distinctions suggest that the ordinary courts followed what we might cautiously call a more "modern" pattern of officeholding, one based on education, skill, mobility, and liquidity of office. Unlike their counterparts on the sovereign benches in Rouen, local magistrates were largely self-made or recently made men. They neither inherited their judgeships from fathers and uncles in their youth, nor held them as official patrimony for their own sons and nephews. They bought these offices with recent capital accumulation, and liquidated them at the end of their professional careers. They expected (and received) relatively little in the way of patronage favors or transfers from the crown. This was a strikingly different model of royal office from the model used to understand the behavior of parlementaires, for example. Insofar as we know the officeholding patterns in the sovereign financial courts such as the Court of Aids or the Chamber of Accounts (about which little has been written), these patterns were also somewhat distinctive from the those in the parlements. Mark Potter has shown that of fourteen offices created in the new, combined Cour des Comptes, Aides, et Finances in Rouen in 1705 (apart from the office of president), more than half the new officers came from outside the sovereign courts altogether, five were lawyers from the parlements of Paris and Rouen, and only one had known family ties to the old Chamber of Accounts and Court of Aids.[65]

At the same time, the social and fiscal gulf between rural court families and those of sovereign court magistrates in Rouen widened in the seventeenth century. The chief judgeship of an ordinary royal court was the highest judicial office in France that did not enoble its buyer, indicating an important fracture line in status. In the late seventeenth and early eighteenth centuries, as the financial crisis in local offices deepened, one of the most common requests from the king's ordinary courts was that the crown at least confer personal nobility, if not hereditary nobility, on the officers not already noble through other means. They were continually rebuffed, despite the fact that the king had recently conferred nobility on a raft of lesser posts, including the much-ridiculed *noblesse de cloche,* or bell-tower nobles. (The only exception was made for the judges of the Châtelet of Paris, and then only after 1768). The obvious choice for many legal men was to simply buy up these ennobling municipal posts, a far cheaper expedient than buying patents of nobility outright.

Perhaps the most dramatic split between sovereign and lower courts occurred in the mid-seventeenth century as the gates slammed shut on recruitment of judges from bailliages and vicomtés into the ranks of the highest magistracy. The rise of parlementaire fortunes into the stratosphere in this period separated them ever further from the world of the village and bourg judges. Intensifying family recruitment within the Parlement sealed their fates. Parlementaire records confirm that neither rural judges nor their sons had any prospect of continuing directly up the ladder of the magistracy into sovereign courts after the mid-1650s. Their further social ascent required them to make a long detour through the accumulation of land, rentes, and dignities, or through the financial courts. The largest contingent of outsiders came from the sovereign financial courts of the Court of Aids and the Chamber of Accounts in Rouen, which provided nearly a fifth of parlementaires between 1649 and 1715.[66] There were certainly strong intermarriage practices between the families of bailliage courts in the Caux and those of financial courts in Rouen (see below), which indicates that sons of rural judges recognized the parquet of the financial courts as a crucial step on the narrow ladder to the top. But they no longer had hope of moving more directly into judgeships in the Parlement, which their predecessors had still entertained as late as the mid-seventeenth century. Mousnier has also speculated that families of local bailliage officers may frequently have detoured through the Chamber of Accounts, the Court of Aids, or treasury posts before aspiring to the Parlement, and that more families were becoming marooned in middling positions even by the time of Louis XIII.[67]

Nor was there an intake mechanism from the rural bailliages into the présidial of Caudebec, the intermediate appelate court for the Caux. An examination of présidial officeholding offers a simple explanation: the officers of the présidial were recruited almost exclusively from the urban bailliage court of Caudebec in the same town, most of whose members owned their présidial and bailliage offices cumulatively. There was no reason to extend recruitment into the hinterlands; the bailliage produced enough legal men to more than fill its appellate court. (A few Cauchois attorneys did make their way into the tax élection of Caudebec, as will be seen below.) The intake mechanism to the présidial of Caudebec from the countryside may in fact never have existed, given the faltering status of some of these courts almost since their inception.[68] Christophe Blanquie has noted that at least since the time of Richelieu, présidials enjoyed very diverse powers and status in different towns, and particularly suffered from competition with the parlements for cases.[69]

One of the few exceptions to the pattern of parlementaire recruitment in this period proves the rule. Between 1649 and 1715, only two Norman parlementaires of 255 accepted into office came from royal bailliage families.[70] Between 1715 and 1740, only one succeeded from a family of bailliage court judges outside Rouen, Michel Alphonse Subtil de Beauchamel.[71] In its inquiry, the Parlement underlined the oddity of his rise from a bailliage family. In an age when the sovereign court's required examination of the mores, religion, and legal ability of new councillors had become cursory at best or was even waived, Beauchamel's stood out for the intensity of the inquiry. The magistrates interviewed no fewer than forty-nine colleagues and acquaintances, ranging from his law-school professors to merchant drapers and treasurers in the tax bureau.[72]

The inquest also laid bare Beauchamel's instructive career trajectory. His father had been the sieur Subtil, lieutenant leneral of the vicomté of Vire. The son had studied law in Caen, then became a lawyer in the Bureau of Finances and a lawyer at the Parlement. In 1727 he bought an office of treasurer of France in the Bureau of Finance for 16,000 livres. The Parlement was supposed to examine his moral, legal, and Catholic qualifications, but they were more intent on probing his finances and his manners. Nearly every witness was asked to estimate his father's income and the size of his wife's dowry. Beauchamel's wife, a mademoiselle de Fontenelle, had brought 50,000 livres to the marriage, a handsome sum for the son of a rural judge, and his father had mysteriously accumulated the enormous sum of 250,000 livres, the going price for the ennobling post of a king's secretary. As a result of his marriage the son became the seigneur and patron of a parish and acquired the property of Franquetville.

Politesse and noble behavior was also much on the examiners' minds. The merchant draper and mercer testified that Beauchamel had never acted in a way unworthy of an "honnête homme," while a king's councillor in the Bureau of Finance stated approvingly that he had "beaucoup de politesse." An attorney in the Parlement confirmed that the Beauchamels came from the "moient genre de robe," but had nevertheless lived nobly.[73] Beauchamel's brother-in-law was involved in a small scandal in a legal case in the Bureau of Finance, but the Parlement was unable to bring anything definite to light. Evidently Beauchamel was accepted into the elite corps, but their spotlight on his fortune and his behavior speaks volumes about the gulf separating rural bailliage families from direct ascent into the sovereign courts. A scandal in the bureau would have provided a convenient excuse for rejecting him had he not squeaked by his financial inspection. Although Beauchamel's ambitions and fortunes were considered extraordinary for the times, his detour through the Bureau of Finance may not have been. If so, this pattern of shifting from regular lower courts to financial jurisdictions links these two distinct branches of the Norman judiciary much more closely together than their differing functions might lead one to assume.

But how are we to explain the fact that the increasing financial and social disparity between local magistrates and parlementaires in Rouen apparently did not translate into professional hostility toward the Parlement? On the contrary, there was a dramatic reversal in the political alignment of local officers after the Fronde in the mid-seventeenth century, when they shifted their loyalty away from the crown and toward the provincial Parlement. Local Norman bailliage officers had been cool or even hostile toward the higher court during the Fronde, generally siding with the king. By the late seventeenth century that allegiance appears to have reversed itself: the ordinary courts answered to Parlement alone.

The reasons for local officers' reversal of loyalties after the mid-seventeenth century can best be sought locally. Despite placing obstacles in the way of their direct ascent, the Parlement allowed local officers to consolidate their powers in their own bailiwicks. An examination of appellate cases heard in the Norman Parlement shows that the higher court had a surprisingly strong history of upholding the judgments of both royal and seigneurial courts on appeal, thus reinforcing their authority in the countryside.[74] They also protected the lower courts from interference by the intendants and from undue royal pressure, repeatedly delaying or refusing to enforce edicts that would have robbed the main branch of the court system of its autonomy or authority.[75] Sovereign magistrates were also quick to dispute any attempts by the king's financial courts to encroach on the jurisdiction of the ordinary courts. Despite the Parlement's fitful attempts to regulate the fees and professional behavior of lower court judges, and despite the staggering hauteur of its members, the Parlement of Normandy jealously defended the independence of both the province and the judiciary.

The sovereign magistrates were handsomely paid for their patronage during the later eighteenth century, when conflicts between crown and Parliament intensified. During the rebellion over the Brienne edicts in 1788, the royal bailliage court of Cany defied both king and intendant in support of the high court. "We cannot dissimulate," they noted in a speech, "our repugnance at letting ourselves be enriched by the spoils of the high magistrature."[76] The officers made good on their professed revulsion. On June 12, the bailliage of Cany adjourned sine die until the edict was revoked and the Parlement fully reinstated. This pattern was no by means universal in France; in urban bailliages and sénéchaussées, where professional and social hostility toward the Parlements could be intense, the lower courts sometimes sided against the sovereign courts.[77] But the relative isolation of rural bailiwicks endowed them with the kind of independence and autonomy that their wealthier city counterparts often lacked. That confidence in their local powers had been more than a century in the making, and it carried them well into the Revolution.

Parlement and the Ordinary Courts: Appellate Cases and Judicial Oversight

The Parlement of Normandy had two routine tools for supervising the lower courts: its appellate jurisdiction and its right to police and discipline the judiciary itself. We can best gauge the relationship between the sovereign magistrates and the lower-court judges by looking at their treatment of the high justices. These were large jurisdictions in many Norman districts, and they were also the jurisdictions that some sixteenth and seventeenth century legal treatises had insisted were both corrupt and useless, most famously Guy Coquille and Charles Loyseau. If the Parlement had a policy of closely policing the lower courts, it is surely here that it would do so. And yet the records leave a dramatically different impression. Not only did the Parlement treat the high justices as the lowest rung of the royal court system, but it also had a strong record of upholding their judgments on appeal.

The crown had in fact been long at work integrating high justices into the standards and procedures followed by royal justice. The king ensured that new baillis were licensed in law and confirmed by the Parlement; he also actively restricted the creation of new offices in high justices without royal permission.[78] As Pierre L'Hommeau wrote in his *Maximes générales de droit Français* in 1612, "one can therefore class, as we have done, the officers of seigneurs among the servants of the king."[79] But the seigneurial system was also independent of the crown in the same ways that the local royal courts were. Venality or ownership of office, distance from the center, and the force of provincial customary law and local usages gave them wide latitude for independent action.

Other legal commentators of the time recognized this fundamental integration into the body of ordinary royal courts. As Houard argued in his commentary on high justice in the custom, "in a word, there is no difference between the judge of a high justice and a royal judge." The sovereign origin of high justice was why judges of high justice were required to take an oath before the Parlement, and why the procurator general of the Parlement could insist that men of sufficient quality be chosen.[80] By law, high justice partook of delegated sovereignty from the king and was granted by royal will alone. Low and middling justice were considered to be inherent in the fief as a function of land ownership, not of sovereignty. Moreover, the sentences in such courts were always passed in the name of the judge, not in the name of the seigneur. The *seigneur haute justicier* was strictly forbidden to act as a judge in his own court, even in the most inconsequential cases. In legal terms, the office and the fief were entirely distinct, both as property and as privileges. In Houard's expressive phrase, high justice was a "decoration" to the property, not a right inherent in it.[81]

The fundamental breaking point in the court system of Normandy was not between royal and seigneurial justice, but between high justice and the lesser forms of purely landed justice beneath it, middle and low justice. The Parlement of Normandy seemed to recognize this breaking point as well, consistently treating high justices as the lowest rung of the royal judicial system. Parlementary arrêts regulating fees and épices, appellate supervision of cases, and attempts to control judicial practices all extended to the high justices, but these regulations seldom took much notice of middle or low justices in the province. This interest seems to reflect the practical fact that high justices heard cases that extended far beyond the fiscal interests of the seigneurie and involved the broader interests of the king's subjects. Their caseloads involved loans and debts, inheritances and contracts, and the movement of property in the countryside. This was closely related to the daily work that went on in the lower royal courts and required the same kinds of procedures and judgments.

Another long-standing assumption about royal sovereignty over seigneurial justice is called into question by the court records. Both royal apologists and modern historians have often described the transfer of justice from lords' courts to royal courts as a fundamental shift in the French state. In larger terms, this was really the transfer of private jurisdiction to the state, a watershed in the emergence of a more recognizably modern state system. Many commentators have specifically pinpointed the transfer of certain categories of criminal cases to the crown in the Criminal Code of 1670 as a turning point in seigneurial-royal relations. The Criminal Code expanded the category of cas royaux, felonies that attacked the majesty, sovereignty, or person of the king.

But the court records of upper Normandy suggest that any perception of this change as a crisis in seigneurial justice be strongly nuanced. The crown was first of all expressly interested in the transfer to royal courts of *grand criminal* cases, which were relatively rare in the rural jurisdictions where seigneurial justice was most widespread. In the seigneurial courts of the pays de Caux studied here, the Criminal Code of 1670 resulted in no more than one to four cases a year being evoked into the royal courts, and in smaller jurisdictions, no more than one to two cases a decade. In the large ducal high justices of Longueville and Estoutteville, there is no convincing evidence that royal courts ever made a serious attempt to evoke grand criminal cases from them, the more so since these courts acted as bailliage courts and had the right of direct appeal to the Parlement. Nor do cas royaux make up a significant category of crimes in studies of lower courts in Toulouse, the Auvergne, and elsewhere. Although the transfer of grand criminal cases into the royal system is certainly an interesting symbolic expression of state ambition, it is important to recognize that its effect on the real jurisdiction and case loads of seigneurial high justices was quite negligible.

As several historians have recognized, seigneurial courts had an economic interest in shedding criminal cases that were notoriously long, expensive to prosecute, and often featured defendants without enough property to pay their court and legal fees. Studies by Guy Cardineau in Brittany, Pierre Goubert, and others have all emphasized the economic rationality of lords' courts transferring criminal jurisdiction into royal hands.[82] Seigneurial high justices were not withering away by so doing; they were engaging in an economically advantageous agreement with the royal courts. Their principal focus had always been civil cases, and in a sense they agreed to specialize more fully in the regulation of civil society and property in the countryside. The Parlement records contain no protests against the evocation of grand criminal cases from high justices, although some seigneurs may have felt the symbolic sting of losing a privilege. Here again the trend suggests not so much the iron hand of absolutism at work, but a complex and mutually agreeable symbiosis between royal and seigneurial courts.

The most accessible sources on seventeenth- and eighteenth-century lower courts have perhaps led us partly astray in understanding the shift towards royal justice. As Pierre Goubert and Daniel Roche noted, until a decade or two ago legal and political treatises largely formed our ideas about the daily functioning of lower justice during the ancien régime, despite the inherent dangers of relying on these records alone.[83] Seigneurial justice has perhaps suffered most from this tendency. Charles Loyseau, the most prolific writer on high justice in the seventeenth century and one who was widely quoted by legal commentators in the eighteenth century, took a sharply antiseigneurial tone in his *Des abus des justices de village*. Both Loyseau and the commentators who followed after him have often been cited as evidence that seigneurial justice was both profoundly corrupt and a dying, if not actually dead, institution.[84] These perceptions have begun to change under new scholarship on the court system in the past twenty or so years. Recent studies of seigneurial high justice within the context of lordship as a whole have added substantially to the understanding of the daily functions of high justices. Those of Jean Meyer and Jean Gallet in Brittany, and Jeremy Hayhoe in Burgundy, have resculpted much of the earlier scholarship on these institutions as a whole.[85]

The most detailed evidence of the relations between seigneurial high justices and the sovereign courts comes from cases appealed to the Rouen Parlement. If the crown or Parlement had a policy of removing jurisdiction from seigneurial or local courts, we would expect to see significant numbers of cases appealed or evoked into the higher court and a high rate of appellate cases being overturned. The records of the Tournelle, or criminal chamber, provide a useful index of royal or parlementaire intervention, since these were precisely the lower-court cases that the crown had expressed an interest in controlling. The 1670 Criminal Code required that all crimes meriting afflictive punishment, perpetual banishment, civil or actual death, galley service, or other dishonorable amends, be mandatorily appealed to the Parlement. (It should be noted here for clarity that the category of crimes that had to be appealed mandatorily into the Parlement were not simply cas royaux, or crimes that had to be heard in royal courts in the first instance. Cas royaux were only a very small subset of those crimes meriting afflictive punishment and therefore requiring sovereign appellate review.)

The appellate records of the Tournelle tell a rather interesting story about the relationship between the sovereign and seigneurial courts. Of 764 cases heard by the Tournelle in four sample years–1672, 1695, 1709, and 1728–only fifty-three, or just under 7 percent, came from high justices. This ranged from a high of eighteen cases in 1695, after a terrible famine, to a low of ten cases heard in 1672. Of the fifty parties to the seigneurial cases whose occupation or *qualité* is clear, 68 percent were royal officers, sieurs, or nobles. An additional 14 percent were merchants, surgeons, or priests, and the remaining 18 percent were laboureurs or artisans[86] (see table 5.2).

These numbers suggest two things. The Parlement's criminal chamber was not engaging in any widespread surveillance of criminal cases in high justices, despite the consistently strong royal rhetoric about such cases throughout the period. Even at its peak activity, if the approximately two hundred known high justices in the présidial districts of Rouen and Caudebec-en-Caux were the only ones serving in the province, they could expect to have a case before the Tournelle once every twelve years. If the high justices of the other five présidial districts are considered (a number of courts on which there is no clear agreement), one might expect the average number of years between cases to at least double. This unusually low level of high-justice cases appealed to the Tournelle is all the more striking, given that the majority of seigneurial jurisdictions in the généralité of Rouen and all of the largest titled high justices had the right of direct appeal to the Parlement.

Table 5.2. High justice appellate cases, Parlement of Rouen,
Tournelle Chamber

Sample years: 1672, 1695, 1709, 1728

Year	No. of total cases	No. of high justice cases	Percentage of high justice cases	No. of nobles, sieurs, dames, officers	No. of merchants, surgeons, priests	No. of laborers, artisans, weavers
1672	278	10	3%	6	1	0
1695	260	18	6%	14	1	3
1709	112	12	10%	4	1	2
1728	114	13	11%	10	4	4
TOTALS	764	53	–	34	7	9
PERCENTAGE	100%	–	6.9%	64.2%	13.2%	17.0%

Source: ADSM B 3576, 3581, 3583, 3586.

The average number of cases was naturally higher for the largest seigneurial jurisdictions. In the pays de Caux, the high justice of Longueville had three cases before the Parlement in 1695, whereas its subordinate seat at Grainville-la-Teinturière had one. On the other hand, the ducal high justice of Longueville was a larger jurisdiction than the royal bailliage of Cany or the royal bailliage of Caudebec-en-Caux. Yet 93 percent of all cases that arrived in the Tournelle from lower jurisdictions came from other royal courts, not from high justices.

The second feature of interest is the social rank of the appellants. This was not a random cross section of seigneurial court appellants by any means. Most of the parties (64 percent) were among the wealthiest, most highly educated, most privileged members of rural society. In part, this composition of appellants reflected the distance and expense involved in pursuing a case in Rouen. But what this also suggests is that their appeals were voluntary, not forced by the Parlement. The civil nature of some of the cases reinforces the impression that the appellants sought out the Parlement, and not vice versa. They included such clearly civil matters as a contested inheritance, a contested tutorship, a contested seigneurial due, and a debt of 500 livres.[87] Those that were criminal in nature included one verbal insult, one abduction (*rapt*), one *scandale,* one theft of a coffer of linen, one case of bodily harm, and two false judicial seizures of property. Although it is probable that many if not most of the summary cases were crimes, this profile of cases suggests that the Tournelle was acting as a *tournelle civile* as well as *criminelle*. It was neither a chamber of terror nor even entirely a criminal court. Above all, it was not the scourge of local justice in the Norman province.

Perhaps the best index of the relationship between Parlement and local courts is the percentage of appeals that were upheld. One can assume that the majority of summary cases, if not all such cases, were upheld; the court found no need to call further witnesses or hear testimony, nor did it direct that a prisoner be released. Among the cases in which there was some discussion or dispute in the Tournelle, the rate of upheld lower court decisions was still very high. In 1709, for example, the Tournelle heard 112 cases, of which twelve arrived from high justices. In two of the twelve, the case was granted to the appellant by default. A baker in the high justice of Emenville who had been called a "mal honnête homme," for example, was given 12 livres amends when his opponent failed to show up in court. But in none of the twelve cases that year did the sovereign court rule to *casser et annuler,* or overturn, the ruling of a high justice.[88]

In 1695 the Tournelle heard 260 cases, which may have reflected the misery of people driven to desperation during the famine of the previous years. Eighteen of these cases, or 6 percent, came from high justices in Normandy. Two defendants again defaulted, and in one appeal the court ordered a purely administrative action in favor of the appellant. No orders to overturn were recorded.[89] In a few instances the records indicate that the attorneys adjudicated the cases as they were being heard in the Parlement, particularly where numerous parties were involved. Here the sovereign court merely catalyzed the clients and lawyers of lower courts to arrange matters among themselves before the magistrates did it for them.

Increasing the penalties for those convicted in high justices was not uncommon in the sovereign court of Normandy, either. The laboureur François Macy successfully sued Sergeant Jacques Duval for committing bodily harm in the market at Beuzeville in 1695. Sergeant Duval appealed to the Parlement. The Parlement let stand the 10-livre judgment against the violent sergeant, slapped him with another 12 livres amends toward the king, and threw in Macy's court expenses for bringing a meritless case to the Tournelle.[90] In 1672, another sergeant who had been condemned to pay a 50-sol fine to a man in his jurisdiction appealed to the Parlement and found his fine was amended upward to 12 livres.[91] Increasing the severity of lower-court penalties was perhaps the strongest possible endorsement of lordly and local justice that the sovereign magistrates could offer the lower courts.

This support was also a most cautionary warning to malcontents who might be tempted to make frivolous appeals to the royal courts from high justices. Parlements were not in the business of encouraging the popular classes to flout the authority of their seigneurial lords. Nor did they wish to give seigneurial clients a sense that they could exploit conflicts between seigneurial and royal authorities. The rationale was simple: by undercutting the legitimacy of seigneurial justice, parlementaires would have been undercutting their own position in society as seigneurial landlords. They would also have compromised their ability to keep provincial order, perhaps the fundamental definition of their responsibility as royal magistrates.

The types of civil cases that were accepted on appeal into the Parlement from the pays de Caux also reveal something interesting about the reasons for sovereign court intervention in lower-court cases. Three types of civil cases were particularly common: exceptionally complicated property cases, disputes between nobles that could not be settled by a single seigneurial jurisdiction due to the privileges of the combatants, and cases that crossed jurisdictional boundaries. These appellate cases tended to reflect the natural borders of seigneurial jurisdiction, both legal and geographic. They show us the precise points where seigneurial justice was becoming vulnerable to a society where individuals and property were increasingly mobile and ranged beyond the borders of the smallest jurisdictions. Yet at the same time, the nature and number of these cases does not support the notion that the Parlement was attempting to encroach on seigneurial courts' legitimate jurisdiction.

In appellate property cases the parlementaires, it turns out, were often as challenged as the local judges in determining the rights and customs that applied. In 1667, the Parlement heard an appeal from the high justice of Cany-Caniel. The dispute was over who would inherit 725 livres in capital from a marriage contract signed in 1610. The contract had tried to establish community property between husband and wife, although this was against the Custom of Normandy. The Parlement needed a year to sort the case out, and finally condemned the losing party to pay 64 livres to the original high justice of Cany-Caniel for court costs. These cases highlighted not so much incompetence on the part of the high justices as the disorganization or complexity of property law itself.[92]

Geographic and professional mobility also drove some appeals from high justices to the Parlement. A professor at the University of Paris who was also a curé in the Norman village of Portmort failed to pay his debts to one of his relations. The high justice of Portmort sent an usher from the Châtelet in Paris to the professor's collège and seized his mobile property. The Parlement and the Conseil d'État ruled that high justices could not dispatch ushers outside their jurisdiction to seize property, whatever their claims against the individuals.[93] Commoners, like the noble clients of the courts, were sometimes propelled by necessity to seek the larger and more powerful jurisdictions the state could offer.

Nevertheless, the interests of order, property, or justice did lead magistrates to give swift and serious attention to certain types of cases that originated in rural high justices and royal bailliages alike. These cases are a fascinating gauge of where the crown and sovereign magistrates felt most compelled to bring a new sense of state order into the countryside. But here again, the axis of tension was more urban-rural than it was royal-seigneurial. Sorcery, abuses of petty officials in the countryside, and snarled cases of criminal complicity that caught up whole villages in their net, were the main focus of parlementaire interest.

Even here the interdependency of all levels of the court system remains a strong countertheme. The magistrates were not entirely divorced from the raisonnement of the popular classes that led into the morass of these crimes or accusations. Perhaps first President Claude Pellot's bitterest tournament against the Parlement of Normandy occurred after the magistrates upheld a rash of sorcery convictions from the lower courts. The sentences led to the execution or death in jail of several rural shepherds, shepherdesses, and peasants. With direct intervention from Colbert, the first president eventually forced the parlementaires to vacate their own appellate sentences. The documents from these trials leave a tantalizingly ambiguous impression about the nature of elite legal culture. Did the Norman magistrates believe in sorcery, or did they believe in the fabric of local society, which the peasant communities and local justices expected them to uphold?[94]

The best-documented of the sorcery cases to arise from a high justice in this period suggests some unusual answers. The bailli of the barony and high justice of Écouis heard evidence in the summer of 1700 against the Le Levres, father and son, and a third villager, Haubert. The three were accused of using poison and malefice to kill animals and to dry up the milk of cows in the district. The judge, Nicollas le Monnier, sieur de Hamal, was also an attorney practicing in the royal bailliage and présidial of Gisors. He appears to have been quite reluctant to prosecute the case in the high justice. His trial documents pointedly note over and over that he was hearing the trial at the express request of the seigneur, that is, not at the request of the clients of the court, to whom he may have refused to give a hearing before. Curiously, the seigneur was not a rusticated local haute justicier. He was Nicolas de Forment, marquis du Rofay, councillor of the king in his councils, and a *maître des requêtes ordinaire du roy de son hôstel.*

In this case, it would appear that the court of high justice was only reluctantly pursuing a sorcery case at the behest of a royal officer of state and titled noble. Nevertheless, the wheels once set in motion inevitably ground fine: Le Levre père was sent to the galleys in perpetuity, and his son and Haubert were condemned to row for the king's navy for six years. They did not, however, receive capital punishment from the high justice, a penalty Judge Le Monnier was fully authorized to impose. This case strongly suggests that belief in sorcery had faded out among many seigneurial and royal lower-court officers as it had elsewhere by this period, perhaps aided by the connection of the most important of these judges to higher royal jurisdictions. We are left with the odd impression that élite magistrates and nobles in Normandy were doing more to keep sorcery alive than local authorities.[95]

Despite its supervisory role over rural justice, the Parlement of Normandy always stood in solidarity with the lower royal courts and high justices against the encroachments of the crown financial courts. Royal ordinances had long granted jurisdiction over the *voirie* (public roads) to the trésorier-général, not the regular courts, for example. In 1750, the officers of all three bureaus of finance in the province sent a stern protest to the Parlement about the pretensions of high justices in Normandy to jurisdiction over the road networks. The financial corps warned the sovereign court that they had been forced to complain directly to the crown. "The seigneurs haute-justiciers contest with them every exercise of voirie in the extent of their high justices," they argued. The Parlement had sustained these high justices by rendering numerous arrêts in their favor. Far from backing down, in a later case the Parlement condemned the king's prosecutor in the Bureau of Finance to pay all expenses for challenging a lower court's jurisdiction. The next year the magistrates gave high justices and royal bailliages clear authority over all the network of crossing roads, neighboring roads, and trees near the royal roads.[96]

A secondary indication that seigneurial courts were indeed considered a vital part of the royal system, even by the early seventeenth century, are the arrêts on judicial administration issued by the Parlement of Normandy. The fees, épices, *vacations* (travel expenses),[97] and other emoluments of the high justices were regulated on much the same footing as those of the royal vicomtés. In most instances their judges were given the same or just slightly lower status and privileges, with comparable financial emoluments, as the lowest rank of royal judges. In the extensive regulations handed down by the Parlement in June 1671 for judges and officers of the lower seats, they clearly specified that they applied "as much to royal justices as to high justices." When judges were working at home, they were to restrict themselves to an hourly wage and clearly mark down their time in the register: councillors of the Parlement could charge 3 livres, 4 sols in vacations for an hour and a half of work; vicomtal officers 16 sols per hour; and seigneurial officers 12 sols per hour.

Seigneurial judges in the high justices were allowed to take the same emoluments for their signature on definitive acts and decrees as vicomtal judges. Their clerks were allowed the same 15 deniers for each two pages of paper they filled, and their clerks could charge the seigneur's fiscal agent for any seizures or proclamations he brought into the court to be written up, just as a royal judge would. The courts did regulate the low justices in a severe manner, however. They were strictly forbidden to charge more than 5 sols for a signature on any aveux, no matter how large the fief involved, and the clerks received significantly less for an equal amount of work.[98] In a society where such wage scales indicated the degree of honor and status attached to the office, the Parlement's almost obsessive level of detail in regulating these matters actually spoke volumes about its view of the judicial hierarchy.[99]

The sharpest wage and emolument distinctions for all types of officers were naturally those between the sovereign courts in Rouen and the local jurisdictions, which mirrored the abrupt disparity in social status and wealth between the two levels of courts by the mid-seventeenth century. They also tended to single out the lowest of officials—the clerks, ushers, sergeants, and notaries—for the most precise and even demeaning regulation. In order that none might plead ignorance, the Parlement ordered its fee schedule, in table form, nailed to the door of every bailliage and lower jurisdiction. The regulations were seen as necessary to remedy the numerous "inconveniences which are introduced by the passage of time in the administration of justice, to the trampling and oppression of the king's subjects of this jurisdiction."[100] Again, the tension here was not primarily or even noticeably seigneurial-royal. Rather, it followed larger fault lines in provincial society and royal administration: urban-rural and noble-commoner.

Where both Parlement and intendant really wanted to intervene was not in the suppression of lordly justice, but in the professional behavior of its officers. In December 1678 the Parlement published in its secret registers an arrêt on the reception of seigneurial judges. The king's procurator general reminded the assembly that the majority of these local judges were "young men leaving college without experience and without having haunted or frequented the bar," yet they were placed as sole judges over criminal and civil affairs in their jurisdiction. "Such an abuse," he warned, "is greatly injurious to his majesty's subjects." The Parlement voted to accept only baillis who were twenty-five years of age, and who had "pleaded before, haunted, and frequented this bar" or practiced in a royal jurisdiction for two years.[101] The education and age of judges were also persistent concerns of the central government throughout this period, not only because of a growing desire to professionalize state functions but also because these regulations returned some residual authority to the king over the selection of judges.[102]

The documents of the Parlement's examination and reception of judges indicate that this quickly became a waning problem in high justices. In the larger high justices of the pays de Caux, which are the basis of this study, it was the norm rather than the exception for judges to have practiced as attorneys in the Parlement itself. The Parlement's receptions of the bailli of Valmont, Jean Baptiste Alexandre, in 1698; the bailli of Cany-Caniel, Alexander Baudry, in 1704; and the succeeding bailli for the same court, Philippe Louis Bréard, in 1727 indicate that the first two judges had practiced as avocats au Parlement, and the third was an avocat en Parlement. The same was true for the baillis of other large Norman high justices, such as that of the duchy of Elbeuf.[103] Both André Corvisier and Jonathan Dewald have found similar patterns for other Norman high justices.[104]

Of twenty-seven seigneurial baillis accepted into office by the Norman Parlement between 1692 and 1727, only one was given a dispensation from the legal examination he was supposed to undergo because he did not hold the degree of avocat. Of the remaining lawyers, five were avocats au Parlement, two were avocats en Parlement, and one was an avocat au grand conseil for the king.[105] The majority of baillis for high justices also moonlighted as officers or attorneys in local royal courts, or, perhaps more accurately, these royal officers moonlighted as baillis in seigneurial courts. This fact goes far toward explaining the perception by Parlements and intendants that seigneurial courts were the lowest rung of the French court system and not merely an enclave of lordly resistance and privilege opposed to the state.

Présidials and Bailiwick Courts

Rural bailiwick courts were little affected by an awkward level of appellate justice inserted in 1551–52 between their courts and the Parlement, the présidiaux. Typically, a Norman présidial court had three to seven bailliages or vicomtés in its jurisdiction. The présidial's legal jurisdiction, laid out in an edict of 1552, gave these courts the right to hear appeals in cases over property or cash worth up to 10 livres in rent or 250 livres in capital and provisional jurisdiction over cases up to 20 livres in rent or 500 livres capital.[106] These figures were adjusted upward in the seventeenth century. In 1670 the crown made the présidials the final appellate court for maréchaussée crimes, which also included the right to judge the competency of the maréchaussée to hear cases within three days after a crime was committed.

In theory, the présidials were to be a means of relieving the Parlements and bailliages of some of their appellate load. In truth, they were created by Henri II largely as a money-raising expedient. Although the présidials did perform their later function of supervising maréchaussée jurisdictions to a certain extent, many were stymied in their primary function of hearing appellate cases from the regular courts. The stubborn unwillingness of the Norman Parlement and the bailliages to relinquish their jurisdiction over lucrative civil cases left the présidial of Caudebec-en-Caux empty of clients. The présidials of Normandy were evidently not unique in this regard. Almost all appellate cases that came to the présidial of Quimper in Brittany were judged by the sénéchaussée court, not by the présidial.[107] Some French présidials, such as those of Nantes in Brittany and Angers in Anjou, were functional, especially those in cities far outside the orbit of a Parlement, where they could fulfill more of their statutory functions.[108]

As a practical matter the présidials of Caudebec-en-Caux and Rouen thus became fused with lower-ranking bailliage courts beneath them through multiple officeholding, just as the bailliages to a lesser extent had become fused with lower-ranking vicomtés in the same towns. Presumably incumbent bailliage officials bought most of these offices to prevent newcomers from diluting their jurisdiction, and perhaps to some extent for honorary purposes. Although we do not know for certain, this state of affairs had in fact probably existed since the institution of the Norman présidials in the sixteenth century.[109]

Cumulative officeholding within the bailiwick courts could reach ridiculous extremes. An arrêt du conseil from the early eighteenth century confirmed that eleven councillors' offices in both the présidial and bailliage courts of Rouen would remain united to the office of the lieutenant general civil.[110] All twelve offices in both jurisdictions were owned by the sieur de Boisguilbert, Jean Pierre Adrien Augustin le Pesant, who thereby had even more offices than names.[111] In fact, there was only one set of officers for both Rouen courts from the judge down, including the subordinate judges (the lieutenants particular civil and criminal), the councillors, and the king's attorneys. The more rural présidial and bailliage of Caudebec-en-Caux followed precisely the same pattern.[112]

This odd pattern of officeholding immediately becomes understandable when we turn to look at the real jurisdictions of présidial courts in upper Normandy. The surviving records of the présidial of Caudebec-en-Caux indicate that its caseloads in the late seventeenth and early eighteenth centuries were thin at best. In 1698, for example, the court heard just forty-four cases. Only two cases were clearly appeals from the vicomté or bailliage. On the other hand, at least eight cases involved disputes between royal court officers from the présidial, the élection, or other jurisdictions, who seemed to be using the présidial as an internal officers' court to settle their own affairs. The remainder of the cases involved primarily jurisdictional cases of the maréchaussée and disputes between sieurs over sums in the several hundreds of livres.[113] In 1730, after the maréchaussée had been expanded by the crown, the présidial of Caudebec-en-Caux heard sixty-seven cases during the year, at least fifty of them being clearly *cas prévôtaux*.[114] This was a slight improvement over the late seventeenth century, but the court still averaged little more than one case per week. The présidial court of the Caux thus had a precarious status, throughout the ancien régime.

In truth, the présidial jurisdictions had been in distress in Normandy since at least the early decades of the seventeenth century, and perhaps since their inception. In 1633 and again in 1649, the Grand Conseil and Conseil Privé sent arrêts to the Parlement for registration, chastising the Rouen bailliages and high justices for taking cases and appeals away from the présidial (as well as for ignoring repeated edicts and arrêts on this subject). The crown insisted that lower jurisdictions clearly record the value of cash, land, or rights in play in civil cases so that the présidial could take jurisdiction over those due to it. In criminal matters, all appeals were to be sent to the pré-sidial—as long as the penalties did not involve afflictive punishment, civil or actual death, the galleys, perpetual banishment, or honorable amends, which went to the Parlement.[115]

The real state of affairs is instantly transparent here: the Parlement retained its right to hear criminal cases that were of any real interest, and the bailliages and high justices had not the least intention of giving up lucrative civil cases to this interloper. Orders of the privy council notwithstanding, the présidials were unable to make inroads into local justice. Like many other royal jurisdictions, their legal borders were contested or eroded by the advance of the bailliage.

Intendants and Bailiwicks: *"Pain, Paille, Gîte et Gaol"*

The second leg of the governing tripod, the intendancies, consolidated an important administrative role in the province during the collapse of the Estates. The ordinances of the intendants of Rouen between 1642 and 1788 show them to have been consistently involved in impositions of the dix-ième and vingtième (income tax), the levying of soldiers for the militia, and actions against renegade manufacturers.[116] But Normandy, a geographically sprawling province, was split between three intendants by the late seventeenth century: those of Rouen, Caen, and Alençon. Moreover, between 1672 and 1715 the intendancy of Rouen was rotated at a rate that would have made it difficult for the commissaires to develop their own lines of personal authority in the province. Nineteen intendants circulated through the office in forty-three years, serving on average a little more than 2.2 years. It was not until 1715 that the intendants of Rouen began serving long tours of duty; the next two served seventeen and twenty-two years, respectively.[117]

Despite their sweeping mandate, the intendants had only two regular forms of contact with the ordinary courts. They reimbursed the *frais de justice* (judicial expenses) to seigneurial courts that had tried royal criminal cases, such as bread, straw, lodging and jail (*pain, paille, gîte, et gaol*) for prisoners. After 1730 intendants attempted, with a notable lack of cooperation, to collect the *statistique criminelle* in the local courts. The insouciance with which local officers ignored the intendants' requests to send progress updates on criminal prosecutions gives us some index of their immunity from the intendants. Here too the Parlement vocally backed the local jurisdictions. Belbeuf, the king's prosecutor of the Norman Parlement and twice over a *haute justicier* on his own estates, wrote a letter railing against such pettifogging nonsense on the part of the intendants.[118] The local courts, he clearly implied, did not have to answer to the intendant and certainly didn't need to waste their time filling out statistical forms for him.

The intendants' traditionally small staff of *subdélégués,* who were no more than a handful of men in each intendancy, made it even more imperative for the intendant to rely on local notables. Not surprisingly, in Normandy these local arms of the intendant were often lower royal judicial officers.[119] The lieutenant general of the bailliage of Arques, for example, was one of the subdélégués of the intendant of Rouen in the 1690s. He performed occasional commissions for the intendant in the pays de Caux and distributed forms and inquests sent out by the king's commissaire. But most of his professional time was spent sitting on the royal bench at Arques as its presiding judge.[120] The tendency for lower judicial officials to assume administrative roles in the countryside was thus reinforced by the intendants as well as the Parlements.

Hilton Root has argued that intendants played a role in weakening seigneurial justice in the village in Burgundy by interfering in seigneurial court cases on behalf of peasants.[121] But the intendants present a significantly different face in Normandy. Cases of intervention in local justice were exceptional rather than normal, despite the persistent suspicion of the intendants that criminal cases were not being diligently pursued. The principal evidence of the intendants' relationships with the lower courts comes from the frais de justice and statistique criminelle records in Normandy. (The intendant of Rouen did not have a permanent office before the eighteenth century, which means that many records antedating that period have been lost. For the sake of continuity, the records used here extend to the Revolution.) The royal declarations of both 1687 and 1745 mandated that the controllers and receivers of the king's domain immediately reimburse the officers of lower courts for expenses in royal criminal cases, including payments to witnesses, stamped paper, bread and transport for prisoners, captures and travel by court ushers, and the nourishment of abandoned children.[122] This in turn reinforced the crown's desire to fix the rates of payment for both royal and seigneurial court officials, since both could draw on the domain for these sums.

This financial necessity tended to draw the high justices even closer into the royal orbit. In exchange for the crown's reimbursement when they apprehended or jailed individuals suspected of committing crimes in royal jurisdictions or suspected of committing cas royaux in their own jurisdictions, the high justices were regulated into the existing court system. As Louis XVI explained, this mutual arrangement was strongly in the interests of public order and justice. "It will be acknowledged that if, for the good of Justice and . . . the maintenance of order and public tranquillity, it is indispensable to assure limitless funds to underwrite the payment of expenses. . . . [I]t is not less just to take wise precautions which . . . can also foresee and prevent the dissipation of these funds."[123]

Otherwise, the king noted, crimes simply went unpunished "for lack of funds" to put the accused on trial when there was no civil party to pay the fees. The crown charged the intendants with verifying expenses and weeding out claims that were illegitimate. The intendant had to recover these illicit expenses from the high justices, royal bailliages, defendants, civil parties, or royal *engagistes* who should have been responsible for them. In return, high justices, royal judges, sworn surgeons of the courts, and even prison concierges petitioned the intendant to reimburse them for specific expenses. As an *arrêt du conseil d'état* noted in 1774, the sums that were advanced by the king's domain to cover judicial expenses in lower jurisdictions were "très onéreux."[124] We have little idea how much it actually cost the French state to pay the frais de justice, a subject currently being researched by Albert N. Hamscher, but the sum must have been substantial.

Ordinary courts had rather frequent correspondence with the intendant about these financial matters. In the two-year period 1762–64, thirty-seven high justices or engagistes corresponded with Intendant La Michodière to recover their expenses.[125] One of the later requests from a high justice was for payment of a bill for 63 livres, 13 sols for removing a cadaver from the parish of Roquefort in the Caux. The parish was partly dependant on three separate high justices and on the royal court at Caudebec-en-Caux. The trick was in convincing the intendant that the body was recovered on a street in someone else's jurisdiction, preferably the king's.[126] Although we do not know exactly how many of these claims were eventually reimbursed, they suggest that the high justices, with the powerful sponsorship of noble engagistes, were not shy about negotiating with royal intendants or demanding royal funds. This does not seem a likely profile for a court system under attack by the intendants.

The picture that emerges out of the intendant's financial records reinforces the impression that finance, not judicial sovereignty, was the real bone of contention between crown commissioned officers and local courts. The king's intendants were encouraging the seigneurial courts to take local responsibility for crimes committed in their jurisdictions, and the high justices were busy trying to fob off expenses and responsibility onto the crown. These were legitimate fiscal issues, particularly for small high justices. Several of them pled insolvency to the intendant, stating that they simply could not reimburse the expenses on the royal rolls, such as the 31 livres the domain tried to collect from the small high justice of Neufeuillete for a prisoner's bread and straw.[127] Although the intendants attempted to tighten up collection, we can assume that in the end the crown simply absorbed many small sums from high justices.

Without the royal courts' and the king's deep pockets as backstops, some of the functions of seigneurial justices would have been impossible or at least unprofitable. This much has been noted before. But the crown had a compelling reason to choose to fund them. Without seigneurial cooperation, the exercise of royal justice would have been impeded. The only solution that would keep public order and justice functioning, as the king astutely recognized, was for the crown to embrace every level of the court system in the countryside, whether royal or seigneurial. The only way to exercise financial control in such a vast undertaking was to standardize court operations and fees, including those of the high justices, within a single system. What appear to be tensions in the intendants' records over who would pay for local criminal justice are perhaps more accurately recognized as symptoms of symbiosis and of a reordering of responsibilities between the royal and seigneurial courts.

Aside from finances, the second principal responsibility of the intendant for local justice during the eighteenth century was collecting the *statistique criminelle*. This attempt to monitor the diligence of lower courts in pursuing criminals was also an outgrowth of seventeenth-century initiatives, above all the Criminal Code of 1670. This led to the development of one of the first truly bureaucratic survey forms, outside of the tax system, in common use in Normandy, a printed sheet sent to each bailliage with exact spaces for each piece of information to be filled in.

In 1733, the chancellor outlined a plan for collection of criminal statistics to be carried out jointly by the Parlement and the intendant, the better to supervise the judicial system. He sent a letter to Intendant de la Bourdonnaye complaining that "the pursuit of crimes is more neglected than ever, in the majority of the kingdom's provinces," and that the lower courts had demonstrated "such negligence on this point, whether in the seigneurial justices or even in the royal seats, that a great number of crimes and even very graves crimes remain unpursued." From this point forward, the chancellor demanded that the king's procurator general in the Parlement send him an exact memoir of all crimes judged worthy of death or afflictive punishment in the province. In fact, the intendant's office ended up with responsibility for the task.[128] Collection of the criminal statistics, according to the chancellor, was required for both "la justice & pour l'ordre public," which had been damaged by the lack of zeal in the lower courts.

The lower courts remained quite resistant to the intendants' demands for the *statistique criminelle* throughout the eighteenth century. In 1735, 1739, and 1741, Chancellor d'Aguesseau wrote from Versailles to Intendant de la Bourdonnaye, chastising him for the incomplete records he collected. Numerous accusations pursued by the courts of Caudebec-en-Caux and Pont-Audemer were missing, and most other entries were undated, so it was impossible to know if the pursuit of crimes has been neglected. "I pray you, therefore, to recommend to your subdélégués to take care to be better informed," the chancellor admonished him.[129] In 1739, the royal bailliages of Dieppe, Le Havre, Eu, and Andelay simply refused to give *états*, or official statistics, to the subdélégués. D'Aguesseau again jumped in to investigate, and the courts disingenuously replied that they had never been enlightened on the subject, or they would have filled the forms out willingly.[130] As late as 1784 the clerk of Pont-Audemer refused to give information for the état.[131] Delay and obfuscation were powerful local tools against state meddling, and the ordinary courts were masters of the game.

Local Court Relations: Seigneurial and Royal Jurisdictions

Despite the growing integration of royal and seigneurial justice on most levels, they naturally suffered the same conflicts of jurisdiction that the royal courts had with each other. Higher-ranking officers in vicomtés and bailliages sometimes resented competition with seigneurial courts for civil cases and felt burdened with royal responsibility for the criminal cases, which seldom paid much. The lieutenant of the bailliage of Le Havre wrote the intendant, asking him to suppress the high justice of Graville altogether. He first made a high-flown appeal against the abuses of seigneurial justice, which he acknowledged was drawn straight from the same treatises from which historians have drawn much of their understanding of seigneurial justice:

> The most enlightened jurisconsults have all . . . raised their voices against the high justices, against the abuses of all types which they produce. All these abuses have been so well demonstrated, the necessity of suppressing this first degree of jurisdiction so well established . . . that there is no magistrate who doesn't desire this beneficial resolution.

But the lieutenant quickly got to the real heart of the matter. The high justice of Graville extended right up to the walls of Le Havre, which were about to be expanded into the *banlieu*. The judges of this court, he complained, were already "disposed to send all criminal matters to the royal judge in order to keep only the useful affairs, those that produce some emoluments." This competition was cutting off the lifeblood of the royal court, money and offices. Two offices of councillor assessor in the bailliage were already standing vacant in the royal court, he charged. "Why? Because the bailliage is extremely enclosed."

The provincial records seem to indicate that what hostility existed toward seigneurial justice came from local competitors, the royal bailliages, rather than from the upper reaches of the French state. This competition was of course considerably muddied by the fact that many local officers owned charges in both courts. Moreover, this hostility appears to have been grounded in economics and professional survival, not in a philosophy of state advancement, as the lieutenant of Le Havre tells us. But he knew very well how to frame this complaint in a way that the crown would respond to.

The town of Le Havre was becoming more immense, he noted, and it was essential for the

> police of good order that the bailliage be composed of numerous magistrates who can quickly expedite all criminal and police affairs, [which] have been greatly multiplied by vagabonds and the poor who abound everywhere, attracted by the work of the new town.

The themes of growing cities, expanding dangerous classes, and the need for unified police and jurisdiction to keep "bon ordre" were music to an intendant's ears. Unfortunately the lieutenant had just bumped up against that other powerful force, the personal property of a lord. The high justice of Graville stayed right where it was.[132]

Seen from this local perspective, the advance of royal justice in rural Normandy appears to have been more an organic process than it was a studied seizure of power by the crown. The steady march forward of bailiwick courts followed the principle of economies of scale. Small jurisdictions, whether royal or seigneurial, faded; large jurisdictions, whether royal or seigneurial, were drawn into a more unified system. Moreover, this process was largely driven by local officers and by changing local power structures, not by the direct intervention of the crown. Historically, the French crown had relied in part on the nobility to perform many local functions for the state; now it found the ordinary courts were its indispensable allies in the countryside. To what are we to attribute this local devolution of power on the bailiwick officers, if not to the will of an absolutist state? If the crown was not the sole actor, then we must turn to look at the changing needs of both local officers and ordinary people, who shaped and used the local Norman jurisdictions to solve their most pressing daily problems, those of property and family.

Chapter 6

VILLAGERS AND TOWNSPEOPLE

CIVIL LITIGANTS

The other day I went to the place where justice is rendered. . . . I entered the sacred spot where all the secrets of families are revealed, and all the most hidden actions are brought to the light of day. . . . One hears only of irritated fathers, abused daughters, unfaithful lovers and chagrined husbands.

Montesquieu, *Lettres persanes*

A week before the Christmas feast of 1728, Judge Jean Rousselet, in his black robes, took the bench at the Croix Rouge tavern, opening the year's last royal assizes in the town. The tavern was a warmly familiar setting for the villagers and townspeople assembled at the audience.[1] Rousselet's court had circulated from inn to inn in Grainville-la-Teinturière for more than two decades, after his chambers were flooded by the Durdent River in the winter of 1703. Royal edicts and arrêts repeatedly forbade holding court in taverns, but finding the village publican a more congenial landlord than the king, some Norman judges cheerfully violated the rule. Under the sign of the Three Merchants, the Red Cross, or the Image of Saint Francis in Grainville-la-Teinturière, the tavern was a natural crossroads where state and local justice merged.[2]

Rousselet's assizes remind us that justice was a far more fluid and community-based practice in the early modern world than in our own. Local judges relied less on written law and considerably more on equity, case precedent, and community traditions than do modern courts. The inhabitants of the bailiwick continued to practice ancient forms of community regulation within and around the courts, above all arbitration, witnessing, composition, and raising the hue and cry (*clameur de haro*). Moreover, the normal social mechanisms of early modern society, including kinship, rank, reputation, and gossip, operated just as well at the assizes as they did in the church or the tavern. Villagers and townspeople thus exercised significant control over

159

who could be prosecuted and for what offenses through a formidable array of legal and social tools.

In English counties these social mechanisms were formalized through petty jurors and grand jurors, who "wielded considerable discretionary power" over prosecutions.[3] In French local courts, public influence was not institutionalized in the jury, but it was powerful nonetheless. In the bailiwicks of the Caux, justice had long been a flexible marriage of royal and community practices, both less standardized and less dependent on written texts than its modern counterpart.[4] Officers contributed to this bricolage of justice with three key legal tools of their own: discretionary sentencing, equity, and restitution. Virtually no sentencing guidelines were available to early modern judges (save in cas royaux), leaving ample scope for local influence in the sentencing and punishment phases of criminal trials. The ancient legal practice of equity, which required judges to fill the gaps in written laws and customs with fairness and educated reason, remained a guiding principle in civil settlements. Tribal and medieval traditions favoring monetary restitution or composition by the guilty party (as opposed to the royal preference for corporal punishment) were still much in favor at the bar. Taken together, these community-based practices became law in a powerful secondary sense. They were gradually enshrined in case precedents that were useful for judges and litigants in settling new cases that appeared before the assizes.

The deepest community influence on the courts came quite simply from the decisions of the litigants themselves. The men and women who brought their daily problems to the assize doors defined the kinds of issues that judges and attorneys would spend most of their time litigating. What they wanted resolved at the bench was not the king's business but their own: just over 86 percent of cases were civil matters, most about property or family law. Moreover, this was a true court of common pleas, in which 94 percent of litigants were commoners.[5] Vivid and interesting as studies of criminal cases have been, we need to connect them to the courts' larger and more common civil roles. As Steven G. Reinhardt has commented, what is needed is "a formidable task: to consider the relationship of royal justice to society as a whole."[6]

By viewing courts in the round, we can begin to understand these broader political and social functions.[7] In the late-seventeenth-century bailiwicks of the Caux, litigants used ordinary courts far more frequently to regulate status and power within the community than to regulate relations between the community and outside elites. Commoners' impassioned disputes about ownership, usage, and income rights over the district's arable land and mobile wealth lay at the bottom of myriad suits. The community also kept order and calibrated power through inventive moral and social litigation. Church benches, burial plots, parish funds, tavern hours, grain prices, blasphemy, and slander were vigorously litigated at the king's bench or those of the seigneurs.

The crown was only a distant party to most of these cases. Few civil suits in the district required the king's law; indeed, royal edicts or statutes governed scarcely more than 2 percent of civil cases. Provincial and local customs, equity, or privileges that often predated the annexation of Normandy to the French crown regulated nearly all cases. Prosecution of villagers by their seigneur in his or her court was also comparatively rare in the Caux by the late seventeenth century. With the exception of rent collection (an important category addressed later), only the occasional rabbit poaching or refusal to use the lord's grain mill rises above the common pleas. Indeed, so much noble property in the Caux had been leased and subleased to sieurs and laboureurs that they were principally suing each other over rents and other property issues. As one historian of England has noted of the same period, seigneurial courts had long become a place where "order is maintained collectively by the tenants" rather than by the active involvement of the lord or his steward.[8] Yet the court system was eminently useful to both king and local lords, if not quite in the way we had once assumed. The courts were a key mechanism of self-regulation, bringing nearly a quarter of a million inhabitants into a judicial system with some real authority to regulate property and order.

"All the Secrets of Families": Civil Cases of the Common Courts

Judge Rousselet opened his assizes in the Croix Rouge on December 16, 1728 with an altogether typical docket. Seven cases were brought to his makeshift bench, requiring two or three attorneys, a dozen or so parties, and an audience of villagers milling around to stay warm. In his black judicial robes, the judge called the widow Marguerite David forward to confront her neighbor, the laboureur Jean Desportes. The wealthy peasant had sued the widow David after she had driven his animals off her pasture in the neighboring hamlet of Canouville. Rousselet summarily found in her favor despite the fact that she was female, poor, and widowed. He fined Desportes 30 sols damages to underscore the sentence.

The day of her favorable audience saw a parade of such small but vitally important matters pled before the tavern bench. A male plaintiff brought the abbess of Montvillier into court, opposing her seizure of his property. The sieur François de Thunes presented his royal letters from Fontainebleau, installing him as the new king's prosecutor for the court. Marie Orenge, a widow, was sued by a relative of her late husband, possibly over the terms of her dower. The sieur Oursel asked for a default judgment of 101 livres against the sieur Monflard. Two men were thrown out of court for bringing a frivolous suit and then fined the expenses.[9] None of the cases copied out by the royal clerk on that winter afternoon in the Croix Rouge had the excitement and drama of crime, and only the reception of the crown prosecutor had the obvious interest of the king apparent in it. And yet in the quiet and even somnambulant humming of a village court, we can hear the overtones of something much more interesting: the meaning of justice, even the ordinary meaning of the state, to the subjects who made up the vast majority of the French population.

Marguerite David's audience, unspectacular as it was, presents to us the everyday face of the king's justice. The regulation of family, property, and status in the community was the chief function of the common courts. In sample periods taken from seven royal and seigneurial courts in the Caux district between 1670 and 1745, some 3,098 litigants participated in 1,360 cases (see table 6.1.) Of these cases, only 183, or 13.4 percent, were criminal affairs, ranging from theft to priestly concupiscence. Among the civil cases that made up most of the quotidian business of these rural chambers, perhaps 10 to 25 percent were clearly identified by cause, depending on the court and the abilities of the clerk. The majority of the cases were summary, resolved without so much as a comment. But there is no evidence that they would have fallen far outside of the usual round of customary cases whose identity was recorded. Then as now, civil litigation tended to follow distinctive crests and whorls, creating a visible pattern in the records over time. Individual cases thus have a great deal to communicate about the lively and typical interests in family, property, village, and state that frequently collided in the ordinary court chambers.

Four principal types of cases kept the judges and attorneys in fees. First among them were property issues. These were dominated by debts, possessory actions, inheritances, income rights from land (héritages), boundary disputes, contracts, rents, sales, and mortgages. Next in frequency were family issues, most of which closely intersected with property issues: contested inheritances again, curatorships (curatelles), tutorships (tutelles), widows' dowers (douaires), marriage dowries (dots), declarations of legal majority, and property separations for married couples. Virtually all of these property and family cases were regulated by customary law. Two new widows who came before the petty assizes in Cany-Caniel, for example, were the highly literate Catherine Jennette and the illiterate Marie Doray. Both women asked that the court liquidate their dowries "according to the Custom." This was a standard tag line in asking the court to regulate property and family cases of all types.[10]

A distant third down the list in importance were cases derived from seigneurial privileges. These privileges formed what could be considered microcustoms, laws unique to each estate or seigneury. Poaching, wood theft, refusal to use the lord's mills or ovens that were the seigneurs' monopoly disputes over entry fees (relief) due on succession to a tenant's property, and the occasional police matter such as a chimney about to fall through a village house made up the bulk of these cases. The apparent absence of feudal

Table 6.1. Civil and criminal litigation with *qualité* of litigants, 1670–1745, lower courts of the pays de Caux

Court	Civil	Percent	Criminal	Percent	Total cases	Total litigants	No. of nobles	Percent of nobles	No. of sieurs	Percent of sieurs	No. of other commoners	Percent of other commoners
Bailliage de Cany	208	84.0	40	16	248	546	31	5.6	99	18.1	416	76.1
Bailliage de Grainville-la-Teinturière	59	75.4	19	24.3	78	162	8	4.9	20	12.3	134	82.7
Haute justice, Cany-Caniel	716	87.0	107	13.0	823	1892	111	5.8	233	12.3	1548	81.8
Haute justice, Grainville-la-Teinturière	30	94.2	2	6.2	32	76	5	6.5	11	14.4	60	78.9
Haute justice, Longueville	86	89.7	10	10.4	96	240	8	3.3	60	25.0	172	71.6
Haute justice, Vittefleur	46	95.0	2	4.1	48	100	3	3.0	16	16	81	81.0
Haute justice, Valmont	33	93.6	3	8.5	35	82	5	6.0	11	13.4	66	80.4
TOTALS	1178	86.6	183	13.4	1360	3098	171	5.5	450	14.5	2477	80

Percentage noble litigants: 5.5%
Percentage commoner litigants: 94.5%

dues on land held by commoners (*cens* and *champarts*), and the relatively light work obligations (*corvées*) that were part of the lord's prerogatives obviated many of the traditional seigneurial disputes.[11] Ground rent was naturally a common matter of court adjudication, but rents had been largely drained of feudal or even seigneurial content in the Caux and can be considered more tenurial in nature. They were almost always paid in money by the later seventeenth century and were a relatively modern property arrangement.[12]

Fourth, local courts regulated moral and communal life, increasingly displacing the church as the favored venue for morals cases. The crown had gradually stripped the officialités, or ecclesiastical courts, of jurisdiction. The Ordinance of 1539 allowed church courts to judge laypersons only in spiritual matters, and by the Edict of February 1678 clerics accused of crimes had to be judged by royal magistrates. Intensifying litigation over management of the parish church vestry (fabrique) and its accounts became a legal epidemic during the early decades of the eighteenth century. Who was leasing church lands in the parishes and for how much and where the money went to were sources of escalating quarrels.[13] Parishioners engaged in lively contests over pews and burial plots in the parish church, condemned priestly misbehavior and turned in parishioners who came to mass drunk. Yet only a handful of cases appear in which issues of the legal village community (communauté) proper are raised, including use of the common lands or repartition of the tax burden, cases which we see with some frequency in the courts of Burgundy.[14] The weakness of the Cauchois communauté, whose affairs were largely controlled by a small group of wealthy peasants and landlords, is reflected in the silence of court records.

The domination of the courts by commoner litigants is also striking. Of the 3,098 litigants, only 5.5 percent were noble. The percentage of noble litigants remained fairly small, at between 3 and 6.5 percent, for both royal and seigneurial courts. Nobles' use of the courts was therefore several times higher than their percentage of the population, but they by no means dominated the use of the courts. Of these nobles, very few were titled; most were resident lords of the lesser variety. Of the remaining 94.5 percent of commoners, 14.5 percent of these were sieurs or dames. This ranged from a probably anomalous high of 25 percent sieurs or dames in one very small seigneurial court sample to a low of 12.3 percent in both the royal bailliage of Grainville-la-Teinturière and the high justice of Cany-Caniel. (See table 6.1).

The remaining 80 percent of litigants were therefore mostly commoners without sieuries. Clerks only occasionally threw light on litigants' occupations in the assize registers, although the much smaller universe of cases that went to a full trial almost always recorded litigants' and witnesses' occupations. Royal and seigneurial officers, parish priests, and occasionally laboureurs received the honor of having their occupations recorded. It is exceptionally rare to see the designation of merchant, master, or artisan in the records, even in cases that clearly involved mercantile contracts, debts, or activities in the market. The Cauchois records thus draw an opaque curtain across the exact economic and social identity of most of their litigants, except to reveal that they were members of the third estate and had property or family interests to protect in court.

What we might call the "middling sorts" in the villages and towns were thus the heaviest users of the courts. Typical visitors to the assizes were the laboureur and his brother who in 1681 passed a contract before the high justice of Longueville on a 200-livre mortgage, for a fee of 14 livres, 5 sols, 8 deniers.[15] Cases involving cash or property in the 10- to 200-livre range were common, but far smaller amounts were adjudicated as well. The social hierarchy of the district was strongly reflected in court use. Sieurs, laboureurs, officers, and priests (who were often sieurs themselves in the Caux) wore a path to the assize doors. But the number of the poor who also came into the courts to assert their rights should temper our perceptions of these institutions. Cottagers, day laborers, and widows brought suits, too: over debts, work implements, stolen chickens, or even a widow's contractual right to sit by the fire in her son's house. A day laborer, for example, appeared before the winter petty assizes in Cany-Caniel to protest that he had not been paid his wages or the five measures of wheat promised to him during the harvest. The judge condemned his employer to pay back wages.[16] The Caux was not unusual in this strong emphasis on commoner litigants and civil law. Similar profiles of court use appear in the case records of royal and seigneurial courts under the parlements of Paris, Burgundy, and Brittany.[17]

We can also see some surprising features of local justice rising above the horizon of the everyday in Judge Rousselet's audience. His docket shows the frequency of female litigants before the local bench. Women were involved in three of his seven cases. In fact, throughout the Caux, women were parties to 23.6 percent of cases and were the plaintiffs or pursuing parties in half of these. The frequency of female court use closely corresponds to women's rate of land ownership in the Caux. Just over 23 percent of land parcels in the jurisdiction of the high justice of Cany-Caniel were held by or through women.[18] As Amy Louise Erickson has pointed out for England, the "ideal" cycle of property transmission from adult male to adult male was rarely completed, and a "considerable minority of litigants" in English common-law, equity, and borough courts were also female.[19] In a court system dominated by property issues, the system would virtually have ceased to function if women were not admitted to court to adjudicate property disputes.

Women also had vital roles to play in court as curators and tutors for their children; as creditors, inheritors, business owners, landlords, and owners of the financial value of public offices; and even as seigneurs haute justicières. More than 97 percent of cases in the Caux involving women were civil cases, and women used the courts in much the same way as men did: to stabilize families, control property, and protect their honor. There was a strong presumption toward choosing widowed mothers as both the tutors and curators of their children, giving them both financial and physical responsibility for their children. This granted women interim control of the family's estate and gave them the legal status necessary to appear in court on their own behalf.[20] As Barbara B. Diefendorf has pointed out for Paris, the presumption of the law was often not so much toward men as towards heads of households.[21]

The clerk's account also allows us to glimpse the small triumphs of the legally disadvantaged at Rousselet's assizes in the Croix Rouge. When the widow David defeated the trespassing male laboureur, or when the tenant triumphed over his landlord, the noble abbess, we see the usual presumptions of early modern privileges tempered in practice. The law sanctioned and upheld France's many hierarchies of privilege, including gender and estate, but it also gave those privileges certain legal boundaries. Nor was illiteracy an absolute barrier to success in court; indeed, customary law was a spur to both literacy and numeracy in the countryside. These small victories and flexibilities allow us to see a face of royal justice seldom turned toward us in political tracts or administrative documents. It is a human face, a more ordinary face; it is the face of the village and town, and not of a king, that looks back out at us from the court chronicles. Yet precisely because the village was reflected in the state in such a human and mundane way, the state came to be rooted more firmly in the village.

"Good Sense and Good Order": Property and Family Litigation

The interest of villagers and townspeople in regulating family property through the courts was strongly shared by the kings of France.[22] Not only was the family still the single most important mechanism for transferring wealth and land among French subjects, but it was also a fundamental unit for state taxation and borrowing. As David Sabean has suggested, the state's intensifying interest in matters of marriage and family formation went hand in hand with the crown's decision to codify French customary laws in the sixteenth century. Both developments, he argued, "attest to the intense concern of the state with the family holding of property."[23] Given the collective nature of property ownership during the ancien régime, precise laws channeling property from one legitimate family member or generation to the next in a strict hierarchy were essential.

Family uses of the courts in upper Normandy usually clustered around the dramatic moments of transition in the lives of villagers: births, marriages, separations, and deaths. Each event rewove the dense net of kinship in the community, and each implied the transfer of property and wealth in the community. Indeed, law was intimately connected with the life cycle of every villager before the light of his or her first day. Inheritance rights were determined at the moment of conception by the individual's birth order and sex. Not far into childhood, many Cauchois children would find themselves placed under legal tutorship and curatorship on the death of a parent.

The four orphaned Desmarests children were already veterans of the wardship court at Cany-Caniel before the eldest had reached fifteen. They were first placed under their mother's wardship on their father's death, then moved to their uncle Nicolas Desmarests' wardship on their mother's death. After Nicolas Demarests died, they were making their third appearance in chambers to be transferred to the care of another uncle, Jean Boutard.[24] By custom, the surviving mother or guardian would convene with twelve male relatives or friends in the judge's chambers to select those responsible for the children's education and financial management. The tutor or curator could then expect to be called back into court later to show the accounts, and the children would often reappear before the magistrate on attaining their majority.

With marriage, a new set of customary laws came into play. The marital régimes controlling dowries, marital property, widows' portions, and separations were all governed by custom.[25] Indeed, the frequency of second and third marriages during the ancien régime made these services essential for untangling family finances. Typical was the case of Marie Barbe Dubosc, widow of the tavernkeeper Jean Hauthorne. When he died, he left four children from his first marriage and a three-year-old son from his marriage to Dubosc. At the wardship hearing, two separate sets of maternal relatives had to appear, thus filling the small courtroom in Cany with interested parties from three lineages. Two weeks later, Marie Barbe Dubosc returned to the Cany-Caniel assizes to renounce her right of succession to her husband's property and to have her dowry and her own acquisitions during the marriage liquidated according to the Customs.[26] The assizes also handled marital separations (séparations de biens), primarily of couples in the laboureur and sieur classes in the Caux. Most separations were not prompted by violence (although this was allowed under extreme circumstances). Rather, they were initiated to save the family fund from bankruptcy when creditors pursuing the husband attempted to attach property belonging to the wife's dowry or inheritance.[27]

Death closed the circle, and here too the customs placed severe restrictions on the individual's disposition of property by wills or testaments. Even as a man or woman drew his or her last breath, the customs held the property in its iron grip and transferred it to begin the cycle anew. Here was the heart of the ancient legal maxim "The dead seize the living."[28] The eighteenth-century legist Basnage decried the Norman customs for defying "the wisdom and good conduct of man," and placing all individuals, as if they were children, under "a general and perpetual curatorship."[29]

Few were so poor and so bereft of relations as to escape the customary laws entirely. Many contested their custom-ordained lot in life, protesting the management of their life's resources by parents, curators, elder brothers, and husbands. One of the greatest family tensions created by customary laws began at birth: that between a brother and his siblings, generated by the unequal Cauchois inheritance customs of both noble and commoner preciput.[30] The death of a father must often have been the beginning of sibling strife, as two or more children of the same parents were placed on dramatically different life courses.

In the parish of Rocqueville, the merchant-butcher Jacques Hannier found himself embroiled in a sadly typical family lawsuit. He had been made his brother's curator and tutor in 1723, on their widowed mother's death. At twenty-two, his younger brother filed a case against him in the nearby royal bailliage court at Longueville, demanding to see the accounts of his portion of the inheritance. Under court order, the butcher produced the accounts. He stated that he did so not only because of the court's demand, but because "good sense and good order demand that a curator give a just account of his administration . . . in the most succinct and irreproachable manner."[31] Hannier's accounts showed that on taking the succession from his widowed mother, he had paid 56 livres in debts, leaving more than 2,500 livres in real property and a large quantity of wool. He claimed to have spent 725 livres on the upkeep of his younger brother—that is, almost the younger's full one-third share of the succession—and to have given him large quantities of valuable wool besides. The cadet argued that those expenses should be wiped out because he had worked his brother's land and flailed his grain. Jacques Hannier retorted that his brother had only been nine years of age on the death of their mother and moreover had always been too sickly to perform much work on the farm.

The complexity of the family's economic activities and legal status in this small village is illuminating. They were simultaneously merchant-butchers, peasant grain farmers, and involved in the wool trade or in textile production in some manner. Their family capital was tied up in two successive curatorships—their mother Marguerite's and Jacques Hannier's. They were also bound by their father's last testament, customary provisions regarding male preciput and female inheritance, and merchant contracts that were due on the death of their mother. Neither Jacques Hannier nor his discontented younger brother could entirely disentangle themselves from the customary laws and contracts that bound them, to one's benefit and the other's dismay.

The provisions on women in customary law also generated an enormous volume of family and property litigation in the ordinary courts. Jacques Hannier's sisters were a source of contention in his family lawsuit, and they had plenty of company in courtrooms everywhere. Hannier's parents had made some provision for their two daughters under the customary portion of mobile property (as opposed to real property, usually land) that they could voluntarily designate to daughters. The cadet brother wanted a portion of that back as well. He protested that before her death, his mother, Marguerite, had liquidated some real property with the consent of their relatives to provide the daughters with a cash portion of their father's succession.[32]

As the Hannier case reveals, Normans were highly creative in skirting the exacting provisions of the law in order to provide women with property. Liquidating real estate to provide cash was one of the most common strategies. Among the officer classes, by the later seventeenth century, case precedent was used to allow women to take royal offices as a portion of their inheritance. This effectively transformed offices from real property into mobile property and gave women certain powers over the disposition of public offices. These small but important loopholes were expanded into real breaches of customary law, giving villagers and townspeople more control over the disposition of their property. They also invited litigation by disgruntled family members who wanted a stricter interpretation of the Custom.[33]

Recent research has also emphasized the ability of women in early modern England to understand and exploit property law, aided by the passage of quiet legal changes in marriage settlements and trusts. Moreover, "judges had very considerable room for maneuver" in women's property cases, given that both English and French judges were mindful of the need to keep women and children from becoming a charge on the parish. These flexibilities coexisted in England, however, with attention-getting measures that stiffened the courts' presumption of maternal guilt in infanticide, eliminated divorce for women (men could obtain divorce by private Parliamentary bill), and aided in witchcraft prosecutions.[34] In French royal law, as Sarah Hanley has pointed out, a complex of measures were passed during the early modern period requiring women to declare pregnancies in court (déclarations de la grossesse), increasing punishments for clandestine pregnancies and marriages, and reinforcing male authority in the family. This was one of those crucial points where the public and private realms collided "during a time of interrelated family formation and state building."[35] How those laws were negotiated (and sometimes evaded) at the local level is a complex story. In bailiwick courts, the simple fact that women were also part of families and lineages, with male relatives who were allied with them in many cases, mitigated some of the impact of the law.

Landlord-tenant cases form another prominent crest in the legal landscape of upper Normandy. These bring us out into the larger world of village and town relationships, a vast net that tied renters, cottagers, laboureurs, sieurs, seigneurs, and court officers into an economic pattern as complex as the pattern of fields and forests they shared. Law courts were one of the natural nexuses of local property exploiters, the more so since they were usually presided over by judges and attorneys who were significant property owners in the district. Here nearly every important contract, mortgage, sale, exchange, or inheritance of property passed through the hands of a notary or lawyer to be recorded and thus publicized. The court served multiple other property functions in local society: acting as a newspaper of record, a land office, and the permanent guardian of family and village property.

The long line of men and women parading through the assizes for arrears in rent are a somber background to the seventeenth-century as a whole. The cases are simple, usually summary: widows or widowers without sufficient resources, struggling cottagers with fewer than 2 hectares under cultivation, a few who were drinking away their rents in the taverns, or the thousands of victims of terrible harvests and killing winters. Like the villager in Reauville who lost his cottage, barn, fruit orchard, and garden close to the sieur de Houdetot in 1694, many were only one or two failed harvests away from disaster.[36] Landlord-tenant relations, which naturally form such an enormous part of the quotidian work of a rural judge and his court, remind us over and again of the precariousness of both life and money for early modern villagers. The power of landownership was indeed enormous and was often enough abused as the sad litany of property seizures attests.[37]

Yet from the perspective of seventeenth-century Cauchois peasants, the customs offered them a certain protection from their sieur or seigneur by specifying the precise conditions under which the landlord could take their property. This protection may seem a minor enough shelter amid a sea of troubles, but it was in fact one of the few firm walls that stood between villagers and the forces that surrounded them. There were certain clear conditions under which Normans could retain the use of their land and goods and pass them on to their children. They were in writing: they had to make an aveu et dénombrement (avowel and enumeration of obligations due on a fief); they had to pay the *lods et ventes* (sales fees) and the *relief* (succession fees) on buying or succeeding to property under some circumstances; they had to make a reasonable pretense of keeping up with their rents. Neither the seigneur nor their other creditors could seize their moveable property, beasts, money, implements, or household effects without fulfilling the legal formalities and publishing their intent to make a seizure (*saisi*) in the parish.[38] No doubt the Custom's most important function, however, was to act as a prior restraint on the most egregious actions of landlords. It also served as the collective memory of peasants that they had certain rights, however flimsy, that marked them off from serfs and slaves. Those rights were guaranteed by no less a person than the king.

Occasionally the meek, or at least the legally disadvantaged, inherited the earth. In the royal court at Cany in 1720, a sieur sued a peasant over the grazing rights of their respective flocks of sheep. Unexpectedly, the peasant won the case: he was authorized to take his flock to graze on the sieur's land for three days, and the sieur was condemned to pay two chickens for the use of the peasant's herbage.[39] Small as these cases were, the conflicts that spawned them wore on villagers, straining the fabric of social relations and even threatening the economic survival of many. The hundred petty tyrannies that might be exercised by a coq de village or a sieur over his neighbors' pastures and property, neighbors whom he might hope one day to supplant, could sometimes be assuaged by royal courts.

Privileges and property were protected by law in France, but they were also bounded by law. The forty-year prescription rule specified that if a villager had enjoyed the use of a piece of property peaceably for forty years without anyone contesting his possession or demanding an aveu, neither the property nor the seigneurial rights over it could be reclaimed by its original owner.[40] In a later case dating from 1761, a villager even obtained letters from the Chancellery in Parlement requiring a sieur to appear before the high justice and show title to a piece of land, for which the sieur claimed 184 livres in rents were due.[41] This insistence on legal titles by tenants during the eighteenth century may be one of the reasons that seigneurs often hired *feudistes* to research their rights, privileges, and titles in the so-called feudal reaction. In reality this may have been partly a legal reaction to rural society's increasingly sophisticated grasp of property law and rights. In his *Fin du féodalisme dans le Pays de Caux,* Guy LeMarchand has questioned whether the region was a feudal society at all after the late seventeenth century, arguing that "characteristic traits of capitalism had already appeared in the Pays de Caux in the seventeenth century."[42]

The courts provided key services for the rapidly expanding market economy along the Atlantic perimeter. Cotton and linen textiles, fish, grain, and small luxury goods were mainstays of the rural district's economy until cheaper English cotton led to a downturn in the mid-eighteenth century.[43] The Caux was one of the most intensive areas of textile production in France by the seventeenth century, producing everything from handkerchief linen and lace to sailcloth for international markets.[44] The ports of Saint-Valéry-en-Caux and Dieppe harbored fishing fleets that roamed from Poland to Newfoundland and sold fish to the markets of Paris.[45] Along with land exploiters and families, rural merchants and master artisans were thus a third segment of Cauchois society that depended on the courts to act as a basic market regulator.

The need for dedicated merchants' courts was so pressing in the larger ports such as Dieppe that the crown successfully expanded consular jurisdictions in the early eighteenth century, adding several courts in Normandy alone.[46] But these tribunals were two to three days' travel from the central Caux, which like most rural areas continued to use regular assize sessions for market cases. The assizes were also used to settle disputes between masters and artisans. The courts worked to uphold the contractual duties of both, enforcing their mutual obligations for reasons of social peace. Like justices of the peace in England, they showed a "great reluctance to do anything which, by throwing men out of work, could merely aggravate the problems of pauperism and vagrancy."[47]

High justices and royal courts had always held specific mandates from the customs and from their charters to police the districts' markets, including supervision of weights, measures, markets, fairs, and mercantile disputes. In the town of Cany, the sworn masters and guards of the trades were required to attend the twice-annual grand assizes of the seigneury. When they balked, as they did in the summer of 1716, Judge Cabot slapped the masters of fifteen trades with 10-livre amends each.[48] They may have been absent in protest, since many other leaders of middling rural society were represented in the chambers that day: twenty-four judges, lawyers, notaries, and royal officers, most in the land-exploiting classes, all crowded into the session.

The Custom of Normandy specifically recognized the business needs of master artisans, wholesale and retail merchants, peasant producers, and even tennis-court proprietors. Articles 535 and 536 set *prescriptions,* or statutes of limitations, on claiming wages, payment, or merchandise where no written obligations or accounts had been kept. Drapers, mercers, grocers, goldsmiths, and other wholesale merchants, along with masons, carpenters, barbers, and laboureurs had one year to file an action. *Gens de metier* and retail merchants such as pastry cooks, dressmakers, embroiderers, saddlers, harness makers, butchers, cooks, and roast-meat sellers had six months to act.

Tavern and cabaret keepers, as well as those who kept tennis courts, were not so well protected. Innkeepers could take "no actions for wine nor for any other things" sold retail in their establishments, "nor equally the masters of tennis courts." Tavern-keepers in the ports and harbors such as Saint-Valéry and Dieppe were better protected, in theory, against their footloose clientele. If they furnished food to journeymen working on the ships, they could demand that the owner or master of the vessel turn them over for action.[49] Consumers even received a certain measure of protection from swindlers, whether they were merchants or officers. Dame Marguerite Petit charged that her husband had lost "his wits and . . . all his reason" and had been swindled out of his land and cash by the scheming king's prosecutor for the bailliage of Arques. The prosecutor was handed a default judgment against him in an intermediate sentence by the judge at Longueville.[50]

As Liana Vardi has demonstrated for northern France during the eighteenth century, textile merchants were among the most frequent visitors to the assizes to settle debts.[51] The true magnitude of their activity in the Cauchois courts is probably obscured by the nature of record keeping there. Many of the summary actions for debt in the royal and seigneurial courts list no occupation for the parties involved; we can be certain only that they were not sieurs or seigneurs. Additionally, a number of substantial Cauchois peasants were also rural merchants who dealt in raw agricultural products, principally grain, flax, and cotton. Some of these Cauchois *laboureurs* listed weavers among their servants, which suggests that they may have been working for rural merchants. In the cases where their occupation was given, these men were almost always identified in the court records as *laboureurs* rather than as merchants.

Even into the last decades of the ancien régime, local market regulation continued to be a key function of the local courts. The judge of Valmont's court was regularly vexed with suits during the markets and occasional fairs held in the parish of Fauville. The prince of Monaco's *procureur* accused peasants of selling their grain in the boutiques and private houses of the town to avoid paying the market hall duties owed to the prince. The halls were also a natural site for public disorder. The overseer of markets, Jean Follet, complained indignantly to the judge about the rowdy crowds that regularly invaded the public markets at Fauville. Large assemblies had turned into a "frightful bacchanal," with children and even "Great persons" pouring out of the taverns and making merry at the stalls. The magistrate agreed, forbidding assemblies, dances, and games in the halls on Sundays and feast days, on pain of 10 livres amends.[52]

Morality, Community, and Church

Villagers found the erastian functions of the secular courts quite useful, since the bailiwicks had long assumed jurisdiction over most morals cases from ecclesiastical courts. Indeed, the crown's ascendency over canon law was one of the key areas where the state had actually suppressed a significant jurisdiction, just as the state had done in England. In a parish belonging to the high justice of Valmont, a few kilometers northwest of Cany, two neighboring male peasants had apparently developed a quarrelsome relationship with one another. On Saint Michael's day, at about four or five o'clock in the afternoon, one peasant's wife and thirteen-year-old daughter were standing near the common border of their fields. To their amazement, their provocative neighbor walked up "entirely nude" and began insulting and propositioning them. Whether their neighbor was taking revenge against the woman's husband, or merely under the sway of a few pots of Norman cider on a feast day, the judge was not visibly amused. He fined the nude promenader 600 livres and had the clerk publicly post his offense on the village doors. The size of the judgment may have been intended to set an example rather than actually to be collected, but the records offer no more insight into this morals case.[53]

The bland nature of the church's parish visitation records in the eighteenth century implies that the post-Tridentine church had been successful in rooting out the more colorful clerical irregularities by this period. But problems of morals and discipline among the clergy had not been quite so thoroughly rooted out as this silence would suggest. Rather than relying on ecclesiastical intervention, parishioners apparently were simply taking their priests into secular courts for correction and punishment. The bishop d'Aubigné's parish visitation records for the Caux dating from 1710 and 1717 are focused on practical matters: he commented on the parish schools, the physical condition of the churches, and the revenues of their fabriques.[54] Yet in the same year of 1710, extensive trials involving clergy in four separate parishes were underway in the bailiwick court of Cany. Curés and priests were called to the bench at thirteen assizes before the end of June, in most cases over fiscal irregularities. Although the judge ordered civil restitution as high as 2,000 livres in one case, no mention of these problems appears in the bishop's records.[55]

Some of the more animated morals cases brought by Cauchois villagers were also against their own parish priests. Concupiscence with village girls, theft of sacramental objects, and dereliction of duty were among the most common complaints of parishioners.[56] Dame Madeleine Claude de la Champagne successfully prosecuted the vicar priest of Auberville for omitting some of the weekly masses he had been well paid to say for her husband's soul. An arbitrated settlement refunding some of her money had fallen through, so the judge ordered 67 livres, 10 sols seized from the priest for the missing masses. Whether the rebate had any spiritual effect is unrecorded.[57] But the king's courts and lords' courts could be useful weapons in the hands of an angry parish saddled with clergy who had repeatedly offended the community. Priests and curés were typically appointed to their benefices in the Caux by the haute justicier, by a lesser seigneur, or by the distant abbey of Fécamp[58] and were subject to only intermittent religious discipline from the church.

Clergy even sued each other in the secular courts for moral offenses, as when Simon Bossard, curé of Bosville, and his mother sued the canon de Charles for "most outrageous and infamous words." The canon had publicly stated in the hearing of a candlemaker that Bossard's mother was a "little whore" and that curé Bossard himself kept a mistress.[59] Disputes over appointments to church benefices were settled in royal courts, too. In June 1710, after the Parlement declined to hear the case, the royal bailiwick court in Cany determined that the abbey of Fécamp should continue to appoint the curé at Anneville.

Judicial Discretion: Equity, Custom, and Precedent

Just as civil cases dominated the assize sessions of the common courts, customary laws and equity dominated the resolution of those cases. Of the total caseload, just over 2 percent can be clearly identified as falling under the purview of royal law. These included several cas royaux: four murders, one counterfeiting, and two cases of sacrilege aggravated by theft. The dossiers also turned up one case of army desertion; three cases involving questions of debt payment with devalued currency after the scandal of John Law and the Mississippi bubble during the 1720s; and a few more than two dozen disputes involving receptions of royal officers, unmarried pregnancy declarations (déclarations de grossesse), and subornation of witnesses, all subjects of royal edicts or competency. We can speculate that summary cases rarely involved royal crimes or royal laws, because crown cases tended to be more serious and technically complicated, requiring more than summary judgments.

Although the records do not allow us to gauge the exact number of cases settled by equity or by case precedent (precedent was typically set in previous equity decisions), the extremely compact nature of the Norman Custom certainly raises the probability that the proportion was significant. With only slightly more than six hundred customary laws on the books, many civil petty-assize cases would naturally be based on the judge's interpretation of contracts, oral agreements, or local traditions. (Typical of these types of cases was a boundary dispute that erupted when a stream changed course, a case that could not be settled by reference to any written law). Equity also played a secondary role in criminal law. Since civil disputes were often at the bottom of criminal acts between villagers, the judge typically had to adjudicate the underlying civil disagreements in criminal cases as well. Criminal cases required the use of equity in the restitution or composition phase, since there were no written guidelines for making the victim or the community whole at the expense of the criminal.[60]

Equity was the broadest and most subjective tool available to local magistrates in judging both civil and criminal cases. Developed by Aristotle in the *Nicomachean Ethics,* the principle of equity became one of the cornerstones of Roman legal practice and later one of the most widely adopted legal principles in France.[61] Jean Bodin, like many legists, emphasized that equity was the noblest part of judging. "In every commonwealth," he wrote, "there are two principle points which the magistrate ought always to have before their eyes: that is to say, the law, and equity. . . . [O]ne is servile, the other is noble. . . . [O]ne understandeth but of the fact, the other of the right."[62]

Daniel Jousse, a widely published legist and présidial court councillor, appreciated the practical necessity of judging by equity in French courtrooms. He observed that a magistrate ought to judge by written customs, ordinances, or laws when they applied. But in the many cases to which no written laws could be applied, "reason and equity ought to be the rule of his decision, and of his judgment." In essence, equity required the magistrate not to treat the parties as equals (which they often were not), but to give to each party what was due to it in justice. In Jousse's eyes, the two standards of equity and law were really coequals in the courtroom, since in all his decisions the judge ought "principally [to] have justice in view."[63] The rigor of law could thus be moderated by equity, since "one should always prefer equity to that rigor, and rather follow the spirit and intention of the law, than the narrow and hard maxim."

Jousse, like his contemporaries, believed that even written laws were open to judicial interpretation in light of larger social or political goods. Law had been created to promote public utility, humanity, and religion and "should be interpreted with all the breadth which can favor these motives, joined with equity."[64] The individual judge's ability to reach a standard as high as Jousse's depended greatly on his education and personal integrity. Notions of what was equitable, or of what served public utility and social order, varied locally too. Nevertheless, all judges understood that written law was only a general guide to their behavior on the bench. And how they exercised their wide powers of interpretation and equity was often influenced by the community at large.

The king, for his part, was keenly aware that judges and parlementary magistrates relied on equity to enlarge their freedom of action. When the civil ordinance of 1667 was published, he warned judges in the first title of the book not to deviate from his code "under pretext of equity (or) the public good."[65] In trying to impose royal law over customs, usages, equity and precedents, the Habsburgs in Spain faced obstacles similar to those confronting the Bourbons in France. Yet as one historian has pointed out, "this did not reflect any aversion to law or legal practice; on the contrary, it made justice more accessible at every level of society."[66]

The Court of Common Opinion: Popular Legal Strategies

The extensive use of civil litigation in the bailiwick courts presumes a broad legal culture in local communities. It also raises important questions about how villagers and townspeople were able to understand and use the French legal system, one that for long was assumed to be oppressive and even foreign. As recent studies by Olwen Hufton and Liana Vardi have suggested, communities may have been far more adept at law and shrewder in court tactics than even their judges liked to admit. "Civil litigation," argues Vardi, "which took peasants into a broader arena reveals how rural communities, losers and victors, could manipulate the legal system."[67] Their access to these systems and procedures depended in large part on their ability to understand the ways of the courts and the basics of customary law.

The *Clameur de Haro:* Raising the Hue and Cry

When the wealthy peasant Pierre Grandcourt collected four sergeants and clerks and his pregnant daughter Anne to set out after her seducer in 1692, he was following a track that led back through at least seven hundred years of Norman history.[68] The right of any Norman to stop another in flagrante delicto, and in effect to issue his or her own arrest warrant, was one of the most deeply held tenets of customary law. But what had originated as a procedure to stop criminal or public offenses had gradually shifted over the years into alignment with the rest of the customary laws. Pierre Grandcourt was using the hue and cry (clameur) for private and civil purposes, to protect his daughter's honor and to ensure the financial upkeep of her child. Family and property, not crime, propelled him to use the popular legal procedure.

When Intendant de Vaubourg surveyed the Norman province in 1698, a few years after Grandcourt's case, three features in its legal landscape stood out to his eye. "This province is ruled by a custom that one honors with the title 'wise,'" he noted, but "one should not forget to speak of the Norman charter and of the clameur de haro." The *clameur de haro,* whose modern successor is the citizen's arrest, was a revered tradition in Normandy. The clameur was popularly assumed to have originated during the tenth-century reign of Raoul I, duke of Normandy, "whose justice and equity were so known by his subjects and so revered that at the sound of his name alone [Raoul], he who had acted injustly would be arrested by whoever pursued him by an effect of the authority of this prince."[69] Whether the story was apocryphal or not, it had become part of Norman mythology. The clameur, in other words, provided a route by which any Norman could assume the judicial authority derived from his sovereign to arrest an act of injustice.

Although lesser versions of the clameur were practiced in other provinces, notably Brittany, it reached its apogee in the Norman Custom. In the belief that all Normans had the right to exercise certain judicial functions, the clameur was still widely practiced in the province during the seventeenth and eighteenth centuries. During the revolt of the nu-pieds, rioters used the clameur as one of their justifications for sacking the houses of tax collectors. The king even complained of the numerous officers in Rouen who "abused the privilege of the clameur de haro" against the crown.[70] Clameurs were used in calmer circumstances in the villages to prevent marriages and property seizures, thefts, and judicial abuses.

The clameur was not unique to France. H. Pissard, one of the few legal historians to have treated the clameur de haro, noted that it was related to the *ligatio* in Germanic law and analogous to the English and Scandinavian "hue and cry." But other French provinces also had versions of the clameur during the ancien régime. In Beaumanoir's version of the *Coutumes de Beauvais,* a husband had the right to kill his wife taken in flagrant adultery, on raising a cry of "*hareu, hareu.*" The neighbors were obliged to come running, and the wronged husband had the duty as well as the right to deliver instant justice.[71] The ancient custom of Brittany had similar provisions for clameurs, which were still exercised in the seventeenth century.

Normandy was unique, however, in the strength and breadth of legal powers invested in the hue and cry. The clameur was available to those whose legal rights were normally restricted under customary law. Women and minors had full authority to cry haro, arrest an actor, and force a court hearing in a royal jurisdiction. This broad mandate was particularly suited to the Norman temperament, noted Pissard, being "of that spirit so supple and so procedural, so conservative and so enterprising."[72] Cases involving the clameur de haro give us one of the few insights we have into popular ideas about justice and law in a long period that provided no serious revolts or rebellions for us to work with in deciphering popular ideas.

The ancient custom of Normandy had restricted the cry of haro to criminal acts, including fire, theft, and homicide, "comme si quelqu'un court fus à un autre le couteau trait."[73] As Natalie Zemon Davis has pointed out, "[i]t should be remembered how often conditions in sixteenth-century cities required groups of the *menu peuple* to take the law into their own hands. Royal edicts themselves enjoined any person who saw a murder, theft, or other misdeed to ring the tocsin and chase after the criminal."[74] But during the redaction of the *Coutume de Normandie* in 1583, the clameur was expanded to include civil matters. Articles 54 to 62 specified that a haro could be invoked not only for bodily harm and imminent peril, but also for matters involving movables, héritages, and church property. Both parties had to proceed to the judge, either to be imprisoned or to post a bond. The judge was bound at least to levy an amend against one party or the other at the conclusion of the case, to discourage frivolous or malicious clameurs from being raised.[75] Civil clameurs were considered important enough procedures that the Custom listed them first in the catalog of cases in the jurisdiction of a royal vicomtal court.[76] By the late seventeenth century, clameurs were almost exclusively exercised in civil matters, although the occasional good citizen still cried haro when he or she surprised a crime in progress.

Clameurs also opened a legally sanctioned route to political protest. A clameur could be raised against government officers, including the king's judicial officers. Three years before Pierre Grandcourt's hue and cry, a cry of haro against officers in the royal bailliage of Pont-Audemer prompted a full-scale investigation by the Parlement of Normandy of judicial corruption in the bailiwick.[77] The royal Edict of May 15, 1725 eventually forbade the use of clameurs against royal sergeants, ushers, and employees of the tax farms, a strong indication that during the eighteenth century, Normans were still using the law as a form of tax protest and of resistance against local royal officials. But other lawyers and judges continued to argue that it could legitimately be used against magistrates and sergeants who abused their powers.[78]

Over the years, the Norman populace invested the practice with an even sharper political meaning of its own. In the early seventeenth century, the haro was a dangerous cry to arms in the province. During the revolt of the nu-pieds in 1639, the head of the insurgents of Rouen was said to have run through the streets of the town crying "Rou! Rou!" as he indicated financiers' and tax collectors' houses for fire and pillage.[79] Thus the rioters were designating one of the ordinary functions of the state, revenue collection, as a criminal attack on their property and well-being. The subjects' legal cry for justice was turned against the king's men with violent effect. An arquebusier was shot at the abbey of Saint-Ouen, the president of the parlement was attacked in the street, and several partisans' houses were burned to the ground.[80]

Family matters and property were often at the bottom of clameurs in the Caux, however, as they were for Pierre and Anne Grandcourt. The clameur was a particularly reliable legal companion at the rituals where family and property crossed paths in the village: birth and death, marriage and separation, inheritance and orphanage. As a clerk in the Parlement noted, the haro was appropriate for all matters of "imminent peril, as for moveables or income rights, and for introducing all possessory trials."[81] Inheritances were particularly fertile ground for the hue and cry, since they typically involved so many individuals and such an irrevocable transfer of lineage property. Disputes were also resolved at quite reasonable cost in most cases. In 1727, two sieurs cried haro over another sieur, possibly their eldest brother, in a dispute over an inheritance of 900 livres. Given the size of the inheritance, the court costs were surprisingly moderate: 9 livres to the judge for holding an extraordinary session for the case, 3 livres for his decision, and 15 sols for the usher. The costs of resolving the dispute in court were not much over 1 percent of the total value of the inheritance, a judicial bargain even by modern standards.[82] (This does not, of course, tell us what illicit transfers, gifts, and bribes were offered to the court, which was quite a heavy traffic in some jurisdictions.)

The clameur was invoked in commercial disputes in the Caux by the later seventeenth century as well. Ancient customary law thus adapted to the quickening pace of market transactions, helping to fill a void in the legal system. In the spring of 1699, Pierre Bruquois, the valet of an oil mill at Barville, was dragged before the bench of the high justice of Cany in a haro. The oil mill had been newly leased by an élu of the élection at Caudebec, displacing Bruquois' employer. When the élu arrived to take possession, he found the old valet still operating the mill and interjected haro. The remedy was efficient; the wheels of the mill stopped grinding as soon as the miller's man was led across the river Durdant to court by the royal élu's agent.[83] At a rather lower level on the social scale, Nicolas LeFrançois cried haro in the market of Cany in the fall of 1699, after a rural merchant sold ten young sheep with their wool to another buyer. They walked across the street to the courtroom with witnesses, including the illiterate shepherd, and sheep in tow to settle their differences.[84]

The procedure provided an uncommon meeting ground for different social classes in the village, one where the ordinary rules of engagement could be subtly or even dramatically changed. Under customary law, the individual who cried haro was bound to appear in court on his or her own behalf, rather than by the proxy of an attorney or seigneurial agent. In 1730, we find a clameur in the royal bailliage of Cany that pitted a noble royal officer against an illiterate merchant in the marketplace. Jean Baptiste le Bataille, an auditor in the sovereign Chambers of Accounts, Aides, and Finances in Rouen, and also seigneur of Omonville in the pays de Caux and a king's counsellor, cried haro against one of the merchants in the Cany market, François Leseigneur. Le Bataille had sent one of his domestics to the peasant merchant's stall to buy goods, and found the desired items already being sold to another buyer. In countertestimony, François Leseigneur charged that the king's auditor, in a fit of temper, had run up to his stall and rapped him with his baton. Le Bataille felt compelled to respond to the local judge that he hadn't actually maltreated the man but merely complained to him of bad faith.[85]

The seigneur's physical punishment of a social inferior violated the merchants' traditional rights to personal security, which the local courts upheld. Under the roof of the market, even nobles were bound by commercial, customary, and royal laws, not class. The law thus occasionally leveled all parties to a dispute through the mechanism of a few broad-based rights. The merchant's use of the hue and cry in this case further challenged the social barriers between them. Clameurs performed a rather radical function merely by demanding that a privileged individual appear on the legal field of battle to do personal combat with a vile commoner. The privileged party also had to be prepared to lose that combat publicly, as indeed happened from time to time. A simple gesture, but one perhaps freighted with symbolic meaning for such men as Le Bataille and Leseigneur.

Haros cut across authority in another direction as well. Villagers and townspeople raised the hue and cry against the king's men in the Caux. This provided them with a limited but valuable tool for disputing the actions of individuals who exercised royal offices. In 1680, Sergeant Piard of Cany appeared at a villager's door without a warrant and attempted to seize the family's movables in payment for a debt. The villager cried haro against the hasty sergeant and in his testimony forthrightly called the sergeant's actions "an abuse." The two men came to blows before they came to court. But the villager demonstrated a clear knowledge of acceptable court procedures and was confident enough of the law to begin prosecution against the local royal sergeant. Sadly, the outcome is lost.[86] But there are sufficient examples of village haros against local court officials to indicate that villagers were getting some kind of satisfaction from their suits.[87]

A Village of Judges: Arbitrators and "Amiable Compositors"

Clameurs lead us to another central judicial role played by Cauchois inhabitants through the medium of their tongues, that of arbitration. Lay judging
was a natural outgrowth of a society organized into self-regulating corps, and
one where seigneurial or royal officials had traditionally been very thin on
the ground. Unfortunately the documents on lay arbitration are scattered far
and wide in notarial, judicial, corporate, and private records, which makes it
difficult to see more than the broad outlines of popular adjudication within
the whole judicial system. The laconic nature of local court records usually leaves out any prior history of arbitration in a case, except in cases that
required witnesses to be deposed. (Arbitral sentences were by law supposed
to be homologized or confirmed by the court in order to be valid, but were
only occasionally.) Yet a vast reservoir of judicial self-regulation underlay local
society during the ancien régime, one that almost certainly dwarfed the activities of the official courts. Fewer than 20 percent of Cauchois assize cases list a
definitive judgment by the court (although summary civil cases would not typically record a courts' decision), leaving a large number of cases open to the
possibility of arbitrated settlement before final judgment.[88] In England, the
diary of the eighteenth-century Wilshire J. P. William Hunt indicated that 60
percent of the cases initiated in his court were settled by arbitration.[89] Unlike
the English petty assizes, French bailiwick courts had barristers, solicitors, and
clerks with a monetary interest in seeing cases concluded in court. But many
cases were likely too small to be worth pursuing, and arbitration relieved bailiwick officers of burdensome or nonremunerative cases.

Here too, there appears to be increasing integration between popular
and official methods of justice, rather than straightforward colonization by
the crown. Community and corporate arbitration was a royally sanctioned
part of the French justice system. From the mid-sixteenth century onward,
the crown invested considerable ink in trying to mandate that many family,
property, and merchant affairs would go through lay arbitration in the first
instance. Royal laws such as the Edict of August 1560 obliged the parties to
choose arbiters in certain types of family-property cases.[90] Notably, community arbiters were required at most of the important junctures where large
amounts of family property were transferred: the division of inheritances,
restitution of a woman's dowry or delivery of her widow's dower, and emancipation of a minor from tutorship.[91]

As the crown reinforced community arbitration with its left hand, it also
funneled arbitration business to existing royal court personnel with its right
hand. A clarification passed by the Parlement of Normandy in 1666 confirmed
that judges could act as informal arbiters, even in cases involving relatives or
domestics, as long as the arbitration occurred in their private residences and
not in their courtrooms or council chambers.[92] Soon after, by the Edict of

March 1673 the crown created the office of clerk of arbitrage, an office available in both royal and ducal seigneurial justices. (Most of these offices were
naturally enough bought up by royal notaries, who were forced to buy functions they had already been performing.)[93] Clerks of arbitrage were allowed
to settle the compromise between the parties and to write up the documentation, which guaranteed extra fees. By the late eighteenth century, in part of
northern Burgundy arbitration was entirely in the hands of legal professionals:
all were lawyers, and some were seigneurial judges as well.[94]

The two kinds of justice, informal arbitration and court litigation, were
thus increasingly conducted by the same people in the villages of the Caux.
This blending of personnel led to a gradual, though never complete, merg-
ing of community practices into the royal system. Royal notaries, attorneys,
and judges were frequently involved in mediating out-of-court settlements.
They practiced here alongside other kinds of local authorities: priests, sworn
guards of the trades, the village communauté, dames, sieurs, or other local
notables such as syndics and mayors (who were often royal judicial officials
anyway).[95] Individuals tended to choose those with the natural authority to
resolve their particular disputes. Women in the linen trade in Cany went to
the sworn guards of their trade to settle artisanal disputes; peasants often
went to notaries; attorneys tended to pick senior lawyers or judges in settling
their own affairs.

By royal law, arbiters were to be chosen from among those in the community who had a natural ability to judge the facts in the affair. The arbiters
chosen for a child's emancipation, for example, were to be three "bons et
notables personnages," drawn from the relatives, friends, or neighbors of
the child reaching majority.[96] Under Colbert's Commercial Ordinance of
March 1673, merchants and *negociants* were required to establish arbitration
procedures in the contracts of their societies. Those whose contracts did not
provide for arbitration could be assigned arbiters by a royal judge. The arbitral sentences were then recorded in a consular court, if one existed, or in
the regular royal courts.[97]

Those prohibited from conducting binding arbitration in France were
surprisingly few in number. Slaves (perhaps included with an eye to the
colonies), deaf-mutes, infamous individuals, minors, and the insane were
excluded. Women were allowed to act as binding arbiters (despite fierce
debates among jurists), thus granting them significant public judicial authority. Madame de Lavardin's arbitral sentence between two domestics, for
example, was upheld by the Parlement on the grounds that her sentence
was "just and reasonable" and moreover was consistent with the Parlement's
own case law.[98] Arbitration thus created a large potential pool of lay judges
in the community. The law recognized two distinct kinds of community
adjudicators. More specialized were the arbiters, who had to observe the
legal ordinances and were sometimes appointed by judges. Less formal were

the *amiables compositeurs,* who were required to judge only the facts in the case, not the law. Yet the decisions of these lay judges had the force of law in a powerful institutional sense. They could be appealed only to the sovereign courts of Parlement.[99]

Arbitration meant that many in the community could choose their own natural judges in both legal and personal matters. Both parties to a dispute selected a pair of arbiters and under pain of stunning royal penalties (upward of 1,000 livres, to be split between a hospital and the opposing party) agreed to be bound by the agreement.[100] All those who could legally introduce a trial in regular court could ask for arbitration. "One must be free to compromise" was the general rule, which therefore excluded both slaves and serfs from arbitration in most property matters.[101] This exclusion also meant that minors could not proceed without the authority of their tutors and that married women could not submit their property cases to arbitration without the consent of their husbands. Widows and wives who had formal separations were allowed to submit matters for arbitration on their sole authority, if the matter involved property that was legally their own. But in general even the poorest of the poor, if they were free and male, could choose community judges over the king's courts or their seigneur's. Once the parties had come to an accommodation, the Criminal Code of 1670 forbade courts to intervene in the decision unless it was a crime meriting corporal punishment or banishment.[102]

Early modern villagers used the courts of the ancien régime in a substantially different way than litigants use a modern court system. They may often have viewed formal litigation as merely one tactic by which an opponent could be brought to agreement or submission, as an intermediate skirmish in a much more complicated dispute, or as a means of restoring public honor. As Dewald concluded for the village of La Neuville in Normandy, "formal litigation was seen to be only a stage in the process by which settlements were reached. In most instances . . . village laboureurs arranged final settlements through arbitration."[103]

The crown had two pressing motives for promoting community arbitration: finance and order. The state could never hope to field a judicial bureaucracy large enough and specialized enough to settle the enormous range of personal and property disputes that plagued local society, disputes that in the Caux ranged from an argument over shipbuilding contracts between wealthy *armateurs* in Le Havre to a peasants' quarrel over the size of a capon in the Cany market. Public order was still most efficiently and cheaply maintained through self-regulation. These royal motives ironically helped to underwrite much of Normandy's provincial independence in justice. Like local customary laws and the quasi-legislative role of the provincial Parlement, binding community arbitration was a locally driven mechanism of public order.

The jurist Daniel Jousse pointed out the public utility of having such a dual system of justice in the community, although much the same group of people participated in both mechanisms. Arbiters had a singular advantage over judges in that "they could sometimes prefer the considerations of public good and the peace to the exactitude of justice."[104] Then as now, the results of court litigation did not always serve the best interests of the parties, their families, or their communities. But as a royal officer, Jousse argued that the arbiters' power to promote the public good did not constitute a true public authority. They did not share in the *"puissance publique,"* being unable to constrain witnesses to appear, for example, or to publish monitoires. Nevertheless, he stated that their activities were one of "the most advantageous for the public good. . . . They can become the judges of the most illustrious families [and] of all reasonable persons."[105]

Others did view arbitration as a powerful public, and not merely private, institution. An anonymous arbiter wrote to Pussort's judicial commission around 1665, lauding the arbiters' power to promote the bien publique precisely because they possessed a genuine puissance publique. There arose "few trials which cannot be reconciled" in the district, the arbiter of the poor explained, because "when even one of the parties wants to use [my services], the adverse party is forced to come to an accommodation."[106] Although their posts were not considered a public dignity as were royal and seigneurial offices, arbiters commanded both power and authority in the village. Arbitration was so well integrated into local society that the practice survived the Revolution almost intact, as Anthony Crubaugh has shown. After 1790 justices of the peace frequently funneled cases that couldn't be mediated to binding arbiters. Often the parties still chose the judge himself or his assessors to arbitrate. It was the straightforward recognition, Crubaugh explained, that many civil cases "centered more on facts (easily ascertained at the site) than on points of law (argued by legal professionals before a judge)."[107]

The blending of arbitration and litigation is perhaps the strongest possible argument against an absolutist court system. Karl Wegert, in his study of German courts, speculated that "in light of what we know about the vitality of early modern culture, it is surely worth asking how the drive to control engineered from above might have been influenced, perhaps partly facilitated, from below."[108] The Cauchois district's high justices and royal bailiwick courts had absorbed many recognizable features of community justice even as they projected new ideas about law and justice back onto the village community. The blending together of these two modes of law in the state's lower courts was the essence of their strength and their utility. Had villagers and townspeople not found the royal courts useful and comprehensible, despite their sometimes alarming shortcomings, the king's and lords' courts could never have become so deeply woven into the culture of ordinary Normans.

Oral and Written Access to Law

Access to legal information in the towns and villages of upper Normandy was surprisingly widespread. The number of local lawyers who appeared at the mandatory annual summer assizes of the bailiwick courts was many times greater than the number of lawyers who actually practiced at the bar on a regular basis. Some of those with law degrees earned their living as notaries; a few were on retainer to titled nobles or seigneurial lords; some practiced in the tax courts or administered hospitals; a lucky few had retired to sieuries. The number of Cauchois villagers with practical information about how the courts worked was even greater. With the ushers, clerks, notaries, solicitors, and sergeants added in, it would have been difficult to walk through a sizeable village without running into someone who had a knowledgeable connection to the courts.

Printed access to law was affordable and increasingly available. The printers of Rouen did a brisk business in inexpensive paperback editions of the *Coutume de Normandie,* as well as in the more luxurious bound editions. Chez Maurry, the printers to the king and to the archbishop of Rouen, produced a new paper-covered edition of the Customs in 1704 for 15 sols.[109] This was about the price of an almanac, which ranged from about 8 to 18 sols, or of two or three fairy tales in the *bibliothèque bleue* sold in Rouen at the printer Lacrene-Labbey.[110] The same year they offered a tract on how to liquidate the marital law regarding daughters under the customs of the Caux and of Normandy, a more substantial investment at 1 livre, 10 sols; a collection of parlementary edicts since 1672; and no fewer than three major commentaries on the Customs, those of Pesnelle, Berault, and Basnage.[111]

Copies of the Customs were almost invariably in the death inventories of rural lawyers and judges, but they were also in the inventories of villagers and townspeople. One researcher has asserted that "*coutumes* were more common than Bibles" in ordinary French households, and were often the only book in the house.[112] This is not so astonishing as it might seem. Almost the whole of a family's wealth distribution was bound up in customary laws. From cradle to grave, and at every division or addition of the family in between, the Customs governed the allotment of family resources to each member and to each lineage. Customary law was not the sole preserve of the elites; it involved the deepest interests of a village family, the survival and well-being of their children and heirs. As Hufton noted, seigneurial justice dealt with "problems as crucial for the peasant as for the rural community."[113] Peasants who did not know the law would surely be at the mercy of those who did.

Both customs and court procedures encouraged legal literacy in the countryside. Men or women who were granted curatorship of a minor child's property were responsible for keeping an account of their expenses on behalf of the child, an account the child could legally demand to see on achieving his or her majority. Although account keeping for wards had been required by the Norman custom from ancient times, its use by the peasantry had been understandably quite limited in previous centuries. But by the late seventeenth century, as Jonathan Dewald has noted, "extensive collections" of wardship accounts appeared in peasants' death inventories in the barony of Pont-Saint-Pierre in Normandy, "two or three generations before the appearance of printed books." As a result, "the demands of justice also worked to encourage, in some instances even require, literacy and numeracy."[114]

The growth of courts accustomed villagers to legal calculation as well as to numeric calculation. They had to frame their actions on a daily basis to meet legal requirements, satisfy attorneys and judges, and avoid possible lawsuits years down the road. Their relations with their own family members increasingly came to be mediated by law and the courts. This was quite apart from the courts' older role in mediating villagers' relationships with outsiders: their feudal lord, landlord, or king. The entry of public law and justice into what the modern world thinks of as private life was one of the most fundamental transformations of political culture in ancien régime France.

Literacy gave certain advantages in court, the more so since it presumed oral fluency in the French language, which had been made the official language of law courts in 1539 under the Ordinance of Villers-Cotterêts.[115] Since the common language was the Cauchois patois, not the king's French, the role of such wordsmiths as attorneys, solicitors, notaries, and clerks was vital for many clients. Indeed, the parish schoolmaster had his work cut out for him in Cauchois villages. In 1690, the outlying parishes of Doudeville and Bacqueville in the bailiwick of Cany had male literacy rates hovering between 36 and 51 percent. That was significantly below the rather high Norman standard, which exceeded 80 percent in some regions. When Monseigneur d'Aubigné began his parish visitations twenty years later, from 1710 to 1717, he found that 70 percent of the 662 Caux parishes in his records had a boys' school; only 36 percent had a girls' school. The percentage of men who could sign their marriage acts had risen to just 59 percent by the end of the eighteenth century.[116]

The Caux was also an area of striking female illiteracy, with an unusually wide disparity between men and women. At the end of the seventeenth century, female literacy was just 4 percent; by the end of the eighteenth century it had risen to only 34 percent. This was an eightfold increase, but women still lagged far behind their male compatriots.[117] Village notables in Cauchois parishes were universally literate by the mid-eighteenth century, whether male or female. Men in the comfortably off classes of rural laboureurs and merchants enjoyed literacy rates of between 75 and 84 percent.[118] To a certain extent, the literacy threshold among the Cauchois corresponded to both the litigation threshold and to property ownership. But the courts were often and successfully used by nonreaders in the parishes too.

Illiteracy was not as much of a barrier to royal or seigneurial court use as it might seem. In 1710, two illiterate opponents appealed a case from the seigneurial court of Saint Martin into the royal bailiwick court at Cany.[119] This action presumed a reasonably sophisticated understanding of the appellate process on their part. More typical was a complex marriage agreement hammered out in 1684 between two families of substantial peasants, all illiterate. Both the bride's and groom's families appeared before the high justice of the comté d'Eu on the far eastern edge of the Caux, negotiating a half-dozen different types of legal contracts in order to settle the marriage. The family of the husband, Pierre Gemeval, was evidently much less well off than that of the bride, Anne Ferand. Gemeval had to borrow 200 livres from his brother-in-law to bring to the marriage. In consequence, he had to sign a separate donation to his new wife granting her "full dower over all her goods and landed income, following the Custom," which he acknowledged doing with "free will." Her contribution included at least five pieces of property in two hamlets.

Anne Ferand in turn had separate contracts with her mother and brother. Her brother recognized that she gave up her rights to her mariage avenant in favor of sharing her father's succession. Her mother, Elizabeth Panneteau, promised her a piece of land, a red and white cow, five goats with their kids, clothing, and movables. Elizabeth Panneteau also promised food to her new son-in-law's sister and mother, "with all property in common, all working together."[120] This elaborate contra dance of obligations, donations, dowries, widow's portions, inheritances, renunciations, and transfers of property formed the paper trail that made Anne and Pierre's marriage possible. Not one of the numerous family members present could do more than mark his or her assent at the bottom, but this did not make the contracts any less useful to them.

The culture of rural lawyers, who were intermediaries between the state and the village, also blended into the oral traditions of their clients. Natalie Zemon Davis has noted that the fluid medium of proverbs provided a method of thinking and argumentation in both cultures. "Villagers both expected an exchange of proverbs to have some role in legal argumentation and probably used them themselves before manorial courts and in village disputes. . . . Moreover, lawyers had their own proverbs, regulae, and maxims, which they memorized to help them learn the law and plead."[121] Indeed, earlier printed versions of the Norman customs were produced in rhyme, using biblical or proverbial phrases instead of those in the legal text to make it easier for lawyers and clients to remember.[122]

The wider popular press reveals a surprising variety of written material available to ordinary readers that touched on the ways of the courts.

Almanacs and tales from the bibliothèque bleue highlighted spectacular trials, rogue criminals, and stock figures of the courts.[123] Popular editions of fables and fantasies by such writers as La Fontaine and Perrault included tales of arbitration and judging. Many villagers and townspeople could sympathize with La Fontaine's complaint about litigation in his tale of the arbiter judge and two pleaders. "Since he comes from laws, man, for his sins/ is condemned to plead half his life," he lamented. "Half: three-quarters, and often enough his whole life."[124] For the more literate, the Louvain edition of the Old Testament translated into French, with its dramatic parallels to customary law, was also part of a generalized legal culture. The introduction to Exodus reads like a legal gloss rather than a spiritual guide. Subheadings included "punishments and amends for larceny and damages . . . On suborned girls . . . On not detracting from magistrates."[125]

To a certain extent, the courts also fostered a broader state culture. Through the assize readings they connected the district to distant events in the kingdom, and reminded the audience of the interests of the royal administration. The court assizes and the pulpit served as the two licensed broadcasters for the news of the kingdom. In April 1720, the Cany bailiwick court read out royal orders from the past six months: an edict regulating expeditionary bankers from the Court of Rome, the king's declaration forbidding people to carry diamonds on pain of confiscation, an order from the Council of State on burned trees in the forest of Alençon, and a ruling on the resignation of church benefices.[126] Of these, only the last was of any local interest. Transporting diamonds and consorting with papal bankers were not often on the event horizon of town and village residents. Yet such orders did give those in the audience a sense of the broad interests and even broader ambitions of the royal state. From a stand of dead trees in a remote Norman parish to the heights of the Vatican, the crown broadcast its presence through the local courts.

This increasingly widespread legal culture in the villages and towns was a significant force for integration in France, although in a slightly different manner than English common law. For the English, law was "essentially something in which people participated, part of the broad culture of the nation."[127] In France, the translation was less national, but no less universal, in character. Without a unified common law, and with royal statutes so disorganized that the most able jurists of the age failed at codification, French laws provided much less in the way of national identity. And yet the courts were still a powerful force for local order and identity with local and provincial state institutions, as well as a spur to literacy in a common French language. Moreover, the variations in local customary laws and local courts across France were often more cosmetic than real. They performed similar functions in most regions, regulating property, family, and local power. They also introduced the court's users to modes of argument and reasoning that were important elements of a common mental culture in France. As Roger Chartier has eloquently argued, the traditional polarization of elite and popular culture often "obliterates the bases shared by the whole of society."[128] One of the most crucial of those shared bases was the culture and practice of the law, the invisible ligaments that tied all of French society into one body. Through its medium, villagers wove their own ideas and practices of justice into the royal system, even as the royal system knit its reasoning and discipline into theirs.

Chapter 7

UNCIVIL ACTS

CRIME AND PUNISHMENT

A valet fails to give you a clean glass?
Sentence him to amends, or if he breaks it, to the whip.

Racine, *Les plaideurs*

As the pall of smoke lifted from the town square of Grainville-la-Teinturière in the spring of 1693, the bourg's inhabitants were left looking at a pile of ashes representing villager Jacques Lefrançois. The ashes were not those of Jacques Lefrançois himself; they were his straw effigy, which had been hanged and set afire according to the court's order. Judge Pierre Alexandre and the king's prosecutor, Robert Maribrasse, were presiding over a theater of death in which the sentence was read out before an empty prisoner's stool and a straw man burned in justice for a very real murder.[1] The spectacle would have displeased Cardinal Richelieu, who had written a few decades earlier (perhaps not intending the double entendre), that "ordinances and laws are entirely useless if they are not followed by executions."[2]

Preserving security and order was the principal function of the French state at every level, and local magistrates were deeply conscious of their duty to keep the king's peace. But the preservation of order was exercised very differently in the bailiwicks by local officers than it was practiced in the minds of ministers. Local judges could seldom afford to be so contemptuous of common opinion as Richelieu was when he advised that in criminal matters one should scorn the "discourse of an ignorant populace."[3] Keeping the king's peace among their neighbors and fellow parishioners, judges had to engage in a delicate calibration of criminal justice. This sometimes led to very different outcomes from those foreseen in royal laws. As in civil cases, magistrates drew on a panoply of legal, procedural, and customary options to tailor justice to the community. Especially in cases involving settled inhabitants of the bailiwick, judges availed themselves of discretionary sentencing, reduced charges, composition, and restitution to satisfy both the demand for public justice and the need for private peace.

This was not so much a sign of enlightened jurisprudence (though some judges clearly wished to temper the harshness of the law) as it was a matter of political prudence. Draconian application of the crown's criminal laws could have dramatic and destabilizing consequences on families and ultimately on public order. Removing working adults from the labor force through corporal punishment, banishment, or death increased both poverty and vagrancy in the community. Fueling private feuds between families with harsh verdicts increased, rather than decreased, violence. And despite their standing in the community, bailiwick judges had remarkably limited means of physical coercion at hand. Rural magistrates had no effective police force at their command (save a local sergeant and the distant company of archers for the maréchaussée), and no secure jail facilities. They also had little hope of timely reinforcement from the central or provincial government if they failed to keep the peace.

Ultimately, establishing security against crime and disorder in early modern society required constant cooperation from the villagers and townspeople of the district.[4] Without their willingness to report delicts, raise clameurs, bear witness in court, and serve in the many lesser posts of the peace, the criminal courts would have ceased to function. Villagers and townspeople wielded this influence to great effect in the well of the court, prosecuting their own local grievances under the guise of royal or seigneurial violations, settling old scores and protecting family interests. Perhaps the most compelling evidence of public involvement is the fact that local criminal prosecutions were overwhelmingly plaintiff driven. Over 74 percent of all criminal cases in the pays de Caux were initiated by private individuals, not by the king's or seigneur's public prosecutor for the jurisdiction.

Bailiwick and seigneurial courts throughout France displayed the same pattern of plaintiff-driven criminal dockets. Stephen G. Reinhardt's study of the royal sénéchaussée of Sarlat during the eighteenth century found that 71 percent of all criminal cases were privately prosecuted, not publicly prosecuted by the king's prosecutor. Indeed, as he pointed out, "even for royal cases, the prosecution of all offenders . . . would have bankrupted the court." He also noted that the vast majority of criminal cases were brought by nonnobles.[5] Despite being the private jurisdiction of nobles, lords' courts followed substantially the same pattern of commoners prosecuting cases. In the châtellenie and high justice of la Motte-de-Gennes in Brittany, 77 percent of those privately prosecuted cases were brought by peasants alone.[6]

Taken together, these facts require us to rethink what order and security meant at the bailiwick level, where most French criminal cases were tried.

The involvement of broad sections of the community in criminal justice, and the judges' use of criminal justice not simply to punish individual malefactors but to keep the wider civil peace, should lead us to reconnect crime with civil society. The long-standing practice of looking at early modern criminal registers in isolation from the civil registers has partially obscured the broader meaning of justice.[7] The presence of so many outstanding studies on early modern crime has also tended to leave the impression that local courts were primarily about crime and punishment. But they were in fact about a larger kind of order, of which criminal punishment was but one piece of the puzzle.

Indeed, it was usually a very narrowly defined part of the picture. In the pays de Caux, for example, only 13.4 percent of the courts' entire traffic was in criminal justice.[8] Of 1,360 cases from this period that were tried in seven courts, 183 were clearly criminal in nature (see chapter 6, table 6.1). Earlier studies of Norman and Burgundian courts have turned up similarly small percentages of criminal cases. Some historians have criticized the small number of cases used in earlier statistical studies on Norman crime. Apparently they did not realize that those were the total number of criminal cases actually tried in the courts.[9] Crime was therefore an exciting, but decidedly subsidiary, part of the courts' functions.

Moreover, the attempt to categorize crimes in the Caux using the older dichotomy of *vol/violence* (crimes against property versus crimes against persons) falls apart when we look at the larger context. Many violent confrontations were in fact property related. The most distinctive case pattern in the criminal records, as in the civil records, is the prominence of family and property issues. Crime typically erupted out of long-standing civil conflicts in the community that had burst their bounds. When the assizes convened to hear a criminal case in the bailiwick, the judge was frequently looking at the reverse side of a civil dispute, one whose underlying causes had also to be resolved.

Rare was the dangerous stranger, the hardened deviant, in the ordinary courts of the Caux. The perpetrator of a crime was far more likely to be found closer to home, among neighbors and family: the angry laboureur too often denied access across his neighboring sieur's road, the violent son left out of the inheritance, the avaricious court sergeant. The sensational bibliothèque bleue stories that circulated in Normandy fueled the popular imagination with visions of bands of thieves, desperate vagabonds, and footloose soldiers as the face of crime. These masterless men (and occasionally women) were indeed an important part of the equation and a source of great unease for settled society. But in early modern society, the insecurity of life and property began closer to home. The bailiwicks' criminal assizes were largely filled with those who were not strangers, either to each other or to their judges.

Crime, Public Order, and the State

Despite the fact that crime was only a small fraction of the caseload of local bailiwick courts, it had a large political footprint due to its connections to public order, governance, and sovereignty. Crime and punishment bring us directly into the realm of the state's coercive powers. If the courts' civil jurisdiction was derived from the state's monopoly of justice, its criminal jurisdiction was derived as much from the state's monopoly of force. The two powers together formed the Janus-faced majesty of the crown. Through its criminal jurisdiction, the French state graphically reinforced a powerful political idea: that the private disobedience of subjects was a public affront to sovereign authority.

In early modern society, the link between misbehavior (on a private level) and disorder (on public level) was always explicit. Through criminal justice, the state defined not only deviance, but also heresy; not merely disobedience, but treason. There were strong religious and philosophical reasons for this linkage. As in all European countries, the sovereign's authority (and its monopoly of both force and justice) was ultimately derived from religious sources. That was especially true of the highest and most fearsome of those delegated powers, the monarchs' right to deliver judicial death to their subjects. Indeed, from an early modern religious standpoint, no other justification could have excused judicial killing from the taint of mortal sin. In the king's coronation oath, an explicit contract, he was bound to do both justice and mercy. Through justice, the crown was enjoined to keep each individual, family, or corps in its proper place in the realm. Individuals who challenged that order by violating the Decalogue, the laws of the realm, or the laws of the church, were a threat to public and godly order writ large.

Just as the punishment of crime graphically demonstrated the king's majesty, his power to pardon offenses displayed his divine mercy. Louis XIV extolled "the charm of clemency, the most royal of all the virtues, since it can never belong to any but kings."[10] The *lettre de rémission* for unpremeditated homicide was the corollary to the power of execution; with it the king restored life to a convict considered legally dead.[11] Despite the gradual shift since the sixteenth century towards the notion of the sovereign as lawmaker, some seventeenth-century writers such as Bossuet still burnished this image of the king as judge.[12] Bossuet was regarded as a quaint anachronism by many of his contemporaries, but his view of the king as judge was nearer to that still held by most of those living in rural bailiwicks. When a culprit was sentenced to honorable amends in court, he or she still knelt to ask pardon of God and the king.

The political and ideological functions of criminal justice have been a source of lively debate among both Continental and English historians. In 1975, Michel Foucault argued in *Surveiller et punir: Naissance de la prison* that dramatic shifts in criminal punishment over the eighteenth century paralleled the rise of the bourgeoisie and the emergence of a new state. When crime was viewed as an affront to the king's person, the sovereign enacted violent punishment on the bodies of criminals; but as the rising middle classes claimed political control, the state began disciplining minds and bodies in more rigorous penal systems.[13] The reality of ancien régime criminal justice was considerably more complicated, however. As we will see, the king's ordinary courts in fact relied on a broad panoply of punishments, of which afflictive punishment was only one element.

In the same year that Foucault's work appeared, Douglas Hay, in *Albion's Fatal Tree,* emphasized the extent to which English criminal law and the courts were used to uphold the rule of property owners. The law, he argued, was useful in reinforcing "bonds of obedience and deference, in legitimizing the status quo, in constantly recreating the structure of authority which arose from property and in turn protected its interests." Hay identified three principal ideological functions of the law, those of majesty, justice, and mercy, all of which he argued were placed in the service of the ruling class and of property.[14] E. P. Thompson later tempered that view, noting that the law in turn imposed restraints on the propertied classes' abuses of the courts. "The essential precondition for the effectiveness of law, in its function as ideology, is that it shall display an independence from gross manipulation and shall seem to be just," he pointed out. "It cannot seem to be so without upholding its own logic and criteria of equity; indeed, on occasion, by actually *being* just."[15]

The gradual accumulation of empirical knowledge in recent decades about how law actually functioned in early modern communities suggests that we should move even further away from reification of the law. Law reveals itself in ordinary courts to be the expression of multiple powers and multiple interests, and not simply the expression of a unitary sovereign or a single abstract class. In the courts of upper Normandy, there can be no doubt that broadly construed, the property-holding and tax-paying classes were the principal beneficiaries of law. Furthermore, legal procedure channeled conflicts into disputes between individuals and families; it did not allow space for the expression of broad social grievances against classes, institutions, or the state. But this did not prevent law from being regularly used as a form of dialogue, a means of advancement, a weapon of choice, or a tool of survival by many other individuals, classes, and orders in the community. Judges and prosecutors recognized these wider functions of the courts, and within their broad mandate of order allowed many other practices and forms of justice to invade the written codes. There was not one law in France, but rather many overlapping sources of law, custom, equity, and tradition that provided room for ordinary people to maneuver.

Yet because of the broader political functions of royal laws, criminal defendants in early modern Europe risked significant penalties for what modern courts might deem misdemeanors, lesser felonies, or acts outside of criminal jurisdiction entirely. There is no question that criminal procedure in France enhanced those risks. Criminal procedure was inquisitorial procedure and had become more so from the sixteenth century. In 1539, the Ordinance of Villers-Cotterêts formally denied counsel to most defendants. The Criminal Ordinance of 1670, which strengthened the admissibility of hearsay in criminal proceedings, disallowed counsel in those few cases in which it had previously been allowed. Even contemporary jurists found much to denounce in the protocols. Criminal defendants were not only denied legal counsel, but they were also formally left in the dark about both the charges and the identity of the witnesses until a late stage of the trial. Moreover, defendants in capital cases who could not be convicted on testimony of two eyewitnesses, and who refused to confess, could be subjected to the *question préparatoire,* that is, judicial torture (see appendix C).

But numerous studies in recent years have demonstrated that the full penalties of the law fell on only a small portion of those convicted of criminal offenses and on an even smaller portion of those initially charged with a crime. In the Bordeaux region, Julius Ruff found that only 12 percent of criminal cases ended in conviction. Only 5 percent of defendants were convicted in cases that were privately prosecuted by the plaintiff. Moreover, nearly a third of those convicted in capital cases fled the jurisdiction before execution. Conviction rates in other local courts in Normandy ranged from about 8 to 21 percent.[16] The reasons were both legal and social. The lack of a police force or forensic science made it difficult to provide sufficient proof against many malefactors; the ease with which some defendants fled flimsy jails or rural jurisdictions kept others out of court; and the willingness of judges and prosecutors to use their wide discretion in charging and sentencing yielded noncorporal penalties for other defendants.

Moreover, the Ordinance of 1670 allowed judges to assign lesser convictions and penalties in those capital cases that lacked two eyewitnesses or a confession. Torture was no longer necessary to bring in a verdict and assign a penalty, since defendants could be found guilty of a lesser charge. As John H. Langbein and Julius Ruff have pointed out, this virtually eliminated use of the question préparatoire in local courts roughly a century before its formal abolition in 1780.[17] As will be seen below, the number of executions in capital cases was also unexpectedly small, given the reputation of old-regime justice.

This still left criminal suspects at the mercy of the competency or temperament of local magistrates, however. French bailiwick judges, like English J. P.s, "always laid emphasis on some aspects of the law and overlooked others, tackling a limited number of problems with periodic bouts of enthusiasm."[18] The Ordinance of 1670, which revised criminal procedure, had relatively little effect in standardizing outcomes. As Albert Hamscher has noted, judges "retained great discretionary power in determining what constituted a crime and its appropriate punishment,"[19] so the accused ran different risks before different magistrates. This could work both for and against defendants in early modern courts. Yet overall, the most severe punishments in bailiwick courts were reserved for a particular segment of the population: the gens sans aveu, vagabonds or repeat offenders who were considered moral or geographic outsiders to the settled population.

Crimes and Misdemeanors: Cauchois Criminal Records

The traditional distinction between vol/violence, theft and violence, first elaborated by Pierre Chaunu, posited a dramatic change in criminal activity over the course of the seventeenth and eighteenth centuries. Violent crimes, Chanu argued in tandem with Bernadette Boutelet, were overtaken by property crimes such as robbery and fraud.[20] But the idea that the birth of capitalism is reflected in the shift from attacks on persons to attacks on property has come under sustained debate in recent decades. V. A. C. Gatrell has argued that if anything, "it was the law that changed most visibly as a prelude to industrialization, and not the practices, needs or identities of those who most commonly broke it."[21] Or as Yves Castan suggested in his earlier work on honesty, it can be entirely misleading to argue from ancien régime criminal statistics alone, unless they are paired with substantial textual analysis.[22]

The attempt to categorize crimes in the Caux is clouded by the simple fact that property disputes were so often the proximate cause of violent acts. Property disputes were the single largest common denominator in violent criminal complaints in the Caux, including disputes over inheritances and boundaries, usage rights, debts, trespassing, and theft of animals, tools, or money. Family disputes, which strongly overlapped with property issues, were a second common denominator; alcohol and honor were the common solvents. This escalation from civil to criminal complaints seen in the Caux was far from unusual in the province. Alain Margot's study of the Norman bailliage of Mamers also pointed out the property context of many crimes: they were the single largest source of violence, accounting for approximately one-third of all violent crimes. Of lesser frequency were attacks fueled by alcohol, honor, vengeance, official malfeasance, or other causes.[23]

A typical constellation of civil conflicts that suddenly turned brutal burst like an afternoon thunderstorm in the late summer of 1727 near Cany-Caniel. The labitureur Guillaume LeFevre and his son Guillaume were traveling with their cart and plow on a small road that crossed the Sieur de Graville's property. Adrien d'Iel, a noble *escuyer* and the sieur de Graville, attempted to turn back two peasants crossing his property boundaries. Enraged, the men began raining blows on d'Iel. A neighboring farm wife who was out searching for her pastured animals came running to d'Iel's defense. She found the men maltreating the petty noble with "blows from a lever and mallet," then pummeling him with their fists while he lay on the ground.

Marie (whose last name is lost) staunchly kicked the younger LeFevre in the stomach, but he recovered and chased her down. The court surgeon François Pelle found Marie "very incommoded and gravely wounded" after the attack. Both laboureurs fled the jurisdiction before sentencing, but Judge Bréard awarded the sieur 200 livres from their seized property, and the village woman 100 livres for her pains.[24] As in many such cases, violence erupted from a rural recipe of confused property rights, disputed traditions of usage, class conflicts, family loyalties, and the daily frictions of neighbors who knew each other only too well. The boiling point was never far away in the village, with a civil stew such as this always on the back burner.

Violent behavior over property was not solely the province of the bailiwick's commoners. François Toustain, a nobleman and the sieur de Fulton, protested to Judge Cabot before the bench of Cany-Caniel that he had been menaced and gravely injured by his brother Adrien Toustain, also noble and a sieur of Anglesqueville. François Toustain was the inheritor of his late aunt Marie Magdalen Toustain's mobile property, and he had ridden up to his brother's house one day to take possession of her legacy. He was soundly beaten by the entire household, including his brother and the domestics. Judge Cabot considered Adrien Toustain's threat to the plaintiff's life so genuine that he ordered out several cavaliers of the maréchaussée on horseback to take possession of Marie Magdalen Toustain's goods. The Punch-and-Judy conclusion of their story, however, was just the criminal tip of a civil iceberg. The Toustain brothers had left a long trail of civil litigation behind them before escalating to blows. The two petty nobles had judgments dating back more than six months from Judge Cabot at Cany-Caniel and from the appellate court of the Parlement of Rouen, upholding François Toustain's claim.[25]

Family, like property, was another flash point for conflict in the parishes and towns of the Caux. Nicole Castan's work in the early 1970s on family criminality in Toulouse identified the ways in which violent crimes erupted out of the family milieu, born of its deep dependencies and sharp stresses.[26] In Normandy, even the officers of the ordinary courts were arraigned before the bench for their disorderly family disputes. The court sergeant François Racine was among the visitors to the wrong side of the criminal tribunal for domestic violence. His neighbor Robert Davoult deposed that he was walking home from his barn one day when he heard a cry of "Thief!" and saw Racine dragging his mother by the hair to the end of their house. Another witness testified that they had seen him threaten his mother with a knife in the kitchen, although modesty prevented the witness from repeating Racine's curses. On a third occasion, Racine's sister was trying to escape his assault by fleeing up a staircase, when his mother grabbed her son from behind. He struck his mother in the head with a musket, sending her to the surgeon for a plaster. Racine admitted to the judge that he and his parents had had a few disputes in the past. He had separated from his family for a time, and since they had prevented him from taking his thread and linen with him, he had clambered into the house through a window and a fight ensued. But after all, he argued, he had come back to live with his parents in good harmony afterward.[27]

Apart from family and property, alcohol was perhaps the most frequent culprit in village disturbances. One night the maréchaussée captured two shoemakers from Hocqueville after they fled toward their family home in the Lyons Forest to avoid being drawn into the militia. At eight in the evening, the escort of cavaliers and their captives stopped at an inn to drink "several cups" of cider. At three in the morning, the emboldened and drunk shoemaker Mottin sent the innkeeper to fetch a glass of eau de vie. He then grabbed a cavalier's musket from beside the fireplace and shot him in the chest at close quarters. The court surgeon was taken aback by the violence of the scene when he viewed the cavalier Frebourg laid out before the fireplace in his red coat and brown culottes, his chest and lungs entirely laid open.[28] Although the murder was made more complex by the addition of the feared militia, the setting of alcohol and taverns was entirely typical of many disputes. "While drinking at the fair"[29] was the musical prelude to many prosecutions at the petty assizes.

In criminal litigation, as in civil, the plaintiffs were the lead engine of justice; inhabitants of the bailiwick filed suit without the participation of the public prosecutor in nearly three-quarters of criminal cases. Charles Hauthorn, a shepherd from Cany, brought suit when he was ambushed and insulted at supper in the cabaret by a disguised laboureur and his four valets. Two months later he filed suit again when the same laboureur attacked him in the sheepfold, and he won 25 livres from the culprit. He was almost certainly supported in his suit by his master Adrien Anquetil, who may have been engaged in a proxy feud with the attacker.[30]

Townspeople and villagers naturally used the normal social mechanisms of seventeenth- and eighteenth-century communities to influence magistrates' interpretations of law and justice. The judge's inclinations could be shaped by case precedents set in the bailiwick or in neighboring jurisdictions, by employers or patrons interceding on behalf of the accused, by social rank, by gender, or by simple bribery. This sometimes left a wide gateway open for local corruption of the judicial process. As we have seen in the Norman bailliage of Pont-Audemer, officers expected gifts of fruit, salmon, and wine from middling defendants, and favorable land leases and cash from sieurs in more serious trouble.[31] On a more benign level, however, the system allowed judges to take into account the reputation and past behavior of plaintiffs and defendants in judging cases. These were a traditional part of jurisprudence. As a local judge circulated in the taverns and church, in his chambers, and among his circle of friends and dependents, the roomy authority in sentencing left to him by the king's law could quickly be invaded by other opinions and influences in the community.

Tailoring Judgments to Fit the Community: Reducing the Charges, Composition, and Discretionary Sentencing

Despite royal theories on deterrence through swift and sometimes cruel punishment, it is crucial to remember that these state powers were often exercised differently in practice in French bailiwick and seigneurial courts than in the imaginations of jurists or ministers. Propertied villagers, townspeople, officers, and judges wielded considerable control over who would be prosecuted, who convicted, and who actually punished. Many of these mechanisms are already familiar to us from the previous chapter's discussion of civil cases, including private accommodation or arbitration of disputes as well as equity judgments.

In the criminal realm, three additional mechanisms of judicial discretion deserve special mention here. The first of these were composition and restitution, or the settlement of criminal grievances through monetary amends rather than corporal punishment. (Technically, "composition" referred to monetary damages for bodily harm and restitution to damages for financial harm, but they were sometimes used interchangeably.) The second mechanism was discretionary sentencing, which was a near absolute right of French magistrates in all but the most serious cases. It is rather surprising to remember that early modern France had neither a penal code nor mandatory sentencing, except for recommended sentences in cas royaux. Even then judges were not required to carry out those recommendations.

The third power was the ability of judges or king's prosecutors to reduce the charges in a case in order to impose an appropriate punishment for a crime, especially when the consequences of convicting on the highest charges seemed draconian. Convicting on lesser charges allowed judges to exercise their highest function, distributing justice, and not merely carry out their administrative function, enforcing the law. This was common procedure in other European states. In Spain, one historian found that in more than half of criminal cases, the charges were reduced, and the plaintiff settled for a lesser fine.[32] It also allowed judges to take into consideration the larger good of public order and stability. Prominent among these considerations was the economic goal of keeping whole families from falling into poverty and becoming a charge on the parish when an able-bodied adult was thrown out of work.

Composition of cases enjoyed a long history in France. Some observers have argued that in fact two competing forms of criminal justice were practiced in early modern Europe, the punitive and the restitutive. The king's justice under this formulation was punitive, meting out corporal punishment and discipline on the guilty party, whereas the village's justice was restitutive, or focused on making the victim whole. Composition or restitution from the responsible party to the victim was a signature of settlements in ancient customary justice and a feature of all tribal European law codes. Punitive justice, on the other hand, was an expression of sovereignty, of the crown's power over the bodies and actions of its subjects. According to this theory, they were two distinct systems of justice within the European context, and the replacement of restitution by punitive penalties was a sure sign of growing sovereignty.

Sentencing patterns across the Cauchois courtrooms, however, quickly blur any sharp distinctions between community and royal punishment. Bailiwick judges and prosecutors almost invariably required financial or in-kind restitution to the victim alongside any physical punishments they might impose. Recent work on Burgundian seigneurial courts by Jeremy Hayhoe has also shown that restitution was commonly awarded to ordinary litigants "because judges agreed with them on how to treat minor crimes over property and reputation."[33] At the same time, lesser corporal punishments such as confinement in the stocks were handed out freely by the crown courts. Yet these lesser punitive sentences apparently met with the approval of much of the community. Bruce Lenman and Geoffrey Parker have argued for other European countries that Emile Durkheim's notion of a transition from restitutive to punitive law "will have to be abandoned,"[34] and the local courts of Normandy support the same analysis for France.

The marriage of punitive and restitutive justice was brought home to a starving Cauchois villager named Pierre Planage. In early spring 1693, Planage was arrested and charged with stealing wheat from the granary of Anthoine Martin, the baker of Grainville-la-Teinturière. Planage's theft was especially serious because of the famine raging through the Caux, which had already led to fearsome mortality. Every measure of grain the villager had stolen was bread taken from the mouths of his neighbors, and his theft raised the specter of grain riots or pillaging for public authorities. It was these aggravating factors that led the king's prosecutor to recommend the kinds of punishment usually reserved for repeat offenders or violent criminals. From a modern perspective the penalties seem both grim and excessive.

Yet the prosecutor for the jurisdiction, the ambitious young attorney Robert Maribrasse, asked for no extraordinary corporal punishments for the single culprit who had been caught. Planage's corporal sentence was to be publicly exhibited in the square on market day for three hours, with a placard labeled "wheat thief" hung about his neck. The sentence further banished him from the province for nine years. But Maribrasse asked the judge to sentence Planage's two accomplices to the far more dangerous penalty of the king's galleys. This, he knew, was a sentence unlikely to be meted out, since both men had fled the jurisdiction before trial. All three men were further condemned to make restitution to the court and to the miller, with a judgment of 100 livres each in amends. The court's sentence was a studied blend of restitution and public humiliation, topped off with a severe galley sentence for the two culprits who were already beyond reach.[35] The punishment was a stern warning to imitators and ensured that Planage and his accomplices would steer clear of the bailiwick. But it stopped far short of bringing the full force of the law to bear on the starving grain thief who had been caught. Both state justice and community considerations had been served by the ruling.

Sentencing was one of the most powerful tools wielded by early modern magistrates, and one that allowed them to tailor judgments to fit the community's expectations as well as their king's or seigneurs' demands. An early modern magistrate's panoply of options was far greater than that of modern judges: monetary amends, public humiliation, corporal discipline (including the pillory, flogging, or branding), banishment, galley service, or death formed the standard repertoire. The last three sentences, the most severe options, included the penalty of *mort civile*. This was aptly called "civil death"; it made the convicted ineligible to act in a civil capacity, including making a will, entering into contracts, or holding office. Depending on the province, those under *mort civile* could also have their property seized.

Incarceration, however, was a much less common punishment. Local jails were neither designed nor intended for long-term captivity. In France as in England, rural jails were largely reserved for prisoners awaiting trial, drunk-and-disorderlies in the lockup for the night, vagrants, or debtors.[36] The ruinous state of most French jails (and the incompetence of their jailers) was endemic. Crumbling buildings lacking barred windows; jailers who took the post only for the lodging it provided; and the temptations of bribery, which led many jailers to liberate their charges, made jails a poor choice for long-term punishment. In Brittany, as one historian has noted, the average sénéchaussée court held only ten prisoners a year.[37] Able-bodied men and women were expected to work. On the whole, bailiwick and seigneurial judges tended to favor public humiliation and monetary amends for lesser delicts and banishment for greater misdeeds, as the court did for Pierre Planage. As Julius Ruff has pointed out, magistrates at the local level generally used their discretion in sentencing "not so much to inflict brutal punishments as to exclude criminals from society."[38]

Where judges and prosecutors were most likely to cast a severe eye on culprits were in cases of repeat offenders who threatened the order-keeping classes of laboureurs, masters, and merchants in the district. François Saumon was sentenced to death by hanging in the présidial court of Caudebec for stealing 156 livres worth of wood near the parish of Valmont. But Saumon had a long rap sheet before the day of his death sentence. He was also convicted of stealing wheat from his master, the miller of Crasville; slipping 6 écus from a sleeping victim on the road to Saint-Vaast; assaulting a sieur; and filching 700 livres from a rope maker in Anglesqueville. Saumon had developed a network of female fences in Saint-Vaast who concealed and later sold his takings, one of the more common occupations of female criminals. In short, he had graduated from an opportunistic thief on the high road to a professional criminal. Insubordination to his master, vagrancy, and assault made him seem a genuinely threatening figure to the middling sorts of property exploiters who dominated the courts in the community.[39]

Saumon's case reminds us that concerns about order and security were not confined to the state and royal agents alone. As Robert M. Schwartz has demonstrated, the slowly growing effectiveness of police measures in eighteenth-century Normandy was partly a response to the real concern of settled society about rising numbers of vagabonds, beggars, and the poor in general. Both crown and rural society were thus united by a "common concern to preserve public security."[40] Other Continental and English criminal studies in recent years have also mitigated the impression of an absolutist judiciary, delivering punishment to defenseless or uncooperative subjects.[41] Despite the very real uses of torture and corporal punishment in certain types of cases, justice was neither so bloodthirsty nor so divorced from the needs of the community as its unsavory reputation suggests. Or as J. A. Sharpe put it for England, rural and village justice probably did well enough, "given contemporary expectations of what law enforcement might have been about."[42]

When local justice failed, however, the community occasionally went over the heads of local magistrates to prosecute offenders. When villagers in the high justice of Brionne felt the judge had not sufficiently punished a marauding sergeant at the petty assizes, they appealed the case to the Parlement. The accusers caught the attention of the crown prosecutor by charging the culprit with the heinous crime of dismembering his illegitimate child and throwing the body into a well. Dozens of witnesses then appeared to give testimony about his more plausible acts of violence, theft, and official misconduct in the neighborhood. By the time the trial ended, more than three dozen villagers and officers had participated in the case.[43] Yet only in rare circumstances like this one, or in the final rash of Norman sorcery cases dating from the last decade of the seventeenth century and the first decade of the eighteenth, did the Parlement or the crown intercede in local sentencing.[44]

Perhaps the most dramatic evidence of a magistrate's discretionary sentencing powers and the community's influence comes from the death penalty. The paucity of convictions and executions for capital crimes in upper Normandy is striking, particularly given the greater likelihood that trial records would be preserved in such cases. The high justice of Grainville-la-Teinturière had always held the right to condemn to death, the more so as it was a court of one of the most powerful ducal families in France, the Longuevilles. Yet the case of Marin LeRouge, discussed below, is the only existing death sentence in seventy years of records from 1622 to 1692–and the sentence was only carried out *en contumace,* by hanging a straw effigy of the offender in the village square. Although there are serious gaps in the early seventeenth-century registers for the court, enough records remain to indicate that such sentences would have been rare. Moreover, this low rate of executions was well known to the parlementaires of the sovereign court, since all capital convictions were automatically appealed to their court. It was also well known to the crown, which complained repeatedly about the failure of local courts to pursue serious crimes. The intendant's *statistique criminelle* in the eighteenth century attempted to force lower courts to track crimes and prosecutions, but to no avail (see chapter 5).

Other jurisdictions in Normandy, Brittany, Burgundy, and Bordeaux displayed the same reluctance to impose or execute capital punishment as well. Marie-Madeleine Champin's study of the Norman bailliage of Alençon from 1715 to 1745 uncovered ten capital punishment convictions in nine hundred criminal cases, of which seven convicts were sentenced to hang and three were condemned to the wheel. But records indicate that only four of the ten condemned were in fact executed. The capital punishment rate was thus 0.4 percent for all convicted criminals over a thirty-year period.[45] Ian Cameron and Julius Ruff have turned up a wide variety of penalties, often favoring exclusion from the jurisdiction or province, in both sénéchaussée and maréchaussée courts in Bordeaux, Guyenne, and Auvergne. Cameron noted that even those convicted in the quasi-military maréchaussée courts suffered "bewilderingly diverse" punishments, of which death was reserved for only a hardened few.[46] Although these statistics were of no comfort to those actually hanged or decapitated (or, in particularly infamous cases, drawn and quartered, broken on the wheel, or burned at the stake), most convicts faced lesser punishments. English courts used a different mechanism to arrive at the same result. Juries showed themselves deeply reluctant to bring in a conviction on many of the new eighteenth-century charges that carried mandatory death sentences, feeling that the punishment was too draconian even when the evidence of guilt seemed overwhelming.[47]

The strong feelings stirred by capital punishment were reflected in public treatment of the *bourreau,* the executioner. Perhaps no figure besides a military conscriptor or a sorcerer excited so much public revulsion in the bailiwicks. Unlike jailers, executioners were a privileged corps in France. They enjoyed explicit financial rights and considered themselves members of a skilled trade. Until the middle of the eighteenth century, executioners were granted a *droit de havage* from the king, or the right to take a portion of the grains and other produce in the sold in market each week. But communities often forced the bourreau to take his measure of grain from the sacks with a long-handled spoon, to prevent him from touching the food.[48] The king had to issue repeated arrêts to prevent children and adults from running after the bourreau in the markets and streets with insults. Even the executioners' families were condemned to virtual endogamy, since no trade would intermarry with them, and few trades would accept their children as apprentices. The intendant of Rouen called these royal tradesmen in death the "victims of a widespread prejudice that would be impossible to destroy."[49]

By the eighteenth century, the bourreaux had so little business that they were in danger of extinction until the Revolution revived their fortunes. In the province of Brittany, only thirteen people were condemned to death in the thirty-one years before the Revolution. The architect of the Parlement of Rennes, Joseph-Anne le Compte, stated that the scaffold in the Place des Lices had fallen into such miserable disrepair that the executioner couldn't vouch for its functioning.[50] Because of their special relationship with the crown through their droits, executioners were the only occupational group in the local courts that had a connection with the royal intendants. In Normandy during the eighteenth century, they petitioned the intendants to rescue them from financial ruin when the droits were reduced and their business declined. The crown in return seemed to recognize a certain responsibility to these artisans in death, apparently shunned as a foreign body by the regular court system and the parlements alike.

The key role played by local communities and officers in carrying out the death penalty raises important questions about sovereignty in the ancien régime. Jean Bodin had stated in 1576 that the power to condemn to death was the "highest mark of sovereignty."[51] In 1681, John Locke emphasized in his *Second Treatise on Government* that the right to inflict the death penalty was synonymous with sovereign power. "Political power," he remarked, "I take to be a right of making laws with penalties of death."[52] In France, both seigneurs haut justiciers and royal magistrates had always recognized death as a power explicitly derived from their king, not from feudal tenure or from the ordinary prerogatives of judicial office. Only the king could create a high justice with the right to inflict the death penalty, an authority that French kings continued to exercise with only occasional usurpation until the Revolution.[53] But the symbolic power of the gibbet cast a far longer shadow than the actual executions that took place there.

The reasons for the French judiciary's recoiling from execution may be very complex. From the state's perspective, convicted criminals could be more useful rowing in the king's galleys than hanging from the king's gallows. There is indeed a strong inclination toward impressment as punishment for all types of male criminals in the Parlement's Tournelle records.[54] Practically speaking, the galleys were merely a form of slow execution.

From the perspective of a local magistrate, a disappearance was often as good as a hanging. Banishment from the province or galley service had two obvious benefits: it removed the culprit from the jurisdiction, and it usually allowed his or her property to be seized for amends or transferred to family members under the presumption of mort civile. From the community's perspective, the network of solidarities and family relations were not torn apart by the shame and violence of a public hanging, however much they might have been rent by the condemnation and disappearance of a villager.

Wagging Tongues, Open Eyes: Testifying and Hearsay in Court

The sights and sounds of the village and town were preserved in the collective memory of the inhabitants. Their ideas about reputation, honor, guilt, and justice, and their willingness to bear witness to it all, were the seemingly evanescent material that made up the whole backbone of the ancien régime court system. In a world with little access to scientific evidence, few police in the modern sense, and an enormous volume of oral contracts and agreements, witnessing and rumor were the foundations of justice. Their importance was emphasized in the Criminal Code of 1670, which affirmed that rumor was admissible evidence in criminal cases. As Champin has stated, "the practice of witnessing constitutes the foundation and the condition of judicial operations."[55] Through the simple act of witnessing, villagers wielded surprising amounts of control over what kinds of royal laws, customary codes, and seigneurial privileges could actually be executed in the countryside.

The importance of witnessing can be readily found in cases concerning the forest and game laws, the source of a perpetual cat-and-mouse contest between authorities and villagers. The medieval Normans have been censured for developing some of the harshest game laws in Europe, which the Anglo-Norman kings passed on to the English.[56] Although France's seventeenth-century hunting laws never approached the terrifying rigor of the English Black Act of 1723, which made poaching a capital offense (and which was seldom enforced to the letter in any case),[57] hunting rights remained a potent symbol of lordship. They were also a constant temptation to the poor and the hungry. Yet the relatively few who were caught and convicted were not always vagrants or paupers. Among them were substantial men in the community, including millers, laboureurs, or even artisans. They were men with a taste for wild game and sometimes a firm belief that the lords had usurped their natural right to fish and hunt in the countryside. As Roger B. Manning noted, poaching could be a potent kind of "political protest and covert discourse" with local lords or authorities.[58]

For the witnesses too, testifying at the assizes could become a political act as well as a legal one. Their decision about whether to participate in the trial defined which privileges and laws could actually be enforced, and against which inhabitants, since the culprit was seldom caught by officers in flagrante delicto. In desperation, the crown or seigneurial court could resort to the publication of monitoires to force witnesses to come forward. Read out on three successive Sundays by the parish priest, monitoires threatened villagers with excommunication if they failed to report evidence in a case.[59] (Bailiwick courts were sometimes reluctant to publish monitoires, because the widespread popular belief that monitoires would bring hail in their train created panic). The dire nature of the threat indicates how central community witnessing was to the capture and punishment of malefactors. It also allows us to gauge the stubborn resistance of the community to cooperating in certain prosecutions, if only the threat of eternal damnation was deemed sufficient to move them.

Witnessing in the well of the court, like gossip outside of court, was thus one of the inhabitants' most important tools for policing the community according to their own notions of justice. But we are often left to speculate about the expression of popular politics in misdemeanors such as poaching and woodcutting, or in the refusal to bear witness. Early modern courts were little concerned about the interior motives or private feelings of suspects, and their interrogations seldom waded into the muddy waters of psychology. Indeed, judges and lawyers often seem lamentably incurious to us, accustomed as we are to modern legal voyeurism. Their different construction of the self as an individual agent, moreover, made it unlikely that seventeenth- and early eighteenth-century actors would describe their acts in the ways we might expect them to.[60] Nevertheless, there is a strong undercurrent of civil disobedience to acts that were commonly committed against seigneurial privileges and some royal laws by settled members of the community. The court records are full of fortuitous information about daily life, including the surprising number of illegal firearms in the bailiwick. Although commoners who were not part of the courts were not supposed to have guns (having no legal use for them), court cases tell us incidentally that a good number of peasants had an old fowling-piece or arquebus proudly mounted above the fireplace.[61] Neither the king nor the seigneur, it seemed, had an absolute monopoly on force.

We can be more certain in saying that these unlawful acts assumed life-or-death importance in the lean years, which were not uncommon in the seventeenth century. The year 1685 had been terrible in the Caux, but the summer of 1692 was fraught with harbingers of an even more devastating mortality in France. The harvest was poor, and that which followed in 1693 was catastrophic. Men, women, and children of the district were eating acorns and grass by the early fall, and illness and famine swept in with

November. During the killing winter of 1693–94, the parish curé in Saint-Vaast-Dieppedalle buried sixty-six members of his flock, in a village that counted well under two hundred taxable hearths.[62] Poaching was no longer political or even recreational; it was sheer survival.

In the unlucky case that the culprit was caught in the act by the seigneur's forest guard, the court expenses could be staggering. When the butcher Pierre Lecoustre was caught stealing wood from the copse of the marquis d'Houdetot and dragged into the seigneurial court of Grainville-la-Teinturière during the first hard winter of 1692, the expenses rained down on him. He was condemned to pay the forest guard Jean Bréant 30 sols for his testimony and for losing half a day's work, 50 livres to the judges, and twenty-nine other fees for various documents and officers involved in the trial. The expenses were then "moderated" to 47 livres. This was more than a hundred times the cost of a bundle of wood in the Caux, which then sold for about 4 to 8 sols.[63]

But many of the complaints made by seigneurial agents to the courts about anonymous poachers were abandoned for lack of evidence. The villagers' legal tactic of refusing to produce witnesses often carried the day, even under the threat of excommunication by parish *monitoires*. In March 1693, a few months after Lecoustre's conviction for pilfering wood, the marquis de Cany, Pierre de Becdelièvre II, sent his agent up to the high justice of Grainville-la-Teinturière. His agent complained to the judge, Pierre Alexandre, about numerous thefts of timber and illegal hunting and fishing in the marquis' handsome woods, which stood on the heights overlooking the village. His complaints indicated that far more than the usual number of villagers were turning to the underground economy of nature to survive the famine. The veteran judge and his lieutenant duly noted the abuses, and fingered three men from the outlying parish of Bosville for a single case of rabbit poaching. The other charges conveniently dropped out of sight for lack of witnesses.[64]

Failure to find witnesses for many of the infractions may have been convenient for village authorities in Grainville, too. From a public-order perspective, theft of natural resources from the woods was in many ways preferable to the theft of property from other villagers, or to the rioting that shortly broke out in the streets of Rouen during the famine.[65] This was not an entirely far-fetched scenario, even in the rural parishes of the Caux. In 1775, the inhabitants of Grainville-la-Teinturière would sack the bakeries of the village in a bread riot.[66] Grain and bread riots were perhaps the most endemic form of disturbance in early modern Europe. Rural areas of Brittany experienced them in the early seventeenth century, and city governments across Europe made control of the grain supply one of their top priorities.[67] For English J. P.s, it was both a "duty" and a "public expectation" that they would prevent famine.[68] Subsistence, as one historian has pointed out, "was the precondition of social order."[69] Ultimately, the maintenance of order was a higher charge for a seigneurial judge than protecting his lord's individual privileges.

Community silence protected the majority of the marquis' trespassers, but community indignation sank the poachers of Bosville. On April 2, five witnesses appeared before Judge Alexandre's bench, including a tanner, an artisan, a domestic, the priest of Bosville, and a minor. The thirty-eight-year-old priest testified that in August he had heard three hunters–Pierre Jacques Filu, Charles Doré, and François Manouay–heading into the woods with their fowling pieces to hunt rabbits. The cleric heard shots being fired, then saw his parishioners emerge with game that he thought belonged to the marquis. Two of the witnesses, including the artisan Denis Monnaud from Grainville, testified that they had seen the trio hunting in the woods again during Holy Week. The culprits ran out of the forest with rabbits, boasting that they had shot them "to make paté for Easter."[70] The parishioners had spent a pleasurable day hunting game in the woods during Lent, when everyone else was expected to eat sparingly. Perhaps the delectable smell drifting out of the kitchen was simply too much for their neighbors. The community gave the paté makers their comeuppance in court, where it was reinforced with heavy fines.

Here we have a likely example of Hughes Neveux's maxim that villagers often tried different grievances in the courts from those their judges thought were being tried there. Royal and customary laws had an "exterior function," that of legitimizing internal village complaints before the external circle of public authorities.[71] The courts allowed villagers to frame their private grievances as affronts to published law codes, to seigneurial rights, or to the king's authority. Neveux's assertion, however, that French peasants appealed to the king as the fount of law, as opposed to German peasants, who appealed to local custom, does not hold true for the courts of Normandy. Although pleaders did have a sense of the king as the ultimate fount of justice and pardons, virtually all of their appeals to the court are framed by the customs or by traditional rights or practices.[72] Only in exceptionally rare cases was the king or royal law invoked in the court records at all.

Paradoxically, the inhabitants' ability to prosecute according to their own notions of justice depended on their knowledge of the official law and of court procedures. The witnesses in the paté makers' case provided corroboration that fitted with the several rules governing proof, including the number of witnesses needed to establish different facts in the case. Other cases show witnesses' shrewd grasp of written laws, religious injunctions, and the pervasive concern with order among local authorities. Curé Jean Noel arrived at the tavern assizes of the royal bailiwick court one July with thirteen witnesses in tow to testify against the cabaret keeper and the miller in Grainville-la-Teinturière. At Judge Rousselet's bench he described the scandalous behavior of the taverner, who kept the cabaret open on Sundays during mass "against the edicts" and allowed it to remain open "throughout the night . . . against the police [and] the public repose, and at the same time occasioning unfortunate accidents." The curé asked the king's prosecutor to use the "authority which the king has confided in you to reprimand these abuses and scandals." (This was, interestingly, one of the few recorded instances in the Cauchois records in which a petitioner invoked the king's name).

The crux of Noel's complaint, however, was against the village miller. The curé described how the miller had drunk during the entire night from Friday to Saturday, then stumbled into mass "full of wine" and shouting impieties during special prayers for good weather. But his most impassioned statement to the court laid out his parishioner's economic offenses against the community. The village miller, accused Noel, was "too fat with the blood of the poor people, whom he robs every day." Among the thirteen witnesses against the miller were five women who were forced to grind grain in his mill to feed their families. He leased his business from their seigneur, the marquis de Cany, who held the right of the ban de moulin for the entire seigneurie. Here we can see the enormous resourcefulness of the village in using royal edicts, religious laws, and arguments about public order dear to a magistrate's ears to punish a very different sort of offense against the community.[73]

Despite the tantalizing difficulties posed by early modern records in defining exactly what villagers and townspeople in the bailiwick courts meant by "justice," there is ample evidence that their notion was sophisticated, flexible, and pragmatic. Justice was deeper than written law and was expressed in far more settings than in the assize sessions. Among the more literate classes, for example, we find a dame making a clear distinction between written law and abstract justice before the bailiwick court at Longueville. She explained to the assize judge that she had gone to visit an adversary, hoping to appeal to his sense of justice, "but instead was forced to go to law."[74] This larger meaning of justice was informed by religious narratives, proverbs, customary laws, local traditions, and a broad notion of equity. The precise definition might differ greatly depending on class or occupation, yet villagers and townspeople of almost all classes seemed able to engage in the common argument about what was just and equitable. As David Sabean has noted for German communities, this did not imply that the community agreed on matters, but that they were "engaged in the same argument, the same raisonnement, the same *Rede*."[75]

L'affaire LeRouge: A Case Study in Community Justice

A few seconds before he was shot point blank by a royal sergeant from Grainville-la-Teinturière in 1692, the weaver Marin LeRouge uttered his last words about the law. "You cannot take men by force," witnesses recalled him saying.[76] LeRouge had been a bystander in a civil drama that had been unfolding in the Caux village of Saint-Vaast-Dieppedalle over the course of several months. Anne Grandcourt, the daughter of the prosperous laboureur Pierre Grandcourt, had become pregnant by her fiancé, the weaver Nicolas LeFromager. But the fickle Nicolas had his priest post the banns of marriage to another woman on the doors of the parish church. On the last day of May 1692, Pierre and Anne Grandcourt announced a clameur de haro against Nicolas to prevent the marriage.[77] Grandcourt père rounded up two heavily armed royal sergeants, Jean Huezé of Cany and Jacques Lefrançois of Canville, and two minor court functionaries, Richard LeMarchand and Jaques LeMaistre. Together with Anne Grandcourt, the men hunted down the reluctant fiancé. In hot pursuit of LeFromager across his family farm, Huezé collared him hiding in the fossé, a typical Norman hedgerow planted with trees. At his shouts, LeFromager's neighbor Marin LeRouge, a forty-two-year-old fellow weaver, rushed to his aid. As the men stood wrestling at the top of the hedgerow of the quiet Caux village, Marin LeRouge shouted out his surprisingly legalistic objection to the sergeants who had arrived without a court warrant. Sergeant Jacques Lefrançois ran up with a pistol in each hand, and replied with lead shot. In an instant LeRouge lay dead, with royal ammunition in his head.

The homicide of Marin LeRouge could be read simply as a tale of ancien règime police brutality, a miscarriage of justice that resulted in the death of an innocent villager. But if we look more attentively, an entirely distinct story begins to unfold from the trial documents and parish records. From the raising of a civil clameur by a peasant, through the phases of testimony, sentencing, and punishment, the fingerprints of the village community were everywhere in the records of *l'affaire* LeRouge. The temperamental outburst that took the life of a village weaver was an unexpected twist in a routine civil matter, one where justice went fatally wrong. But it was an outburst that momentarily lights up the darkness of these often laconic records and allows us to see inside the complex workings of village justice.

From the outset, the LeRouge case was set in motion by village dynamics and legal strategies. Sergeants Jacques Lefrançois and Jean Huezé were not acting on a bench warrant from the royal or seigneurial judge in pursuing Nicolas LeFromager.[78] They were instead responding to a popular clameur de haro raised by a peasant villager, the laboureur Pierre Grandcourt, on behalf of his pregnant daughter Anne Grandcourt. As one of the *coqs du village,* Grandcourt was able to command the services of four petty-assize officers to pursue his family interests. He had used the courts for family cases before and would again.

Although well below the Grandcourts on the village social ladder, the victim LeRouge was no stranger to the courts either. He was identified in court documents as a *tisserand en toile,* a weaver of inexpensive and locally sold cloth. But he too had brought a case to the petty assizes barely a year before, suing in an unspecified civil matter. At his burial in the parish church of Saint-Vaast on the first of June, one of the relatives mentioned by name in the parish register was Charles Thibault.[79] Thibault had at one time held a minor office in a seigneurial court and had remained close to his relations, who were weavers and farmers like Marin LeRouge.

LeRouge was also steeped in the legal culture of early modern communities. To his mortal sorrow, he was engaged in a rather sophisticated legal argument with the royal officers over allowable arrest procedures when his discourse was cut short. Sergeants were required to have a formal warrant for court-ordered seizures or arrests, and the lack of bench warrants was a common complaint at the assizes against these officers. In another case, a thief had cried haro against his arresting sergeant, for an unwarranted arrest and seizure.[80] Pierre Grandcourt had indeed fudged the difference between a popular clameur and a court arrest by taking along royal strong-arms who carried no warrants. The customs forbade the use of court officers during a clameur, but villagers sometimes brought them along to provide official witness as well as an element of intimidation. LeRouge's objection that the sergeant could not "take men by force" reflects this common legal knowledge about bench warrants and clameurs in the district. Marin LeRouge knew the law.

On March 4, 1693, Robert Maribrasse, the public prosecutor for the high justice of Grainville-la-Teinturière, handed down his conclusions in l'affaire LeRouge. The court's judgment was a masterpiece of legal and cultural blending. Maribrasse combined restitution, corporal punishment, capital punishment, and the wry acceptance that many of the penalties would never be carried out. Judge Pierre Alexandre convicted his distempered subordinate, Sergeant Jacques Lefrançois, of murder, sentencing him to hang by the neck in the village square after making honorable amends at the church door. The practicien Richard LeMarchand was condemned to the king's galleys in perpetuity. The judge and public prosecutor demanded a stiff 100 livres in amends from each of the civilly responsible parties, Pierre Grandcourt, Anne Grandcourt, sergeant Jean Huezé and the practician Jacques Lemaistre, as well as 300 livres from the criminally responsible party, Jacques Lefrançois. Part of the 700 livres amends were designated by the court to go to LeRouge's widow (although it is doubtful whether the seizure of property from the guilty sergeant provided his full share of the composition owed to the weaver's widow). A centuries-old tradition of composition was seamlessly blended into an almost equally ancient royal insistence on exemplary public punishment.

Before the assembled crowd in the courtroom, the clerk read out the chilling legal formula that announced an execution in the ancien régime. The directions were theatrically precise: the culprit would be led by the executioner with "head and feet bare in a chemise, carrying a two-pound burning torch in his hands, the rope around his neck, from the courtroom to the door of the church, demanding pardon of God and King." He was then to be strangled, and his body exhibited for twenty-four hours in the market square.[81]

Apparently the most factual of chronicles, the death sentence copied out by the court clerk of Grainville-la-Teinturière is really a legal *trompe l'oeil*. Not a man of the five ever swung or rowed for his king, nor spent more than a few weeks in his lord's jail, for the death of Marin LeRouge. Lefrançois and LeMarchand had long since fled the jurisdiction and had to be sentenced en contumace. Some part of the community possibly conspired in their escape, effectively commuting the men's sentences to perpetual banishment. The peasant Pierre Grandcourt and Sergeant Jean Heuzé were to have been imprisoned during the course of the year-long trial. But in July, after the murder, the prosecutor Maribrasse frankly admitted that "the prisons of this place are in no state" for actually keeping suspects, so he allowed Grandcourt and Huezé to post bond and go home.[82]

Robert Maribrasse's wry legal humor shone through his concluding remarks in this trial of village ghosts. He noted that he had held an "imaginary confrontation" with the missing murderer, reading out the witnesses' evidence against Lefrançois to an empty prisoner's stool. This was theater with a point, however: it allowed the court to pronounce him civilly dead, if not bodily dead, and therefore to seize his property. The village turned out for the rest of this judicial theater, when they hung a straw effigy of their former sergeant in the market square with a placard identifying him to the audience. The complex brew of villagers' complicity, judicial reluctance or incapacity, and the willingness of both to use the old customary tradition of composition to settle conflicts transformed harsh state laws into local village justice. Death had been cheated, though sadly not for Marin LeRouge.

Chapter 8

UNRULY GOVERNORS

FUNCTIONS AND DYSFUNCTIONS
OF THE COMMON COURTS

The reemergence of bailiwicks as units of provincial governance, and of the common courts as their hub, was in some respects an elegant solution to problems of royal order in the ancien régime. A class of legally educated, propertied men stationed in the ordinary courts was a logical successor to the authority of the high nobility and aristocracy. Indeed, the French legal class had become so indispensable to local government that it largely crossed the watershed of the Revolution unscathed, becoming a key part of the country notability of the late eighteenth and nineteenth centuries.[1] From the crown's perspective, the local legal elites had perhaps done a better job than anyone might have dared hope in protecting property, social order, and the family structure that underpinned the state. They thereby preserved the tax base of the French crown, not to mention the security of the privileged classes and the governing elites.

But the magistrates' position in the countryside and towns was so distinct from that of magistrates in the sovereign courts, and from other central royal administrators, that we need to see them from a new perspective. To understand their roles, we have to look in unexpected places: not in the urban centers of France but in the countryside of England, where the gentry had inherited much the same sort of power and for much the same reason. That so little comparison has made between the two systems can perhaps be explained by the mesmerizing effect of contemporary English commentators, who are still routinely cited to prove that English justice was the enlightened polar opposite of French despotism. Scholars describe a France where magistrates were mere "salaried functionaries who took office 'that they might eat Bread,' and governed those whom they have never seen before." England, by contrast, was a realm where "magistracy rested upon unpaid justices of the peace, men of 'Ample fortunes' who administered the communities in which they resided."[2]

213

Yet surely this last sentence is as good a description of French lower magistrates as we can find. They administered their districts as substantial landowners, men whose fortunes and families were embedded in the countryside they helped to govern. As fate would have it, they were almost as unpaid by the state as their English counterparts. This meant of necessity that they were men of substance, and in Normandy often of the lower nobility, before ascending the bench. In early modern France as much as in England, the challenge was to draw on men of "sufficient wealth and standing to command the respect due to the office," but who were "not so important as to become leaders of local faction."[3] In order for justice to function smoothly, they had to occupy a social and economic berth that made them the natural judges of almost all who would pass before their rural benches.

The primary condition of local government by magistrates in England and France was, of course, the weakness of state finances. "Local government in the seventeenth century was cheap, but it was often too cheap," observed G. C. F. Forster of the English counties.[4] Few state-tax levies remained in rural communities, and those that survived were insufficient to provide more than rudimentary public services. Bridges, roads, and dikes received occasional ad hoc levies; in both France and England, parishes often taxed themselves for pressing local needs.[5] Lacking regular revenue, administration was as poorly funded as infrastructure. Central states also lacked the resources to back up their local governors in times of disorder or disobedience, save in exceptional circumstances. Localities had little choice, then, but to rely on the largely unpaid services of propertied men. A judge's personal status within the community was the ultimate guarantor of public obedience.

In France, the price of the office ensured that substantial men of property ascended to magisterial power. In England, where the commission of the peace was technically not sold, a formal property qualification was used instead.[6] By 1731, justices were required to have an annual income of at least 100 pounds.[7] William Hunt, a fairly typical J. P. in Wiltshire, held land in at least four parishes and enjoyed "the comfortable circumstances of the middle ranks of the country gentry." His fellow justices in the district "were, like himself, prosperous country gentlemen."[8] The justicing notebooks, or working journals, of English J. P.s show plainly why private income at a gentry level was so necessary. Justice Robert Doughty of Norfolk, who served in the peace commission from 1662 to 1665, was at work about 180 days per year, or roughly three and a half days a week (though not all justices were so diligent).[9] By statute, J. P.s were paid an annual wage only for their twelve days at quarter sessions.[10] French bailiwick judges usually took the bench twice a week for petty assizes, and worked roughly ten months a year, holidays excepted. They too held a roughly equivalent gentry status in rural society, giving them the leisure to exercise public office.[11]

Over the sixteenth and seventeenth centuries, central governments further loaded these offices with jurisdiction and responsibilities. Just as the Estates General and royal ordinances had done in France, the Parliament concentrated local authority in the English judiciary. English J. P.s had already become the pivotal figures in local government by 1363, and the county had emerged as the key unit of governance. J. P.s' broad governing responsibilities were expanded when Parliament revised the commission of the peace in 1590, empowering J. P.s to hold regular sessions and inquests, try cases, and keep the peace. But their administrative powers were vastly increased by Parliamentary law. More than three hundred statutes enacted in Tudor and Stuart times placed J. P.s squarely in charge of parish supervision, taxation, and local governance. The Poor Law Acts of 1597, 1601, and 1662 placed especially heavy burdens on English judges. J. P.s supervised the overseers of the poor, who in tandem with churchwardens were charged with assessing and collecting the poor rates from taxpayers, and with resettling poor arrivals in their last known settlement.[12] The magistracy was the natural locus of these new responsibilities on both sides of the English Channel. Judges in early modern communities enjoyed wide jurisdictions, the prestige of exercising the religious and royal functions of justice, and the highest social status attached to secular offices.

In both states, changes in county or provincial governance over the course of the seventeenth and early eighteenth centuries brought more new responsibilities to local magistrates. James M. Rosenheim has emphasized the dramatic withdrawal of English elites from provincial governance after the Restoration in 1660, a pattern that continued through the eighteenth century. "Whereas the landed elite's engagement with the centre rose during this era," he noted, "its participation in local governance faltered."[13] Judging in England was left to the middling gentry as the greater gentry and nobility found their social and political identity on a more cosmopolitan stage.[14] As we have seen, robe nobles and the older titled nobility in France had also withdrawn from direct governance in the countryside, preferring to see their country seats as places of private sociability. They exercised their public authority in more urban or national settings, leaving local officers to fill many of their functions.

The remaining pool of men who might take on such wide-ranging public responsibilities was not large, and the accumulation of multiple offices became both normative and necessary. For both French bailiwick judges and English J. P.s, holding a constellation of mutually reinforcing offices in the police, tax, and judicial administration actually simplified their ability to fulfil their primary mandate: to keep the king's peace. Cumuls were just as common, and indeed sometimes even more pronounced, among county judges in England. The J. P. William Hunt's responsibilities in Wiltshire were both global and time consuming. He became a churchwarden, a land-tax commissioner, and an army recruiting commissioner all in one year. As a J. P., he continued in harness as the land-tax and window-tax commissioner.[15] In English parishes, there was even less separation between church and state than in France, as rectors and vicars were allowed to hold secular posts in their parishes and counties. Justice Edmund Tew of Northamptonshire was the rector (pastor) of Boldon parish for more than thirty-five years, but this was not thought at all incompatible with his fourteen years on the bench as a J. P. Wearing his third hat as a governor of Newcastle Infirmary, Tew sat among "governors drawn from a wide range of wealthy and locally influential men such as fellow-clergy and magistrates."[16]

As with his counterpart in the pays de Caux, the judge and sieur Pierre Doré, it would be difficult to overestimate the influence Tew had over the inhabitants of his jurisdiction.[17] On Sundays he preached to them; in petty sessions and quarter sessions he judged them. He collected their church tithes and commissioned their national taxes, sent them to the bridewell for punishment when they erred, and administered their hospital when they were sick or lame. He was also the landlord of those whose farms and meadows were in the living of his parish. From death to taxes, Tew, like Doré, must have been well nigh unavoidable.

The magistrates' functions in the towns and villages were largely parallel, too. We might find a justice of the peace in Kent and a lieutenant general in the Caux carrying out much the same daily business in their bailiwicks: supervising roads and bridges, determining parentage, punishing Sabbath drinkers, ruling on parish church pews. They calibrated the interests of families and the security of the community in court, two of the most insistent challenges in early modern jurisdictions. Like French judges, who were charged with police functions and often responsible for raising the feudal levy, English J. P.s were in charge of the local militia, making the justices rural administrators par excellence.[18] In criminal cases, French judges held a larger brief than their counterparts in Albion. They continued to try most grand criminal cases locally, despite the requirement that capital convictions be confirmed by the parlements. (After the 1590 peace commission reforms, English judges had largely ceded grand felony cases to the assize circuit judges.)[19] French judges also enjoyed a wider property jurisdiction, some of which English judges had lost to the Court of Common Pleas in London.

Both sets of judges had seen their dockets enlarged with cases once tried in other jurisdictions, especially as secular courts gradually leached jurisdiction from church courts. A popular seventeenth-century law manual for English J. P.s laid out their expanding authority over a wilderness of such issues: adultery, bawdery, and bastardy; evesdropping, slander, and drunkenness; rape and ravishment. Social regulation of the parish was crucial on a daily basis, but their statutory responsibilities included grave threats to order. Rebellious assemblies, plague, treason, and the problems of Catholic recusancy or Protestant nonconformity were in the J. P.s' port-folios.[20] Finally, their royal commissions gave them broad peacekeeping powers, quite apart from their statutory powers from Parliament. Although England differed in points of law and in administrative approach to some social issues, this was generally the same set of concerns that occupied French bailiwick judges.

The most notable distinction between their local roles was that English justices were statutorily empowered to supervise and even set the parish rates, or taxes, for a wide variety of local and national government costs. Justices of the peace were typically the commissioners of the national land tax and window tax, frequently commissioners of the salt tax, and always supervisors of the parish poor rates, overseeing the assessors and collectors in each case. (J. P.s often held additional posts as treasurers of the Parliamentary rates for lame soldiers and poor prisoners). On the ecclesiastical side, justices were responsible for approving church rates in the parishes.[21] Local English justices thereby controlled almost all direct taxation paid in England. In France, the system of tax assessment and tax courts was distinct from the ordinary courts. But as we have seen, French judges and lawyers often held posts in the tax and financial administration cumulatively with their ordinary judicial offices.

French local magistrates were indeed different from their English brethren, but less in their local roles than in their position within the state as a whole. What impresses us about the English justices is their participation in a national political culture. Their multiple relationships with a lawmaking Parliament and the central royal courts of Common Pleas, King's Bench, Exchequer, and Chancery formed a strong fabric of national governance after the Restoration.[22] The commissions of the peace had long carried with them the natural expectation of wielding influence in local elections to Parliament, whether one was a candidate or simply a local broker of "interest," or patronage for other candidates. J. P.s became central players in the budding, and often bare-fisted, world of national party politics from the 1680s through the early eighteenth century. The relationships between center and locality were rich.

Within their counties, English judges were visited winter and summer by magistrates from the three royal benches in London, who rode the six assize circuits of the realm. County J. P.s also increasingly made up the grand juries that decided on presentments or charges during the assizes.[23] French local magistrates, in contrast, were formally visited by commissioners from the parlements or the crown only in cases of grave danger, misconduct, or on ad hoc tours. The legal contrast is stark as well: English local judges were vital participants in a genuinely national common law. Consolidated by Henry II, the common law had been written down and collected in yearbooks beginning in the reign of Edward I in 1292.[24] The fragmentation of French customary laws worked against a sense of national legal culture. Moreover, French local judges ceased to participate in creating national legislation after the Estates General of 1614.

No better description exists of the deep political river that flowed between the English counties and the central government in London than Francis Bacon's. As lord chancellor in 1618, he gave the Star Chamber address to the assembled assize judges and justices of the peace of the realm. The key to the justices of the peace, he explained, was that "those that have voices in Parliament to make laws, they for the most part are those which in the country are appointed to administer the same laws." The English justices' judicial and administrative powers in the counties were naturally united to national legislative power, giving them a complete political identity. "If a man would make a commonwealth by a level," Bacon concluded, "he could not find better than these."[25]

Dysfunctions of the Local State

Swirling under the surface of the French common courts were also serious dysfunctions, which coexisted with the courts' many functions. Judicial corruption existed, and it was understood by contemporaries as such. The bailiwicks of France, like all early modern jurisdictions, had a unique set of opportunities for malversation (and a unique set of limitations as well) that were conditioned by the bailiwicks' relationship to the larger state. Although English observers relished the idea that French judges were mere tools of a despotic regime,[26] bailiwick judges were in fact considerably more independent of the central state than English J. P.s. Officers of the French ordinary courts were subject to no assize-circuit supervision by higher magistrates. They were also irremovable from office by the crown, except under the most extreme circumstances. The use of parlementary commissions or royal grands jours inquests to root out local abuses, although dramatic, was exceptional and rare.[27]

In contrast, English J. P.s served at the pleasure of the monarch and did not legally enjoy the right to hold office during good behavior until after the Act of Settlement in 1701.[28] Local judges on the seventeenth-century English peace commissions were routinely cashiered by the sovereign for political or confessional reasons and could be removed for corruption as well.[29] The central courts in London sent assize judges on twice-yearly circuits to hear appeals from the counties, give a harangue from the bench to local justices and residents, and try most capital cases. In practice, however, "neither the central government nor the Parliament told them what to do, closely supervised their activity, or even insured that they act at all."[30] This is a fair description of the independence of rural French bailiwick judges, who only rarely suffered any direct inter-ference from parlements, intendants, or the crown.

Given French local judges' broad independence from the central admin-istration, as well as from the paternal but distant parlements, we might well ask whether these growing powers were used merely to produce a new kind of tyranny. In fact, the local courts' independence from the central state did in some ways magnify the possibilities for arbitrariness and abuse. This was, after all, a court system without juries, assize circuits, or quarter sessions to provide supervision. More seriously, it was run by a judiciary of venal offi-cers who bought and sold their public powers on the market in a state lack-ing a unified common law. These were indeed potentially menacing features of the common courts. The evidence of petty and occasionally grand abuse was often sobering enough. But it stemmed as much from the social and economic conditions of early modern states as from anything peculiar to the French system. English "basket justices," or trading justices as they were sometimes called in London, were famous for trading on their offices for profit. Selling alehouse licenses, exacting bribes, and other forms of creative extortion were perhaps less common in England, but hardly foreign.[31]

Where the controls on the local English system were formalized and obvi-ous to the eye, though, those in the French system tended to be informal. Public influence was brought to bear at the Cauchois benches through testify-ing, rumor, clameurs de haro, and organized jail escapes. Outside the court-room proper, both arbitration and notarized settlements were only some of the popular features that left the crown and lords' courts permeable to the ebb and flow of public justice. Moreover, almost all cases brought before the bench were privately initiated. The vast majority of both criminal and civil prosecutions were brought by the parties to the suit, not by the king's or lords' public prosecutors of the courts. As J. A. Sharpe and Marjorie McIn-tosh have argued for the early modern English village, the community exer-cised "considerable discretion" in determining who would be prosecuted in the first place. In France as much as in England, this was a "natural conse-quence of the dependence upon the participation of the population at large, as prosecutors and officers, in the law enforcement system."[32]

What made the French system perhaps least of all the tool of a police state was the willingness of ordinary villagers to bring civil suits in the courts. The simple fact that rural court dockets were saturated with civil cases involving family and property set much of the agenda for justice, determining on what kinds of cases the king's or lord's men would expend most of their time and resources. The profits of court officials were largely dependent on their ability to render some sort of predictable justice in the civil affairs that mattered most to the king's subjects. Prosecution of villagers by their seigneur in his or her court was also comparatively rare in the Caux by the late seventeenth century. With the exception of rent collection, only the occasional rabbit poaching or refusal to use the lord's grain mill rises above the common pleas. The same held true in seigneurial jurisdictions in Burgundy and Brittany.[33] As one historian of England has noted in the same period, seigneurial courts had long since become places where "order is maintained collectively by the tenants" rather than by the active involvement of the lord or his steward.[34] Here, in the weekly litigation brought in by ordinary villagers and townspeople, was the real source of profit, authority, and growth in the common courts. The true sovereign authority in the Cauchois courts appears not to have been one that could mandate death, but one that could regulate civil society, that is, property and family.

The notion that the courts were blunt tools of royal or seigneurial domination does little to describe the daily affairs handled in the Cauchois assizes. By the late seventeenth century, ordinary courts were used far more frequently to regulate status and power within the community than they were used to regulate relations between the community and outside elites. Commoners' impassioned disputes about ownership, usage, and income rights over the district's arable land and mobile wealth were at the bottom of most suits. The community also kept order and calibrated power through inventive moral and social litigation. Church benches, burial plots, parish funds, tavern hours, grain prices, blasphemy, and slander were vigorously litigated at the king's bench or the seigneur's. The crown or seigneur was only a distant party to most of these cases. Although this did not preclude officers from seeking illicit gain from clients and cases, they were bounded by the many corps and privileged groups in local society that demanded predictable services from the courts.

Other dysfunctions of the common courts were more judicial and political in nature. The local legal classes were among the harshest critics of these defects, and their complaints would figure prominently in *cahiers* (lists of grievances) from the Caux to the Estates General in 1789.[35] Chief among these grievances were the still-unresolved nightmare of jurisdiction and the breakdown of the royal model of venal officeholding at the local level. Both of these institutional issues were sources of unremitting conflict within the local officer corps and have already formed part of this story. But three deeper issues troubled the ordinary courts. These were the problem of property law, the problem of legal petrification more generally, and the problem of connecting local governance to central governance in a satisfying way. All three issues were in fact deeply linked, like branches of the same tree, and should rightly be treated together.

The fossilization of law, and particularly property law, was near the heart of these matters. In a state where crown and parlements had been deadlocked over customary law and droit privé since the reformation of the customs in the late sixteenth century, the natural result was a kind of accelerating sclerosis throughout the whole legal system. Indeed, it may help to explain the mysterious and near universal decline in legal cases observed by some scholars in the four or five decades before the Revolution.[36] The changing nature of the French economy and of social relations had been gradually eroding the foundations of customary law since at least the early eighteenth century. During the same period in England, "law was increasingly being brought into line with the needs of new forms of property."[37] Louis XIV and his ministers instead repeatedly dismissed the parlements' requests to redact the customary codes anew. The parlements, for their part, were utterly unwilling to allow the central state to invade their privilege of controlling customary or private law.[38] Under such a deadlock, we might hypothesize that justices would increasingly be thrown back on equity and case precedents to resolve issues about which the law had little useful to say. For local assize justices, this deadlock must have created a growing sense of disconnect between their local responsibilities and the legal apparatus they had been given to execute their duties.

Property, which was the legal heart of all French customary laws, was thus becoming one of the thorniest problems for the state. In Normandy neither the *Très Ancien Coustumier,* nor the reformed version produced after 1583, proffered an actual definition of property. To the extent that the customary laws assumed a definition of property, that definition was based on property concepts that had been formed in the High Middle Ages. As Emily Tabuteau has demonstrated, both tenurial and feudal ideas about land and real property were already thoroughly mixed together in legal practice in the eleventh century, even before the Custom was written down.[39] By the late seventeenth century, changes in actual land practices in Normandy left these already mixed customary assumptions about property mired in further confusion or disuse. Like a spongy marsh spreading at the center of law in Normandy, new economic and social conditions further eroded the already infirm ground of medieval law. The property issue was slowly becoming a dangerous and inextricable morass.

The increasingly problematic connection between local governance and central governance was intimately related to these legal issues. After all, the local courts were charged with managing the crucial frontier that Bodin so insightfully marked out in the late sixteenth century: the border between the private realm and the public.[40] Property law and family law were the two most important domains that lay on that contested border. The sovereign state had a deepening public interest in regulating both, not least because they were the foundation of the state's ability to tax and to maintain order. Naturally enough, private individuals, families, and early modern corps were equally intent on controlling their families and their property. The courts were the local nexus where those interests met and were adjudicated.

But how were local magistrates during the eighteenth century to exercise their proper functions? With sclerotic law codes, little access to the upper magistracy, and few ties to the central administration, they were a nascent bureaucracy increasingly cut adrift from their state. Moreover, the state had shown such increasing contempt for their own property in office (and thus for their families and for their corps) over the late seventeenth and eighteenth centuries that alternatives seemed thinkable. It was not so very remarkable that some magistrates came to view themselves, not the crown, as the real guardians of the bien publique in the towns and villages of France. Their libraries attest that they had a long line of judicial philosophers to hand, from Aristotle to Jean Bodin, to justify an expansive notion of themselves as men ranked among the proper guardians of the public realm.[41]

Unlike the English J. P.s with their justicing notebooks, French magistrates have left us so few of their own thoughts or notes about their work that we can read more deeply into their self-identities only through circumstantial evidence. Not until we reach the revolutionary watershed do we hear their cumulative voices in the protests that erupted in May 1788 over the Brienne edicts and in the cahiers of 1789. Yet these illuminate attitudes that are clearly connected to long-standing conditions in the bailiwicks. These attitudes also challenge the prevailing notion that officers enjoyed and profited greatly from the dysfunctions of the system. In the spring of 1789, the seigneurial judge Jacques Philly took the bench at Cany to preside over the drawing up of Cany's cahier. The proceedings were dominated by seigneurial and royal officers, yet these officers unequivocally demanded the suppression of all high justices as well as the royal courts of exceptional jurisdiction. Their opposition to both venality and épices was fierce. They insisted that the "venality of all judicial offices in the bailiwick courts be irrevocably abolished, that judges render justice for free; that . . . the justiciables of the said bailiwicks be allowed to present candidates to fill vacant offices to the king, and that no one be elected a judge except lawyers who have continuously exercised their profession for six years in a bailiwick."[42] Seigneurial officers did not object to the elimination of their offices; instead they asked for a wider window of opportunity in filling state offices. The cahier's contents are unexpected, given that scholars have often contended that local officers were the ultimate beneficiaries of confused jurisdictions, multiplying offices, and the imbroglio of ancien régime justice.

We might have expected this to be the manifesto of the clients, not the officers, of the courts. But the similar cahier of Saint-Vaast-Dieppedalle, a few kilometers down the road, was presided over by Pierre-Jacques-Louis Dufay, a king's councillor and the assessor civil, criminal, and police for the royal court. Judicial reform took up most of the ink in the Saint-Vaast document, surprisingly outweighing calls for royal fiscal reform. The Saint-Vaast officers too called for suppression of useless multiple jurisdictions, "as annoying to the judges as to their justiciables."[43] What the cahiers of Cany and Saint-Vaast-Dieppedalle projected was an entirely state-paid judiciary, chosen from resident practicing attorneys who would work in a unified jurisdiction. The inhabitants would have the right to present candidates for judgeships to the king. Attorneys would have clear responsibilities toward their clients, including the responsibility to "work diligently"[44] to conclude their cases.

This was a thoroughgoing critique of the entire ancien régime judicial edifice, including its financial, legal, and jurisdictional underpinnings. It was largely drawn up by the judiciary itself. It was also *for* something: a certain rationalizing of the judicial structure, one that was so clearly to their advantage that local practitioners were willing to throw venality, heredity, épices, and even their own jurisdictions on the bonfire to participate in it. They had the confidence of knowing that their place in rural society, though purchased from the king, was largely exercised independently of him. Ultimately, we need look no further than the revolutionary reforms of the Estates General and the Constituent Assembly to see how thoroughly committed the legal classes were to dismantling the crumbling framework of ancien régime justice. The lawyers who dominated the third estate and later the Assembly were the same experts who drew up the legislation abolishing venality, dismantling the court system, and establishing an entirely new system of justice. At the end of the day, they were consummate artisans in the law. Their society could no longer do without law and lawyers, regardless of whose name the law was issued in.

The elections sent several members of the legal class from the new grand bailliage of the Caux to the Estates General. Of the six members of the third estate elected, three were the king's prosecutors of Cany, Caudebec, and Arques. (Two were laboureurs, a rather surprising percentage, and the last was an armateur from Le Havre). This top-heavy representation of the judicial corps was reflected in the Estates General as a whole. Of the 598 deputies to the Third Estate, 212 were attorneys, and 162 were judges of royal bailiwicks.[45] As David Bell has noted, these men were "overdetermined" to take the lead in the early revolution.[46] Their independence of mind and confident political authority had been gestating for more than century, in a localized political world far removed from the French court.

Power and Politics

But in what sense can we think of local French judges prior to 1789 as political? Certainly not in the early modern English sense, which has come to seem the modern sense. English justices of the peace were expected to influence their counties' voters beneath them, and in turn to be appointed and dismissed by the lord chancellor above them, for reasons of party and politics. Moreover, the commission of the peace was a calling card to the

English Parliament. The majority of members of the House of Commons were active or former J. P.s, and their national political influence was thus a very natural extension of their local interest.[47] French rural judges had no local or national elections to influence, few fears of dismissal by the crown from their venal offices, and precious little hope of ascending into positions of obvious national power. The horizon of national politics began with the provincial sovereign courts and ascended up through offices of state. Both sets of higher offices were financially and socially beyond the reach of most bailiwick judges, and of their sons, by the mid-seventeenth century.

If we step aside from the notion that politics is expressed mainly through national institutions and elections, however, we can see French judges in another light. Political theorists have described politics broadly as the "authoritative allocation of values," the ability to make a governing group's values binding on the community.[48] In their different ways, local courts and the church were the frontline guardians of governing values, which were defined in laws, customs, and privileges. On these depended very concrete matters: the allocation of economic resources, privileges, and social status, and the burden of local or national taxes. The courts' powers of enforcement were significant, too. Judges could revoke property, freedom or life from members of the community who repeatedly challenged those values. This did not necessarily give local courts a share in making national decisions, but it created the preconditions for the state to do so. Had they withdrawn from their functions and their support of those values, as many did in 1789, the state could not long have stood.

If we employ James M. Rosenheim's distinction between "national rulers and local governors," we can also understand early modern politics as a set of functions. In seventeenth- and eighteenth-century England, rulers and governors shared strong social and professional identities; indeed, they were often the same people.[49] In France, those who exercised local governance did not rule. But governing itself was a public power that disposed of the lives, properties, and behavior of a judge's neighbors and communities. English justices of the period described themselves politically, as historians still do today, as governors. They were "the premier exemplars of two traditions of governance which the English considered unique to their island: the practice of self-government at the king's command and acceptance of responsibility by the elite."[50] But perhaps they were unique only in degree. French bailiwick judges were men who understood the art of self-governance at the king's command; no phrase better describes their position. Despite the increasing fiscal disadvantages of remaining in the king's service as the eighteenth century progressed, they showed a broad public-mindedness in their sense of duty. Many of those holding judgeships and king's prosecutors' posts continued to accept their local responsibilities, something neither vanity nor illicit gain can entirely explain away. That they did so tells us something rather remarkable about their view of themselves as men who shared in the governance of the *chose publique.*

How, then, should we characterize the powers of the men who mastered the local judicial system? Neither the French central administration, which largely engaged in benign neglect of the local bailiwick courts, nor the English one, which vilified them, seem to have given us a useful sense of their identity. Nor do we have a ready name for their style of governance. Did the officers of the ordinary courts merely dilute the crown's pretensions to absolutism in the countryside? Or did they effectively create a new kind of local governance, a rural commonwealth that was responsive to the towns, villages, and families they helped to regulate? If they had power, what did they use it for?

Their power was, as we have noted before, of two kinds: one personal and familial, one public. Officers, lawyers, and functionaries avidly exploited their posts to elevate their family fortunes through their supervision of land transactions, contracts, rents, loans, wardships, wills, legal fees, and local markets in their districts. In the time-tested way, they also parlayed their posts into advantageous marriages and into new local offices. They thus accumulated access to and influence over the tight rural world of laboureurs, sieurs, merchants, artisans, and peasants, all of whom needed the services of the bench. Here we see the officers blending private wealth and the public weal in ways that are entirely typical of the ancien régime and that illustrate both the hazards and the opportunities of a world where private and public overlapped so inextricably. Here too is the gray zone where we find the more avaricious members of the bailiwick abusing their offices in ways that their own contemporaries considered corrupt and that were the negative expression of their public powers.

But the petty- and grand-assize records more often than not display the officers' use of public powers in positive (or at least more normative) ways. By piecing together the mosaic of thousands of cases brought before the parquets of the common courts, we discover three broad fields of power. The most significant was surely that the courts provided security of property by enforcing or negotiating the rules of inheritance, ownership, income, and usage rights across the entire countryside. Criminal prosecution was the courts' last bulwark against property threats, but the criminal docket was decidedly secondary to the use of civil litigation and contracts to protect the property order. Prosaic as it seems, order and property security were also the yardstick used by ministers, political philosophers, and the king to measure their own command of the French state.

Bailiwick officers next underwrote the social order of their districts, holding together the complex framework of rights and privileges attached to almost every individual or corporate body. In a world where so much of the social order was written into contracts and laws, they were almost the only body with a broad enough jurisdiction to calibrate the rights of cities, communities, corps, guilds, and churches (in the public realm), and of nobles, officers, clerics, commoners, and merchants (in the private realm), against each other. In a France where rights were largely personal or corporate, not broad based and public, this was a work of almost unimaginable complexity. The right to pronounce on those rights and privileges was the power to uphold or upset the social balance of the community.

Lastly, the men of the common courts ensured that the broad framework of the central state remained standing in the villages and towns. Attacks on tax collectors and royal officers were punished or at least pursued. Royal and seigneurial officers continued to endorse the legitimacy of the crown by securing official commissions as judges and as king's prosecutors and by nominally meeting the king's professional requirements (however lax their observances may sometimes seem in hindsight). Ultimately, they guaranteed for the king that the daily tensions of families, parishes, and entire districts seldom escalated into riots, tax rebellions, or attacks on crown property. That this mattered becomes clear to us only in perfect hindsight. When the legal corps sitting in the common courts refused to endorse the royal judicial and political system in the localities any longer, the system collapsed.

In the aggregate, their daily activities in the Cauchois courtrooms had wide repercussions for the crown's claims to legislative and administrative sovereignty. Bailiwick judges underwrote local order, but they limited the king's direct control of both law and property. Chief among these limitations was the fact that the king's judges overwhelmingly relied on provincial and local customary laws, case precedents, and equity, not positive royal laws, to settle the vast majority of cases that came before their benches. Indeed, the fracturing of provincial and local laws across France made it impossible for the crown to do otherwise than to rely on local codes and interpretations. Even where royal laws applied, they were only selectively enforced. The application of the death penalty, that high mark of royal sovereignty, was the clearest case in point. Despite the harsh rhetoric of capital punishment during the ancien régime, the judges and public prosecutors of the local courts seldom pronounced the king's death penalty in capital cases. It was even more seldom actually executed. France's royal edicts and ordinances, like those of early modern Spain, "served as only a vague guide to judicial behavior" for magistrates.[51]

Their power was largely confined, however, to a circle whose horizons we can see clearly. From the roof of the royal bailiwick and seigneurial court in Cany, it spanned just under a hundred parishes across the cereal plains of the plateau. In Longueville, the horizon stretched a little wider: perhaps a hundred five parishes. In other Norman bailiwicks it was no more than thirty. The officers' power had grown measurably within the charmed circle of the bailiwick during the seventeenth and early eighteenth centuries, but their power had shrunk considerably outside of that circuit.

The dissolution of the Estates of Normandy, the doors firmly closed to parlementary careers in Rouen, the urban inbreeding of the présidial court at Caudebec, the crown's failure to call legal commissions to redact local and provincial customs, were cumulatively crushing.

All of these political developments gave bailiwick judges a significantly smaller role to play in provincial and national governance than they had enjoyed in the sixteenth century. Only a century earlier, Jean Bodin, a seigneurial judge, had been a delegate to the Estates General of France and a pivotal political theorist. By the late seventeenth century, not even royal bailliage judges dreamed of such prominence. These men had paled and grown nearly invisible in the records of the central administration even as they become more prominent in maintaining local security and property for the state. This made them something much more than administrators; they exercised governance across the green downs and villages of the Caux. But it also made them something much less than full partners in the French state.

At the end of the day, it is this disconnect between the local state in the countryside and central authority that strikes us about French local governance. At many points the central state seems to hover mysteriously above the Caux, with little immediate influence over the laws, officers, and clients who together embodied the local state at the weekly assizes. Yet the crown did create a framework for the local state in the broadest sense. It generated and sold offices, set the structure of the court system, exercised certain influence over the qualifications and education of its members, and drew them into its own concerns with order and property. Above all, the central state was the ultimate guarantor of that mass of contracts and customs that held France together in family, village, and town. Thousands of ordinary courts in the countryside executed those contracts and customs on a daily basis. They did so with wide discretionary powers and under sometimes decisive local influence by villagers and townspeople alike. But that they did so at all may still strike us as a remarkable form of governance.

The court system was immensely useful to both crown and local lords, if not quite in the way we once assumed. They helped make the villages and towns of the Caux self-regulating, bringing nearly a quarter of a million inhabitants into a judicial system with some real authority (however honored in the breach) to regulate order. Moreover, the legal system channeled discontents into a forum where they could be framed only as disputes between individuals or corps, not as disputes against classes, orders, or the king. Whatever symbolic protest value such actions as poaching or woodcutting might have had for villagers against privileges or power writ large, they were recast in court as illegal acts against written laws or named individuals. The courts were not designed to litigate social ills, the system of privileges, or the injustice of royal rule. The courts did provide relief against certain kinds of injustice and an outlet for public rage against some malefactors. But they also contained discontent within the narrow channels of law and the adversarial system of litigation.

The common round of activities in the ordinary courts of Normandy thus strongly confirms the more nuanced idea of royal governance offered by recent antiabsolutist historians. The kings had indeed extended the realm of public law and royal jurisdiction over the previous two centuries, in retrospect perhaps even more successfully than the conditions of the age would seem to have made plausible. But whether we look at failed royal reforms, fractured law codes, vibrant seigneurial courts, stubborn provincial officer corps, or resourceful and cunning pleaders at the king's bench, the limitations placed on a would-be absolute king are clear.

And yet everywhere we look we have the impression that the state—that is, the force of political order and of bureaucratic standardization—was advancing in the villages and towns of France. What are we to make of this seeming contradiction of power everywhere foiled and mediated, and everywhere creeping forward? The court records give us a tantalizing, though only partial, answer. The judicial system, a fundamental arm of the royal state, was largely inhabited by and used by individuals and groups with their own reasons for advancing certain aspects of state power even as they impeded or shaped others. In the villages of the Caux, peasants and rural merchants found the larger royal jurisdictions useful as their monetary and family circuits expanded, while local royal court officers found a rich vantage post atop the king's bench for acquiring property and authority in their communities. The result of all these contradictory forces was that the state system itself grew in size and authority, but the king controlled it only very conditionally. Out of such contradictions was born a state for which we no longer have an adequate paradigm, or even a name.

These multiple contradictions should not obscure the practical nature of justice in French society. It was above all about ordinary men, women, and communities attempting to order their lives in the overlapping circles where the private realm met the public commonwealth. But for all their practicality, the ordinary courts were deeply problematic for ordinary people. Law and the judicial system were under multiple ownership from above and suffering increasing stresses from below. The changing nature of property and the changing needs of French society were gradually washing the ground out from under the judicial system. As the permanent outposts of the king in the village, the courts rooted much of what we have come to consider the modern state in local society. All the while, the courts continued to display open dysfunctions and an impressive independence from the central state. But the irreducible ambiguity of justice in the village, and of the king's legislative sovereignty in the state, should not be entirely discouraging. Many people found it as elusive at the time. Justice, like bread, was necessary to all in the ancien régime, and sometimes as difficult to find.

Appendix A

COURTS OF THE GÉNÉRALITÉ OF ROUEN (UPPER NORMANDY), 1670–1740
(WITH APPROXIMATE NUMBERS OF COURTS IN EACH JURISDICTION; SOVEREIGN COURTS ARE SHOWN IN ITALICS)

Ordinary Jurisdictions	Privileged Jurisdictions		Extraordinary Jurisdictions	
Parlement (1)			*Cour des Aides Comptes et Finances (1)*[a]	*Table de Marbre (1)*
Présidials (4)	(Seigneurial)	(Other)	Bureaux de Finance (3) (appellate tax courts, in theory)	Admirautés (7) (admiralty courts)
Bailliages and vicomtés (15)[b]	Hautes justices (high justices)	Consulaires (merchants' courts)	Élections (13) (direct-tax courts)	Eaux et forêts (11) (water and forests)
	Moyennes justices (middling justices)	Officialités (ecclesiastical courts; no appeal to Parlement)	Greniers à sel (18) (salt-tax courts)	Marechaussées (7) (constabulary courts)
	Basses justices (low justices)		Traites foraines (7) (customs duties)	

a. Numerous bailliages and vicomtés were exercised simultaneously; if counted as separate jurisdictions, there were twenty-seven in total.

b. The Cour des Aides and Chambre des Comptes in Normandy were united after 1705; the Cour de la Monnaye lost its legal functions.

Appendix B

Jurisdictions of the Ordinary Courts, Upper Pays de Caux

The diagram shows approximate sizes and overlapping of royal and seigneurial jurisdictions. The royal bailliage of Cany is shown in gray; seigneurial jurisdictions are in outline.

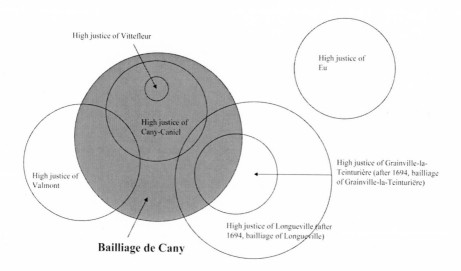

Appendix C

CRIMINAL TRIAL PROCEDURE, ORDINARY COURTS

Most criminal trials were concluded at an intermediate stage with one of the verdicts listed below. Only more serious cases would proceed after the first deliberations of the judge and councillors.

Complaint	(*Plainte*) Accusation made before the judge by either a private individual or the public prosecutor for the jurisdiction
Inquest	(*Information, instruction*) Criminal judge's inquiry, either in court or in the field; written down by the court clerk as a *procès-verbal*
Testimony	(*Témoins*) Witnesses are heard in closed court, in the presence of the judge, councillors (in royal courts), and usually the king's or seigneur's prosecutor
Summons	*Decrèt d'assigné pour être oui:* defendant must appear in court on stated day; summons delivered by sergeant or usher
	Decrèt d'ajournement personnel: second summons; defendant may be arrested for nonappearance
	Decrèt de pris de corps: arrest order; issued as the first summons in crimes meriting corporal or capital penalties
Interrogation	(*Interrogatoire*) Defendant appears without counsel to answer questions under oath before the judge, prosecutor, and councillors (in royal courts)
Conclusions (1st)	(*Conclusions du procureur*) Public prosecutor recommends either definitive conclusions (*conclusions définitifs*) for the judges to deliberate, or recommends continuing to next stage of trial (*conclusions préparatoires*)

Deliberation	Judge and councillors decide whether to proceed with trial; if case is not thrown out or a clear verdict reached, they proceed as below
Verification of testimony	*(Récolement)* Witnesses must swear to truth of testimony; any revisions make them liable to perjury charges
Confrontation	*(Confrontation)* Witnesses are revealed and their testimony presented to the defendant; defendant may refute witnesses, and judge may question witnesses
Conclusions (2nd)	*(Conclusions définitifs)* The prosecutor sums up the case and recommends a verdict and sentence
Deliberation	Judge and councillors deliberate the case after the councillor appointed as *rapporteur* (reporter) reads out the facts and conducts the final questioning of the defendant. Defendant may now call witnesses at his/her own expense and present justification *(faits justificatifs)*
Torture (preverdict)	*(Question préparatoire)* If insufficient evidence exists to convict on a capital charge (including two eyewitnesses) and the defendant does not confess, judge may use torture to force a guilty confession
Verdict	Judge and councillors proceed to majority vote on guilt, innocence, or continuing suspicion
	Coupable (guilty): court imposes sentence, taking into consideration the recommendations of the public prosecutor
	Plus amplement informé à temps: defendant remains incarcerated for up to one year to see if additional evidence surfaces
	Plus amplement informé: Defendant released, pending new information
	Mis hors cour: acquittal for lack of evidence, but does not eliminate all suspicion
	Non-coupable (innocent)
Torture (postverdict)	*(Question préalable)* Used to extract the names of accomplices from the defendant prior to execution

NOTES

Chapter 1

1. Historians have scaled back earlier estimates that there were seventy to eighty thousand functioning courts in France; nevertheless, the court system remained considerably denser than modern Western judiciaries.

2. Charles Louis de Secondat de Montesquieu, *Lettres persanes* (Paris: Bokking International, 1993), 158.

3. The crown issued a stream of prohibitions against cumulative local officeholding right through the eighteenth century, with the usual lack of success advertised by the laws' repetition.

4. On policing Normandy, see also Robert M. Schwartz, *Policing the Poor in Eighteenth-Century France* (Chapel Hill: University of North Carolina Press, 1988).

5. G. C. F. Forster, *The East Riding Justices of the Peace in the Seventeenth Century* (York: East Yorkshire Local History Society, 1973), 7–67; J. A. Sharpe, *Crime in Early Modern England 1550–1750* (London: Longman, 1999), 40–44; David Underdown, *Revel, Riot and Rebellion: Popular Politics and Culture in England, 1603–1660* (Oxford: Oxford University Press, 1985), 10, 23, 109–10.

6. Bodin, *Six Livres de la République* (Paris: 1583), 1.

7. David Parker, "Sovereignty, Absolutism, and the Function of the Law in Seventeenth Century France," *Past and Present* 122 (Feb. 1989): 36; Pierre Goubert and Daniel Roche, *Les français et l'ancien régime* (Paris: Armand Colin, 1984), 1:275; Robert Mandrou, *La France aux XVIIe et XVIIIe siècles* (Paris: 1971), 267–68.

8. For recent works on urban présidials and sénéchaussées, see especially Christophe Blanquie, *Les présidiaux de Richelieu: Justice et vénalité (1630–1642)* (Paris: Éditions Christian, 2000); Séverine Debordes-Lissillour, *Les sénéchaussées royales de Bretagne: La monarchie de l'ancien régime et ses juridictions ordinaires (1552–1790)* (Rennes: Presses Universitaires de Rennes, 2006); Joël Hautebert, *La justice pénale à Nantes au grand siècle: Jurisprudence de la sénéchaussée présidiale* (Paris: Michel de Maule, 2001); and Sylvain Soleil, *Le siège royal de la sénéchaussée et du présidial d'Angers (1551–1790)* (Rennes: Presses Universitaires de Rennes, 1997).

9. Recent revisionist works on prerevolutionary seigneurial justice include Anthony Crubaugh, *Balancing the Scales of Justice: Local Courts and Rural Society in Southwest France, 1750–1800* (University Park: Pennsylvania State University Press, 2001); Antoine Follaine, *Les justices locales dans le villes et les villages du XVIe au XIXe siècle: Administration et justice locales,* vol. 2 (Rennes: Presses Universitaires de Rennes, 2006); Jeremy Hayhoe, *Enlightened Feudalism: Seigneurial Justice and Village Society in Eighteenth-Century Northern Burgundy* (Rochester, NY: University of Rochester Press, 2008); and Steven G. Reinhardt, *Justice in the Sarladais, 1770–1790* (Baton Rouge: Louisiana State University Press, 1991): 238–75.

10. See chapter 7 for a list of works on criminal justice.

11. Steven G. Reinhardt, "Crime and Royal Justice in Ancien Régime France: Modes of Analysis," *Journal of Interdisciplinary History* XIII (Winter 1983): 460.

12. Peter Heylen, *A Full Relation of Two Journeys: The One into the Main-Land of France. . . .* (London: 1656), 7.

13. Bodin, *Six Livres,* 392–409.

14. Some historians estimate the ratio to be even lower, at about one royal (not seigneurial) judge per thousand of population; see Richard Mowery Andrews, *Law, Magistracy, and Crime in Old Regime Paris, 1735–1789* (Cambridge: Cambridge University Press, 1994), 1:45.

15. The judiciary of France in 1990 had approximately 5,800 judges for a population of 61 million; the United States in 2006 had approximately 30,000 judges for a population of over 299 million, or one judge for roughly every ten thousand inhabitants. Institut National de la Statisque et des Études Economiques (INSEE), Doc. # 236298, 1990; U.S. Census Bureau, 2006 American Community Survey, B24020.

16. John Phillip Dawson, *A History of Lay Judges* (Union, NJ: Lawbook Exchange, Ltd., 1999), 72.

17. Norman Landau, *The Justices of the Peace, 1679–1760* (Berkeley: University of California Press, 1984), 44–45.

18. ADIV 1 Bh 13–15, Parlement de Bretagne, 1701. A revolt against the sénéschal of the court of Chateaugiron, who attempted to impose road repairs on the parishioners, ended with a number of substantial tax-paying laboureurs imprisoned in the conciergerie in Rennes.

19. Ralph E. Giesey, "State-Building in Early Modern France: The Role of Royal Officialdom," *Journal of Modern History* 55 (June 1983): 191–207.

20. Louis XIV, *Mémoires* (Paris: Le livre club du librairie, 1960), 186.

21. Judges also raised the monetary payments that often took the nobles' place; active service in the "feudal host" was discontinued in 1636, but revived under protest in 1652 and in 1675, for example. See Jonathan Dewald, *Pont-St-Pierre, 1389–1789: Lordship, Community, and Capitalism in Early Modern France* (Berkeley: University of California Press, 1987), 172–73.

22. David Parker, "Sovereignty, Absolutism," 73.

23. Underdown, *Revel, Riot,* 106.

24. James R. Farr, *A Tale of Two Murders: Passion and Power in Seventeenth-Century France* (Durham: Duke University Press, 2005), 203.

25. John Locke, *Second Treatise on Government,* in *Political Writings of John Locke,* ed. David Wooton (New York: Mentor, 1993), 325.

26. See David Warren Sabean, *Property, Production, and Family in Neckarhausen, 1700–1870* (Cambridge: Cambridge University Press, 1990), 208–22 on similar functions of courts in Germany.

27. Marc Bloch, *Les caractères originaux de l'histoire rurale Française,* 2ième ed. (Paris: Armand Colin, 1952), 232–33.

28. See Jean Bart, *Histoire du droit privé de la chute de l'empire romain au XIXe siècle* (Paris: Montchrèstien, 1998), 137–38 on the decline in ecclesiastical jurisdictions. On similar trends in England, see Marjorie Keniston McIntosh, *Controlling Misbehavior in England, 1370–1600* (Cambridge: Cambridge University Press, 1998), 5–6, 23–45; Keith Wrightson and David Levine, *Poverty and Piety in an English Village: Terling,*

1525–1700 (Oxford: Clarendon Press, 1995), 201; J. M. Beattie, *Crime and the Courts in England 1660–1800* (Oxford: Clarendon Press, 1986) and Sharpe, *Crime in Early Modern England*, 7–9.

29. Marc Raeff, *The Well-Ordered Police State: Social and Institutional Change Through Law in the Germanies and Russia, 1600–1800* (New Haven, CT: Yale University Press, 1983), 75; David Warren Sabean, *Property, Production and Family in Neckerhausen, 1700–1870* (Cambridge: Cambridge University Press, 1991), 29, 72–74.

30. Sara Hanley, "Engendering the State: Family Formation and State Building in Early Modern France," *French Historical Studies* 16, no. 1 (Spring 1989): 25.

31. See also Dewald, *Pont-St-Pierre*, 130, and V. A. C. Gatrell et al., *Crime and the Law: The Social History of Crime in Early Modern Europe Since 1500* (London: Europa, 1980), 9.

32. *La Saincte Bible, traduit par les theologiens de l'Université de Louvain* (Rouen: 1572): Exod. 20–23, 67–70; Lev. 24, 112. The standard Louvain Bible is a strikingly legalistic French translation.

33. Underdown, *Revel, Riot*, 106.

34. William Beik, *Urban Protest in Seventeenth-Century France* (New York: Cambridge University Press, 1997), 28–48; 252–53; James B. Collins, *Classes, Estates and Order in Early Modern Brittany* (Cambridge: Cambridge University Press, 1994), 251–70; Julius R. Ruff, *Violence in Early Modern Europe 1500–1800* (Cambridge: Cambridge University Press, 2001), 184–215; and Tommaso Astarita, *Village Justice: Community, Family, and Popular Culture in Early Modern Italy* (Baltimore: Johns Hopkins University Press, 1999) explore the variety of responses to the violation of community norms.

35. Charte aux Normands, in *Ordonnances des Rois de France* (Paris: 1902), i, 551, 557. The customary laws of the Charter were in turn based on earlier codes, particularly the Consuetudines et Iusticie of William the Conqueror (1091) and the Très Ancienne Coustumier of Normandy from the latter twelfth century. See Charles Homer Haskins, *Norman Institutions* (Cambridge, MA: Harvard University Press, 1925), 277–84.

36. As Parker has pointed out, "Indeed, for some contemporaries, the rule of justice was virtually synonymous with the preservation of customary rights." David Parker, *The Making of French Absolutism* (New York: St. Martin's, 1983), 1.

37. Michel de L'Hôpital, *Oeuvres completes,* ed. P. J. S. Durey, t. V, *Traité de la reformation de la justice* (reprint: Genève: Slatkine Reprints, 1968), 20–21; Cardinal Richelieu, *Testament politique* (Paris: Robert Laffont, 1947), 231–43.

38. William Doyle, *Venality: The Sale of Offices in Eighteenth-Century France* (Oxford: Oxford University Press, 1996); Roland Mousnier, *La venalité des offices sous Henri IV et Louis XIII* (Rouen: Éditions Maugard, 1945). On local and provincial venality, see especially Maurice Gresset, *L'introduction de la vénalité des offices en Franche-Comté* (Paris: Belles Lettres, 1989); Pierre Goubert, "Les officiers royaux des presidiaux, bailliages et élections dans la société française du XVIIe siècles," *Dix-septième siècle,* 42–43 (1959): 54–75; and Blanquie, *Les présidiaux,* 189–216.

39. Even the parlements were struggling to defend their property interests against the crown during the Dutch and Spanish wars; see John J. Hurt, *Louis XIV and the Parlements: The Assertion of Royal Authority* (Manchester: University of Manchester Press, 2002), 68–75, 95–103.

40. Debordes-Lissillour, *Les sénéchaussées royales,* 236, 239, 421.

41. James B. Collins, *The State in Early Modern France* (Cambridge: Cambridge University Press, 1995): 213. On the changing nature of provincial nobility in Normandy, see also Dewald, *Pont-St-Pierre,* and James B. Wood, *The Nobility of the Election of Bayeux, 1463–1666* (Princeton, NJ: Princeton University Press, 1980).

42. Jonathan Dewald, *Aristocratic Experience and the Origins of Modern Culture: France, 1570–1715* (Berkeley: University of California Press, 1993), 16. See also Dewald, *Pont-St.-Pierre,* 187, 252; and Sharon Kettering, *French Society 1589–1715* (Harlow: Longman, 2001), 77–79. On nobles and revolt, see Mack P. Holt, *The French Wars of Religion, 1562–1629* (Cambridge: Cambridge University Press, 1995), and Orest Ranum, *The Fronde: A French Revolution, 1648–1652* (New York: Norton, 1993). On noble patronage, see Kettering, *Patrons, Brokers and Clients in Seventeenth-Century France* (Oxford: Oxford University Press, 1986) and Kettering, *Patronage in Sixteenth and Seventeenth Century France* (Aldershot: Variorum, 2002).

43. Collins, *The State in Early Modern France,* 84, 129–38.

44. James M. Rosenheim, *The Emergence of a Ruling Order: English Landed Society 1650–1750* (London: Longman, 1998), 129.

45. Ordonnance de Blois, 1579; see also Jean Bart, *Histoire du droit privé, de la chute de l'empire romain aux XIXe siècle* (Paris: Montchrestien, 1998), 137–38.

46. Gérard Hurpin, *L'administration de Normandie,* 206.

47. Édit de Cremieu, 1536, in Ordonnances des Rois de France: François Ier, t. VIII, 104–12.

48. On the history of bailliage and sénéchaussée jurisdictions in late medieval and early modern France, see Gustave Dupont-Ferrier, *Les Officiers royaux des bailliages et sénéchaussées et les institutions monarchiques locales en France à la fin du Moyen Age* (Paris: Bouillon, 1903); Bernard Guenée, *Tribunaux et gens de justice dans le bailiage de Senlis à la fin du Moyen Age (vers 1380–vers 1550)* (Paris: Société des Éditions Les Belles Lettres, 1963); and Jean Guerout, "La question des territoires des bailliages royaux: L'example de la prévoté et vicomté de Paris (XIIIe–XVIIIe siècles)," *Actes du 100e congrès national des sociétés savants* 2 (Paris: Comité des Travaux Historiques et Scientifiques, 1978), 7–18.

49. Leopold Soublin, *Les grandes bailliages de Haute Normandie en 1789* (Rouen: 1972); and Soublin, *Le premier vote des Normands, 1789* (Fécamp: E.M.T.N., 1981) document the prominence of Norman lawyers and officers in the early Revolution.

50. In Charente-Inférieure, for example, 77 percent of the new justices of the peace whose occupations are known had been lawyers or notaries in the ancien régime. See Crubaugh, *Balancing the Scales of Justice,* 144–45.

51. This view can still be found in contemporary English history; see, for example, Sharpe, *Crime in Early Modern England,* 58, in which the English judicial system is described as one that "caused less oppression, and indeed, less distortion of society" than Continental justice.

52. Soleil, *Le siège royal,* 288.

53. Robert Muchembled, *Popular Culture and Elite Culture in France 1400–1750,* trans. Lydia Cochrane (Baton Rouge: Louisiana State University Press, 1985), 183.

54. Parker, "Sovereignty, Absolutism," 37; see also Parker, *Class and State in Ancien Régime France: The Road to Modernity?* (London: Routledge, 1996), 168–73.

55. Jacques-Bénigne Bossuet, *Politique tirée des propres paroles de l'écriture sainte* (Turin: 1824), 188.

56. For further discussion of Bodin, see Richard Bonney, "Bodin and the Development of the French Monarchy," in *The Limits of Absolutism in Ancien Régime France,* 43–61 (Aldershot: Variorum, 1995); A. London Fell, *Origins of Legislative Sovereignty and the Legislative State,* vol. 4 (New York: Praeger, 1991); Julian Franklin, *Jean Bodin and the Rise of Absolutist Theory* (Cambridge: Cambridge University Press, 1973); and David Parker, "Law, Society and the State in the Thought of Jean Bodin," *History of Political Thought* 2 (1981): 253–85.

57. Collins, *Classes, Estates,* 13.

58. Claude Seyssel, *La Monarchie de France,* ed. Jacque Poujol, Part I, Chap. 8, 115 (Paris: Librarie d'Argences, 1961).

59. Bodin, *Six livres,* 221.

60. Bodin, *Six livres,* 215–16.

61. Bodin, *Six livres,* 223.

62. See also Sara Hanley, "The Monarchic State in Early Modern France: Marital Regime Government and Male Right," in *Politics, Ideology and the Law in Early Modern Europe,* ed. Adrianna E. Bakos, esp. 109–15 (Rochester, NY: University of Rochester Press, 1994), on the French law canon.

63. Bodin, *Six livres,* 222.

64. Bodin, *Six livres,* 135.

65. Bodin, *Six livres,* 160.

66. Louis XIV, *Mémoires,* livre I, 1661 (Paris: Le livre club du librairie, 1960), 20; see also Albert N. Hamscher, *The Conseil Privé and the Parlements in the Age of Louis XIV: A Study in French Absolutism* (Pittsburgh: American Philosophical Society, 1987).

67. Parker, "Sovereignty, Absolutism," 71.

68. Collins, *Classes, Estates,* 14.

69. Cardinal Richelieu, *Testament politique* (Paris: Robert Laffont, 1947): 248–49.

70. Bodin, *Six livres,* 15.

71. Bodin, *Six livres,* 1.

72. Nannerl Keohane, *Philosophy and the State in France: The Renaissance to the Enlightenment* (Princeton, NJ: Princeton University Press, 1980), 69, 72; on dualism, see also Parker, *The Making of French Absolutism,* 2, 91. We can see this distinction between public sovereignty and the private realm expressed elsewhere in Europe; see, for example, Bartolomé de las Casas, *A Short Account of the Destruction of the Indies,* trans. and ed. Nigel Griffin (London: Penguin Books, 1992), 52–53.

73. Bodin, *Six livres,* 429; see also 373.

74. de L'Hôpital, *Traité de la réformation de la justice,* 8.

75. Aristotle, *Nicomachean Ethics,* trans. and ed. Roger Crisp (Cambridge: Cambridge University Press, 2000), 83.

76. Cicero, *On Obligations (De officiis),* trans. P. G. Walsh (Oxford: Oxford University Press, 2000), 9.

77. Bodin, *Six Livres,* 436. Bodin also conceded that seigneurial jurisdictions were a form of personal property, as long as the seigneur rendered faith and homage to the sovereign.

78. Phillipe du Plessis-Mornay, *Vidiciae Contra Tyrannos* (1579), in *Constitutionalism and Resistance in the Sixteenth Century: Three Treatises by Hotman, Beza, and Mornay,* ed. and trans. Julian Franklin (New York: Pegasus, 1969), 161–62.

79. Theodore Beza, *Right of Magistrates,* in *Constitutionalism and Resistance in the Sixteenth Century: Three Treatises by Hotman, Beza, and Mornay,* ed. and trans. Julian Franklin (New York: Pegasus, 1969), 111. See also Robert Descimon and Alain Guery, "Un état de temps moderns?" in *L'état et les pouvoirs,* ed. André Burguiere and Jacques Revel, 224 (Paris: Éditions Sevil, 1989).

80. François Hotman, *Francogallia,* in *Constitutionalism and Resistance in the Sixteenth Century: Three Treatises by Hotman, Beza, and Mornay,* ed. and trans. Julian Franklin (New York: Pegasus, 1969), 95.

81. Henri-François d'Aguesseau, "L'amour de son état," in *Oeuvres choisies* (Paris: 1863), 10–18, quoted in Andrews, *Law, Magistracy and Crime in Old Regime Paris,* 265.

82. William Beik, *Absolutism and Society in Seventeenth-Century France* (Cambridge: Cambridge University Press, 1985), 13.

83. See Albert N. Hamscher, *The Parlement of Paris After the Fronde, 1653–1673* (Pittsburgh: University of Pittsburgh Press, 1976), 142–46, 200–1.

84. Beik, *Absolutism and Society,* 309.

85. Hurt, *Louis XIV and the Parlements,* 95–124, 195–98.

86. Roger Mettam, *Power and Faction in Louis XIV's France* (Oxford: Basil Blackwell, 1988), 258.

87. See Jean-Laurent Rosenthal, *The Fruits of Revolution: Property Rights, Litigation, and French Agriculture, 1799–1860* (Cambridge: Cambridge University Press, 1992), 15–18, 139–40, on local property law in the postrevolutionary period.

88. BN 500 Colbert 260, Voysin de la Noiraye, *Mémoire sur la généralité,* 1665, fols. 180–205.

89. Jonathan Dewald, "Magistracy and Political Opposition at Rouen: A Social Context," *Sixteenth Century Journal* 2 (October 1974): 66–78.

90. Lloyd Moote, *Louis XIII, The Just* (Berkeley: University of California Press, 1989), 118.

91. See Madeleine Foisil, *La révolte des nu-pieds et les révoltes normandes de 1639* (Paris: E. Frère, 1970).

92. Sharon Kettering, *Judicial Politics and Urban Revolt in Seventeenth-Century France* (Princeton, NJ: Princeton University Press, 1978), 6.

93. Grainville-la-Teinturière and Longueville were high justices until they escheated to the crown in 1694 and were converted to royal courts.

94. There are serious limitations to large-scale statistical studies using local court records, because of the vagaries of record keeping from one court to the next and the hazards of record preservation, but these limitations can be partly mitigated. Wherever complete bound registers were available, those registers were used to build smaller-scale statistical analyses spanning one or several years. When combined with the general patterns of the nine courts taken together, they allow reasonably accurate generalizations to be made about functioning of the system as a whole.

95. Louis XIV, *Mémoires,* 20.

96. Beik, *Absolutism and Society;* Collins, *The State in Early Modern France;* Collins, *Classes, Estates and Order;* and Mettam, *Power and Faction.*

97. John Northleigh, *Topographical descriptions, with historico-politico and medico-physical observations made in two voyages. . . .* (London: 1702), 106.

98. Alexis de Tocqueville, *L'ancien régime et la révolution,* ed. J.-P. Meyer (Paris: Gallimard, 1967), 122.

99. Crubaugh, *Balancing the Scales,* 144–45. As several historians have noted, some legal men lost their enthusiasm for Continual revolution after the early reforms, but the legal class prospered in the nineteenth century. See David Bell, *Lawyers and Citizens: The Making of a Political Elite in Old Regime France* (New York: Oxford University Press, 1994), ix; Lenard R. Berlanstein, *The Barristers of Toulouse in the Eighteenth Century (1740–1793)* (Baltimore: Johns Hopkins University Press, 1975),168–71; Phillip Dawson, *Provincial Magistrates and Revolutionary Politics in France, 1789–1795* (Cambridge, MA: Harvard University Press, 1972); and Timothy Tackett, *Becoming a Revolutionary: The Deputies of the French National Assembly and the Emergence of a Revolutionary Culture, 1789–1790* (Princeton, NJ: Princeton University Press, 1996).

Chapter 2

1. On protoindustrialization and weaving in Normandy and northern France, see Liana Vardi, *The Land and the Loom: Peasants and Profit in Northern France 1680–1800* (Durham: Duke University Press, 1993); Gay Gullickson, *Spinners and Weavers of Auffray: Rural Industry and the Sexual Division of Labor in a French village, 1750–1850* (Cambridge: Cambridge University Press, 1986); and Jacques Bottin, "La production des toiles en Normandie, milieu XVIe siècle–milieu XVIIe siècle," in *L'homme et l'industrie en Normandie* (Alençon: Sociétés Historiques et Archéologiques de Normandie, 1990), 77–86.

2. By the early eighteenth century, the Caux had lost its eastern frontier near Neufchâtel to the pays de Bray, leaving an eastern boundary running roughly from Gournay north to Dieppe.

3. Antoine Follaine, *Les juridictions royales subalterns en Normandie du XVI au XVIII siècle* (Rouen: Mémoire D.E.A., Université de Rouen, 1989), 239. This is the best modern source for Cauchois jurisdictions.

4. Rouen had a population of roughly eighty-eight thousand, but estimates of its population in the seventeenth and eighteenth centuries still vary widely. See Guy Lemarchand, "La fin du féodalisme dans le pays de Caux" (thèse d'état, Université de Paris, 1985), 11.

5. *Coutumes du pays de Normandie* (Rouen: Chez Jean B. Besonge, 1697).

6. Christophe Blanquie, *Les présidiaux de Richelieu: Justice et vénalité (1630–1642)* (Paris: Éditions Christian, 2000), 7.

7. Pierre Gouhier, Anne Vallez, and Jean-Marie Vallez, *Atlas historique de Normandie* (Caen: Centre de Recherches d'Histoire Quantitative, 1972), 2:pl. 25; see Claude Marin Saugrain, *Dictionnaire universel de la France ancienne et moderne, et de la Nouvelle France* (Paris: Saugrain, 1726). In 1665, for example, Cany had 77 non-*utile* hearths for its 206 *utile* hearths; by 1713 there were 235 *utile* hearths. The 1713 *dénombrement* failed to list the number of hearths below the tax threshold.

8. Léopold Soublin, *Le premier vote des Normands: 1789* (Fécamp: E.M.T.N., 1981), 48.

9. Soublin, *Le premier vote.*

10. The lower courts under the presidials were technically chartered by the crown as "bailliages vicomtals," but their judges were quick to take advantage of the ambiguity and styled their courts as "bailliages et vicomtés" at the top of their records.

Bailliage has been favored over *vicomté* here, not only because they were so called by their officers, but because they exercised full bailliage jurisdiction according to the Custom of Normandy. They also did not appeal cases into the bailliage and presidial of Caudebec but directly into the Parlement of Normandy.

11. ADSM C 1619, Bureau des Finances, Aveu de Cany-Caniel, 1750.

12. ADSM 7 BP 25, Présidial de Caudebec en Caux, avr. 1721.

13. ADSM 13 B 9, bailliage de Cany, 1671.

14. Jacques La Gallisoniere, *Recherche de la noblesse,* t. 1 (1672).

15. ADSM C 1619, Bureau des Finances, aveu de Cany-Caniel, 9 mai 1750.

16. ADSM 13 BP 52, bailliage de Cany, 9 déc. 1720.

17. See R. Villand, F. Lamotte, and A. Dubuc, "Notes sur les foires et marchés en Normandie," in *Circuits commerciaux, foires et marchés en Normandie,* 165–70 (IXe congrès des sociétés historiques, archéologiques, et ethnologiques de Normandie, Rouen, 1975).

18. ADSM 46 BP 25, haute justice de Cany Caniel, juin 1716.

19. ADSM 5 E 3, haute justice de Cany-Caniel, Arts et Métiers, Drapiers de Cany, 1736.

20. Similar functions can be seen in the Norman high justice of Pont-Saint-Pierre; see Jonathan Dewald, *Pont-Saint-Pierre, 1398–1789: Lordship, Community, and Capitalism in Early Modern France* (Berkeley: University of California Press, 1987), 252–53.

21. Claude Saugrain, *Dictionnaire universel de la France* (Paris: Chez Saugrain, 1726).

22. Duc de Saint-Simon, *Mémoires* (Paris: 1842), 3:223.

23. Here I have used the multiplier 4.5 for the number of persons per household.

24. ADSM C 1619, Bureau des Finances, Cany-Caniel aveu, 1750.

25. Arrêt du conseil, 24 déc.1695; see also Dom Michel Toussaint Chrétien Duplessis, *Description géographique et historique de la haute Normandie* (Paris: Veuve Ganeau, 1740), 191–92.

26. ADSM 71 BP 9, bailliage de Grainville-la-Teinturière, 16 déc. 1728; ADSM 71 BP 3, bailliage de Grainville-la-Teinturière, 1693–97.

27. ADSM G 738, Visites pastorales de Msgr. d'Aubigné, 25 mai 1714.

28. On the career of Anne-Geneviève de Bourbon, duchess of Longueville, see Arlette Lebigre, *La duchesse de Longueville* (Paris: Perrin, 2004); Madeleine Foisil, *Femmes de caractère au XVIIe siècle, 1600–1650* (Paris: Fallois, 2004), 71–92; and Jacques Debu-Bridel, *Anne-Geneviève de Bourbon, duchesse de Longueville* (Paris: Gallimard, 1938).

29. Duplessis, *Description géographique,* 191–92.

30. Follaine, *Les juridictions royales,* 243–60.

31. ADSM C 2798, Procès verbaux de prise de possession du duché de Longueville, 1694–95.

32. Comte d'Estaintot, *Un procès entre deux seigneurs haute-justiciers (Valmont et Cany-Caniel) au XVIII siècle* (Rouen: 1891). On Valmont and the duchy of Estouteville, see also Duplessis, *Description géographique,* 723–25; and Jacques Bottin, *Seigneurs et paysans dans l'ouest du pays de Caux (1540–1650)* (Paris: Sycamore, 1983), 79, 239. The number of parishes counted in the jurisdiction ranges from forty to more than sixty, because of the overlap of jurisdictions in parishes.

33. Seigneurial baillis (active chief judges) should not be confused with royal baillis, sword nobles who technically sat at the head of a royal bailliage court, but who after 1579 were forbidden to actually judge in court.

34. Daniel Jousse, *Traité de l'administration de la Justice* (Paris: Debure Père, 1771) 1:630.

35. See n. 1.

36. The Caux was among the most densely populated countrysides in France, with between fifty-one and fifty-eight inhabitants per square kilometer, above the average for the *généralité* of Rouen as a whole and well above other heavily populated, grain-producing regions such as the Beauce. (See LeMarchand, "La fin du féodalisme," 15–16). As a rough guide, the élection of Caudebec, one of six in the Caux, had eighteen thousand taxable and exempt hearths in 1713, for a total population of approximately eighty-one thousand solvent inhabitants. The early eighteenth-century taille records do not record non-utile households. The rural élection of Caudebec-en-Caux had more taxable hearths than the élection of Rouen, but only a tenth as many exempt or privileged hearths. On tax figures for populations, see Gouhier et. al., *Atlas historique de Normandie* and Edmond Esmonin, *La taille en Normandie au temps de Colbert, 1661–1683* (Paris: Hachette et cie, 1913), 545 passim.

37. Arthur Young, *Travels in France during the Years 1787, 1788, 1789* (Paris: 1808), 83.

38. ADSM 1 B 5528, Parlement de Normandie, Arts et métiers, Arrêt du conseil d'état du roi, 24 déc. 1701.

39. Marc Bloch, *Les caractères originaux de l'histoire rurale Française,* 2ième ed. (Paris: Armand Colin, 1952), 232.

40. Jacques Bottin, *Seigneurs et paysans,* 255–56.

41. James M. Rosenheim, "County Governance and Elite Withdrawal in Norfolk, 1660–1720," in *The First Modern Society: Essays in English History Written in Honor of Lawrence Stone,* ed. A. L. Beir, David Cannadine and James M. Rosenheim, 95 (Cambridge: Cambridge University Press, 1989); see also Lawerence Stone and J. C. F. Stone, *An Open Elite? England 1540–1880* (Oxford: Oxford University Press, 1984), 269–75.

42. Gerard Hurpin, "L'administration de la Normandie au temps de Louis XIV," *Bulletin de la Société Libre d'Emulation de la Seine Maritime* (Rouen: 1986): 34–36.

43. James Debu-Bridel, *Anne-Geneviève de Bourbon, duchesse de Longueville* (Paris: Gallimerd, 1938), 9.

44. *Mémoires de M. de ***,* 1648, in *Collection des mémoires relatifs a l'histoire de France,* ed. A. Petitot et al. (Paris: 1829), 58:62.

45. ADSM 1 Mi 871, de Becdeliévre family papers, 13 avril 1683, shows the extent of absentee management of the duchy of Longueville.

46. Duplessis, *Description géographique,* 214. See Mary-Claude Gricourt, "Etude d'histoire démographique, sociale et religieuse de 5 paroisses . . . ," *Annales de Normandie,* no. 3 (1963): 474, on other absentee noble families in the bailiwick.

47. ADSM 71 BP 14, bailliage de Grainville-la-Teinturière, 1745; Claude Pellot, *Notes du premier Président Pellot sur la Normandie (1670–1683),* ed. G. A. Prévost (Rouen, Paris: 1915), 26–27, 195; see also Gricourt, "Etude d'histoire," 445–555, for a discussion of landholding and social patterns in five parishes near Cany.

48. James M. Rosenheim, "Landownership, the Aristocracy and the Country Gentry," in *The Reigns of Charles II and James VII and II,* ed. L. K. J. Glassey, 154 (New York:

St. Martin's Press, 1997); Jonathan Dewald, *Aristocratic Experience and the Origins of Modern Culture: France, 1570–1715* (Berkeley: University of California Press, 1993), 150.

49. LeMarchand, "Le fin de féodalisme," 241–55.

50. LeMarchand, "Le fin de féodalisme," 157–58, 168; see also David Roger Hainsworth, *Stewards, Lords, and People: The Estate Steward and His World in Late Stuart England* (Cambridge: Cambridge University Press, 1992), 13.

51. Jonathan Dewald, *The European Nobility 1400–1800* (Cambridge: Cambridge University Press, 1996), 118, 165.

52. Mark Venard, *Bourgeois et paysans au XVII siècle* (Paris: S.E.V.P.E.N, 1957), 110; Gricourt, "Étude d'histoire," 474.

53. James M. Rosenheim, "County Governance and Elite Withdrawal in Norfolk, 1660–1720," in *The First Modern Society: Essays in English History in Honor of Lawrence Stone,* ed. A. L. Beier, David Cannadine, and James M. Rosenheim (Cambridge: Cambridge University Press, 1989), 122–24.

54. ADSM C 1728, Taille, Aubermesnil, 1695. Thanks to James B. Collins for these tax rolls.

55. ADSM C 1728, Taille, Aubermesnil, 1695.

56. LeMarchand, "La fin du féodalisme," 122–24.

57. J. A. Sharpe, *Early Modern England: A Social History 1550–1760,* 2nd ed. (London: Arnold, 1997), 208; David Underdown, *Revel, Riot and Rebellion: Popular Politics and Culture in Early Modern England 1603–1660* (Oxford: Oxford University Press, 1985), 26.

58. BMR Ms Y 169, Intendant de Vaubourg, *Mémoires concernant la généralité de Rouen, 1698,* fols. 5–9.

59. Vaubourg, *Mémoires,* fols. 5–9.

60. Soublin, *Le premier vote,* 35–38.

61. Vaubourg, *Mémoires,* fols. 27–29.

62. Racine, *Les plaideurs,* Théâtre de Racine, ann. par Pierre Mélèse (Paris: Imprimerie Nationale de France, 1951), 131–32.

Chapter 3

1. ADSM 71 BP 6, haute justice de Grainville-la-Teinturière, 1693–1698; 71 BP 10, bailliage de Grainville-la-Teinturière, 1698–1700; André Lecole, "La haute justice et vicomté de Grainville-la-Teinturière aux XVIIe et XVIIIe siècle" (mémoire de maitrise, U.E.R. des lettres de Rouen, 1978), 42–43.

2. John Locke, *Travels in France, 1675–1679,* ed. John Lough (Cambridge: Cambridge University Press, 1953), 48–49.

3. William Doyle's *Venality: The Sale of Offices in Eighteenth-Century France* (Oxford: Oxford University Press, 1996) has shed important new light on the system of venal officeholding as a whole; on the provinces, see particularly Maurice Gresset, *L'introduction de la vénalité des offices en Franche-Comté* (Paris: Belles-Lettres, 1989); and Doyle, "Venality and Society in Eighteenth-Century Bordeaux," *Sociétés et groupes sociaux en Aquitaine et en Angleterre* (Bordeaux, 1979), 201–14. Earlier scholarship on local venality rested on a handful of older works, principally Roland Mousnier, *La vénalité des offices sous Henri IV et Louis XIII* (Rouen: Éditions Maugard, 1945); Gaston

Dupont-Ferrier, *Les officiers royaux des bailliages et sénéchaussées et les institutions monarchiques locales en France à la fin du Moyen Age* (Paris: 1903); and Jean Droualt, *Les vicomtés en Normandie aux XVIII siècle* (Caen: L. Jouan et R. Bigot, Librairies de l'Université de la Société des Antiquaires de Normandy, 1924).

4. Despite royal attempts to root out judicial officers from the municipalities, beginning with the reorganization of the towns in 1692 through the reforms of 1774, they retained control of many of these offices at least through the middle of the eighteenth century. For a discussion of municipal reforms in relation to judicial officers, see John Carey, *Judicial Reform in France before the Revolution of 1789* (Cambridge, MA: Harvard University Press, 1981), 103–4; and Hilton Root, *Peasant and King in Burgundy: Agrarian Foundations of French Absolutism* (Berkeley: University of California Press, 1987), 52–53. On the "municipalizing" of villages, see Antoine Follain, *Le village sous l'ancien régime* (Paris: Fayard, 2008), 376–420.

5. Edmund Tew, *The Justicing Notebook (1750–64) of Edmund Tew, Rector of Bolton,* ed. Gwenda Morgan and Peter Rushton, 1–4 (Woodbridge: Boydell, 2000).

6. Lionel K. J. Glassey, *Politics and the Appointments of Justices of the Peace 1675–1720* (New York: Oxford University Press, 1979), 24–31; Norman Landau, *The Justices of the Peace, 1679–1760* (Berkeley: University of California Press, 1984), 6–9, 19–45; Tew, *Justicing Notebook,* 2–25.

7. David Bell, *Lawyers and Citizens* (New York: Oxford University Press, 1994), 6–7; Doyle, *Venality,* 193; Philip Dawson, *Provincial Magistrates and Revolutionary Politics in France, 1789–1795* (Cambridge, MA: Harvard University Press, 1972), 205–7, 340–43; Paul R. Hanson, *Provincial Politics in the French Revolution: Caen and Limoges, 1789–1794* (Baton Rouge: Louisiana State University Press, 1989), 193–96; Lenard R. Berlanstein, *The Barristers of Toulouse in the Eighteenth Century (1740–1793)* (Baltimore: Johns Hopkins University Press, 1975), 186; and William J. Bouwsma, "Lawyers and Early Modern Culture," *American Historical Review* 78, no. 2 (1973): 303–27.

8. Landau, *Justices of the Peace,* 69–95; Glassey, *Politics,* 100–34, 262–69.

9. André Corvisier, "Un lien entre villes et campagnes: Le personnel des haute justices en Haute Normandie au XVIIIe siècle," *Annales de Normandie, Recueil d'études offert en homage au doyen Michel de Boüard,* vol. 1 (Caen: Université de Caen, 1982) 163; Pierre Goubert, "Les officiers royaux des presidiaux, bailliages et élections dans la société française du XVIIe siècle," *Dix-septième siècle,* 42–43 (1959): 74; Mousnier, *La venalite des offices,* 455–94.

10. Goubert, "Les officiers royaux," 74.

11. William Doyle, "The Price of Offices in Pre-Revolutionary France," in *Officers, Nobles and Revolutionaries: Essays on Eighteenth-Century France* (London: Hambledon Continuum, 1995), 108; Doyle, *Venality,* 187; Phillip Dawson, *Provincial Magistrates and Revolutionary Politics in France, 1789–1795* (Cambridge, MA: Harvard University Press, 1972), 80–83.

12. Goubert, "Les officiers royaux," 69–70.

13. Victor-L. Tapié, "Les officiers seigneuriaux dans la société provinciale du XVIIe siècle," *Dix-septième siècle,* 42–43 (1959): 133.

14. Landau, *Justices of the Peace,* 22–23.

15. Anette Smedley-Weill, ed., *Correspondance des intendants avec le contrôleur général de Finances, 1677–1689: Naissance d'une adminstration,* Sous-serie G. Inventaire analytique (Paris: Archives Nationales, 1989), 1:353 (16 nov. 1689).

16. ADSM 1 B 5612, Parlement de Rouen, Interrogatoire de vicomte de Form-ville; ADIV C 1828, Intendant, Bretagne, Augmentations des gages 1716–18; ADIV C 1835–1836, Intendant, Bretagne, Officiers, 1740–41; see also Séverine Debordes-Lissillour, *Les sénéchaussées royales de Bretagne: La monarchie d'ancien régime et ses juridictions ordinaires (1532–1790)* (Rennes: Presses Universitaires de Rennes, 2006), 264–66.

17. Goubert, "Les officiers," 55.

18. Morgan and Rushton, in Tew, *Justicing Notebook*, 25.

19. ADSM 46 BP 39, HJ de Cany-Caniel, 3 mai 1730.

20. ADSM C 1619, Bureau des Finances, Cany-Caniel aveu, 1750.

21. Glassey, *Politics*, 25.

22. ADSM 71 BP 14, bailliage de Grainville-la-Teinturiére, déclarations de gros-sesse, 1746.

23. See, for example, ADSM 1 B 5697, Parlement de Normandie, Tournelles, 18 juin 1717.

24. Richard Gough, *The History of Myddle,* ed. David Hey (Harmondsworth: Penguin, 1981), 15, 254–64.

25. Glassey, *Politics,* 25.

26. ADSM 13 BP 49, bailliage de Cany, 27 jan. 1710; 10 fév. 1710.

27. ADSM 13 BP 57, bailliage de Cany, 20 mars 1730.

28. Arrêt de 8 mars 1736; see also Houard, *Dictionnaire analytique, historique, et étymologique de la coutume de Normandie* (Rouen: Le Boucher le jeune, 1781), 239–46. The pattern of misusing church funds and properties was a problem in Brittany as well that the Parlement at Rennes attempted to control.

29. On communal property and the communes in Normandie, see Follaine, *Le village,* 160–214.

30. Lemarchand, "La fin de féodalisme," 110–18, 122–24.

31. For Burgundy, see ADCO B 165 15, bailliage de Nuits-Saint-George, 1717–1730.

32. Lemarchand, "La fin du féodalisme," 110–11.

33. Debordes-Lissillour, *Les sénéchaussées royales,* 276–80.

34. ADSM C 1619, Bureau des Finances, Cany-Caniel aveu, 1750.

35. ADSM 19 BP 2, bailliage de Longueville, pièces isolées, 1694–1770, n.d.

36. ADSM 1 ER 1084, de Becdelièvre family papers, 1 juillet 1949.

37. ADSM 1 ER 1084, de Becdelièvre family papers.

38. James B. Collins, *From Tribes to Nation: The Making of France 500–1799* (Toronto: 2002), 454.

39. Liana Vardi, *The Land and the Loom: Peasants and Profit in Northern France, 1680–1800* (Durham: Duke University Press, 1993), 181.

40. ADSM 13 BP 52: bailliage de Cany, 1720–1723.

41. Intendant Le Blanc à le contrôleur générale, 6 fév. 1679, 8 mai 1679, in Smedley-Weill, *Correspondence,* 293, 294.

42. BMR Ms Y 169, Intendant de Vaubourg, "Mémoires concernant la généralité de Rouen," 1698–1699, fols. 35–41.

43. On consular courts in Normandy, see Gayle Brunelle, *New World Merchants of Rouen 1559–1630* (Kirksville, MO: Truman State University Press, 1991).

44. ADSM 1 ER 1084, de Becdelièvre family papers, 1711.

45. Déclaration de 12 jan. 1680.

46. ADSM 71 BP 15, bailliage et vicomté de Grainville-la-Teinturière, réceptions d'office, 1722–29.

47. ADSM C 1619, Bureau des Finances, Cany-Caniel aveu, 9 mai 1750.

48. Landau, *Justices of the Peace*, 191–93; Morgan and Rushton, in Tew, *Justicing Notebook*, 14–15; Glassey, *Politics*, 25.

49. Jonathan Dewald, *The European Nobility 1400–1800* (Cambridge: Cambridge University Press, 1996), 118.

50. Voysin de la Noiraye, *Mémoire sur la généralité de Rouen (1665)*, ed. Edmond Esmonin (Paris: Librairie Hachette, 1913), 230–32. For the entire généralité of Rouen, there were only fifty-one archers, plus an additional twenty-three belonging to the the the prévoté générale of Upper Normandy.

51. Intendant Marillac à le controlleur générale, 29 jan., 28 fév. 1685, in Smedley-Weill, *Correspondence*, 327–29.

52. BMR Ms Y 169, Vaubourg, "Mémoires," fol. 2.

53. ADSM 5 Mi 863, Registres paroissales, Saint-Vaast-Dieppedalle, 1692–94.

54. ADSM 71 BP 6, Grainville-la-Teinturière, 1694; elsewhere in France, see James B. Collins, *The State in Early Modern France* (Cambridge: Cambridge University Press, 1995), 153.

55. William Beik, *Urban Protest in Seventeenth-Century France: The Culture of Retribution* (Cambridge: Cambridge University Press, 1997), 259–62, shows how intimidating urban riots could be even for parlementaires. See also Alexander Cowan, *Urban Europe 1500–1700* (London: Arnold, 1998), 184–86; and Sharon Kettering, *French Society 1589–1715* (Harlow: Longman, 2001), 35–36.

56. ADSM 71 BP 6, HJ de Grainville-la-Teinturière, héritages, ventes, etc., 1692–94.

57. ADSM 46 BP 18, HJ de Cany-Caniel, 2 jul. 1694.

58. ADSM 46 BP 18, HJ de Cany-Caniel.

59. Intendant Le Blanc à le controlleur générale, 6 mai 1678, in Smedly-Weill, *Correspondence*, 291.

60. BMR MS Y 169, Vaubourg, "Mémoires," fols. 5–9, 24, 35–41.

61. BMR MS Y 169, Vaubourg, "Mémoires." On the crisis of 1693–94, see also Jean-Paul Bardet, "Mourir à Rouen au temps de Boisguilbert: Les faux-semblants de la crise de 1693–1694," in *Boisguilbert parmi nous: Actes du Colloque International de Rouen, 22–23 mai 1975* (Paris: INED, 1989), 201–17.

62. ADSM 71 BP 14, bailliage de Grainville-la-Teinturiére, 11 déc. 1738.

63. ADSM 71 BP 13, bailliage de Grainville-la-Teinturière, 4 nov. 1743.

64. Albert N. Hamscher, *The Parlement of Paris After the Fronde, 1653–1673* (Pittsburgh: University of Pittsburgh Press, 1976), 179.

65. Isambert, Dieussy, Jourdan, et al., *Recueil générale des anciens lois françaises, depuis l'an 420 jusqu'a la Revolution de 1789* (Paris: Belin-le-Prieur, 1821–33), 19:530–34.

66. ADSM 19 BP 2, bailliage de Longueville, 1697.

67. Dewald, *European Nobility*, 116.

68. ADSM 13 BP 29, bailliage de Cany, oct. 1680.

69. Jacques La Gallisonière, *Recherche de la noblesse*, t. 1 (1672).

70. ADSM 13 BP 52, bailliage de Cany, 5 jan. 1720, 29 jul. 1720.

71. Glassey, *Politics,* 6, 22.

72. Cardinal Richelieu, *Testament politique* (Paris: Robert Laffont, 1947), 236.

73. Goubert, "Les officiers royaux," 63.

74. ADSM 1 B 3654, Parlement, réceptions des Lieutenants Général, 1705–1746; réceptions des officiers, 1702–1718.

75. On Brittany, see Debordes-Lissillour, *Les sénéchaussées royales,* 191–95; on Bordeaux, see Julius R. Ruff, *Crime, Justice and Public Order in Old Régime France: the Sénéchaussées of Libourne and Bazas, 1696–1789* (London: Croom Helm, 1984), 30–31.

76. Ibid.

77. ADSM 46 BP 19, haute justice de Cany-Caniel, 4 oct. 1713.

78. ADSM 46 BP 23, HJ de Cany-Caniel, registres du greffe, lettre à Mme. Baudry de M. D'Angouville, 23 sep. 1713. Documents often use the word *tutelle* to encompass both tutorship and curatorship.

79. ADSM 71 BP 6, HJ de Grainville-la-Teinturière, tutelles, 1693–94.

80. ADSM 46 BP 24, HJ de Cany-Caniel, tutelles, 4 oct. 1713.

81. See also Maurice Gresset, *Gens de justice à Besançon, de la conquête par Louis XIV à la Révolution française (1674–1789)* (Paris: Bibliothèque Nationale, 1978), 197–98, 202–3, for marriage patterns in urban Besançon, where fewer than 51 percent of lower magistrates married wives from judicial families.

82. Landau, *Justices of the Peace,* 386.

83. Claude Pellot, *Notes du premier président Pellot sur la Normandie (1670–1683),* ed. G. A. Prévost (Rouen and Paris: Société de la Histoire du Normandie, 1915), 193–94.

84. Pellot, *Notes.*

85. De la Noiraye, *Mémoire,* 207–35.

86. Ordonnance de Blois, Article 15; Ordonnance d'Orléans, Articles 100–101.

87. Tapié, "Les officiers seigneuriaux," 122–31.

88. In Brittany, for example, a seigneurial office of procureur fiscal was sold for 2,000 livres; in the Caux the marquis de Cany leased the clerkship in his high justice at Cany, as did the duchess of Longueville in the high justice of Valmont.

89. Tapié, "Les officiers seigneuriaux," 122–31.

90. The percentage of all officers who were noble over this period would drop slightly if complete records were available; the list of receptions for middling officers ends in 1718, whereas the list of receptions for judges extends to 1746.

91. Rentes on the Hôtel de Ville in Paris were less common in rural portfolios.

92. J. A. Sharpe, "The History of Crime in Late Medieval and Early Modern England," *Social History* 7 (1982): 201.

93. ADSM C 308, Intendant de Rouen, Roles de la capitation des officiers et employées du Roi en la Généralité de Rouen, 1701.

94. ADSM C 317, Intendant de Rouen, Roles de la capitation des officiers et employées du Roi en la Généralité de Rouen, 1713.

95. Goubert, "Les officiers royaux," 63.

96. Comte d'Estaintot, *Récherches sur les hautes justices féodales existant en 1789* (Rouen: 1892), 29.

97. ADSM 71 BP 6, haute justice de Grainville-la-Teinturière, 1693–1698; 71 BP 10, bailliage de Grainville-la-Teinturière, 1698–1700; André Lecole, "La haute justice

et vicomté de Grainville-la-Teinturière aux XVIIe et XVIIIe siècle" (mémoire de maitrise, U.E.R. des lettres de Rouen, 1978), 42–43.

98. ADSM 13 BP 46, bailliage de Cany, assizes, avril 1692; ADSM 46 BP 14, haute justice de Cany-Caniel, 1680–1681.

99. ADSM 46 BP 18, haute justice de Cany-Caniel, 1688–1698; 71 BP 7, haute justice de Grainville-la-Teinturière, 1691; 13 BP 46, bailliage de Cany, 1689–1693; 13 BP 48, 1708–1710.

100. De la Noiraye, *Mémoire,* 229.

101. ADSM 5 Mi 863, Registres paroissiale de Saint-Vaast-Dieppdale, 1694. Unfortunately, the name of the bride's father is effaced.

102. Lécole, "La haute justice et vicomté de Grainville-la-Teinturière aux XVIIe et XVIIIe siècle" (mémoire de maitrise, U.E.R. des lettres de Rouen, 1978), 43–44. Lécole was able to trace Maribrasse's offices outside of the main courts, in the élection and the salt warehouse.

103. ADSM 13 B 9, bailliage de Cany, assize mercuriale, 1671; ADSM 13 B 46, bailliage de Cany, assize mercuriale, 10 mai 1689; assize mercuriale, 10 octobre 1690.

104. See Berlanstein, *The Barristers of Toulouse,* 19–23, for a discussion of how a few lawyers came to dominate urban courts as well.

105. ADCO B2 149/1, bailliage de Beaune, fols. 51–52, 7 fév. 1668; fols. 53–54, undated, late 1660s to early 1670s.

106. On earlier seventeenth-century "urban oligarchies"of magistrates and mayors, see Christophe Blanquie, *Les présidiaux de Richelieu: Justice et vénalité (1630–1642)* (Paris: Éditions Christian, 2000), 10.

107. On cumuls in the urban sénéchaussée and présidiale of Nantes, see Hautebert, *La justice pénale,* 32.

108. Tapié and Goubert recognized the prevalence of seigneurial court cumuls in the tax élections and the existence of royal cumuls in the seigneurial courts. But Goubert chose to emphasize here the traditional view of hostility between royal and noble jurisdictions, rather than their integration or controlled competition.

109. ADSM C 2798–2799, Administration des domaines, procès verbaux, 1694–1695.

110. Smedley-Weill, *Correspondance des intendants,* 291, 333.

111. ADSM, C-Serie Inventaire, Intendants de Normandie, fols. 11–12. A twentieth intendant was sent but immediately recalled.

112. Debordes-Lissillour, *Les sénéchaussées royales,* 173–77.

113. Other examples of cumuls among legal families can be found in 71 BP 11, bailliage de Grainville-la-Teinturière, 1706–1725; 46 BP 25, haute justice de Cany-Caniel, assizes, juin 1716; and 71 BP 11, bailliage de Grainville-la-Teinturière, 1712.

114. ADSM 19 BP 2, bailliage de Longueville, 1721.

115. ADIV C 1828, Augmentation des gages, 14 aout 1716.

116. ADIV C 1823, Intendant, Sénéchaussées royales, 1704–1789.

117. ADSM 46 BP 19, haute justice de Cany-Caniel, assizes mercuriales, nov. 1700; 46 BP 22, 1704, jul. 1707; 46 BP 24, 1714; 13 BP 49, bailliage de Cany, jan. 1710; 13 BP 48, mai 1710; 13 BP 49, oct. 1712; 13 BP 52, bailliage de Cany, assizes mercuriale, 5 oct. 1716.

118. For other examples of officers exercising royal and seigneurial cumuls, see ADSM 46 BP 19, haute justice de Cany-Caniel, 1700–1701; 46 BP 22, 1704; 46 BP 24, mai 1714; 46 BP 25, juin 1716; 13 BP 48, bailliage de Cany, 1 oct. 1708, 2 avr. 1709; 13 BP 49, oct. 1712; 13 BP 52, 5 oct. 1716. ADSM 46 BP 39, haute justice de Cany-Caniel, 1726–1772. In the high justice of Vallase in the eighteenth century, André Corvisier found that two of the seven baillis were known to be councillors in royal bailliages; of the three judges at the high justice of Fresles, one was a lieutenant criminal in the bailliage of Neufchâtel. See Corvisier, "Un lien entre villes et campagnes."

119. Corvisier found that all four procureurs fiscal for the high justice of Fresle were solicitors or barristers in the royal bailliage of Neufchâtel. Six of twenty seigneurial clerks in the jurisidictions he studied exercised a royal office in the bailliage, the Parlement, or the Bureau of Finance, or served as a royal notary in a larger town. See Corvisier, "Un lien entré villes et campagnes," 157–79.

120. Maurice Gresset, *Gens de justice à Besançon, de la conquête par Louis XIV à la Révolution française (1674–1789)* (Paris: Bibliothèque Nationale, 1978), 74.

121. ADSM 71 BP 6–7, haute justice de Grainville-la-Teinturière, 1691, 1693–1698; 46 BP 19, 25, haute justice de Cany-Caniel, assizes, nov. 1700, juin 1716; 71 BP 10, bailliage de Grainville-la-Teinturière, 1698–1700; 71 BP 15, 1729; 13 B 46, bailliage de Cany, assizes 10 mai 1689, 10 oct. 1690, avr. 1692; 13 BP 52, assizes, 5 oct. 1716; 13 BP 48, assizes, 1 oct. 1708, 22 avr. 1709; 13 BP 49, assizes, oct. 1712; 13 BP 52, assizes, 1723.

122. ADSM 71 BP 9, bailliage de Grainville-la-Teinturière, assizes, juillet 1727; 46 BP 19, haute justice de Cany-Caniel, assizes, nov. 1701; 46 BP 24, assizes, 16 mai 1714; 46 BP 25, assizes juin 1716; 46 BP 13–14, 1679, 1680–1681; 13 BP 24, bailliage de Cany, assizes, déc. 1678, fév. 1679, oct. 1679; 13 BP 46, assizes, 10 mai 1689, 10 oct. 1690, avril 1692; 13 BP 52, assizes, 5 oct. 1716, 1723; 13 BP 48, assizes, 1 oct. 1708, 22 avr. 1709; 13 BP 49, assizes oct. 1712; 13 BP 57, assizes 27 jan. 1727; 13 BP 25, assizes, 1680.

123. ADSM 1 B 3654, Parlement, réceptions des lieutenants générals, 1705–1746; réceptions des officiers, 1702–1718.

124. John Evelyn, *Diary,* ed. E. S. De Beer (London, 1955), 2:140, in John Lough, ed., *France Observed in the Seventeenth Century by British Travellers* (Stocksfield: Oriel Press, 1984).

125. Richard Mowery Andrews, *Law, Magistracy, and Crime in Old Regime Paris, 1735–1789* (Cambridge: Cambridge University Press,1994), 1:70, 241.

126. Andrews, *Law, Magistracy,* 248; Berlanstein, *The Barristers of Toulouse,* 4–6.

127. Cicero, *De officiis* ("On Duties"), trans. P. G. Walsh (Oxford: Oxford University Press, 2000), 9.

128. Jean Bodin, *Six livres de la République* (Paris: 15831), 1, 373, 429, 436.

129. James R. Farr, *A Tale of Two Murders: Passion and Power in Seventeenth-Century France* (Durham: Duke University Press, 2005): 204.

130. Cicero, *De officiis,* 9.

131. Cicero, *De officiis,* 9; Cicero was borrowing from Plato's *Letter to Archytas.*

132. P. G. Walsh, in Cicero, *De officiis,* 131.

133. Cicero, *De officiis,* 67.

134. Cicero, *De officiis,* 107.

135. Cicero, *De officiis,* 67.

136. Édit du juin 1679; Déclaration du 28 mars 1682.

137. Déclaration de 12 jan. 1680, Isambert, Dieussy, et al., *Receuil,* 2:137.

138. Jean-Pierre Royer, *Histoire de la justice en France: De la monarchie absolue à la République* (Paris: Presses Universitaires de France, 1995), 131.

139. Alfred de Curzon, "L'enseignement du droit français dans les universités de France aux XVIIe et XVIIIe siècles," *Nouvelle Révue Historique du Droit Français et Étrangere,* XLIII (1919): 209–269, 305–364; Richard Kagan, "Law Students and Legal Careers in Eighteenth-Century France," *Past and Present,* 68 (1975): 38–72; Bell, *Lawyers and Citizens,* 40.

140. Landau, *Justices of the Peace,* 378–79.

141. ADSM 107 BP1, haute justice de Valmont, plumatifs et pièces isolées, 1757–1786.

142. François Rabelais, *Le tiers livre,* ed. M. A. Screech (Geneva: Droz, 1964), 269–72.

143. Bouwsma, "Lawyers and Early Modern Culture," 303–27.

144. Andrews, *Law, Crime,* 50.

145. On judicial mentalités in the higher courts, see Catherine E. Holmes, *L'eloquence judiciaire de 1620 à 1660: Reflet des problemes sociaux, religieux et politiques de l'époque* (Paris: A. G. Nizet, 1967).

146. Goubert, "Les officiers," 70.

147. Goubert, "Les officiers," 74; on libraries and readers, see Roger Chartier, *L'ordre des livres: Lecteurs, auteurs, bibliothèques en Europe entre les XIVe et XVIIIe siècles* (Aix-en-Provence: Alinca, 1992).

148. Other historians have stressed the great difficulty in reconstructing the fortunes and incomes of local judicial officers. Unfortunately, few jurisdictions provide sufficient family records, testaments, or notarial records to do sos.

149. De la Noiraye, *Mémoire,* 207–35. The office of an ordinary councillor (lower-ranking magistrate) in the Parlement of Rouen could be had for about 88,000 livres.

150. ADSM 46 BP 18, haute justice de Cany-Caniel, règlement des comtes, juillet 1694.

151. ADSM 46 BP 48, haute justice de Cany-Caniel, tutelles, 1726–1747, ADSM 71 BP 14, bailliage de Grainville-la-Teinturière, juillet 1741.

152. Droualt, *Les vicomtés en Normandie,* no pagination.

153. Debordes-Lissillour, *Les sénéchaussées royales,* 116–20.

154. Mousnier, *La venalité des offices,* 462.

155. BMR U 1285–3 II, Recueil PB Normandie, arrêt de la cour de le Parlement de Rouen portent règlement pour les taxes, 9 juin 1671.

156. Règlement de 4 juin 1612.

157. BMR U 1285–3 II, Arrêt de la cour, 9 juin 1671.

158. ADSM 1 ER 1084, Becdelièvre family papers, gages-pleges, 7 juin 1691.

159. Mousnier, *La venalité des offices,* 469, 490–91; Goubert, "Les officiers royaux," 65–75.

160. Goubert, "Les officiers royaux," 64–65.

161. Goubert has suggested that most judicial fortunes came from ground rent, loans, commerce, and shipping, but there is no direct evidence in the pays de Caux that these last two categories figured significantly into official fortunes. See "Les officiers royaux," 54–75.

162. Goubert, "Les officiers royaux," 69–70.

163. John Morrill, "The Stuarts (1603–1688)," in *The Oxford Illustrated History of Britain*, ed. Kenneth O. Morgan (Oxford and New York: Oxford University Press, 1988), 290.

164. ADSM 1 B 5613, Parlement de Normandie, Monitoire de Conséquence, 26 fév.1692.

165. ADSM 1 B 5699, Parlement de Normandie, factums 1694–1733; ADSM 1 B 5700, factums 1685.

166. From data collected from the Bureau des Finances by Voysin de la Noiraye in his *Mémoire*. The taille imposed on Pont-Audemer in 1665 was 19,080 livres, but the élus did not specify how many utile and inutile feux went into this assessment, as they did for other towns in Normandy. The first president of the Parlement put the population figure slightly higher, at perhaps 15,000. Pellot, *Notes du premier président*, 141.

167. ADSM BP 5850, Parlement de Rouen, État des paroisses ressortissantes du présidial de Rouen; Follaine, *Les juridictions royales*, 272, 358. There are several manuscript sources for calculating the number of parishes in each royal bailliage, but all differ in their lists.

168. BN ms. fr. 4286, Mémoires de l'intendant de La Bourdonnaye, f01.10; De la Noiraye, *Mémoire*, 3, 147.

169. Bureau des Finances, *État des offices de la généralité de Rouen en 1665*, in Voysin de la Noiraye, *Mémoire*, 220, 224–225, 227. These jurisdictions included a grenier à sel, with twelve officers; an eaux et forêts jurisdiction, with nine officers; a post of the maréchaussée, with two officers and two archers; and the tax élection, with sixteen officers and solicitors.

170. ADSM 1 B 5613, Parlement de Normandie, Interrogatoire de Lieutenant Général Le Grix, 8 août 1693.

171. Intendant de Vaubourg, "Mémoires"; Edmond Esmonin, *La taille en Normandie au temps de Colbert, 1661–1683* (Paris: Hachette, 1913), 545–46.

172. Voysin de la Noiraye, *Memoire*, 220.

173. AN, Correspondence des Intendants, 26 juin 1687, M. Paniot, 345; ADSM 1 B 5613, Parlement de Normandie, Interrogatoire de Lieutenant Général Le Grix, 8 août 1693.

174. ADSM 1 B 5612, Parlement de Normandie, Interrogatoire de Vicomte Formeville, 11 déc. 1691, and Interrogatoire de Charles le Maistre, huissier, 20 nov. 1691.

175. Édit de 1692; ADSM 1 B 5612, Parlement de Normandie, Interrogatoire de Vicomte Pierre de Formeville.

176. On the towns in ancien régime France, see also T. J. A. Le Goff, *Vannes and Its Region: A Study of Town and Country in 18th-Century France* (Oxford: Clarendon Press, 1981).

177. ADSM 1 B 5612, Parlement, Conseiller De Marest, 3 déc. 1691. On hospitals, see also Kathryn Norberg, *Rich and Poor in Grenoble, 1600–1815* (Berkeley: University of California Press, 1985); and Cissie Fairchilds, *Poverty and Chastity in Aix-en-Provence, 1640–1789* (Baltimore: Johns Hopkins University Press, 1976).

178. ADSM 1 B 5612, Parlement, Conseiller Commissaire De Marest, 23 nov. 1691.

179. Marcel Marion, *Dictionnaire des institutions de la France aux XVIIe et XVIIIe siècles* (Paris: A. & J. Picard, 1968), 387–38.

180. BMR U 1285-3 II, Arrêt de la cour du Parlement de Rouen, portant règlement pour les taxes de Juges, 9 juin 1671.

181. See Jean-Christophe Casard, *Saint Yves de Tréguier* (Paris: Beauchesne, 1992); Marie-Paule Salonne, *Saint Yves: Patron des avocats, avocat des opprimés* (Paris: Éditions Franciscaines, n.d.); and Jean Balcou, "Permanence d'un culte primitif: Saint Yves de Verité," *Mémoires de la Société Historique et Archéologique de Bretagne* 62 (1986): 365–78 for discussion of the cult of Saint Yves and lawyers.

182. ADSM 1 B 5613, Parlement, Interrogatoire de Sr. le Bourg, 17–18 juillet 1693.

183. Some of the bribes listed were obvious exaggerations, but others were not at all implausible, given the status of the defendants (wealthy sieurs) and the severity of the crimes they were accused of (murder and dueling). Although we do not know the commission's conclusions about any of the specific charges, the officers of the court were questioned intensively about several of these large bribes, were accused by multiple witnesses, and were remonstrated for lying to the commission in their denials.

184. See ADSM C 935–936, 939, 943–949, Intendant de Rouen, frais des justice, for examples of the frequent haggling that went on between the intendant and the lower jurisdictions over who was responsible for the expenses of prisoners accused of royal crimes.

185. Sebastien Le Prêtre Vauban, *Le dîme royale,* ed. Emmanuel Le Roy Ladurie (Paris: Imprimerie Royale, 1992).

186. ADSM 1 B 5613, Parlement, Interrogatoire de Sr. de Buisson, avocat, 18 juillet 1693.

187. ADSM 1 B 5613, Parlement, Interrogatoire de Louis Villecoq, 12 août 1693.

188. ADSM 1 B 5613, Parlement, Interrogatoire de Lieutenant Général Le Grix, 8 août 1693.

189. Cas royaux were enumerated in the Ordonnance of 1670; they included lèse-majesté, counterfeiting, rebellion, sedition, and other crimes touching on the person or prerogatives of the king.

190. Vicomte de Formeville was also accused of inventing a sergeantry, to which he claimed he was unable to find the titles. ADSM 1 B 5612, Interrogatoire de Vicomte de Formeville, 11 déc. 1691.

191. ADSM 1 B 5613, Parlement, Interrogatoire de Lieutenant Général Jean Le Grix, 8 août 1693.

192. ADSM 1 B 5612, Supplié de Vicomte de Formeville, 12 déc. 1691.

193. ADSM 1 B 5612, Parlement, Interrogatoire de Vicomte de Formeville, 11 déc. 1693.

194. ADSM 1 B 5612: Parlement, Interrogatoire de Jean L'Enseigneur, déc. 1691.

195. ADSM 1 B 5613, Parlement, Interrogatoire de Lieutenant Général Le Grix, 8 aôut 1693.

196. See ADSM C 317, Capitation de la généralité de Rouen, 1713.

197. ADSM C 317, Capitation, 1713.

198. ADSM C 311, Capitation des officiers, généralité de Rouen, 1703.

199. Chancellier Louis de Pontchartrain à Vernouillet, président à mortier au Parlement de Rouen, in G. A. Depping, *Correspondance administrative sous le règne de Louis XIV* (Paris: Bibliothèque Impériale, 1855), 3:354, no. 187.

200. BN fonds français 32318, Mémoires du Parlement de Rouen, 1693.

Chapter 4

1. ADSM 71 BP 15, bailliage de Grainville-la-Teinturière, nov. 1729.

2. Denis Richet, *La France moderne: L'ésprit des institutions* (Paris: Flammarion, 1973), 30.

3. *Coutume de Normandie, avec l'Ordonnance de 1667, & celle de 1670* (Bayeux: Veuve Briard, 1773. The number of articles varies, depending on the edition and upon whether the local usages were numbered into the General Custom.

4. The customs first appeared as the *Statute et Consuetudines Normandie* between 1199–1204, and were translated into the *Très-ancien Coutumier*. See Jean Caswell and Ivan Sipkov, *The Costumes of France in the Library of Congress: An Annotated Bibliography* (Washington DC: Library of Congress, 1977): 34–37. On the dominance of customary law in Brittany, see Séverine Debordes-Lissillour, *Les sénéchaussées royales de Bretagne: La monarchie d'ancien régime et ses juridictions ordinaires (1532–1790)* (Rennes: Presses Universitaires de Rennes, 2006), 239, 416.

5. ADSM 71 BP 15, bailliage de Grainville-la-Teinturière, nov. 1729.

6. The distinction between private and public law was elaborated by the classical jurist Ulpian in the third century C.E.; see Peter Stein, *Roman Law in European History* (Cambridge: Cambridge University Press,1999), 21.

7. Maistre Guillaume Terrien, *Commentaire du droit civil tant public que privé, observé au pays et duché de Normandie,* 3rd ed. (Rouen: Chez F. Vaultier, 1654), 1–32.

8. Denis Richet, *La France moderne,* 21.

9. See, for example, Denis Richet, *La France moderne,* 32–33.

10. On the arrêts of the Parlement of Normandy, see Virginie Lemonnier-Lesage, *Les arrêts du règlement du parlement de Rouen, fin XVIe–XVIIe siècles* (Paris: Éditions Panthéon-Assas, 1999).

11. On local regulatory sentences and the process of confirmation by the parlements, see Debordes-Lissillour, *Les sénéchaussées royales,* 273–94.

12. ADSM 1 B 5612–13, Parlement de Normandie.

13. ADSM I B 5697, Parlement, Chambre des Tournelles, mars 1749.

14. ADSM 71 BP 15, bailliage de Grainville-la-Teinturière, réception des offices, 1729.

15. *Coutumes du Pays de Normandie* (Rouen: Jean B. Besonge, 1697).

16. Jean Bouhier, *Les coutumes du duché de Bourgogne, avec les anciennes coutumes tant générales que locales* (Dijon: Chez Arnaud-Jean-Baptiste Auge, 1742–46), 183.

17. Michel de Montaigne, "De la coutume et de ne changer aisément une loi reçue," in *Essais* (Paris: Librarie Générale Française, 1972), 175.

18. J. H. M. Salmon, "Renaissance Jurists and 'Englightened' Magistrates: Perspectives on Feudalism in Eighteenth-Century France," *French History* 8, no. 4(1994): 389, 393.

19. On the similar functions of law in England, see E. P. Thompson, *Whigs and Hunters: The Origin of the Black Act* (New York: Pantheon, 1975), 258–69.

20. Règlement du Parlement de Normandie, 6 avr. 1666; ADCO C 3339, Bourgogne, Intendant de Dijon; Charte aux Normands, *Ordonnances des Rois de France* (Paris: 1902), i, 551, 557.

21. Jean Bart, *Histoire du droit privé, de la chute de l'empire romain au XIXe siècle* (Paris: Montchrestian, 1998), 146–48, 293.

22. Sarah Hanley, "Engendering the State: Family Formation and State Building in Early Modern France," *French Historical Studies* 16, no. 1 (Spring 1989): 4–27; see also Hanley, "The Jurisprudence of the Arrêts: Marital Union, Civil Society, and State Formation in France, 1550–1650," *Law and History Review* (2003): 1–40.

23. Bart, *Histoire du droit privé*.

24. R. Filhol, *Le premier président Chrisophe de Thou et la reformation des coutumes* (Paris: 1937), quoted in Robert Descimon and Alain Guery, "Un état des temps modernes?" *L'état et les pouvoirs*, ed. André Burguière and Jacques Revel, 218 (Paris: Éditions Seuil, 1989).

25. J. Brejon de Lavergnée, "Les vicissitudes de l'enregistrement des usances locales de Bretagne lors de la rédaction officielle de la Coutume de 1580," *Revue Historique de Droit Français et Étrangèr*, extrait du vol. 55 (1977): 559–78.

26. Bart, *Histoire du droit privé*, 147.

27. BMR, U 1285 3-2: Lettres patentes de Henri III, 22 mars 1577.

28. BMR U 1285 1, fols. 102–17, *La Charte aux Normans, & confirmations d'icelle: Extraict des registres de la cour souveraine de l'Eschiquier de Normandie, tenu à Rouen, 1462.* Gerard Hurpin, in "L'Administration de la Normandie au temps de Louis XIV," *Bulletin de la Société Libre d'Emulation de la Seine Maritime* (1986): 28–40, called the charter the "sole Norman text which could evoke the notion of public liberty under the old monarchy, although here the word liberty must be partly understood to mean privileges."

29. Stein, *Roman Law*, 84–85.

30. Jean Domat, *Lois civiles dans leur ordre naturel*, vol. 3 (Paris: J. B. Coignard, 1691–94).

31. Robert-Joseph Pothier, *Traités sur differentes matières du droit civil* (Orleans: J. Rouzeau-Montaut, 1770); see also J. H. M. Salmon, "Renaissance Jurists," 400.

32. M. du Bois, in Bouhier, *Les coutumes*, 185.

33. Denis Diderot, in Bart, *Histoire du Droit Privé*, 438.

34. M. de Guiné, *De la répresentation*, and M. d'Argentre, *Preface de son avis, sur le partage des nobles*, quoted in Bouhier, *Les coutumes*, 190 and 185.

35. Brejon de Lavergnée, "Les vicissitudes de l'enrégistrement," 559–78.

36. ADSM 1 B213, Parlement de Normandie, Arrêt de Règlement, 19 jan. 1690.

37. Auguste-Marie Poullain du Parc, *Principes du droit français, suivant les maximes de Bretagne* (Rennes: François Vatar, 1767), 26.

38. Bouhier, *Les coutumes*, 183, 185.

39. Canon law, which made important contributions to English common law, was partially absorbed into the public law of France during the medieval period. Its direct influence on secular law had faded considerably by the seventeenth century, however.

40. The line of demarcation between largely Roman-law and non-Roman-law regions ran along a meandering line connecting the regions of Franche-Comté, Burgundy, and Poitou.

41. Stein, *Roman Law,* 26–27.

42. Bouhier, *Les coutumes,* 185–92, 198.

43. Stein, *Roman Law,* 40–41.

44. Bart, *Histoire du droit privé,*112, 131, 134.

45. See, for example, David Parker, *Class and State in Ancien Régime France: The Road to Modernity?* (London: Routledge, 1996), 172–73.

46. *The Digest of Justinian,* trans. Alan Watson (Philadelphia: University of Pennsylvania Press, 1985), 1.3.31.

47. Aristotle, *Nicomachean Ethics,* Book V, trans. and ed. Roger Crisp (Cambridge: Cambridge University Press, 2000), 100.

48. Stein, *Roman Law,* 47–48.

49. The Latin rule of equity presumed that not all men had the gift; "probabilis quaedam ratio, non omnibus hominibus naturaliter cognia, sed paucis tantum, qui prudentia, usu, doctrina praediti didicerunt, quae ad societatis humanae conservationem sunt necessaria," in Bouhier, *Les coutumes,* 192.

50. Daniel Jousse, *Traité de la administration de justice,* vol. 2, *Justice Civile* (Paris: Debure Père, 1771), 23.

51. Albert Hamscher, *The Conseil Privé and the Parliaments in the Age of Louis XIV: A Study in French Absolutism* (American Philosophical Society, March 1987), 147–48; see also Roland Mousnier, *La conseil du roi, de Louis XII à la révolution* (Paris: Presses Universitaires de France, 1970).

52. Daniel Jousse, *Traité,* 695.

53. Bouhier, *Les coutumes,* 185–92.

54. Robert Génestal, *Études de droit privé normand: La tutelle* (Caen: Librairies de l'Université, 1930), 168.

55. Bart, *Histoire du droit privé,* 132+35.

56. *Coutume de Normandie,* art. 235.

57. Poullain du Parc, *Principes du droit français,* 18–20. The Custom of Paris also helped to fulfill this function.

58. Bouhier, *Les coutumes,* 198.

59. Claude de Ferrière, *Préface sur le coutume de Paris,* in Bouhier, *Les coutumes,* 183. Ferrière expressed similar opinions in his *Dictionnaire de droit et de pratique, contenant l'explication des termes de droit, d'ordonnonces, de coutumes et de pratique* (Toulouse: J. Dupleix, 1799).

60. Charles-Louis Secondat de Montesquieu, *L'ésprit des lois* (Paris: Seghers, 1972).

61. Houard, *Dictionnaire analytique, historique, et étymologique de la Coutume de Normandie* (Rouen: Le Boucher le jeune, 1781), 2:25–36.

62. The terms *droit français* and *droit commun* were used ambiguously during the ancien régime. "French law" sometimes meant royal and customary law together, and sometimes meant only royal law; it is used in this latter sense here to distinguish it from customary law. "Common law" was sometimes used to mean Roman law, but other times referred to customary law.

63. *Coutume de Normandie, Avec l'Ordonnance de 1667, & celle de 1670. . . . instruction sur la marche de la procedure civile & criminelle;* on the process of the reformation of

justice, see Albert Hamscher, *The Parlement of Paris after the Fronde, 1653–1673* (Pittsburgh: University of Pittsburgh Press, 1976), 155–81.

64. Stein, *Roman Law,* 106; see also Jean-Pierre Royer, *Histoire de la justice en France, de la monarchie absolue à la republique* (Paris: Presses Universitaires de France, 1995), 33–38.

65. Bouhier, *Les coutumes,* 179.

66. Pierre Goubert and Daniel Roche, *Les français et l'ancien régime,* vol. 1, *La société et l'état* (Paris: Armand Colin, 1984), 290.

67. Bouhier, *Les coutumes.*

68. Bart, *Histoire du droit privé,* 155–56.

69. Poullain du Parc, *Principes du droit français,* 26; *La Coutume et la jurisprudence coutumière de Bretagne* (Rennes: François Vatar, 1783).

70. On varieties of royal law, see also Richet, *La France moderne,* 30–33.

71. Édit des Épices, mars 1673, in Jousse, *Traité de l'administration,* 216.

72. See, for example, Ordonnance de Blois, 1579, in Isambert, Dieussy, Jourdan, et al., *Recueil générale des anciens lois françaises, depuis l'an 420 jusqu'a la Revolution de 1789* (Paris: Belin-le-Prieur, 1821–1833), 14:380–432; Ordonnance d'Orleans, 1560, in Isambert et al., *Recueil,* 14:63–98.

73. Ordonnance de Villers-Cotterêt, août 1539, in Isambert et. al., *Recueil,* 12:600–40.

74. Arrêt de Règlement du 15 mai 1714, rendu pour le bailliage et Comté de Pont-Chartrain, in Jousse, *Traité de l'adminstration,* 211.

75. Règlement du Parlement de Normandie, 6 avr. 1666.

76. ADCO C 3339, Bourgogne, Intendant de Dijon.

77. BMR 1285 U-3, Lettres patentes du Henri III, 22 mars 1577.

78. Jean Yver, "La rédaction officielle de la Coutume de Normandie (Rouen, 1583): Son ésprit," *Annales de Normandie,* 1, no. 3 (1986): 3–36.

79. BMR 1285 U-3, Procès verbaux des coutumes de Normandie, août–oct. 1586.

80. BMR U 1285 3-2, Procès verbaux de la Coutume de Normandie, 1586–87.

81. BMR 1285 U-3, Procès verbaux de la Coutume de Normandie, 22 oct. 1577.

82. Yver, "La rédaction officielle," 7–12.

83. BMR U 1285 3-1, *Coutumes de pais de Normandie, ancien ressors, et enclaves d'iceluy* (Rouen: Imp. Martin le Mesgissier, 1588). For similar developments in Brittany, see J. Brejon de Lavergnée, "Les États de Bretagne et la reformation de la Coutume sous le regne de Louis XIV," *Mémoires de la Société Historique et Archéologique de Bretagne* 27 (1947): 33–43.

85. BMR U 1285 3-1, Lettres patentes de Henry III, 22 mars 1577.

86. Yver, "La redaction," 5.

87. Georges Duby, *Le Moyen Age 987–1460* (Paris: Hachette, 1987), 100.

88. Some provincial customs, notably that of Paris, underwent a second "reformation" at the end of the sixteenth century.

89. *Coutume de Normandie,* Arts. 54–59.

90. Hugues Neveux, "La justice, norme ambigue de la paysannerie européenne, XVe–XVIIe siecles," *Cahiers des Annales de Normandie* 24 (1992): 120.

91. *Très Ancien Coustumier de Normandie.*

92. See, for example, Emily Zack Tabuteau, *Transfers of Property in Eleventh-Century Norman Law* (Chapel Hill and London: University of North Carolina Press, 1988),

1–3; and B. E. J. Rathery, *Études historiques sur les institutions judiciares de la Normandie* (Paris: Dupont et cie., n.d.).

93. Emily Zack Tabuteau, *Transfers of Property in Eleventh-Century Norman Law* (Chapel Hill: University of North Carolina Press,1988), 2. Tabuteau emphasizes that even by this period, "Normans did not live in a predominantly 'feudal world,' either tenurially or mentally."

94. The commentaries are essential to understanding the actual application of customary law in practice, since customary laws were normally expressed as short maxims and left significant room for interpretation by lawyers and judges. The four most widely used commentaries on the *Coutume de Normandie* were each issued in multiple editions over the seventeenth and eighteenth centuries. The editions relied on here are those of Pesnelle, *Coutume de Normandie* (1727, 1759), Berault, *Coutume Reformée de Normandie* (1632, 1660, 1684, 1776), Basnage, *Les Oeuvres de maître Henri Basnage* (1709, 1778) and Houard, *Dictionnaire analytique, historique, étymologique de la Coutume de Normandie* (1781). Houard is generally cited here because of his sound reliance on the work of the three earlier authors and his clarity, a rare virtue among legal commentators.

95. BMR Ms Y 169, Intendant de Vaubourg, "Mémoires concernant la généralité de Rouen," fols. 27–29, 1698–99.

96. See Charles-Antoine Cardot, "La Bretagne dans le *Répertoire universel de jurisprudence* de Guyot (1784–1785)," *Mémoires de la Société Historique et Archéologique de Bretagne* 53 (1975–76): 95–120 on the successoral régime in Brittany.

97. *Coutume de Normandie,* Art. 237.

98. David Sabean, "Aspects of Kinship Behavior and Property in Rural Western Europe Before 1800," in *Family and Inheritance: Rural Society in Western Europe, 1200–1800,* ed. Jack Goody, Joan Thirsk, and E. P. Thompson, 107 (Cambridge: Cambridge University Press, 1976).

99. *Coutume de Normandie,* Art. 353. If the principal house was *en bourgage,* or in town, the eldest was not automatically entitled to it; but the largest rural habitation still went to him. In all cases under the general custom of Normandy, the eldest had to announce that he intended to exercise his right to the *preciput* before the lots were drawn up (Art. 348–349).

100. *Coutume de Normandie,* Art. 337.

101. *Coutume de Normandie,* Art. 336.

102. *Coutume de Normandie,* Art. 346.

103. *Coutume de Normandie,* Art. 356.

104. *Coutume de Normandie,* Art. 350–352, 356.

105. *Coutume de Normandie,* Art. 353.

106. Joan Thirsk, "The European Debate on Customs of Inheritance, 1500–1700," in Goody, Thirsk, and Thompson, *Family and Inheritance,* 177–91.

107. Thirsk, "The European Debate."

108. Emmanuel Le Roy Ladurie, "Family Structures and Inheritance Customs in Sixteenth-Century France," in Goody, Thirsk, and Thompson, *Family and Inheritance,* 70.

109. Jack Goody, "Inheritance, Property and Women," in Goody, Thirsk, and Thompson, *Family and Inheritance,* 33.

110. Le Roy Ladurie, "Family Structures," 69–70.

111. Emmanuel Le Roy Ladurie helped to establish this view of Norman custom in *The French Peasantry 1450–1660* (Oxford: Scolar Press, 1987), 137–50 and passim, as well as in the article "Système de la coutume: structures familiales et coutumes d'hèritage en France au XVI siècle," *Annales d'Histoire Économique et Sociale* 27 (1972): 825–46.

112. *Coutume de Normandie*, Arts. 248, 250, 258, 271.

113. *Coutume de Normandie*, Arts. 240, 272, 336, 360.

114. *Coutume de Normandie*, Art. 389: "les personnes conjointes en mariage ne sont communes en biens."

115. The douaire, under most customary laws in France, was the usufruct that the widow received of the goods belonging to the husband and wife. Unlike in the *Coutume de Bourgogne*, however, in which the douaire proceeded from the assumption of community property, in Normandy the douaire gave the widow only temporary oversight of property that had never belonged to her. She therefore had more limited rights of disposition.

116. *Coutume de Normandie*, Art. 330, forbade the use of a marriage contract to give to the widow a larger share of the property conquests made during the marriage than her customary share.

117. See also Houard, *Dictionnaire analytique,* 232–86, on provisions affecting women under both the Norman and Caux customs.

118. Quoted by Jacqueline Muset, "Les droits successoraux des filles dans la coutume de Normandie," *La femme en Normandie: Actes du XIXe congrès des sociétés historiques et archéologiques de Normandie* (Caen: Archives Départmentales du Calvados, 1986): 54.

119. Berault, *Coutume reformée,* 1:35. See also Pierre Cinquabre, "Le statut juridique de la femme Normande aux XVIIe et XVIIIe siècles," *La Femme en Normandie* (Caen: Archives Départmentales du Calvados, 1986), 43–51 for an extensive discussion of douaires, *dots,* and other legal provisions relating to women under the coutumes.

120. Yver, "La redaction officielle," 24.

121. Zoe Schneider, "Women before the Bench: Female Litigants in Early Modern Normandy," *French Historical Studies* 23, no. 1 (Winter 2000): 1–32.

122. B. E. J. Rathery, *Etudes historiques sur les institutions judiciaires de la Normandie* (Paris: Dupont et cie, n.d.), 3.

123. Although legally part of the Caux, the bailliage de Neufchâtel east of this line gradually came to be thought of as the pays de Bray.

124. BN, Ms. fr. 22612, *Collection Dangeau,* has a reasonably accurate list of parishes in the Norman présidial jurisdictions.

125. *Coutume de Normandie*, Coutume de la Pays de Caux, Art. 279, 292, 302. The Custom does not specify whether younger sons were given a life interest in the net or the gross income of the estate.

126. *Coutume de Normandie,* Coutume de la Pays de Caux, Art. 279–280; Houard, *Dictionnaire analytique,* 6:284–90.

127. *Coutume de Normandie,* Coutume de la Pays de Caux, Art. 290–291.

128. Yver, "La redaction officielle," 20.

129. See Robert Génestal, "La rédaction des usages locaux de Normandie, 1586–1587," *Bulletin de la Société des Antiquaires de Normandie* 35 (1924): 309–43.

130. BMR 1285 U-3, Procès verbaux de la Coutume de Normandie, 1586–1587.

131. BMR 1285 U-3, *Coustumes du pais de Normandie, anciens ressors, et enclaves d'iceluy* (Rouen: Martin le Mesgissier, 1588), 89–93.

132. BMR 1285 U-3, *Coutumes du pais de Normandie, anciens ressors, et enclaves*, 89.

133. Houard, *Dictionnaire analytique*. The clever peasant who desperately wanted a change of venue could wall up one door and create another.

134. Bouhier, *Les coutumes*, 173.

135. ADSM 1 ER 1084, Familles, de Becdelièvre family papers. In 1734, for example, seventeen of the seventy-two aveus in the seigneurie of Cany-Barville, or just over 23 percent of the *mazures* and land parcels held by roturiers, were noted as being held "a cause de sa femme" or "ayant épouzé la herittiere."

136. BMR U 1286-3, Procès verbaux de la Coutume de Normandie, 22 oct. 1587.

137. Schneider, "Women before the Bench," 1–32.

138. An eighteenth-century clerk of the Norman Cour des Aides helpfully provided several mathematical solutions to the inheritance laws for lawyers and judges who were as befuddled by the problem as their clients. For example, under the Coutume, all daughters together might receive up to one-third of the total succession, but in no case might any daughter receive more than any younger son (*puisné*). In a family where there were more puisnés than daughters, if all the daughters together were to be given one-third of the succession, then each daughter would receive more than each puisné, which the Coutume forbade. To solve the problem correctly, one must therefore count the eldest son (ainé) for twice as much as the puisnés together:

$$3 \text{ puisnés (younger sons)} = 3 \text{ parts}$$
$$1 \text{ ainé (eldest son) } (2 \times 3 \text{ parts}) = 6 \text{ parts}$$
$$2 \text{ daughters} = 2 \text{ parts}$$

Therefore, one-eleventh of the succession goes to each daughter and younger son, and six-elevenths of the succession goes to the eldest son. Astonishingly, however, the author seems to have mistaken six-elevenths for the equivalent of two-thirds, which should alert us to the enormous potential for error among even those who dealt with these cases on a daily basis. See M. Burel, *Elemens de pratique et modèles d'exploits* (Rouen: Et. Vinc. Macheul, 1772), 17–18.

Chapter 5

1. Recent works on provincial authorities have greatly expanded our understanding of these institutions. For Normandy, on the Parlement see Jonathan Dewald, *The Formation of a Provincial Nobility: The Magistrates of the Parlement of Rouen, 1489–1610* (Princeton, NJ: Princeton University Press, 1980); and Dewald, "Magistracy and Political Opposition at Rouen: A Social Context," *Sixteenth Century Journal* V (1974). On the Estates of Normandy, H. Prentout, *Les Etats provinciaux de Normandie* (Rouen: 1915–17); on the governors of Normandy, Célestin Hippeau, *Le gouvernement de Normandie au XVIIe et au XVIIIe siècles, après le correspondence de marquis de Beuvron et des ducs d'Harcourt. . . .* (Caen: G. DeLaporte, 1863–70); and Maurice Veyrat, "Les gouvernors de Normandie du XVIe siècle à la Revolution," *Études normandes* 27 (4th

quarter, 1953). On the intendants, Gerard Hurpin, "L'Administration de la Normandie au temps de Louis XIV," *Bulletin de la Société Libre de la Seine Maritime* (1986): 28–40. On historical development of Normandy, Charles Homer Haskins, *Norman Institutions* (New York: F. Unger, 1960). More specialized works are noted below. A comprehensive study of Norman provincial elites and institutions in this period has yet to be written.

2. BN 500 Colbert 260, fols. 180–205; see also E. Esmonin, ed., *Voisin de la Noiraye: Mémoire sur la généralité de Rouen en 1665* (Paris: 1913), 207–35.

3. Charles Beaurepaire, ed., *Cahiers des Estats de Normandie,* vol. 1 (Rouen: Chez Ch. Métérie, 1880), Art. XXIX, nov. 1593, 17–18.

4. Although the judges of the lower jurisdictions attended the Parlement once a year on a date assigned for their bailliage, this was emphatically not an arena for political deliberation or mutual decision making.

5. See also Prentout, *Les États provinciaux de Normandie.*

6. Séverine Debordes-Lissillour, *Les sénéchaussées royales de Bretagne: La monarchie d'ancien régime et ses juridictions ordinaires (1532–1790)* (Rennes: Presses Universitaires de Rennes, 2006), 180–83, 189–91.

7. Debordes-Lissillour, *Les sénéchaussées royales,* 236.

8. ADSM 6 BP 12–23, vicomté de l'eau de Rouen. The vicomté de l'eau in Rouen contested jurisdiction over the Seine and over river traffic with the admirauté court.

9. The Longuevilles owned the jurisdiction as a private fief. ADSM 1 B 5696, Parlement de Normandie, Arrêt du Grand Conseil, 10 juin 1664.

10. Guy Coquille, quoted in J.-F. Noel, "Une justice seigneuriale en Haute Bretagne à la fin de l'ancien régime: La chatellenie de la Motte-de-Gennes," *Annales de Bretagne et de Pays de l'Ouest* (1976): 124.

11. Robert Descimon and Alain Guèry, "Un état des temps modernes?" in *L'état et les pouvoirs,* ed. André Burguiere and Jacques Revel (Paris: Éditions Seuil, 1989), 259.

12. Charles de Figon, *Arbre des Estats & Offices de France,* reproduced in Emmanuel le Roy Ladurie, *Histoire de France,* vol. 2, *L'état royal, 1460–1610* (Paris: Hachette, 1977), 246.

13. ADSM C 920, Intendant de Rouen, Frais de Justice: Chancellier d'Aguesseau à l'Intendant de la Bourdonnaye, 25 fév. 1740.

14. BN NAF 2496: M. Bertin, *Dictionnaire historique . . . des offices* (eighteenth century, n.d.), fols. 117–24, is perhaps the best set of these eighteenth-century maps, but they are unable to indicate the dozens of enclaves or overlapping jurisdictions that coexisted with the bailliage jurisdictions.

15. For example, Édit de déc.1745.

16. Technically, cases in the Court of Moneys in Rouen could be appealed to the main Court of Moneys in Paris, but Rouen was still considered one of the sovereign courts.

17. Edmond Esmonin, *La Taille en Normandie* (Paris: Hachette, 1913), 23, 32–33; James Collins, *Fiscal Limits of Absolutism: Direct Taxation in Early Seventeenth-Century France* (Berkeley: University of California Press, 1988), 126–29, 151–55.

18. Upper Normandy was a region of grande gabelle. The officers of the greniers, or salt warehouses, had jurisdiction over cases involving salt sales and related conflicts; appeals went to the Court of Aids.

19. James B. Collins, *The State in Early Modern France* (Cambridge: Cambridge University Press, 1995), 17–18.

20. Many bailliages and vicomtés sat together as one court and had substantially the same personnel, so they have been counted as one jurisdiction. If they are counted separately, there were twenty-seven in total in the généralité of Rouen.

21. James B. Collins, *Classes, Estates, and Order in Early Modern Brittany* (Cambridge: Cambridge University Press, 1994), 111–15.

22. The admirauté courts had jurisdiction over the ports, docks, rivers, and streams of the tidal zone, the coast, and the sea itself. Their cases could be appealed from the Table de Marbre to the Parlement.

23. The maréchaussée courts were ultimately supervised by the marshals of France, since they were in essence a domestic military police. Locally they fell under the jurisdiction of the Table de Marbre, but their functions were often performed by lieutenants who were directly attached to the présidials, and the présidial courts were responsible for determining whether the maréchaussée had jurisdiction over a case. In the présidial of Caudebec-en-Caux, for example, the lieutenants of both courts sat together to hear contentious cases. The prévôts of the maréchaussée were often attached to the bailliages in some parts of France, although this was not the case in upper Normandy before the expansion of the maréchaussée in the eighteenth century. By the Édit de mars 1720, registered by the Parlement in 1722, the old prévôtal courts were technically suppressed and replaced by a maréchaussée court in each généralité under the direction of a prévôt général and his lieutenants. They were supposed to have final judgment in cases involving military deserters, vagabonds, beggars, and certain types of thieves. They had no jurisdiction over nobles, royal officers, or clergy.

24. The eaux et forêts jurisdictions, as the name implies, supervised the multiplicity of rights over forest areas and waters, which were strongly contested during the ancien régime. They administered gathering deadwood and minerals, harvesting trees and fruits, the woods of the king's domaine, and woodcutting on communal lands, among other rights. The jurisdictions had their own police in Normandy, the *gruerie,* and the eaux et forêts jurisdiction in Rouen could hear cases involving disputes. But property cases and transactions involving woods and waters were normally heard by the ordinary court system. The surviving documents for the woods and waters jurisdictions in the pays de Caux are very fragmentary, leaving an open question about how well they continued to function during this period.

25. See ADSM B 200 BP. The consular court in Dieppe has left only a few records of its functioning, and those prior to the late eighteenth century are fragmentary. That of Rouen has left substantial records. Created by the Édit de mars 1556, which was not registered by the Parlement until 1563, the Rouen consular jurisdiction was given authority over all cases involving merchandise and over all persons, including nobles.

26. On consular courts in Normandy and elsewhere, see Gayle K. Brunelle, *New World Merchants of Rouen 1559–1630* (Kirksville, MO: Truman State University Press, 1991). On the maréchaussée in the seventeenth and eighteenth centuries, see Iain Cameron, *Crime and Repression in the Auvergne and Guyenne* (Cambridge: Cambridge University Press, 1981); and Malcolm R. Greenshields, *An Economy of Violence in Early Modern France: Crime and Justice in the Haute Auvergne, 1587–1664* (University Park:

Pennsylvania State University Press, 1994); on the sénéchausée courts, Julius R. Ruff, *Crime, Justice and Public Order in Old Regime France* (London: Croom Helm, 1984); and Stephen G. Rheinhardt, *Justice in the Sarladais, 1770–1790* (Baton Rouge: Louisiana State University Press, 1991). Roland Mousnier's *Institutions of France under the Absolute Monarchy, 1598–1789,* 2 vols. trans. Arthur Goldhammer (Chicago: University of Chicago Press, 1979–84) remains an unreplicated work in understanding the basic composition and jurisdiction of the lower royal courts, although their functioning is better understood through more recent works.

27. BN 500 Colbert 260, Voysin de la Noiraye, *Mémoire sur la généralité de Rouen (1665),* ed. Edmond Esmonin (Paris: Librairie Hachette, 1913), fols. 180–205.

28. The most important primary sources on jurisdictions in Normandy are BN Ms. Fr. 32318, *Memoires pour servir à la histoire;* BN NAF, 2496, M. Bertin, *Dictionnaire historique;* BN Ms. fr. 22612, Collection Dangeau, *Memoires;* BN 500 Colbert 260, *Registre des offices en Normandie,* fols. 180–205; and Houard, *Dictionnaire analytique* (1781). The most reliable secondary source is Anthoine Follaine, *Les juridictions royales subalternes de Normandie du XVIe au XVIIIe siècle* (Mémoire D.E.A., Université de Rouen, 1989), which painstakingly reconstructs lower royal jurisdictions in upper Normandy using court records along with royal sources. See also Comte d'Estaintot, *Récherches sur les hautes justices féodales existant en 1789 dans les limites du département de la Seine-Inférieure* (Rouen: A. Lestringant, 1892); Jean Droualt, *Les vicomtés en Normandie aux XIIIe siècle,* ed. L. Jouan and R. Bigot (Caen: Librairies de la Université et de la Société des Antiquaires de Normandy, 1924); Max Gilbert, "Le bailliage de Caux et les autres bailliages de la Normandie," ADSM F 216, Ms. 10 oct. 1952; Léopold Soublin, *Les grands bailliages de haute-Normandie en 1789* (Rouen, 1972); François Burckard, *Guide des Archives de la Seine-Maritime,* vol. 1, *Généralités: Archives Antérieures à 1790.* (Rouen: Archives Départementales, 1990), 183–252.

29. See ADSM 1 B 5444, Parlement de Normandie, Provisions d'office; see also Henri de Frondeville, *Les conseillers du Parlement de Normandie 1641 à 1715* (Rouen: A. Lestringant, 1960); and Alexandre Bigot de Monville, *Mémoires,* ed. Madeleine Foisil (Paris: A. Pedone, 1976) for a comparison with the Parlement of 1640. Michel Le Pesant has corrected Frondeville's prosopography using the ADSM's provisions of office documents, along with AN U 755–767, registre du conseils, and AN subseries VI, lettres de provision. His *"Personnel d'une cour souveraine sous le règne de Louis XIV,"* *Extrait de la bibliothèque de l'École des Chartes* (Paris: École des Chartes, 1972), 129:431–44 analyzes the background of parlementaire magistrats from this period.

30. Debordes-Lissillour, *Les sénéchaussées royales,* 189–91; Collins, *Classes, Estates and Order,* 90.

31. The nine-year cycle was briefly interrupted in 1665, when the paulette was renewed for only three years, and again in 1668, when it was renewed for six years.

32. AN, Correspondance des Intendants, 13 jan. 1684, M. le Guerchois, proc. generale, 319–27.

33. Seong-Hak Kim, "Michel de L'Hôpital: The Vision of a Reformist Chancellor during the French Religious Wars," *Sixteenth Century Essays and Studies* 36 (1997): 18.

34. James Farr, *A Tale of Two Murders: Passion and Power in Seventeenth-Century France* (Durham and London: Duke University Press, 2005), 202.

35. On increasing heredity and family recruitment in the Parlements, see Mousnier, *La Venalité des offices,* 381, 388.

36. ADSM 1 B 5612.

37. André Corvisier, "Un lien entre villes et campagnes: Le personnel des haute justices en Haute Normandie au XVIIIe siècle, *Annales de Normandie, Recueil d'études offert en homage au doyen Michel de Boüard,* vol. 1 (Caen: Université de Caen, 1982), 157–70.

38. Mousnier, *La vénalité des offices,* 351.

39. ADSM 1 B 3654, Parlement, Réceptions des Lieutenants Générals, 1705–46.

40. Mousnier, *La vénalité des offices,* 374.

41. Landau, *Justices of the Peace,* 373–77.

42. Maurice Gresset found somewhat higher rates of heritability in the urban lower courts of Besançon, where two of six lieutenants general of the bailliage had fathers in the post, and fewer than 10 percent of councillors succeeded their fathers. Gresset, *Gens de justice,* 192–93.

43. Debordes-Lissillour, *Les sénéchaussées royales,* 183–85.

44. Exemption from the taille for inferior judicial officers was legally established by the Édit du février 1674, but officers had long unofficially enjoyed an exemption. They therefore resisted paying the tax the crown demanded for this supposedly "new" privilege. See Esmonin, *La taille en Normandie,* 250–51.

45. Goubert, "Les officiers royaux," 68–70; Mousnier, *La vénalité des offices,* 464–65; Andrews, *Law, Magistracy and Crime,* 69.

46. Édit d'avril 1715.

47. De la Noiraye, *Memoire,* fols. 180–205.

48. ADIV C 1828, Intendant de Bretagne, agumentations des gages, 1716–17; ADIV 1 Ba 2 bis, Parlement de Bretagne, Augmentation des gages, 1716–19.

49. De la Noiraye, *Mémoire,* 213.

50. Debordes-Lissillour, *Les sénéchaussées royales,* 115–16.

51. De la Noiraye, *Mémoire,* 207.

52. BMR Ms. G 160, Payment des gages de Mss. les officiers du Parlement de Rouen, 1743.

53. Doyle, *Venality,* 23, 39; on Normandy see also Mark Potter, *Corps and Clienteles: Public Finance and Political Change in France, 1688–1715* (Aldershot: Ashgate, 2003), 46–48, 110–17.

54. BN 500 Colbert 260, Bureau des Finances, généralité de Rouen, fols. 180–205; ADSM 1 B 5610, Parlement, extrait de la greffe, 1634.

55. ADIV C 1828, Intendant de Bretagne, augmentation des gages, 1716–17; ADIV C 1835–1836, Intendant de Bretagne, officiers 1740–41.

56. ADSM C 914, Intendant, Correspondence . . . relative à des nombreux bailliages, offices, états de juridictions, 7 août 1777.

57. ADIV C 1828, Intendant de Bretagne, augmentation des gages, 1716–17; ADIV C 1835–1836, Intendant de Bretagne, officiers 1740–41. On the worsening crisis in Brittany during the later eighteenth century, see Debordes-Lissillour, *Les sénéchaussées royales,* 129–34.

58. Édit de décembre 1665; Édit de décembre 1709.

59. Voysin De la Noiraye, *Mémoire sur la géneralité de Rouen, 1665,* ed. Edmond Esmonin (Paris: Librairie Hachette, 1913), 213.

60. Corvisier, "Un lien entre villes et campagnes," 157–70.

61. ADSM 1 B 3654, Parlement, Réceptions des Lieutenants Général, 1705–46.

62. Édit de décembre 1665; Édit d'août 1669; Isambert, Dieussy, Jourdan et. al., *Receuil générale des anciens lois françaises,* 18:66–67, 325–27; François Bluche, *Les magistrates du Parlement de Paris au XVIIIe siècle* (Paris: Economica, 1986), 17–19.

63. Hamscher, *The Parlement of Paris after the Fronde,* 26, 191–93. See also Colin Kaiser, "The Deflation in the Volume of Litigation at Paris in the Eighteenth Century and the Waning of the Old Judicial Order," *European Studies Review* 3 (July 1980): 309–36.

64. Andrews, *Law, Magistracy and Crime,* 70–71.

65. Potter, *Corps and Clienteles,* 115–17.

66. Le Pesant, *Personnel d'une cour souveraine,* 129:431–44. His study of the Parlement of Rouen found that from 1649 to 1715, 255 councillors were received into the Parlement. Of those whose backgrounds were known, 142 were sons of parlementaires; 48 were sons of officers from the Cour des Aides and Chambre des Comptes; 21 were sons from merchant, échevin, or secretaire du roi backgrounds; only 2 came from royal bailliages. See also Andrews, *Law, Magistracy and Crime,* 108 on Châtelet judges from financial families.

67. Mousnier, *La vénalité des offices,* 388.

68. Zoe Schneider, "The Village in the State: Justice and the Local Courts in Normandy, 1670–1740" (PhD. diss., Georgetown University, 1997), 171–78. On similar circumstances in the bailliage and présidial of Besançon, see Gresset, *Gens de justice,* 23. On a more fully functioning présidial court in Brittany, see Hautebert, *La justice pénale à Nantes.*

69. Blanquie, *Les présidiaux de Richelieu,* 15, 272–76.

70. Le Pesant, *Personnel d'une cour souveraine,* 431–44.

71. ADSM 7 BP 117, Présidial de Caudebec-en-Caux, 1721. One councillor in the Parlement received a dispensation to buy the office of president of the présidial and pailliage of Rouen after becoming a parlementaire, but this was not usual practice.

72. ADSM 1 B 5444, Parlement, Provisions d'office, 22 août 1732.

73. ADSM 1 B 5444, Parlement, Provisions d'office, 22 août 1732.

74. Julius Ruff found that the sénéchaussées of Libourne and Bazas sustained or increased lower court verdicts and penalties in more than 80 percent of cases. Julius Ruff, *Crime, Justice and Public Order in Old Régime France: the Sénéchaussées of Libourne and Bazas, 1696–1789* (London: Croom Helm, 1984), 62.

75. Schneider, "The Village in the State," 203–19; see also G. A. Depping, *Correspondence administrative sous le règne de Louis XIV* (Paris: 1850–55), 3:168–73 for a rare example of an intendant interfering in the king's ordinary courts. In this case, the commissaire intervened in the punishment of the judge of Barbonne in 1669, because he had interfered with collection of the taille for many years.

76. Soublin, *Le premier vote,* 38.

77. Not all provinces followed the same pattern. In Toulouse, the sénéchaussée court opposed the Parlement after the May edict, in part because of long-standing rivalries between the urban courts. See Berlanstein, *The Barristers of Toulouse,* 146–47.

78. The arrêt du 6 juillet 1643 had specified that high justices could not augment their officers beyond a bailli, a lieutenant, and a fiscal solicitor without royal permission. The crown actively enforced this rule. In 1652, the canons of Saint-Marcel were forbidden to name a lieutenant as a second judge in their high justice; in 1748 another haute justicier was forbidden to create the office of fiscal solicitor in his court, since one had never existed before. Houard, *Dictionnaire analytique,* 2:457.

79. Pierre L'Hommeau, *Maximes générales de droit Français,* 1612, quoted in Victor Tapié, "Les officiers seigneuriaux," 121.

80. Houard, *Dictionnaire analytique.*

81. Houard, *Dictionnaire analytique,* 2:704.

82. Guy Cardineau, "Les juridictions de l'ancien régime en Bretagne," *Bul. Mens. Soc. Pol. Morbihan* 112 (July 1985): 24; Pierre Goubert, *La vie quotidienne des paysans français au XVIIe siècle* (Paris: Hachette, 1982), 225.

83. Pierre Goubert and Daniel Roche, *Les français et l'ancien régime,* vol. 1, *La société et l'état* (Paris: Armand Colin, 1984), 275.

84. Charles Loyseau, *Discours de l'abus de iustices de village* (Paris: Chez Abel L'Angelier, 1605).

85. Jean Meyer, *La Noblesse bretonne au XVIIIe siècle* (Paris: Imprimerie nationale, 1966); J.-F. Noel, "Une justice seigneuriale en Haute Bretagne à la fin de l'Ancien Régime: La châtellenie de la Motte-de-Gennes," *Annales de Bretagne* 83 (1976): 127–63; and Hayhoe, *Enlightened Feudalism.*

86. ADSM 1 B 3576, 3581, 3583, 3586, Parlement de Normandie, Tournelles, 1672, 1695, 1709, 1728.

87. It is unclear why these civil cases were heard in the Tournelle, but from what we know of the functioning of royal courts in general, it seems likely that cases were not distributed to the chambers with complete impartiality or according to clear rules of jurisdiction. The interests and connections of the judges in the Tournelle (who presided on a rotating basis) may have determined whether a particular case was heard there.

88. ADSM 1 B 3583, Parlement de Normandie, Chambre des Tournelles, 1709.

89. ADSM 1 B 3581, Parlement de Normandie, Chambre des Tournelles, 1695.

90. ADSM 1 B 3581, Parlement de Normandie, Chambre des Tournelles, 1695.

91. ADSM 1 B 3576, Parlement de Normandie, Chambre des Tournelle, 1672.

92. 1 B 5579, Parlement de Normandie, haute justice de Cany-Caniel, 20 aout 1667 et 20 avr. 1668.

93. ADSM 1 B 5696, Arrêt du conseil d'état privé du roy, 12 Mars 1736.

94. ADSM 1 B 5521–5522, Parlement de Normandie, Sorcières; see also Robert Mandrou, *Magistrats et sorcières en France au XVIIe siècle, une analysé de psychologie historique* (Paris: Plon, 1968), 444–57, on sorcery cases in the Parlement of Rouen. Both Mandrou and the Parlement documents suggest that an element of resistance against the crown also figured into the tenacity of the Parlement's refusal to reverse its decision, but this came after the appellate decisions were made.

95. ADSM 1 B 5521, Parlement de Normandie, baronie et haute justice de Écouis, 1700.

96. 1 B 5449, Parlement de Normandie, arrêts du 20 juillet 1750 et 17 août 1751.

97. *Vacations* had a dual meaning in the courts. The vacation was the fee that could be charged when working away from the court, at home or on the road; it was also the vacation session of the court, which in the Parlement was presided over by a small complement of judges who dealt with any urgent cases.

98. BMR U 1285-3 II, Arrêt de la Cour de Parlement de Rouen, portant règlement pour les taxes des Iuges, 9 juin 1671.

99. For similar regulations in Burgundy, see for example ADCO, D1 0066, Règlements pour les fonctions et droits des officiers, greffiers, procureurs . . . set plusiers arrêts sur des matières importantes (Dijon: 1736).

100. BMR U 1285-3 II, Arrêt de la Cour, 9 juin 1671.

101. ADSM 1 B 205, Parlement de Normandie, Registres secrets, 10 décembre 1678.

102. See also Hamscher, *The Parlement of Paris after the Fronde,* 192–93, on education reform.

103. ADSM 1 B 3646–3648, Parlement de Normandie, Examens et Informations, 1692–98, 1698–1716, 1716–27.

104. Corvisier, "Un lien entre villes et campagnes," 157–79; Dewald, *Pont-Saint-Pierre,* 252.

105. ADSM 1 B 3646–3648, Parlement de Normandie, Examens et Informations, 1692–98, 1698–1716, 1716–27.

106. Édit de janvier 1552; see Isambert, Dieussy, Jourdan et. al., *Receuil générale des anciens lois françaises,* 13:248.

107. See also Hélène Prax-Falcou, *Le sénéschal et siège présidial de Lauragais: Les magistrats, la procedure criminelle (1670–1790)* (Position des thèses, École des Chartres, 1971), which confirms the doubling of court personnel in the présidal and lower jurisdictions in Lauragais.

108. H. Bourde de la Rogerie, "Liste des juridictions exercées au XVIIe et au XVIIIe siècles dans le ressort du Présidial de Quimper," *Bull. Soc. Arch. Finistere* 37 (1910): 256; Hautebert, *La justice pénale à Nantes,* 33–38, 53–64, 142–43; Soleil, *Le siège royale,* 23–24, 286.

109. See Armelle Sabbagh, Conservateur, ADSM, Rep. Numerique 22/1, 1971, who has argued from the sixteenth-century documents that the two courts were fused together from the inception of the présidial of Rouen. In Champagne, the présidial and bailliage officials were formally linked according to the intendant's report in 1688.

110. ADSM 5444, Receptions d'offices, Arrêt du Conseil d'État. The paper was partly torn, making it impossible to give a precise date.

111. From this judicial family, see also Boisguilbert, *Mémoire sur l'assiete de la taille* (Paris: I.N.E.D., 1966 reprint) and *Factum de France* (Paris: I.N.E.D., 1966 reprint). See also *Mémoire à Rouen au temps de Boisguilbert,* especially Bardet, "Mourir à Rouen au temps de Boisguilbert."

112. BN 500 Colbert 260, fols. 180–205; see also Voysin de la Noiraye, *Mémoire,* 209–13. The intendant's records of présidial and bailliage offices being united are confirmed by the Parlement of Normandy's examinations and receptions of officers into these offices; for example, the reception of Nicolas Chambellan as a councillor for both the bailliage and the présidial of Caudebec in 1721 or the registration of letters of nobility for the sieur de la Motte, lieutenant general of the bailliage and présidial of Rouen, in 1697 (ADSM 1 B 3646, 3648, Parlement, Commissaires: examens et informations des officiers, 1721, 1697).

113. ADSM 7 BP 218, Présidial de Caudebec-en-Caux, 1698. The documents for the présidial are unfortunately very erratically preserved and catalogued, making it necessary to rely on several sample years of cases taken from 1697 to 1699, from 1717 to 1723, and from 1730. Many of the early registers indicate that the court was sitting as both "bailliage and présidial" at the same time and dealt with both types of cases together. See, for example, ADSM 7 BP 218, Bailliage et Présidial de Caudebec-en-Caux, décrets des heritages, 1690–91.

114. ADSM 7 BP 31, Présidial de Caudebec-en-Caux, 1730.

115. ADSM 1 B 5696, Parlement de Normandie, Arréts du Grand Conseil et Conseil Privé, 15 juillet 1633, 12 aout 1633, 15 octobre 1649.

116. ADSM C 2215, Intendant de Rouen, Ordonnances, 1642–1788.

117. ADSM, Inventaire, Intendants de Normandie, 11–12. A twentieth intendant was sent to Rouen during this period but was recalled almost immediately.

118. ADSM C 920, Intendant de Rouen, Letter from M. de Belbeuf to the procureur du roy, bailliage de Neufchatel, 1775.

119. On provincial administration and the intendants and governors of Normandy, see Hurpin, "L'administration de la Normandie," Hippeau, *Le gouvernment de Normandie,* and Veyrat, "Les gouverneurs de Normandie." After the death of the duc de Longueville in 1662, the provincial governors in Normandy were in practice superseded by the lieutenant general for Haute Normandie, who watched over the defense of the province.

120. ADSM C 2798–2799, Administration des domaines, procès verbaux de prise de possession du Duché de Longueville, 1694–95.

121. Root, *Peasant and King in Burgundy.*

122. ADSM C 946, Intendant, Frais de justice: Arrêt du conseil d'état du roy du 3 juin 1778; see also Déclaration du 12 juillet 1687 and Déclaration de 26 juin 1745.

123. ADSM C 946, Intendant, Arrêt du conseil d'état du roy du 3 juin 1778.

124. ADSM C 947, Intendant, Frais de justice, Arrêt du conseil d'état, 11 avril 1774.

125. ADSM C 948, Intendant, Frais de justice, 1762–64.

126. ADSM C 949, Intendant, Frais de justice, Intendant de Crosne, 1776.

127. ADSM C 948, Intendant, Frais de justice, 1760.

128. ADSM C 950, Intendant, Statistique criminalle, M. le Chancelier à M. de la Bourdonnaye, 9 octobre 1733.

129. ADSM C 950, Intendant, Statistique criminalle, Crimes et delits de la Généralité de Rouen, Chancelier d'Aguesseau à Intendant de la Bourdonnaye, 20 février 1741.

130. ADSM C 950, Chancelier d'Aguesseau à Intendant de la Bourdonnaye, 21 avril 1739.

131. ADSM C 950, Miromesny à Intendant de Crosne, 18 octobre 1784.

132. ADSM C 920, Intendant, Frais de justice, Statistique criminalle, Graces et remissions: *Mémoire pour la suppression de la Haute Justice de Graville.*

Chapter 6

Epigraph. Charles Louis de Secondat, Baron de Montesquieu, *Lettres persanes* (Paris: Bokking International, 1993), 154–55.

1. ADSM 71 BP 9, bailliage de Grainville-la-Teinturière, 16 déc.1728.

2. ADSM 71 BP 14, bailliage de Grainville-la-Teinturière, 13 juin 1740; ADSM 71 BP 3, bailliage de Grainville-la-Teinturière, 1693–97; see also Lécole, "La haute justice," 38–39.

3. Marjorie Keniston McIntosh, *Controlling Misbehavior in England, 1370–1600* (Cambridge: Cambridge University Press, 1998), 8.

4. See chapter 7 on witnessing, composition, and clameurs.

5. The courts' *plumitifs,* or registers, are the most complete inventory of the uptake of cases. Trials requiring witnesses or expert testimony were typically kept in separate registers or on loose paper; about one-third of the more documented trials in the Caux were criminal affairs, reflecting the greater need for testimony in such cases.

6. Steven G. Reinhardt, "Crime and Royal Justice in Ancien Régime France: Modes of Analysis," *Journal of Interdisciplinary History* 13 (Winter 1983): 460.

7. Anthony Crubaugh, *Balancing the Scales of Justice: Local Courts and Rural Society in Southwest France, 1750–1800* (University Park: Pennsylvania State University Press, 2001), 31–54, also discusses the civil functions of seigneurial justice in the later eighteenth century.

8. Underdown, *Revel, Riot, and Rebellion,* 13.

9. ADSM 71 BP 9, bailliage de Grainville-la-Teinturière, 16 déc.1728.

10. ADSM 46 BP 22, haute justice de Cany-Caniel, 30 sep. 1704, 14 fév. 1708.

11. The cens and champart were rarely enforced in the seventeenth and eighteenth centuries in Normandy; most annual gage-plèges and aveux from Cauchois seigneuries make no mention of them. See also Dewald, *The Formation of a Provincial Nobility,* 166.

12. Lemarchand, "Le fin du féodalisme," 8. See also Dewald, *Pont-Saint-Pierre,* 282.

13. See also Collins, *Classes, Estates, and Order,* 83, on leases of church lands.

14. ADCO B 165 15, bailliage de Nuits-Saint-George, 1717–30; see similar cases in Root, *Peasants and King in Burgundy.*

15. ADSM 19 BP 3, bailliage notarial de Longueville, 1681.

16. ADSM 46 BP 24, haute justice de Cany-Caniel, 24 nov 1713.

17. See for example AN Z2 390, haute justice de Bosc Roger, 1671–1725; AN Z2 1022, haute justice de La Ferté-en-Bray, 1664–95; ADSM 112 BP 1–2, haute justice de Vittefleur, 1648–88; ADCO B 2 149/1; B 2 161 1–2, balliage de Beaune; ADCO B2 164 2–3, bailliage de Nuits-Saint-George; ADCO B 2 942–1, haute justice de Villars Fontaine; ADCO B 2 819 1, haute justice de Quincy; ADIV 1200 1–4, haute justice de Châteaugiron; ADIV 4 B 1251–1253, 1281–1291, 1296–1300, 1337–1340, 1347–1348, 1350 haute justice de Chateauneuf; ADIV 3 B 856–860, prieuré de Hédé; ADIV 3 B 610–613, sénéchaussée de Hédé; ADIV 3 B 234, sénéchaussée de Fougeres. Although the exact profile varies from court to court, the overall emphasis on civil regulation of family and property is the same. Similar evidence can be found in Jeremy D. Hayhoe, "'Judge in Their Own Cause': Seigneurial Justice in Northern Burgundy, 1750–1790" (PhD. diss., University of Maryland, College Park, 2001), 216.

18. Schneider, "Women before the Bench," 16–17.

19. Amy Louise Erickson, *Women and Property in Early Modern England* (London and New York: Routledge, 1993), 5, 223.

20. Schneider, "Women before the Bench," 22–24.

21. Barbara B. Diefendorf, "Women and Property in Ancien Régime France: Theory and Practice in Dauphiné and Paris," in *Early Modern Conceptions of Property,* ed. John Brewer and Susan Staves, 187 (London and New York: Routledge, 1995).

22. ADSM 19 BP 2, bailliage de Longueville, 1736.

23. David Sabean, *Power in the Blood: Popular Culture and Village Discourse in Early Modern Germany* (Cambridge: Cambridge University Press), 137.

24. ADSM 46 BP 48, haute justice de Cany-Caniel, 25 août 1727.

25. Coutume de Normandie, Arts. 330, 389.

26. ADSM 46 BP 48, haute justice de Cany-Caniel, 3–15 sep. 1727.

27. Schneider, "Women before the Bench," 11–12, 20–21; see for example ADSM 71 BP 10, bailliage de Grainville-la-Teinturière, 15 mars 1708.

28. Coutume de Normandie, Art. 235.

29. Henri Basnage, *Les oeuvres de maître Henri Basnage* (Paris: 1778), 1:337. See also Jean Yver, "La redaction officielle de la Coutume de Normandie (Rouen, 1583): Son esprit," *Annales de Normandie* 1 (1986): 35.

30. Coutume de Normandie, Art. 237.

31. ADSM 19 BP 2, bailliage de Longueville, 1736.

32. ADSM 19 BP 2, bailliage de Longueville, 1736.

33. Schneider, "Women before the Bench," 26–31.

34. Susan Staves, *Married Women's Separate Property in England, 1660–1833* (Cambridge, MA: Harvard University Press, 1990), 197–99, 226–30; Erickson, *Women and Property in Early Modern England,* 223–34; and Erickson, "Common Law Versus Common Practice: The Use of Marriage Settlements in Early Modern England," *Economic History Review,* 2nd ser., 43 (1990), 21–39.

35. Sarah Hanley, "The Monarchic State in Early Modern France: Marital Regime Government and Male Right," in *Politics, Ideology, and Law in Early Modern Europe,* ed. Adrianna E. Bakos, 109 (Rochester, NY: University of Rochester Press, 1994); see also Hanley, "Engendering the State: Family Formation and State Building in Early Modern France," *French Historical Studies* 16, no. 1 (Spring 1989): 4–27, and Hanley, "The Family, the State, and the Law in Seventeenth- and Eighteenth-Century France: The Political Ideology of Male Right versus an Early Theory of Natural Rights," *Journal of Modern History,* 78, no. 2 (2006):

36. ADSM 71 BP 6, Grainville-la-Teinturière, 1694.

37. On the use of seigneurial courts for rent and dues collection in Burgundy, which had a more extensive complex of seigneurial obligations than Normandy, see Hayhoe, "'Judge in Their Own Cause,'" 146–207.

38. See also Intendant Louis le Blanc, 29 avr. 1678, on registration of a royal declaration forbidding the seizure of work animals, in Smedley-Weill, ed., *Analytique, Sous-serie G. Inventaire,* 1:291.

39. ADSM 13 BP 52, bailliage de Cany, 23 sep. 1720.

40. Coutume de Normandie, Art. 521.

41. ADSM 107 BP 1, haute justice de Valmont, 1761.

42. Lemarchand, "La fin de féodalisme," 131.

43. On the economy and society of the pays de Caux in the seventeenth and eighteenth centuries, see particularly Jacques Bottin, "La production des toiles en Normandie, milieu XVIe siècle: Approche des voies de développement," *L'Homme et l'Industrie en Normandie* (Alencon: Sociétés Historiques et Archéologiques, 1990), 77–86; and his *Seigneurs et paysans dans l'ouest du pays de Caux: 1540–1650* (Paris: Sycomore, 1983); Marie-Claude Gricourt, "Étude de histoire demographique, sociale et religieuse de 5 paroisses," in *Cahiers des Annales de Normandie,* vol. 3, *À travers la Normandie des XVIIe et XVIIIe siècles* (Caen: 1963), 445–555; and the older but still partly

useful Jules Sion, *Le paysans de la Normandie orientale: Pays de Bray, Caux, Vexin Normand, Vallée de la Seine* (Paris: Armand Colin, 1909).

44. On later textile production, see Gullickson, *Spinners and Weavers of Auffay.*

45. Voysin de la Noiraye, *Mémoire,* 12–13 and passim.

46. On Norman consular courts, see Brunelle, *New World Merchants of Rouen.*

47. Forster, *The East Riding Justices of the Peace,* 54.

48. ADSM 46 BP 25, haute justice de Cany-Caniel, juin 1716.

49. Coutume de Normandie, Arts. 533–536.

50. ADSM 19 BP 2, bailliage de Longueville, juillet 1710.

51. Vardi, *The Land and the Loom,* 184–87.

52. ADSM 107 BP 1, haute justice de Valmont, 1757–86.

53. ADSM 107 BP 1, haute justice de Valmont, juin 1763.

54. ADSM G 736-G 741, visites de Monseigneur d'Aubigné.

55. ADSM 13 BP 49, bailliage de Cany, 27 jan., 10 fev., 24 fev., 24 mar., 4 avr., 28 avr., 5 mai, 12 mai, 26 mai, 2 juin, 16 juin, 23 juin, 30 juin 1710.

56. ADSM 19 BP 2, bailliage de Longueville, 1720.

57. ADSM 13 BP 57, bailliage de Cany, 27 mars 1730.

58. ADSM 13 BP 49, bailliage de Cany, 2 juin 1710.

59. ADSM 19 BP 2, bailliage de Longueville, 1720; see also ADSM 13 BP 57, bailliage de Cany, 24 avr. 1730.

60. See chapter 4 for a discussion of the legal history of equity from Roman times.

61. Aristotle, *Nichomachean Ethics,* 99–100. In the *Ethics,* Aristotle described equity as superior to the law because of its ability to apply principles of justice to widely individual cases.

62. Bodin, *Six Livres,* 439–40.

63. Jousse, *Traité,* 23.

64. Jousse, *Traité,* 30–31.

65. Jean-Pierre Royer, *Histoire de la justice en France* (Paris: Presses Universitaires de France, 1995), 35.

66. Michael R. Weisser, *Crime and Punishment in Early Modern Europe* (Atlantic Highlands, NJ: Humanities Press, 1979), 96.

67. Liana Vardi, "Peasants and the law: A Village Appeals to the French Royal Council, 1768–1791," *Social History,* 13, no. 3 (1988): 296; Olwen Hufton, "Le paysan et la loi en France au XVIIIe siècle,"*Annales ESC.* 3 (1983): 679–701.

68. ADSM 71 BP 5, haute justice de Grainville-la-Teinturière, 1693–94.

69. BMR, Ms Y 169: Vaubourg, "Mémoires."

70. Madeleine Foisil, *La révolte des nu-pieds et les révoltes Normandes de 1639* (Paris: Fallois, 1970), 146.

71. H. Pissard, *La clameur de haro dans le droit Normand* (Caen: 1711), 10 and passim.

72. Pissard, *La clameur de haro.*

73. M. Pesnelle, *Coutume de Normandie, expliquée par M. Pesnelle . . . avec les arrêts et règlements de la Cour* (Rouen: 1704), 52.

74. Natalie Zemon Davis, *Society and Culture in Early Modern France* (Stanford: Stanford University Press, 1975), 168.

75. Coutume de Normandie, Arts. 54–62.

76. BMR 1285 U-3, T.II: *Coutumes de Pais de Normandie* (1588).

77. ADSM 1 B 5612–5613, Parlement de Normandy, enquête, bailliage de Pont-Audemer.

78. Pissard, *La clameur de haro;* see also Houard, *Dictionnaire analytique,* 2:704.

79. Rathery, *Etudes historiques,* 3.

80. Foisil, *La révolte des nu-pieds,* 255–56.

81. M. Burel, *Elemens de pratique et modèles d'exploits* (Rouen: 1772), 155, 181.

82. ADSM 46 BP 28, haute justice de Cany-Caniel, 18 juin 1727.

83. ADSM 46 BP 19, haute justice de Cany-Caniel, 1699.

84. ADSM 46 BP 19, haute justice de Cany-Caniel, oct. 1699.

85. ADSM 13 BP 57, bailliage de Cany, 27 fév. 1730.

86. ADSM 13 BP 26, bailliage de Cany, 1680.

87. See, for example, ADSM 71 BP 5, haute justice de Grainville-la-Teinturière, 16 mars–30 juin 1693.

88. In a study covering fifty-five years of records of the bailliage of Mamers, Alain Margot found sentences in just over 16 percent of criminal cases. Champin found that 20 percent of the cases in the bailliage of Alençon had a final sentence, although another 18 percent had a preliminary sentence. Even if one takes into account gaps in the records and long delays between the initiation and the conclusion of a trial, we must conclude that an enormous percentage of cases were resolved out of court. See Alain Margot, "La criminalité dans le bailliage de Mamers (1695–1750)," *Annales de Normandie* 22 (1972): 185–224; and Marie-Madeleine Champin, "Un cas typique de justice bailliagière: La criminalité dans le bailliage d'Alençon de 1715 à 1745," *Annales de Normandie* 22 (1972): 47–84.

89. Elizabeth Crittall (ed.), *The Justicing Notebook of William Hunt 1744–1749* (Devizes: Wiltshire Record Society, vol. 37, 1982), 28, 51.

90. See also Ordonnance de Moulins, Art. 83; Ordonnance de jan. 1629, Art. 152; Ordonnance civile 1667, Art. 22, Title 29.

91. In some provinces, the parlements may have tried to rein in arbitration; for Burgundy, see Hayhoe, "'Judge in Their Own Cause, '" 479–80.

92. Parlement de Normandie, Placités de 1666, "Instruction sur la marche de la procedure civile," in *Coutume de Normandie, avec l'ordonnance de 1667 & celle de 1670* (Bayeux: Veuve Briard, 1773). This confirmed the Ordinance of 1539 and the Ordinance of Blois, which made similar provisions for judicial arbitration.

93. Édit de mars 1673.

94. Hayhoe, "'Judges in their Own Cause,'" 490.

95. Yves Castan, in "Mentalités rural et urbaine à la fin de l'ancien régime dans le ressort du Parlement de Toulouse d'après les sacs à procès criminels, 1730–1790," in *Cahiers des Annales,* no. 33, *Crime et criminalités en France sous l'Ancien Régime, XVIIe-XVIIIe siècles* (Paris: Armand Colin, 1971), 135–38, remarked on the use of curés to settle disputes in the parlement jurisdiction of Toulouse.

96. Jousse, *Traité,* 722.

97. Ordonnance de Commerce, mars 1673.

98. Jousse, *Traité,* 695.

99. Under some interpretations, arbitrated decisions could be appealed to the présidials as well.

100. Arrêt du conseil, 6 avril 1715.

101. Jousse, *Traité,* 692.

102. Ordonnance criminel de 1670, Titre 25, Article 9.

103. Dewald, *Pont-Saint-Pierre,* 262–63.

104. Jousse, *Traité,* 698.

105. Jousse, *Traité,* 683–84.

106. BN, Melanges Colbert, vol. 33, fols. 332–33.

107. Crubaugh, *Balancing the Scales,* 189.

108. Karl Wegert, *Popular Culture, Crime, and Social Control in 18th-Century Wurttemburg* (Stuttgart: F. Steiner, 1994), 12.

109. Pesnelle, *Coutume de Normandie,* printer's advertisement.

110. René Helot, *La bibliothèque bleue en Normandie* (Rouen: A. Lainé, 1928).

111. Pesnelle, *Coutume de Normandie.*

112. Bruce Lenman and Geoffrey Parker, "The State, the Community and the Criminal Law in Early Modern Europe," in *Crime and the Law: The Social History of Crime in Western Europe since 1500,* ed. V. A. C. Gatrell, Bruce Lenman, and Geoffrey Parker, 11 (London: Europa Pubulications, 1980).

113. Hufton, "Le paysan et la loi en France," 681.

114. Dewald, *Pont-Saint-Pierre,* 262.

115. Ordonnance de Villers-Cotterêts, août 1539, in Isambert, Dieussy, Jourdan, et. al., *Recueil,* 601.

116. ADSM G 738, visites pastorales de Msgr. D'Aubigné, 1710–17; Muriel Jéorger, "La alphabetisation dans l'ancien diocese de Rouen au XVIIe et au XVIIIe siècles," in *Lire et Écrire: L'alphabetisation des Français de Calvin à Ferry* (Paris: Éditions de Minuit, 1977), 128, 131.

117. Jéorger, "La alphabetisation." Individual villages in the central Caux displayed similar patterns. Marie-Claude Gricourt found that male literacy in the parishes of Doudeville and Bacqueville, near the royal court seat of Cany, had male literacy rates of between 36 and 51 percent in the decade 1680–90, whereas female literacy never exceeded 10 percent. Gricourt, "Étude d'histoire démographique," 484–553.

118. Ibid, 143. These figures include rural areas in the département of the Eure as well as Seine-Inferieure, so they would likely be somewhat lower for the pays de Caux alone.

119. ADSM 13 BP 49, bailliage de Cany, 30 juin 1710.

120. AN Z2 1017, haute justice de la comté d'Eu, 16 février 1684. The comté was a Norman jurisdiction, but its cases were appealed to the Parlement of Paris and it practiced a second customary law of its own. This useful confusion no doubt allowed the peasants here to make much more creative use of donations and marriage contracts than the Custom of Normandy would seem to allow.

121. Davis, *Society and Culture in Early Modern France,* 244.

122. *Ancien costumier de Normandie,* c. 1280, quoted in Houard, *Dictionnaire analytique IV,* 132–33.

123. Geneviève Bolleme, "Les Almanachs populaires aux XVIIe et XVIIIe siècles" (École Pratique des Hautes Études, Paris, 1969), 65–66, 71–72; Roger Chartier, *L'ordre des livres: Lecteurs, auteurs, bibliothèques en Europe entre XIVe et XVIIIe siècle* (Aix-en-Provence: Alinea, 1992), 143–44.

124. Jean de la Fontaine, "Le juge arbitre, l'hôspitalier, et le solitaire," in *Fables* (Paris: Garnier-Flammarion, 1966), 368.

125. *La Saincte Bible, Traduit par les Theologians de l'Université de Louvain* (Rouen: 1572), Ex. XX, XXIII, 68–69; Lev. 24:112.

126. ADSM 13 BP 52, bailliage de Cany, 2 April 1720.

127. Sharpe, *Crime in Early Modern England,* 123.

128. Roger Chartier, *The Cultural Uses of Print in Early Modern Europe* (Princeton, NJ: Princeton University Press, 1988), 5; see also David Underdown, *A Freeborn People: Politics and the Nation in Seventeenth-Century England* (Oxford: Oxford University Press, 1996), 49, 59.

Chapter 7

1. ADSM 7 BP 5, haute justice de Grainville-la-Teinturière, jugement définitif, 1693.

2. Cardinal Richelieu, *Testament politique* (Paris: Robert Laffont,1947), 343.

3. Richelieu, *Testament politique,* 342. On Richelieu's attitude toward the judiciary and the "interêts publique," see also Keohane, *Philosophy and the State in Early Modern France,* 175.

4. See also Schwartz, *Policing the Poor,* on the public and the *dépôt de mendicité* and maréchaussées. On England, see McIntosh, *Controlling Misbehavior,* 8, 15.

5. Reinhardt, "Crime and Royal Justice," 442, 452. For the sénéchaussées of Libourne and Bazas in Bordeaux, approximately 75 percent of crimes were privately prosecured; see Julius Ruff, *Crime, Justice and Public Order,* 47.

6. Noel, "Une justice seigneuriale," 138–63.

7. Apart from those listed elsewhere in this chapter, the key earlier studies include Yves Marie Bercé, "Aspects de la criminalité au XVIIe siècle," *Revue Historique* 239 (1968): 33–42; and François Billaçois, "Pour une enquête sur la criminalité dans la France d'ancien régime," *Annales d'Histoire Économique et Sociale* (March–April 1967): 340–47, which laid out general hypotheses and avenues for research. Later works include Nicole Castan's *Justice et répression en Languedoc à l'epoque des lumières* (Paris: Flammarion, 1980) and her thesis "Criminalité et litiges sociaux en Languedoc de 1690 à 1730" (Université de Toulouse–Le Mirail, 1966); sections of Nicole and Yves Castan's *Vivre ensemble: Ordre et disorde en Languedoc (XVIIe–XVIIIe siècles)* (Paris: Gallimard-Juilliard, 1981); and Yves Castan's contribution to *Crime et criminalités en France,* "Mentalités rural et urbaine à la fin de la ancien régime," 109–86. On general trends, see also Alfred Soman, "Deviance and Criminal Justice in Western Europe, 1300–1800: An Essay in Structure," *Criminal Justice History* 1 (1980): 3–28; and Benoit Garnot, "Une illusion historiographique: Justice et criminalité au XVIIIe siècle," *Revue Historique* 570 (1989): 361–79.

8. Nor was the maréchaussée, or mounted constabulary court, a significant presence for handling criminal cases in the rural Caux. There were only nine archers for the entire presidial district of Caudebec-en-Caux, with a sprawling jurisdiction of over eight hundred parishes. The constabulary typically appeared on the roads of the central Caux only when summoned by the regular courts to provide security for court personnel, or to take charge of a prisoner.

9. In eighteenth-century Burgundian seigneurial courts, criminal cases made up less than 5 percent of the caseload; see Jeremy D. Hayhoe, "Neighbors Before the

Court: Crime, Village Communities and Seigneurial Justice in Northern Burgundy, 1750–1790," *French History* 17, no. 2 (2003): 131. Lenman and Parker particularly criticized the small number of cases used in four key studies on early modern crime in Normandy (see below). Although Boutelet's work is based on eighty-eight cases, and Margot's on 704 cases over fifty-five years, they are an accurate representation of the relatively small number of criminal cases tried in royal bailliage courts, compared with the civil caseload. See Lenman and Parker, "The State, the Community," in Gatrell et. al., *Crime and the Law,* 47. Among the best criminal studies on Normandy are Jean-Claude Gegot, "Étude par sondage de la criminalité dans la bailliage de Falaise (XVIIe–XVIIIe siècles): Criminalité diffuse ou société criminal?" *Annales de Normandie* 13 (1966): 103–64; Bernadette Boutelet, "Étude par sondage de la criminalité dans le bailliage de Pont-de-l'Arche (XVIIe–XVIIIe siècles): De la violence au vol; En march vers l'escroquerie," *Annales de Normandie* 12 (Dec. 1962); Champin, "La criminalité," 47–84; and Margot, "La criminalité dans la bailliage de Mamers," 185–224.

10. Louis XIV, *Memoires,* 117.

11. See David Potter, "'Rigueur de Justice': Crime, Murder and the Law in Picardy, Fifteenth to Sixteenth Centuries," *French History* 11, no. 3 (1997): 265–309; and Natalie Zemon Davis, *Fiction in the Archives: Pardon Tellers and Their Tales in Sixteenth-Century France* (Stanford: Stanford University Press, 1987).

12. Bossuet, *Politique tirée des propres paroles,* 195–98.

13. Michel Foucault, *Surveiller et punir: Naissance de la prison* (Paris: Gallimard, 1975).

14. Douglas Hay, "Property, Authority and Criminal Law," in *Albion's Fatal Tree: Crime and Society in Eighteenth-Century England,* ed. Douglas Hay, Peter Linebaugh, John G. Rule, E. P. Thompson, and Cal Winslow (New York: Pantheon, 1975), 25–26.

15. E. P. Thompson, *Whigs and Hunters: The Origin of the Black Act* (New York: Pantheon, 1975), 263.

16. Ruff, *Crime, Justice,* 56, 61.

17. Ruff, *Crime, Justice,* 56; see also John H. Langbein, *Torture and the Law of Proof: Europe and England in the Ancien Régime* (Chicago: University of Chicago Press, 1977) for a full discussion of judicial torture.

18. Forster, *The East Riding Justices of the Peace,* 66.

19. Hamscher, *The Parlement of Paris after the Fronde,* 187.

20. Pierre Chaunu, introduction to Boutelet, "Étude par sondage de la criminalité," 235–65.

21. Gatrell et al., *Crime and the Law,* 9; see also James A. Sharpe, "The History of Crime in Late Medieval and Early Modern England," *Social History* 7 (1982): 187–203.

22. Yves Castan, *Honnêteté et rélations sociales en Languedoc (1715–1780)* (Paris: Plon, 1974), 517–19.

23. Margot, "La criminalité dans la bailliage de Mamers," 185–224.

24. ADSM 46 BP 39, haute justice de Cany-Caniel, 28 août 1727.

25. ADSM 46 BP 39, haute justice de Cany-Caniel, 7 juin 1727.

26. Nicole Castan, "La criminalité familiale," 91–107.

27. ADSM 1 B 5697, Parlement, Tournelles, 1720.

28. ADSM 71 BP 13, bailliage de Grainville-la-Teinturiére, 4 nov. 1743.

29. ADSM 46 BP 39, haute justice de Cany-Caniel, 14 sep. 1729.

30. ADSM 46 BP 39, haute justice de Cany-Caniel, 2 juillet, 19 sep. 1729.

31. ADSM 1 B 5612–13, Parlement de Normandie vs. bailliage de Pont-Aude-mer, 1690–93.

32. Weisser, *Crime and Punishment in Early Modern Europe,* 61.

33. Hayhoe, "Neighbors Before the Court," 147.

34. Lenman and Parker, "The State, the Community," 15.

35. ADSM 71 BP 5, haute justice de Grainville-la-Teinturière, 16 mars-30 juin 1693.

36. See Underdown, *Fire from Heaven: Life in an English Town in the Seventeenth Century* (New Haven, CT: Yale University Press, 1992), 98; Lecole, *Haute Justice,* 30.

37. Debordes-Lissillour, *Les sénéchaussées royales,* 89.

38. Ruff, *Crime, Justice,* 63; see also Ruff, *Violence in Early Modern Europe,* 95, 107. On similar mechanisms in Spain, see Weisser, *Crime and Punishment,* 62–63.

39. ADSM 7 BP 31, présidial de Caudebec-en-Caux, jul. 1730; see also ADSM 7 BP 117, présidial, 1721.

40. Schwartz, *Policing the Poor,* 251. Other notable studies on vagabondage, begging, delinquency, and police include Arlette Farge, *Delinquance et criminalité: Le vol d'aliments à Paris au XVIIIe siècle* (Paris: Plon, 1974); Olwen Hufton, "Begging, Vagrancy, Vaga-bondage and the Law: An Aspect of the Problem of Poverty in Eighteenth-Century France," *European Studies Review* 2 (1972): 97–123; and Hufton, *The Poor of Eighteenth-Century France* (Oxford: Oxford University Press, 1974); and Alan Williams, *The Police of Paris, 1718–1789* (Baton Rouge: Louisiana State University Press, 1979).

41. Among the most important studies on continental justice are, for Italy, Tom-maso Astarita, *Village Justice: Community, Family, and Popular Culture in Early Modern Italy* (Baltimore: Johns Hopkins University Press, 1999); John K. Brackett, *Criminal Justice and Crime in Late Renaissance Florence, 1537–1609* (Cambridge: Cambridge University Press, 1992); Thomas L. Kuehn, *Law, Family and Women: Toward a Legal Anthropology of Renaissance Italy* (Chicago: University of Chicago Press, 1991); and Brian Pullan, *The Jews of Europe and the Inquisition of Venice, 1550–1670* (Totowa, NJ: Barnes and Noble Books, 1983). For Germany, see Karl Wegert, *Popular Culture, Crime, and Social Control in 18th-Century Wurttemberg* (Stuttgart: Franz Steiner Verlag, 1994); and John H. Langbein, *Prosecuting Crime in the Renaissance: England, Germany, France* (Cambridge, MA: Harvard University Press, 1974). For Spain, see particularly Richard L. Kagan, *Lawsuits and Litigants in Early Modern Castile, 1500–1700* (Chapel Hill: University of North Carolina Press, 1981); and Ruth Pike, "Capital Punishment in Eighteenth-Century Spain," *Histoire sociale/Social History* 18 (1985): 376–86.

42. Sharpe, "The History of Crime," 193.

43. ADSM 1 B 5697, Parlement de Normandie, Tournelles, 18 juin 1717.

44. ADSM 1 B 5521, Parlement de Normandie, haute justice de Écouis (1700), bailliage d'Evreux (1709–10); ADSM 1 B 5522, bailliage de Gisors (1692, 1663–64).

45. Champin, "Un cas typique," 47–84; see also Hayhoe, "Neighbors before the Court," 132.

46. Ian Cameron, *Crime and Repression in the Auvergne and the Guyenne, 1720–1790* (Cambridge: Cambridge University Press, 1981), 155–58. Julius Ruff turned up capi-tal sentences in 21.9 percent of all crimes for the sénéchaussées of Libourne and

Bazas, near Bordeaux, but a third of those were not executed because the defendant had fled, making the execution rate approximately 14.7 percent. Ruff, *Crime, Justice,* 60–61; see also Ruff, *Violence in Early Modern Europe,* 107.

47. E. P Thompson, "The Crime of Anonymity," in Hay et al., *Albion's Fatal Tree,* 286; Sharpe, *Crime in Early Modern England,* 36; see also Peter Linebaugh, *The London Hanged: Crime and Civil Society in the Eighteenth Century* (London: Penguin, 1991) for a detailed look at crime and capital punishment in London.

48. Houard, *Dictionnaire analytique,* 2: 704.

49. Michel Bée, "Vivre du métier de bourreau au XVIIIe siecle en Normandie," *Cahiers Leopold Deslisle,* 32 (1982–83): 99–114.

50. Marie-Laure Coquelin, "L'éxecuteur de haute justice sous l'ancien régime (l'exemple Breton au XVIIIe siecle)," *Annales de Bretagne* 1:100 (1993): 53.

51. Bodin, *Six Livres de la République,* 431.

52. John Locke, *The Second Treatise of Government,* in *Political Writings of John Locke,* 262.

53. Foucault, *Surveiller et punir;* and Emile Durkheim, *De la division du travail sociale,* 2nd ed. (Paris: F. Alcan, 1902). See also *Durkheim and the Law,* ed. Steven Lukes and Andrew Scull (New York: St. Martin's Press, 1983).

54. ADSM 1 B 3576 (1672–73), 1 B 3581 (1695–96), 1 B 3583 (1709–10), 1 B 3586 (1728–29), Parlement de Normandie, Tournelles.

55. Champin, "La criminalité," 52.

56. Roger B. Manning, *Hunters and Poachers: A Social and Cultural History of Unlawful Hunting in England, 1485–1640* (Oxford: Oxford University Press,1993), 58.

57. Thompson, *Whigs and Hunters,* 270–77.

58. Manning, *Hunters and Poachers,* 236.

59. ADSM 1 B 5613, bailliage de Pontaudemer, 26 fev. 1692

60. On *mentalités* and identities in early modern Europe, see also Yves Castan, "Mentalités rurale et urbane," 109–86.; Sabean, *Power in the Blood,* 138–43; and James B. Collins and Karen L. Taylor, *Early Modern Europe: Issues and Interpretations.* (Malden, MA: Blackwell, 2006), 7–82.

61. See, for example, ADSM 71 BP 5, 15 juillet 1694; ADSM 71 BP 13, bailliage de Grainville-la-Teinturière, 4 nov. 1743.

62. ADSM 5 Mi 863: régistres paroissales, Saint-Vaast-Dieppdalle, 1692–94.

63. ADSM 71 BP 4, 1692; ADSM 71 BP 6, haute justice de Grainville-la-Teinturière, 31 déc. 1692. Thanks to André Lecole for pointing out this case in *La haute justice,* 47–50.

64. ADSM 71 BP 5: haute justice, Grainville-la-Teinturière, 26 mars 1693.

65. BN Fonds français 32318, mémoires du Parlement de Rouen.

66. Charles LeRoy, *Paysans normands au XVIIIe siècle,* vol. 1, *La vie rurale* (Brionne: 1978 reprint).

67. William Beik has described how even parlementaires could be intimidated by such riots; see Beik, *Urban Protest in Seventeenth-Century France: The Culture of Retribution* (New York: Cambridge University Press, 1997), 259–62. On seventeenth-century grain riots in Brittany, see Collins, *Classes, Estates,* 251; elsewhere in Europe, see Alexander Cowan, *Urban Europe 1500–1700* (London: 1998): 185–86.

68. John Walter, "Public Transcripts, Popular Agency and the Politics of Subsistence in Early Modern England," in *Negotiating Power in Early Modern Society: Order,*

hierarchy and subordination in Britain and Ireland, ed. Michael J. Braddick and John Walter (Cambridge: Cambridge University Press, 2001), 138.

69. Steven L. Kaplan, *Bread, Politics, and Political Economy in the Reign of Louis XV,* vol. 1 (The Hague: Martinus Nijhoff, 1976), 677.

70. ADSM 71 BP 5: Haute justice, Grainville-la-Teinturière, 26 mars–2 avr. 1693.

71. Hughes Neveux, "La justice, norme ambigue de la paysannerie européene, XVe–XVIIe siecles," *Cahiers des Annales de Normandie* 24 (1992): 109–22. Although Neveux's article is based on a few printed collections of parlementaire cases, many of his conclusions are borne out by lower court records.

72. On royal pardons, see also Davis, *Pardon Tales,* 5, 52.

73. ADSM 71 BP 11, bailliage de Grainville-la-Teinturière, 12 juillet 1725.

74. ADSM 19 BP 2, bailliage de Longueville, juillet 1710.

75. Sabean, *Power in the Blood,* 29.

76. ADSM 71 BP 5, haute justice de Grainville-la-Teinturière, affaire LeRouge, 1693–94.

77. See chapter 6 on the clameur de haro.

78. Although the case was tried in the seigneurial high justice of Grainville-la-Teinturière, the accused sergeant leased one of the royal sergenteries of the district from a noble family that held the office as a fief from the king. This intertwining of royal and seigneurial functions was everywhere common in the Caux.

79. ADSM 5 Mi 863, régistres paroissales, Saint-Vaast-Dieppdalle, 1 juin 1692.

80. ADSM 71 BP 5, haute justice de Grainville-la-Teinturière, 16 mars–30 juin 1693.

81. ADSM 7 BP 5, haute justice de Grainville-la-Teinturière, jugement définitif, 1693.

82. ADSM 7 BP 5, haute justice de Grainville-la-Teinturière, jugement définitif, 1693.

Chapter 8

1. Although not all local lawyers and judges prospered in the vicissitudes of the Revolution, their long-term professional and social status continued to rise. Crubaugh, *Balancing the Scales of Justice,* 142–46, shows the prevalence of notaries and lawyers in the ranks of rural J. P.s early in the Revolution. On lawyers during the Revolution, see also David Bell, *Lawyers and Citizens: The Making of a Political Elite in Old-Régime France* (New York: Oxford University Press, 1994); Berlanstein, *The Barristers of Toulouse;* Paul R. Hanson, *Provincial Politics in the French Revolution: Caen and Limoges, 1789–1794* (Baton Rouge: Louisiana State University Press, 1989), and Timothy Tackett, *Becoming a Revolutionary: The Deputies of the French National Assembly and the Emergence of a Revolutionary Culture, 1789–1790* (Princeton, NJ: Princeton University Press, 1996).

2. Norma Landau, *The Justices of the Peace, 1679–1760* (Berkeley: University of California Press,1984), 1; see also Hay, "Property, Authority, and the Criminal Law," in *Albion's Fatal Tree,* ed. Hay et al., 37–38.

3. Sharpe, *Crime in Early Modern England,* 42.

4. Forster, *The East Riding Justices,* 64.

5. James B. Collins, *The Fiscal Limits of Absolutism: Direct Taxation in Early Seventeenth-Century France* (Berkeley: University of California Press, 1988), 16, 114–19; Forster, *The East Riding Justices,* 64.

6. In cities, so-called trading justices or basket justices sometimes did buy and sell commissions of the peace and lived from their fees; all judges had to pay engrossment fees for their official commissions. See Sharpe, *Crime in Early Modern England,* 43; E. G. Dowdell, *A Hundred Years of Quarter Sessions: The Government of Middlesex from 1660 to 1760* (Cambridge: Cambridge University Press, 1932), lxix; and Underdown, *Revel, Riot, and Rebellion,* 23.

7. Justices' Qualification Act of 1731, 5 Geo. 2, c. 18; Justices' Qualification Act of 1744, 18 Geo. 2, c. 20.

8. Crittal, ed., in *The Justicing Notebook of William Hunt,* 3, 4, 8.

9. James M. Rosenheim, ed., in Robert Doughty, *The Notebook of Robert Doughty, 1662–1665* (Norfolk: Norfolk Record Society, 1989), 54:9.

10. Forster, *The East Riding Justices,* 14.

11. By the seventeenth century, the English gentry made up somewhere between 2 and 3 percent of the population. Ranked lower than the small number of noble families who held lay peerages, they nevertheless were expected to be men of landed wealth and considerable leisure and were entitled to a coat of arms.

12. Poor Law Act, 1601, 43 Eliz. 1; Poor Law Act, 1662, 13 & 14 Car. 2, c. 12; Forster, *The East Riding Justices,* 10–18, 34–36, 45–48, 52; Landau, *Justices of the Peace,* 23–45.

13. James M. Rosenheim, *The Emergence of a Ruling Order: English Landed Society 1650–1750* (London: Longman, 1998), 115–23; Sharpe, *Crime in Early Modern England,* 42.

14. Although elites avidly sought peace commissions for their social and political cachet, during the eighteenth century they increasingly declined to qualify to act as justices in their counties.

15. Crittal, ed., in *The Justicing Notebook of William Hunt,* 4, 8.

16. *The Justicing Notebook (1750–64) of Edmund Tew,* ed. Morgan and Rushton, 2–3.

17. See chapter 3.

18. Underdown, *Revel, Riot, and Rebellion,* 10, 23, 109–10; Sharpe, *Crime in Early Modern England,* 40–44.

19. Sharpe, *Crime in Early Modern England,* 33.

20. Michael Dalton, *The Countrey Justice, containing the practices of the Justices of the Peace. . . .* (London: Society of Stationers, 1618), 31–37, 70, 160, 192, 226, 246, 249.

21. Local English tax commissioners' powers were partly assumed by royal appointees after the reforms of the 1670s; see Rosenheim, *Emergence of a Ruling Order,* 167–68.

22. Richard Gough, *The History of Myddle,* ed. David Hey (Harmondsworth, 1981), 86, discusses a typical seventeenth-century Shropshire J. P. who rose to become a master in Chancery and member of Parliament while retaining his local judgeship.

23. Landau, *Justices of the Peace,* 54–57; Sharpe, *Crime in Early Modern England,* 32.

24. David Underdown, *A Freeborn People: Politics and the Nation in Seventeenth-Century England* (Oxford: Oxford University Press, 1996), 56.

25. Francis Bacon, Speech to the Judges Before the Circuits, 1618, in *The Letters and Life of Francis Bacon,* ed. James Spedding (London, 1872), 6:304.

26. See Hay, "Property, Authority, and the Criminal Law," in *Albion's Fatal Tree,* ed. Hay et al., 37–38.

27. ADSM 1 B 5612, Parlement de Normandy, 1691–93; see also Albert Hamscher, "Les réformes judiciares des grands jours d'Auvergne, 1665–1666," *Cahiers*

d'Histoire 1, no. 4 (1976): 425–32; Esprit-Valentin Fléchier, *Mémoires sur les Grand Jours d'Auvergne,* trans. W. W. Comfort (Philadelphia: University of Pennsylvania Press, 1937); and Arlette Lebigre, *Les grands jours d'Auvergne: Désordres et répression au XVIIe siècle* (Paris: Hachette, 1976) for examples of these kinds of commissions.

28. Act of Settlement, 1701, *Statutes of the Realm,* c. 2 12 & 13 Will. 3, 636–38.

29. Landau, *Justices of the Peace,* 73–89.

30. Landau, *Justices of the Peace,* 2, 69–95; Dowdell, *A Hundred Years of Quarter-Sessions,* lx–lxi; Forster, *The East Riding Justices,* 24–29; and Rosenheim, *Emergence of a Ruling Order,* 134–40, on party and politics in appointment.

31. See n. 6.

32. Sharpe, "The History of Crime," 202; see also McIntosh, *Controlling Misbehavior in England,* 8, 15.

33. For additional detail on French seigneurial justice in Burgundy, see Hayhoe, *Enlightened Feudalism.*

34. Underdown, *Revel, Riot, and Rebellion,* 13.

35. C. Romain, ed., "Cahier de Saint-Vaast-Dieppdalle," in *Les cahiers de doléances des paroisses du bailliage de Cany* (Rouen: 1909), 127. Crubaugh, *Balancing the Scales,* 121–30 examines judicial complaints in cahiers from the rural southwest.

36. For example, Colin Kaiser, "The Deflation in the Volume of Litigation at Paris in the Eighteenth Century and the Waning of the Old Judicial Order," *European Studies Review* 3 (July 1980): 309–36.

37. Roy Porter, *English Society in the Eighteenth Century* (Harmondsworth: Penguin, 1982), 151; see also Linebaugh, *The London Hanged,* xxi.

38. See also Jean-Laurent Rosenthal, *The Fruits of Revolution: Property Rights, Litigation and French Agriculture, 1700–1860* (Cambridge: Cambridge University Press, 1992), 176–77.

39. Tabuteau, *Transfers of Property,* 2–3, 51–65, 199.

40. Bodin, *Six livres de la république,* 1.

41. Goubert, "Les officiers royaux," 54–75.

42. Romain, Cahier de Cany, 45. Neither this cahier nor those of the neighboring bailiwicks were simply taken from a model cahier; that of Saint-Vaast, for example, deals with similar issues but in distinctive ways.

43. Romain, Cahier de Saint-Vaast-Dieppedalle, 127.

44. Romain, Cahier de Cany, 45.

45. Soublin, *Le premier vote des Normands,* 312–14.

46. Bell, *Lawyers and Citizens,* 6.

47. Landau, *Justices of the Peace,* 9, 21–23, 65; Rosenheim, *Emergence of a Ruling Order,* 124–29; Forster, The *East Riding Justices,* 24.

48. J. C. N. Raadschelders, *Government: A Public-Administration Perspective* (London: M. E. Sharpe, 2003), 290–92. The concept originated with David Easton's early work on systems theory, *The Political System* (New York: Alfred A. Knopf, 1953).

49. Rosenheim, *Emergence of a Ruling Order,* 129.

50. Landau, *Justices of the Peace,* 1.

51. Michael Weisser, "Crime and Punishment in Early Modern Spain," in *Crime and the Law: The Social History of Crime in Early Modern Europe since 1500,* ed. V. A. C. Gatrell, Bruce Lenman, and Geoffrey Parker (London: Europa, 1980), 77.

GLOSSARY OF LEGAL TERMS

arrêt: Decree or judgment issued by either sovereign courts (arrêt du parlement or de règlement) or by the king's council (arrêt du conseil)

assizes: Court sessions; in lower courts, divided into petty assizes for property matters every one to two weeks (*pleds de quinzaine en quinzaine*), grand assizes for all matters every six weeks (*pleds de six semaines en six semaines*), and mercurial assizes (*assizes mercuriales*) once or twice each year for supervision of the jurisdiction.

assize circuits: (England) Twice-yearly circuits by London central-court judges through English counties; held to hear appeals and judge grand criminal cases.

augmentation de gages: Additional forced investments by officers in the capital of an office, for which they would receive a commensurate rise in the *gages,* or interest paid out. Augmentations were a frequent revenue-raising measure; they were essentially forced loans by the crown.

avocat: Barrister; licensed in civil or canon law, barristers were allowed to submit verbal or written arguments to judges.

avocat du roi: King's advocate; venal office ranked below *procureur du roi* (king's prosecutor). Second-ranking barrister in a lower royal court.

bailli: In seigneurial jurisdictions, the acting judge. In royal jurisdictions, a sword noble in charge of raising the militia in a bailliage. Royal baillis were forbidden to judge in courts after 1579, and their judicial functions were taken over by legally trained *lieutenants généraux.*

bailliage: Basic administrative and judicial unit of the state in northern France. Beneath the parlement and présidial in the court system, but above the vicomté or prévoté. Known as a *sénéchaussée* in the south.

basse justice: Lowest form of seigneurial justice, allowed to adjudicate only dues and rents. Not a true jurisdiction.

cas royal: Crime affecting the king's person or rights, including *lèse-majesté,* counterfeiting, rebellion, and sedition

clameur de haro: Citizen's arrest; Norman custom whereby a victim or witness of a crime could call "haro" to stop the action in progress and require both parties to go to court.

conseilleur: In lower jurisdictions, advisor to a royal judge; consulted before sentence was rendered. The conseilleur in charge of reporting the facts of a case to the group of conseilleurs was the *rapporteur.*

Chambre des Comptes: Chamber of Accounts; sovereign court that audited accounts of royal financial officials in the provinces.

Cour des Aides: Court of Aids; sovereign tax court in the provinces.

coutumes: The customary laws of France; derived from medieval usages and practices, they eventually became written codes with the force of law in their provinces or localities.

coutumier: Collection of customary laws; many were officially redacted in the sixteenth century.

curatelle: Financial and legal curatorship for minors under age twenty-five; necessary for minors who wished to enter into contracts or plead in court.

déclaration: New royal law that modified or interpreted an existing law

droit écrit: Roman law; so called because it was written down before the French customs were codified.

eaux et forêts: Jurisdiction administering woods and waters

édit: New royal law on a specific matter

élection: Tax and financial jurisdiction in a *généralité;* also local tax courts for *aides* and *taille* in *pays d'élection.* Most were approximately the size of the bishopric they covered.

élu: Chief officer in an *élection*

enquêteur, examinateur: Official under the chief judge; supervised administrative ordinances and examined witnesses.

épice: Fee to a judge and other court official from a litigant.

equity: Principle of law that consisted of giving each person their due; based on fairness rather than written law, it was considered the prerogative of judges to use equity when no law applied.

gages: Annuity or interest paid to officers by the crown on the capital investment in their venal offices. Rates varied by office and were influenced by prevailing rates on other investments.

gage-plèges: Annual seigneurial accounting for tenants and vassals, including dues, rents, and changes in tenure

généralité: Regional unit of royal financial administration; subdivided into *élections.* Each *généralité* was adminstered by a Bureau des Finances, but *généralités* later also became the district overseen by an *intendant.*

gens du roi: King's prosecutors and king's advocates in royal courts; venal officers whose functions were a public ministry.

grands jours: Extraordinary sessions of parlementaires; used to investigate official or criminal wrongdoing in the localities.

greffier: Court clerk; secretary to the judges, and responsible for keeping court records.

grenier à sel: Salt warehouse for the state salt monopoly; also a court with jurisdiction over salt taxes.

haute justice: High justice; seigneurial court with right to impose the death penalty. The privilege of high justice was granted by the king. Most had legal jurisdictions similar to lower royal courts, including the right to hear cases involving persons, property, and criminal affairs.

héritage: Right to draw income from the soil; important component of inheritances and marriage contracts.

huissier: Court usher or tipstaff; also a process server.

intendant: Royal (nonvenal) commissioner; after the 1630s, intendants were placed in charge of each *généralité,* representing the crown's interests.

immeubles: Immoveable property; most often real estate, farm implements, and animals, but also fictive real property, including offices and *rentes.* Immeubles were further divided into *propres,* or lineage property, which had to remain in a family line, and *acquêts,* property acquired during the owner's lifetime, which could be more freely disposed of.

information: Judicial investigation into a case, usually involving the deposition of witnesses

justice of the peace: (England) The pivotal judge and administrator of an English county; appointed by commission by the lord chancellor.

lieutenant criminels, civils: Lower-ranking royal judges for criminal and civil cases, respectively, in the lower courts. Assisted the lieutenant général in judging, or replaced him in his absence.

lieutenant général: Lieutenant general; chief judge in a royal bailliage court. Not to be confused with the military lieutenant général of the province.

lieutenant général d'épée: Military office created in all bailliages and sénéchaussées in 1703; these lieutenants were in charge of raising the ban in the absence of the royal *bailli.*

lieutenant particulier: Lowest-ranking judge in a lower court; became the acting judge in the absence of the lieutenant général, civil, or criminal.

maréchaussée: Mounted constabulary; its police court had jurisdiction over deserters, vagabonds, and highroads in rural France.

meubles: Moveable property, usually cash, personal effects, and some offices

monitoire: Admonition from the pulpit to provide information on a case or risk excommunication

moyenne justice: Ill-defined level of seigneurial justice between low and high justice, for seigneurs with both vassal possessors of fiefs beneath them and superior lords above them. Primarily a fiscal court for the seigneurie.

notaire: Notary; venal officer charged with authenticating contracts and acts.

officialité: Ecclesiastical court with limited jurisdiction over spiritual delicts

ordonnance: General law applying to the whole kingdom, usually treating important matters of state administration

parlement: Sovereign court in twelve (later thirteen) provinces; parlements were the highest appellate courts in their provinces, and also key administrative bodies.

parties casuelles: Office collecting royal revenue derived from the paulette, and from occasional forced loans from officers

paulette: Annual fee paid to the crown after 1604 for the right of hereditary survivance in royal offices, if the officer died within forty days of assuming his post. The fee was one-sixtieth the price of the office. The paulette was usually renewed by the crown every nine years.

pays d'élections: Regions in which taxes were levied by royal officers in the *élections;* they covered approximately two-thirds of France.

pays d'états: Regions in which taxes were levied by provincial Estates

plainte: Accusation or complaint by a plaintiff; usually the first step in a court proceeding.

premier président: Highest presiding judge in the parlement; a venal officer appointed by the king.

présidial: Intermediate jurisdiction between bailliages or sénéchaussées below and parlements above; created in 1552, they were often staffed by the same judges as the lower courts.

prévôt: Judge of a *prévôté,* the lowest level of ordinary royal jurisdiction

prévôt-maréchal: Judge of *maréchaussée* (constabulary court); not required to have legal training.

prévoté: See *vicomté*

procureur: Solicitor; procedural expert who prepared cases for the court. Unlike *avocats* (barristers), procureurs were not allowed to plead before judges or submit written arguments directly to the court.

procureur du roi: King's prosecutor; a venal officer who represented the crown's and the public's interest. Highest-ranking barrister in a lower royal court.

procureur fiscal: Seigneur's prosecutor in a high justice; represented the lord's and the public's interest.

quarter sessions: (England) Quarterly court sessions of justices of the peace in English counties; justices empaneled juries, tried cases, approved local rates or taxes, and administered the county.

rentes: Annuities or interest-bearing bonds given in exchange for loans or investments; those living from such income were *rentiers.*

saisie: Property seizure by court decree

seigneurie: The domain and persons over which a seigneur exercised feudal rights. These included rights of justice; economic monopolies that could include markets, milling, or winepressing; and rights to payments or services from tenants.

sieurie: Estate without feudal rights; the owner was a *sieur.* Seigneurs often owned *sieuries* as well as *seigneuries.*

sénéchaussée: See *bailliage*

sergent: Sergeant; minor officer in charge of summonses, arrests, and seizures of property outside of the courtroom proper.

sergenterie: Minor jurisdiction; the extent of a *sergent's* territory. In Normandy the sergenterie was usually a noble fief.

subdélégué: Royal official serving under an intendant in each élection

tutelle: Tutorship of a minor, including education and housing

usement: Area where a particular legal usage or custom was in force

vicomté: Lowest unit of royal jurisdiction, below bailliages. Sometimes called *prévotés* or *vigueries.*

BIBLIOGRAPHY

Abbreviations

AN	Archives Nationales
BN	Bibliothèque Nationale
ADSM	Archives Départementales, Seine-Maritime
ADCO	Archives Départementales, Côte d'Or
ADIV	Archives Départementales, Ille-et-Vilaine
BMR	Bibliothèque Municipale de Rouen

Archival Sources

Archives Nationales

Series Z 2, Seigneurial Justices

1017	Haute justice, comté d'Eu, Insinuations des contracts, 1683–87
1022	Haute justice, Ferté en Bray, châtellenie de duc de Longueville, seventeenth century
388–390	Haute justice, Bosc Roger, plaides and gage-plèges, 1594–1767

Bibliothèque nationale

Cinq Cents Colbert

260	Colbert, register of Norman offices, 1665; Intendant Voysin de la Noiraye, Mémoire sur la generalité de Roen (1665)
259	Colbert, register of Burgundian and Breton offices, 1665
291	Enquête de Duke Mazarini et du Charles Colbert, Bretagne

Manuscripts français

22454–455	Abridged history of the Parlement of Rouen, 1499–1715
22612	Collection Dangeau, memoirs on Norman justice, 1689–90
7648	Norman documents on penalties
32318	Memoir, officers of Norman jurisdictions
25209	*Anciennes coutumes du duché de Bourgogne,* Bouhier

285

Fonds français
32318   Memoir, officers and jurisdictions, Parlement of Rouen, c. 1740

Nouvelles acquisitions françaises
2495–2496   Bertin, Historical and chronological dictionary of offices
8457   Officers of the Parlement of Rouen, 1721

Mélanges Colbert
7   Intendant's notes on Pierre de Becdelièvre
32–33   Memoirs of Pussort on reformation of justice, 1665–66
123   Letters of Intendant de la Noiraye and First President Claude Pellot,
                1664
152   Letter to First President Claude Pellot from H. d'Aguesseau

Fonds Chapée
XXVI   Becdelièvre family papers

Archives Départementales, Seine-Maritime

Series 1 B, Parlement of Normandie
a. Officers and Personnel
5441   Lists of lower court officers; correspondence 1537–1788
5442–5443   Provisions of Offices, 1613–1790
5444   Receptions and letters of honor, 1543–1778
3654   Receptions of bailliage judges; examinations by presidents, 1702–18
5445   Remonstrances of Parlement, 1469–1785
5447   Letters from the king to Parlement, 1650–1788
5449   Memoirs of officers
5451   Parlement's correspondence with the king, sixteenth–eighteenth
                centuries
5471–5473   Relations of Parlement with other Norman jurisdictions
b. Abuse of Judicial Authority
5612–5613   Investigation, bailliage of Pont-Audemer
5686   Abuse of authority cases
5610   Lieutenant Général Le Grix, bailliage of Pont-Audemer
c. Grande Chambre, Registres Secrets
198–199   1670–71
205–209   1680–81
213   1690
219–220   1699–1701
229–230   1710
239–240   1720
248–250   1730
d. Chambre de Tournelle

3576	Arrêts des audience, 1672–73
3581	Arrêts des audience, 1695–96
3583	Arrêts des audience, 1709–10
3586	Arrêts des audience, 1728–29

e. Dossiers of Procedures and Arrêts
| 5696–5701 | Factums and appeals, Tournelle and Grande Chambre |

f. Appellate cases
5579	Haute justice de Cany
5563	Pierre de Becdelièvre
5148	Jacques de Rouville
5548	Duc de Longueville
5576, 5580	Duchesse de Longueville
5181, 5448	Prémier Président Claude Pellot
5610	Jean et Charles Le Grix
5653	Présdial de Caudebec-en-Caux
1 B 5665	Bailliage de Cany
1 B 5572, 5615–5616, 5632	Bailliage of Longueville

g. Other
5530	Arts et métiers, drapiers de Cany, 1737–50
5528	Arts et métiers, filassiers, 1690
5504	Droits de coutume, Cany
3672–3777	Procès verbaux, 1670–1750
3646–3649	Examinations et informations,1692–1743
5521–5522	Sorcerers

Series 7 BP, Présidial de Caudebec-en-Caux
267	Decrèts d'héritages, 1600s
152	Causes du roi, assizes mercuriales, 1698–99
231	Productionnaires, 1699–1726
218	Procès, 1697–99
232	Productionnaires, 1702–11
224	Procès criminels, 1712–23
223	Procès criminels, 1728–55
117	Procès, 1721
25	Procès, 1730
31	Procès, 1730

Series 13–14 BP, Bailliage and Vicomté of Cany
9 Registres, procès, plumatifs, 1671
24 Registres, procès, plumatifs, 1678–80
25 Registres, procès, plumatifs, 1679–80
26 Registres, procès, plumatifs, 1680–81
27 Registres, procès, plumatifs, 1680–81
29 Registres, procès, plumatifs, 1680–82

30 Registres, procès, plumatifs, 1680–82
46 Registres, procès, plumatifs, 1689–93
48 Registres, procès, plumatifs, 1708
49 Registres, procès, plumatifs, 1708–14
52 Registres, procès, plumatifs, 1716–23
53 Registres, procès, plumatifs, 1716–23
57 Registres, procès, plumatifs, 1727–34
24 Registres, procès, plumatifs, 1678–80
35 Registres, procès, plumatifs, 1699–1705
33 Registres, procès, plumatifs, 1702–1706
34 Registres, procès, plumatifs, 1699–1708

Series 71 BP, Bailliage and Vicomté of Grainville-la-Teinturière
8 Plumitifs, 1701–23
9 Plumitifs, 1726–49
10 Procès, 1698–1700
11 Procès, 1706–25
12 Procès, 1730–46
13 Inquests, informations, interrogations
14 Memoirs of expenses, grossesses, tutelles, curatelles
15 Plaintes and requests, receptions to offices

Series 19 BP, Bailliage of Longueville
1   Registres, procès, plumatifs, 1601–1730
2   Registres, procès, plumatifs, 1726–late eighteenth century

Series 46 BP, Haute Justice de Cany-Caniel
13   Registres, procès, plumatifs, 1679–80
14   Registres, procès, plumatifs, 1680–81
18   Registres, procès, plumatifs, 1688–89, 1693–94
22   Registres, procès, plumatifs, 1704–1708
23   Registres, procès, plumatifs, 1708–15
28   Registres, procès, plumatifs, 1726–31
29   Registres, procès, plumatifs, 1730

Series 71 BP, Haute Justice of Grainville-la-Teinturière
   1   Plumitifs, 1622–67
2   Plumitifs, 1669–86
3   Plumitifs, 1686–99
4   Procès, 1688, 1692
5   Procès, 1693, 1694
6   Requests, plaintes, tutelles, curatelles, 1680s–90s
7   Pieces isolées, 1680s–90s

Series 19 BP, Haute Justice of Duchy of Longueville
1 Registres, 1601–1730

2 Procedures, seventeenth and eighteenth centuries
3 Notarial acts (*tabellionage*), seventeenth and eighteenth centuries

Series 107 BP, Haute Justice of Valmont
BP 1   Registres, 1758–89
BP 2   Registres, 1675–83, 1789

Series 112 BP, Haute Justice de Vittefleur
BP 2   Various, seventeenth and eighteenth centuries
BP 3   Plumitifs, 1648–72

Series C, Intendant and Administration
a. Bailliages, haute justices, Parlement:
914–915   Correspondence of the Intendant on lower jurisdictions; nominations and reunions of offices and haute justices, 1709–85
918   Parlement of Normandy, jurisdictional competence
920   Correspondence of intendant on haute justices; suppression of seats
2215   Ordinances of intendants of Rouen, 1642–1788
b. Statistique Criminelle and Frais de Justice
935   Correspondence, arrêts, 1681–1784
936   Correspondence, clerks' fees, gratifications demanded by officers, 1737–89
943   Expenses of prisoners, gages of concierges, state of prisons, 1736–90
944   Treatment of prisoners
945   Cadavers
946   Frais de justice, généralité of Rouen, 1732–85
947   Charges of seigneurs, payment of royal officers, 1732–89
948   Memoir of chirurgien apothecaire, 1748–69
949   Correspondence, frais de justice, 1570–1776
950   Statistique criminelle, 1733–89
1114   Coutume de Normandie
c. Finances:
230–296   Repartition of the taille, 1649–1788
308   Capitation, Officers, 1701–1740s
311–313   Capitation
317   Capitation
324   Capitation
328   Capitation
322   Capitation
330–331   Capitation
d. Duchy de Longueville
2798–2799   Procès verbaux of royal repossession of duchy, 1694–95
2800–2802   Prisées and estimations of rentes and revenues, 1314–1742
2803–2814   Accounts of value and revenue of duchy, 1385–1778
2823–2835   Aveux rendus, 1384–1761
1050–1070   Noblesse

e. Communities and Seigneuries

2302, 2507, 2529, 2556, 2564, 2777, 2800, 2801: Grainville-la-Teinturière
2601, 2805, 2918: Sergenterie de Grainville-la-Teinturière
2503, 2507: Saint-Vaast-Dieppedalle
2768, 1673, 2326, 2893, 2812: Cany and barony of Cany
949: Chateau de Cany
1673: Châtellanie de Cany
2896, 2919: Sergenterie de Cany
1618, 1965, 2154, 2296, 2311, 2867, 2893, 2894, 2912, 2943: Marquisat de Cany
2850: Bailliage de Caudebec-en-Caux

f. Individuals and Seigneuries

1669, 1282,	
1289, 1305	Pierre de Becdelièvre I
1681, 1505,	
293, 1248	Pierre de Becdelièvre II
1619, 1673,	
2912, 2915	Pierre-Jacques-Louis de Becdelièvre
2299	Thomas Charles de Becdelièvre
2307, 1618,	
1828	Marquisat et seigneurie de Houdetot

Series 1 E, Family Papers

1086	Becdelièvre family papers
1087	Seigneurie de Nestanville; seigneurie de Harcanville
1094	Becdelièvre family papers
1083	Fiefs of Arlesqueville-le-Bras-Long, Saint-Martin-le-Canu
1084	Cany-Barville, aveux, gages-plèges, contracts
1147	Houdetot family papers

Series 5 Mi, Registres Paroissiaux (Also Series 4 E)

863	Saint-Vaast-Dieppedalle, 1546–1746
864	Saint-Vaast-Dieppedalle, 1747–91
817	Grainville-la-Teinturière, 1600–1725
2938	Grainville-la-Teinturière, 1655–1715
2928	Cany, 1600–1725
789	Cany, 1720–91

Series 5E, Communautés, Corporations des Arts et Métiers

3	Cany, registers of drapers, 1736–50
4	Caudebec, statutes of métiers, 1495–1782
738	Rouen, community of teinturières, 1725–47

Series Fi, Plans

1590	Norman bailliages, primary and secondary, 1789
1588	Bailliages, vicomtés, sergentries, early seventeenth century
410	Map of Cany

133   Map of Grainville
543   Map of vicomté of Caudebec
1481/14, 15   Map of Caudebec
1589   Généralité and élections of Rouen

Series G, Secular Clergy
738   Pastoral Visits of Msgr. Aubigné, 1710–17

Series 1 Mi, Microfilms
871   Becdelièvre chartrier
1513   Barony of Cany-Caniel
1007   Domaines of seigneurie of Cany, 1463–1789
1385   Archives privées: Chartrier of Caniel; aveux, titres, 1701–89

Series 3PP, Cadastres (land surveys) and Procès-Verbaux des Communes
806A   Grainville, 1825
802A   Cany, 1825
807   Houdetot, 1826

Archives Départementales, Côte d'Or

Series B 2, Bailliage de Nuits-Saint-George
164 2–3   Edicts, ordinances and contracts
165 11–15   Registres des audiences ordinaires, 1669–1730
166 10–11   Registres des audiences extraordinaires, 1669–1731
167 16–30   Sentences, procès verbaux, décrets, 1671–1730
171 1   Registres, donations entre vifs, 1731

Series B 2, Bailliage de Beaune
149 1   Officiers et droits
156 17–29   Sentences, procès verbaux, 1671–1732
160 2   Registres des tutelles, 1704–1707

Series B 2, High Justices, Nuits-Saint-George
941–942 1   Villars Fontaine or Villeferry
818–819 1   Quincy
539 1, 540   Concoeur et Corboin, communauté de Nuits-Saint-Georges, 1699–
               1790

Series C, Administration
3339   *Coutume de Bourgogne,* 1562–1785
3341   Jurisprudence, 1755–90

Archives Départementales, Ille-et-Vilaine:

Series A: Actes du Pouvoir Souverain

2	Edict reestablishing the teaching of civil law and other edicts, 1674–88
5	Royal laws regarding receivers of amends and épices in all jurisdictions, 1691
7	Royal laws regarding judges and officers of seigneurial justice, 1693
14	Royal laws regarding years of legal study required, 1700
2 A 6	Tables of parishes by sénéchaussées

Series 1 B, Parlement de Rennes

1 Bh 14–15	Revolt of inhabitants of Châteaugiron against sénénschal, 1701
1 Bh 6	Organization and police of inferior jurisdictions, seventeenth and eighteenth centuries
1 By 65	Procès verbaux of parlementary prison visits, 1611–97, 1713–81
1 Bc 2 bis	Dossiers of political affairs, remonstrances, correspondence, 1715–32
1 B 53–57	Présidial cases in Parlement
1 B 62	Complaints against sénéchaux
1 B 75	Remonstrances

Series 2 B, Présidial of Rennes

2 B 1951	Criminal cases begun in seigneurial courts, 1668–80 and 1704–24
2 B 2100	Criminal cases begun in seigneurial courts, letters of grace and remission, eighteenth century

Series 3 B, Sénéchausées of Hédé, Rennes, Fougères

3 B 610–612	Hédé, réceptions d'offices, seventeenth and eighteenth centuries
3 B 860–862	Hédé, justice seigneuriale, seventeenth and eighteenth centuries
2 B 371–380	Rennes, réceptions d'offices, seventeenth and eighteenth centuries
3 B 234	Fougères, réceptions d'offices, seventeenth and eighteenth centuries

Series 4 B, Seigneurial Justices

1200–1201	Haute justice de Châteaugiron, late seventeenth and eighteenth centuries
1252	Haute justice de Châteauneuf, receptions of officers, 1721–83
1253	Châteauneuf, receptions of surgeons, eighteenth century
1254–1258	Châteauneuf, registres, 1720–30
1285	Châteauneuf, descentes et visites, 1709–87
1287	Châteauneuf, police, 1716–71
4 B 1290	Châteauneuf, police, grossesse, 1727–57
4 B 1292	Châteauneuf, sentences de rapport, 1713–34
4 B 1298	Châteauneuf, enquêtes, 1703–27
4 B 1335	Châteauneuf, mains-levées, 1717–84
4 B 1336	Châteauneuf, petite jurisdiction, mains-levées, 1753–90
4 B 1337	Châteauneuf, emancipatons, 1727–86
4 B 1339	Châteauneuf, décrets de mariage, 1695–1751
4 B 1344	Châteauneuf, partages rapportées, 1709–11
4 B 1346	Châteauneuf, saisies, baux judiciares 1728–45

4 B 1347   Châteauneuf, procèdures civiles, 1716–73
4 B 1348   Châteauneuf, procèdures appels, 1686–1777
4 B 1350   Châteauneuf, procedures criminels, 1695–1740
4 B 1349   Châteauneuf, ferme des devoirs, serments des commis, 1721–87?

Series 1 Ba, Registres d'Enregistrement Parlementary Arrêts on
Seigneurial Justice
D 11 juill 1682 25/15 ro
D 4 sept 1684 25/118 vo
LP 25 oct 1682 26/33 ro
AC 12 juill 1689 26/33 vo
E déc 1732 37/1
E mars 1707 31/94 vo
D 1 mai 1708 31/193 vo
D 29 déc 1708 31/283 bis vo
D 13 sept 1711 32/153 vo
D 20 fév 1713 32/282 ro

Series C, Intendants and Administration
143   Graces et remissions, 1733–39
144   Graces et remissions, 1740–46
1818   Jurisdictions of Brittany, 1717–66; inquests of subdélégués into royal
            and seigneurial justices, 1717, 1766
1819   État of royal and seigneurial jurisdictions
1823   Sénéchaussées royales, 1724–89
1828   Augmentations de gages, judicial, 1716–17
1835–1836   Memoirs of sénéchausées and présidials, 1740
1897–1902   Frais de justice
2252   Union of justices, 1736–83

Series C, États de Bretagne
2657   Two customs of Brittany, 1665–68
2658   Revocation of judicial edicts, 1671–77
2659   Suppression of judicial offices, 1679–87
2661   Request for new redaction of the custom, seventeenth century
2792   Request for new redaction of the custom, seventeenth century

Series Eb, Families
6   Baude de la Vieuxville, marquisat de Châteauneuf, XVe–XVIIe siècle
22   Beringhen, comté de Plessix-Bertrand en Châteauneuf, 1474–1788

Bibliothèque Municipale de Rouen (BMR)

Ms Y 169   Intendant Jean-Baptiste Desmarets de Vaubourg, *Mémoires concernant
                la généralité de Rouen, 1698.*
500 Colbert 260 Intendant Voysin de la Noiraye, fols. 180–205.

Published Works: Primary Sources

Anonymous. *Popery and Tyranny, or, the Present State of France.* London: 1689.

Aristotle. *The Nicomachean Ethics.* Translated and edited by Roger Crisp. Cambridge: Cambridge University Press, 2000.

——. *The Politics.* Translated by Carnes Lord. Chicago: Chicago University Press, 1984.

Basnage, Henri. *Les oeuvres de maître Henri Basnage . . . contenant ses commentaires sur la coutume de Normandie, et son Traité de hypothèques.* 4th ed. Rouen: Chez Maurry, 1709.

Beaurepaire, Charles. *Cahiers des états de Normandie sous Louis XIII et Louis XIV.* 3 vols. Rouen: Chez Ch. Métérie, 1876.

Berault, M. *Coutume reformée de Normandie.* Rouen: 1620, 1632, 1660, 1684, 1776.

Bertin, M. N. *Introduction à la pratique judiciaire pour les sièges subalternes de Normandie.* Caen: 1748.

Blanchecape, Pierre de. *Explication du titre des prescriptions de la Coutume de Normandie: Procès Verbal du Coutume de Normandie.* Rouen: 1583–87. Caen: 1665.

Bodin, Jean. *Six livres de la république.* Paris: 1583.

Bouhier, Jean. *Les coutumes du duché de Bourgogne, avec les anciennes coutumes tant générales que locales. . . .* Dijon: Chez Arnauld-Jean-Baptiste Auge, 1742–46.

——. *Souvenirs de Jean Bouhier, président au Parlement de Dijon: Extraits d'un manuscrit autographe inédit. . . .* Paris: Imp. Émile Voitelain, n.d.

Bourdot de Richebourg, Charles. *Nouveau coutumier général.* Paris: 1724.

Boutaric, François de. *Explication de l'ordonnances de Louis XIV [de 1667] sur 6 matières civiles [avec texte des édits].* Toulouse: G. Henault, 1743.

Brillon, Pierre Jacques. *Dictionnaire des arrêsts, ou jurisprudence universelle des parlements de France et autres tribunaux.* 3 vols. Paris: 1711.

Burel, M. *Elements de pratique et modelles des exploits.* Rouen: 1772.

Colbert de Croissy, Charles. *La Bretagne en 1665 d'après le rapport de Colbert de Croissy.* Edited by J. Kerhervé, F. Roudut, and J. Tanguy. Brest: 1978.

Cicero. *On Obligations (De officiis).* Translated by P. G. Walsh. Oxford: Oxford University Press, 2000.

Commentaires sur la coutume reformée du pays et duché de Normandie, anciens ressorts & enclaves d'iceluy. 4th ed. Rouen: Imprimerie de David du Petit Val, 1626, 1632.

Conférences des ordonnances de Louis XIV . . . avec les anciennes ordonnances du royaume de droit écrit et des arrêsts. Paris: 1755.

Coquille, Guy. *Les oeuvres de Maistre Guy de Coquille.* Edited by Claude Labottiere. 2 vols. Bordeaux: 1703.

Coutume de Normandie. Avec l'ordonnance de 1667, & celle de 1670. Augm. d'une instruction sur la marche de la procedure civile & criminelle. Bayeux: Veuve Briard, 1773.

Coutumes du pays de Normandie. Rouen: Jean B. Besonge, 1697.

Coutumes du pays et duché de Normandie, anciens ressorts & enclaves d'icelui, augmentées de plusieurs édits, déclarations . . . rendus depuis 1666 jusqu'en 1753. . . . New ed. Rouen, Imp. de feu J. Besonge, 1754.

Coutumes du pays et duché de Normandie, anciens ressorts & enclaves d'icelui, avec les édits, déclarations, arrêts et réglemens, tant du conseil que de la Cour, corriges de nouveau & augmentes jusqu'a present. . . . Rouen: Chez Richard Lallement, imprimeur, 1764.

Coutumes du pays et duché de Normandie, anciens ressorts & enclaves d'icelui. Caen: Jaques Mangeant, 1596.

Dagar, Charles H. *La nouveau Ferrière, ou Dictionnaire de droit et de pratique, civil, commerical, criminel et judiciaire; contenant l'explication de tous les termes du droit, anciens et modernes, et à la suite de chaque mot.* Paris: Chez l'auteur, Garnery: An XII–XIII, 1804–5.

Dalton, Michael. *The Country Justice, containing the practices of the Justices of the Peace.* . . . London: Society of Stationers, 1618.

Depping, G. B., ed. *Correspondence administrative sous le Règne de Louis XIV.* 4 vols. Paris: 1850–55.

Denis, Louis. *Atlas topographique de la Normandie.* 1770.

Domat, Jean. *Les loix civiles dans leur ordre naturale.* 3 vols. Paris: J. B. Coignard, 1691–94.

———. *Oeuvres completes de Jean Domat.* . . . New ed. 4 vols. Paris: 1835.

Duplessis, Michel Toussaint Chretien. *Description géographique et historique de la haute Normandie.* 2 vols. Paris: Veuve Ganeau, 1740.

Du Rousseau de la Combe, D. *Traité des matières criminelles suivant l'ordonnance d'aoust 1670, et règlements intervenus jusqu'a présent.* Paris: 1741.

Encyclopedie Méthodique: Jurisprudence. 10 vols. Paris: Panckoucke, Libraire, 1781–91.

Esmonin, Edmond. *Voysin de la Noiraye: Mémoire sur la généralité de Rouen en 1665.* Paris: Librairie Hachette, 1913.

Fénelon, Abbé François de Salignac. "Traite de l'education des filles." In *Fénelon on Education,* edited by H. C. Barnard. Cambridge: Cambridge University Press, 1966.

Ferrière, Claude Joseph de. *Nouvelle introduction à la pratique; ou, Dictionnaire des termes de pratique, de droit, des ordonnances et des coutumes, avec les jurisdictions de France.* 2 vols. Paris: M. Brunet, 1734.

Figon, Charles de. *Discours des estates et offices, tant du gouvernement que de la justice et de finances de France.* Paris: 1608.

Floquet, Amable-Pierre. *Journal de voyage de Chancelier Séguier en Normandie, 1639–1640.* Rouen: Frère, 1842.

Galtey, H. *Dictionnaire topographique de la Généralité de Rouen.* Rouen: 1788.

Gough, Richard. *The History of Myddle.* Edited by David Hey. Harmondsworth: Penguin, 1981.

Gujot. *Répertoire universel et raisonnée de jurisprudence.* Paris: 1784.

Harcourt. *La grande bailliage: Comédie historique.* Rouen: 1788.

Houard. *Dictionnaire analytique, historique, et étymologique de la Coutume de Normandie.* Rouen: Le Boucher le jeune, 1781.

Jousse, Daniel. *Nouveau commentaire sur l'ordonnance criminelle du mois d'avril [i.e., août] 1670: avec un abrège de la justice criminelle.* Paris: Debure, 1763.

———. *Nouveau commentaire sur les ordonnances des mois d'aout 1669, & mars 1673, ensemble sur l'édit du mois de mars 1673 touchant les épices.* Paris: Debure l'aîné, 1775.

———. *Receuil chronologique des ordonnances, édits & arrêts de règlement cités dans les nouveaux commentaires sur les ordonnances des mois d'avril 1667, août 1670 & mars 1673.* 3 vols. Paris: Debure, 1757.

———. *Traité de la jurisdiction des présidiaux, tant en matière civile que criminelle: avec un recueil chronologique des principaux édits, ordonnances, déclarations et autres réglemens concernant les presidiaux.* Paris: Debure l'aîné, 1757.

——. *Traité de l'administration de la justice.* 2 vols. Paris: Debure Père, 1771.

La Bruyère, Jean de. *Les caractères de Théopraste traduits du grec avec Les caracteres ou les moeurs de ce siècle.* Paris: Bookking International, 1993.

La Fontaine, Jean de. *Fables.* Paris: Garnier-Flammarion, 1966.

La Foy, Guillaume de. *De la constitution du duché ou état souverain de Normandie.* Rouen: 1789.

La Saincte Bible: Traduit par les Theologians de l'Université de Louvain. Rouen: Raphael du Petit, 1572.

Las Casas, Bartolomé de. *A Short Account of the Destruction of the Indies.* Translated and edited by Nigel Griffin. London: Penguin Books, 1992.

Laurière, E. J. de, ed. *Recueil d'édits et d'ordonnances royaux....* Paris: Montalant, 1720.

L'Hommeau, Pierre de. *Maximes générales du droit français, divisées en trois livres. Avec les notes & observations de Paul Challine advocat en Parlement....* 3 vol. Paris: M. Bobin & N. le Gras, 1665.

L'Hopital, Michel de. *Oeuvres completes.* Vol. 5, *Traité de la réformation de la justice.* Edited by P. J. S. Dufey. Genève: Slatkine Reprints, 1968.

Le Bret, Cardin. *Les oeuvres de messire Le Bret.* Paris: Jacques Quesnel, 1642.

Lesage, Alain René. *Crispin, rival de son maitre.* London: T. Hookham, 1786.

Locke, John. *Political Writings of John Locke.* Edited by David Wooton. New York: Mentor, 1993.

——. *Second Treatise of Government.* Edited by Richard Cox. Arlington Heights, IL: Harlan Davidson, 1982.

Lough, John, ed. *France Observed in the Seventeenth Century by British Travellers.* Stocksfield: Oriel Press, 1984.

Louis XIV. *Mémoires.* Paris: Le livre club du librairie, 1960.

Loyseau, Charles. *Discours de l'abus de justices de village.* Paris: Abel L'Angelier, 1605.

——. *Les oeuvres contenant les Cinq livres du droict des offices, les Traitez des seigneuries, des ordres & simples dignités du degeurpissement & delaissement par hypothèque de la garantie des rentes, & des abus des justices de village.* Paris: E. Covterot, 1678.

Martin, Bernard. *Supplement aux oeuvres de jurisprudence de Monsieur le Président Bouhier ou remarques sur la coutume de Bourgogne.* Dijon: 1789.

Maultrot, Gabriel-Nicolas, and Claude Mey. *Maximes du droit public français.* 2nd ed. Amsterdam: M. M. Rey, 1775.

Merville, M. *Décisions sur chaque article de la coutume de Normandie, et observations sur les usages locaux de la même coutume, & sur les articles placitez ou arrêtez du Parlement de Rouen.... et aussi les anciens réglemens de l'exchiquier de Normandie.* Paris: A. Mesnier, 1732.

Molière (Jean-Baptiste Poquelin). *Le bourgeois gentilhomme.* Paris: Belles Lettres, 1949.

Montaigne, Michel de. *Essais.* Paris: Librarie Générale de Française, 1972.

Montesquieu, Charles Louis de Secondat, baron de. *L'ésprit des lois.* Paris: Seghers, 1972.

——. *Lettres persanes.* Paris: Bokking International, 1993.

Morgan, Gwenda, and Peter Rushton, eds. *The Justicing Notebook (1750–64) of Edmund Tew, Rector of Boldon.* Woodbridge: Boydell, 2000.

Noel, S. B. J. *Essai sur la département de la Seine Inferieure ... districts de Gourney ... et Cany.* Rouen: 1795.

Northleigh, John. *Topographical descriptions, with historico-politico and medico-physical observations made in two voyages.* . . . London, 1702.

Nouveau commentaire portatif de la coutume de Normandie. Rouen, Impr. privilegée, 1778.

Nouveau commentaire sur l'Ordonnance criminelle du mois d'août 1670. Paris: Debure l'aîné, 1753.

Observations de droit et de coutume selon l'usage du Parlement de Dijon. Dijon: 1688.

Ordonnances de Louis XIV . . . pour les matières criminelles [1670]. Paris: 1670.

Ordonnance de Louis XIV . . . touchant le reformation de le justice [1669]. Paris: 1669.

Perrault, Charles. *Contes.* Paris: Bookking International, 1993.

Pesnelle, M. *Coutume de Normandie . . . avec un recueil d'arrêts & réglemens, tant du Conseil de la Cour, donnez le plupart sur la coutume.* 2nd ed. Rouen: J.-B. Besonge, 1727, 1759.

Petitot, A., ed. *Collection des mémoires relatifs a l'histoire de France.* Paris: Foucault, 1829.

Piganiol de la Force, J. A. *Nouvelle description de la France.* 6 vols. Amsterdam, 1719.

Pothier, Robert-Joseph. *Traités sur differentes matières du droit civil.* Orleans, 1781.

Poullain du Parc, Auguste-Marie. *La Coutume et la jurisprudence coutumière de Bretagne dans leur ordre naturel.* 3rd ed. Rennes: François Vatar, 1783.

——. *Principes du droit français, suivant les maximes de Bretagne.* Rennes: François Vatar, 1767.

Prévost, G. A., ed. *Notes du Premier Président Pellot sur la Normandie (1670–1683).* Rouen and Paris: Société de la Histoire de Normandie, 1915.

Procès-verbaux des conferences tenues par ordre du Roi pour examen des articles de l'Ordonnance Civile . . . et de Ordonnance Criminel [1670]. Paris: 1757.

Rabelais, François. *Le tiers livre.* Edited by M. A. Screech. Geneva: Droz, 1964.

Racine. *Les plaideurs.* Annotated by Pierre Mélèse. Paris: Imprimerie Nationale de France, 1951.

Recueil des differens règlements, concernant les Frais de Justice, soit à la charge du Domaine, ou autrement. Paris: 1760.

Règlements pour les fonctions et droits des officiers, greffiers, procureurs, huissiers et notaires des provinces de Bourgogne, Bresse, et du comté de Charolais. . . . Et plusieurs arrêts sur des matières importantes. Dijon: Fay, 1736.

Richelieu, Armand Jean du Plessis de. *Testament politique.* Paris: Robert Laffont, 1947.

Rosenheim, James M., ed. *The Notebook of Robert Doughty 1662–1665.* Norfolk: Norfolk Record Society, 1989.

Routier, Charles. *Pratiques beneficiales, suivant l'usage général et celui de la province de Normandie.* Rouen: P. Le Boucher, Libraire, 1745.

——. *Principes Généraux du droit civil et coutumier de la province de Normandie.* Rouen: 1748.

Saint-Simon, Louis de Rouvroy, duc de. *Mémoires.* Paris: H. L. Delloye, 1842.

Salle, M. *L'ésprit des ordonnances de Louis XIV.* Paris: Rouy, 1755–58.

Saugrain, Claude Marin. *Dictionnaire universel de la France ancienne et moderne, et de la Nouvelle France.* 3 vols. Paris: Chez Saugrain, 1726.

——. *Nouveau denombrement du royaume par généralités, élections, paroisses, et feux.* 3 vols. Paris: 1720.

Sauvageau, Michel. *Coutumes de Bretagne.* Rennes: Joseph Vatar, 1742.

Seyssel, Claude. *La monarchie de France et deux autres fragments politiques.* Paris: Librarie d'Argences, 1961.

Skippon, Phillip. *An Account of a Journey Through Part of the Low Countries, Germany, Italy*
and France. London: 1732.

Smedley-Weill, Anette, ed. *Sous-serie G. Inventaire analytique.* Vol. 1, *Correspondance des intendants avec le contrôleur général de Finances, 1677–1689: Naissance d'une adminstration.* Paris: Archives Nationales, 1989.

Smollet, Tobias. *Travels Through France and Italy.* Edited by T. Seccombe. London: 1935.

Spedding, James, ed. *The Letters and Life of Francis Bacon.* Vol. 6. London: 1872.

Taisand, Pierre. *Coutume générale des pays et duché de Bourgogne avec le commentaire de Monsieur Taisand.* Dijon: Jean Ressayre, 1698.

Terrien, Guillaume. *Commentaires du droit civil tant publique que privé, observé au Pays et Duché de Normandie.* 3rd ed. Rouen: 1654.

Texte de la Coutume de Normandie: avec des notes sur chaque article. On y a joint les observations sur les usages locaux de la province de Normandie & les articles & placités du Parlement de Rouen. Rouen: Veuve Besonge, 1781.

Tocqueville, Alexis de. *L'ancien régime et la révolution.* Paris: Galliamard: 1967.

Vauban, Sébastien le Prêtre. *La dîme royale.* Edited by Emmanuel Le Roy Ladurie. Paris: Imp. Royale, 1992.

Watson, Alan, trans. *The Digest of Justinian.* Philadelphia: University of Pennsylvania Press, 1985.

Young, Arthur. *Travels Through France.* 3 vols. Paris: 1976.

Published Works: Secondary Sources

I. Justice, Law and the State

Abbiateci, A., F. Billaçois, N. Castan, et al., eds. *Cahiers des Annales.* No. 33, *Crime et criminalités en France sous l'ancien régime, XVIIe–XVIIIe siècles.* Paris: Armand Colin, 1971.

Ago, Renata. "Rooli familiari e statuto giuridico." *Quaderni storici* 1 (April 1995).

Andrews, Richard M. *Law, Magistracy and Crime in Old Regime Paris, 1735–1789.* Vol. 1, *The System of Criminal Justice.* Cambridge: Cambridge University Press, 1994.

Astarita, Tommaso. *Village Justice: Community, Family, and Popular Culture in Early Modern Italy.* Baltimore: Johns Hopkins University Press, 1999.

Bakos, Adrianna E., ed. *Politics, Ideology and the Law in Early Modern Europe.* Rochester, NY: University of Rochester Press, 1994.

Bart, Jean. *Histoire du droit privé: De la chute de l'empire romain au XIXe siècle.* Paris: Montchrèstien, 1998.

Bataillon, Jacques Henri. *Les justices seigneuriales du bailliage de Pontoise à la fin de l'ancien régime.* Paris: Recueil Sirey, 1942.

Beattie, J. M. *Crime and the Courts in England, 1600–1800.* Oxford: Clarendon Press, 1986.

——. "The Pattern of Crime in England, 1660–1800." *Past and Present* 62 (1974): 47–95.

Bée, M. "Vivre du métier de bourreau en Normandie au XVIIIe: Travail, métiers et profession en Normandie." 16e Congrès Soc. Hist. Archéol. Normandie, Cahiers Léopold Deslisle (1982–83): 99–114.

Beik, William. *Absolutism and Society in Seventeenth-Century France: State Power and Provincial Aristocracy in Languedoc.* Cambridge: Cambridge University Press, 1985.

———. *Urban Protest in Seventeenth-Century France: The Culture of Retribution.* New York: Cambridge University Press, 1997.

Bell, David. *Lawyers and Citizens: The Making of a Political Elite in Old Regime France.* New York: Oxford University Press, 1994.

———. "The 'Public Sphere,' the State, and the World of Law in Eighteenth-Century France." *French Historical Studies* 17 (Fall 1992): 912–50.

Bercé, Yves Marie. "Aspects de la criminalité au XVIIe siècle." *Revue Historique* 239 (1968): 33–42.

Berlanstein, Lenard R. *The Barristers of Toulouse in the Eighteenth Century (1740–1793).* Baltimore: Johns Hopkins University Press, 1975.

Besnier, Robert. *Cours d'histoire générale du droit Français.* Paris: Cours du droit, 1954.

———. *La répresentation successorale en droit normand.* Paris: Recueil Sirey, 1929.

———. "Problèmes des justices seigneuriales en Normandie." *Revue Historique de Droit Français et Étrangèr* (1933).

Billaçois, François. "Pour une enquête sur la criminalité dans la France d'Ancien Régime." *Annales d'Histoire Économique et Sociale* (March–April 1967): 340–47.

Blanquie, Christophe. *Les présidiaux de Richelieu: Justice et vénalité (1630–1642).* Paris: Éditions Christian, 2000.

Bluche, Francois. *Les magistrats du Parlement de Paris au XVIIIe siècle.* Paris: Economica, 1986.

Bonney, Richard, ed. *The Limits of Absolutism in Ancien Régime France.* Aldershot: Variorium, 1995.

Boüard, Michel de. *Documents de l'histoire de Normandy.* Toulouse: Privat, 1972.

———. *Histoire de Normandie.* Toulouse: Privat, 1970.

Bourde de la Rogerie, H. "Liste des juridictions exercées au XVIIe et au XVIIIe siècles dans le ressort du présidial de Quimper." *Bulletin de la Société Archéologique de Finistère* 37 (1910): 248–91.

Bouissel du Bourg. "Observations sur la criminalité et le fonctionnement des justices seigneuriales en Bretagne au XVIIIe siècle (1700–1789): L'exemple du duché pairie de Penthièvre." Thèse hist. du droit, Rennes I, 1984.

Boutelet, Bernadette. "Étude par sondage de la criminalité dans le bailliage de Pont-de-l'Arche (XVIIe–XVIIIe siècles): De la violence au vol; En marche vers l'escroquerie." *Annales de Normandie* 12 (1962): 235–65.

Bouwsema, William J. "Lawyers and Early Modern Culture." *American Historical Review* 78, no. 2 (1973): 303–27.

Brackett, John K. *Criminal Justice and Crime in Late Renaissance Florence, 1537–1609.* Cambridge: Cambridge University Press, 1992.

Braddick, Michael J., and John Walter. *Negotiating Power in Early Modern Society: Order, Hierarchy and Subordination in Britain and Ireland* (Cambridge: Cambridge University Press, 2001).

Brette, Armand. *Atlas des bailliages ou juridictions assimilée ayant formé unité electoral en 1789.* Paris: 1906.

Brewer, John. *An Ungovernable People: The English and Their Law in the Seventeenth and Eighteenth Centuries.* New Brunswick, NJ: Rutgers University Press, 1980.

Burckard, François. *Guide des Archives de la Seine-Maritime.* Vol. 1, *Généralités: Archives Antérieures à 1790.* Rouen: Archives Départementales, 1990.

Cameron, Ian A. *Crime and Repression in the Auvergne and the Guyenne, 1720–1790.* Cambridge: Cambridge University Press, 1981.

Cardineau, Guy. "Les juridictions de l'ancien régime en Bretagne." *Bulletin Mensuel de la Société Polymathique du Morbihan, Rennes* 112 (July 1985): 19–30.

Cardot, Charles-Antoine. "La Bretagne dans le répertoire universal de jurisprudence de Guyot (1784–1785)." *Mémoires de la Société Historique et Archéologique de Bretagne* 53 (1975–76): 95–120.

Carey, John A. *Judicial Reform in France before the Revolution of 1789.* Cambridge, MA: Harvard University Press, 1981.

Carel, Pierre. *Notes sur les magistrats du bailliage et siège présidial de Caen suivi de la liste des dits magistrats.* Caen: 1899.

Castan, Nicole. "Criminalité et litiges sociaux en Languedoc de 1690 à 1730." Thèse de 3e cycle, University of Toulouse–Le Mirail, 1966 (microfiche). Toulouse: University of Toulouse, 1966.

———. *Justice et répression en Languedoc à l'époque des lumieres.* Paris: Flammerion, 1980.

———. "La criminalité familiale dans la ressort du parlement de Toulouse (1690–1730)." In *Crimes et criminalités en France sous l'ancien régime, XVIIe–XVIIIe siècles,* 91–107. Paris: Armand Colin, 1971.

Castan, Nicole, and Yves Castan. *Vivre ensemble: Ordre et désordre en Languedoc (XVIIe–XVIIIe siècles).* Paris: Gallimard/Julliard, 1981.

Castan, Yves. "Mentalités rural et urbaine à la fin de l'ancien régime dans le ressort du Parlement de Toulouse d'aprés les sacs à procès criminels, 1730–1790." In *Crime et criminalités en France sous l'Ancien Régime, XVIIe–XVIIIe siècles,* 109–86. Paris: Armand Colin, 1971.

Caswell, Jean, and Ivan Sipkov. *The Coutumes of France in the Library of Congress: An Annotated Bibliography.* Washington, DC: Library of Congress, 1977.

Cavaignac, Jean. "La sénéchaussée et siège présidial de Libourne." *RHAL* 35 (1967): 89–95.

Champin, Marie Madeleine. "Un cas typique de justice bailliagiere: La criminalité dans le bailliage d'Alençon de 1715 à 1745." *Annales de Normandie* 22 (1972): 47–84.

Chapman, Terry L. "Crime in Eighteenth-Century England: E. P. Thompson and the Conflict Theory of Crime." *Criminal Justice History* 1 (1980): 139–55.

Church, William F. "The Decline of the French Jurists as Political Theorists, 1660–1789." *French Historical Studies* 1 (Spring 1967): 1–40.

Cinquabre, Pierre. "Le statut juridique de la femme normande aux XVIIe et XVIIIe siècles." *La femme en Normandie, Actes du XIXe congrès des sociétés historiques et archéologiques de Normandie.* Caen: Archives Departmentales du Calvados, 1986: 43–51.

Coquelin, Marie-Laure. "L'executeur de haute justice sous l'ancien régime (l'exemple breton au XVIIIe siècle)." *Annales de Bretagne* 1: 100, 1993: 49–60.

Cockburn, J. S. *Crime in England, 1550–1800.* Princeton, NJ: Princeton University Press, 1977.

———. *A History of English Assizes, 1558–1714.* Cambridge: Cambridge University Press, 1972.

Collins, James B. *Classes, Estates, and Order in Early Modern Brittany.* Cambridge: Cambridge University Press, 1994.

———. *The Fiscal Limits of Absolutism: Direct Taxation in Early Modern France.* Berkeley: University of California Press, 1988.

———. *From Tribes to Nation: The Making of France 500–1789.* Toronto: Thomson Learning, 2002.

———. *The State in Early Modern France.* Cambridge: Cambridge University Press, 1995.

Corvisier, André. "Un lien entre villes et campagnes: Le personnel des haute justices en Haute Normandie au XVIIIe siècle." *Annales de Normandie, Recueil d'études offert en homage au doyen Michel de Boüard,* vol. 1 (Caen: Université de Caen, 1982) 157–70.

Crubaugh, Anthony. *Balancing the Scales of Justice: Local Courts and Rural Society in Southwest France, 1750–1800.* University Park: Pennsylvania State University Press, 2001.

Crittall, Elizabeth, ed. *The Justicing Notebook of William Hunt, 1744–1749.* Devizes: Wiltshire Record Society, vol. 37, 1982.

Cummings, Mark. "Elopement, Family, and the Courts: The Crime of Rapt in Early Modern France." *Proceedings of the Western Society for French History* 4 (1976): 118–25.

Curzon, Alfred de. "Le enseignement du droit français dans les universités de France aux XVIIe et XVIIIe siècles." *Nouvelle Revue Historique du Droit Français et Étranger* 43 (1919): 209–69, 305–64.

Dawson, John Phillip. *A History of Lay Judges.* Union, NJ: Lawbook Exchange Ltd., 1999.

Davis, Natalie Zemon. *The Return of Martin Guerre.* Cambridge, MA: Harvard University Press, 1983.

———. *Society and Culture in Early Modern France.* Stanford: Stanford University Press, 1975.

Dawson, Philip. *Provincial Magistrates and Revolutionary Politics in France, 1789–1795.* Cambridge, MA: Harvard University Press, 1972.

Dawson, Philip. "Sur les prix des offices de judicature à la fin de l'ancien régime." *Revue d'Histoire Économique et Sociale* 42 (1966): 390–92.

Debordes-Lissillour, Séverine. *Les sénéchaussées royales de Bretagne: La monarchie d'ancien régime et ses juridictions ordinaires (1532–1790).* Rennes: Presses Universitaires de Rennes, 2006.

Descimon, Robert, and Alain Guery. "Un état des temps modernes?" In *L'état et les pouvoirs,* edited by André Burguière and Jacques Revel, 183–360. Paris: Éditions Seuil, 1989.

Detourbet, Edmond. *La procédure criminelle au XVIIe siècle.* Paris: 1881.

Dewald, Jonathan. *The Formation of a Provincial Nobility: The Magistrates of the Parlement of Rouen, 1489–1610.* Princeton, NJ: Princeton University Press, 1980.

———. "Magistracy and Political Opposition at Rouen: A Social Context." *Sixteenth Century Journal* 5, no. 2 (1974): 66–78.

Dhaille, Marie-Paul. *Étude des contrats de vente d'offices des juridictions siègeant à Rouen dans la seconde moitié du XVIIIe siècle.* Mémoire de maitrise, Faculté des Lettres et Sciences de Rouen, 1968–69.

Dickinson, J. A. "L'activité judiciaire d'après la procédure civile, le bailliage de Falaise, 1668–1790." *Revue d'Histoire Économique et Sociale* 2 (1976): 145–68.

Dowdell, E. G. *A Hundred Years of Quarter Sessions: The Government of Middlesex from 1660 to 1760.* Cambridge: Cambridge University Press, 1932.

Doyle, William. *The Parlement of Bordeaux and the End of the Old Régime, 1771–1790.* New York: St. Martin's Press, 1974.

———. *Venality: The Sale of Offices in Early Modern France.* Oxford: Clarendon Press, 1996.

———. "Venality and Society in Eighteenth Century Bordeaux." In *Sociétés et groupes sociaux en Aquitaine et en Angleterre,* 201–14. Bordeaux: Acter du Colloque franco-brittanique, 1979.

Dupaquier, Jacques. *Mercuriales du pays de France et du Vexin français, 1640–1792.* Paris: 1968.

Droualt, Jean. *Les vicomtés en Normandie aux XVIII siècle.* Caen: L. Jouan and R. Bigot, Librairies de l'Université de la Société des Antiquaires de Normandy, 1924.

Dupont-Ferrier, Gustave. *Les officiers royaux des bailliages et sénéchaussées et les institutions monarchiques locales en France à la fin du moyen age.* Paris: E. Bouillon, 1902.

Erickson, Amy Louise. *Women and Property in Early Modern England.* London: Routledge, 1993.

Esmein, Adhemar. *Histoire de la procédure criminelle en France et specialement de la procédure inquisitoire depuis le XIIIe siècle jusqu'à nos jours.* Paris: 1882.

Estaintot, Comte de. *Un procès entre deux haute-justiciers, Cany-Caniel et Valmont au XVIIIe siècle.* Rouen: Boisel, 1891.

———. *Recherche sur les hautes justices féodales existant en 1789 dans les limites du department de la Seine-Inferieure.* Rouen: 1892.

"Les états de Bretagne et la réformation de la coutume sous le regne de Louis XIV." *Mémoires de la Société Historique et Archéologique de Bretagne* 27 (1947): 33–43.

Evérat, E. *La sénéchaussée d'Auvergne et le siège présidial de Riom au XVIIIe siècle.* 1886.

Farge, Arlette. *Delinquance et criminalité: Le vol d'aliments à Paris au XVIIIe siècle.* Paris: Plon, 1974.

Farge, Arlette, and Michel Foucault. *Le désordre des familles: Lettres de cachet des archives de la Bastille au XVIIIe siècle.* Paris: Gallimard/Julliard, 1982.

Farr, James. *A Tale of Two Murders: Passion and Power in Seventeenth-Century France.* Durham and London: Duke University Press, 2005.

Fell, A. London. *Origins of Legislative Sovereignty and the Legislative State,* vol. 4, *Medieval or Renaissance Origins? Historiographical Debates and Deconstructions.* New York: Praeger, 1991.

Fenet, P. Antoine. *Pothier analysé dans ses rapports avec le code civil, et mis en ordre sous chacun des articles de ce code, ou, Les legislations ancienne et nouvelle comparées.* Paris: 1826.

Flechier, Esprit-Valentin. *Mémoires sur les grands jours d'Auvergne.* Translated by W. W. Comfort. Philadelphia: University of Pennsylvania Press, 1937.

Floquet, Amable. *La charte aux Normands.* Rouen: N. Perieux, 1842.

———. *Histoire du Parlement de Normandie.* Rouen: 1840–42.

Foisil, Madeleine. *La révolte des nu-pieds et les révoltes normandes de 1639.* Paris: E. Frère, 1970.

Follaine, Antoine. "Les juridictions royales subalternes en Normandie du XVI au XVIII siècle: Bailliage et vicomtés de Caux, d'Evreux, de Gisors et de Rouen." Mémoire D. E. A., Université de Rouen, 1989.

——. *Les justices locales dan les villes et villages du XVe au XIX siècles.* Vol. 2, *Administration et justice locales.* Rennes: Presses Universitaires de Rennes, 2006.

Forster, G. C. F. *The East Riding Justices of the Peace in the Seventeenth Century.* York: East Yorkshire Local History Society, 1973.

Foucault, Michel. *Surveiller et punir: Naissance de la prison.* Paris: Gallimard, 1975.

Franklin, Julian, trans. and ed. *Constitutionalism and Resistance in the Sixteenth Century: Three Treatises by Hotman, Beza, and Mornay.* New York: Pegasus, 1969.

——. *Jean Bodin and the Rise of Absolutist Theory.* Cambridge: Cambridge University Press, 1973.

Frondeville, Henri de. *Les présidents du Parlement de Normandie, 1499–1790.* Rouen: A. Lestringant, 1953.

Frondeville, Henri de, and Odette de Frondeville. *Les conseillers du Parlement de Normandie de 1641 à 1715.* Rouen: A. Lestringant, 1960.

Garnot, Benoit. "Une illusion historiographique: justice et criminalité au XVIIIe siècle." *Revue Historique* 570 (1989): 361–79.

Gatrell, V. A. C, Bruce Lenman, and Geoffrey Parker, eds. *Crime and the Law: The Social History of Crime in Western Europe since 1500.* London: Europa, 1980.

Gégot, Jean-Claude. "Étude par sondage de la criminalité dans le bailliage de Falaise (XVIIe–XVIIIe siècles): Criminalité diffuse ou société criminelle?" *Annales de Normandie* 13 (1966): 103–64.

Genestal, R. *Études de droit privé Normand: La tutelle.* Caen: L. Jouan and R. Bigot, 1930.

——. "La Rédaction des usages locaux de Normandie." *Bulletin de la Société des Antiquaires de Normandie* 34 (1927).

——. "La réforme de la coutume de Normandie à la fin du XVI et au cours du XVIIe siècle." *Revue Historique de Droit* 5 (1926).

Giesy, Ralph E. "Rules of Inheritance and Strategies of Mobility in Pre-Revolutionary France." *American Historical Review* 82 (April 1977): 271–89.

——. "State-Building in Early Modern France: The Role of Royal Officialdom." *Journal of Modern History* 55 (June 1983): 191–207.

Giffard, Andre. *Les justices seigneuriales en Bretagne aux XVIIe et XVIIIe siècles (1661–1791).* Paris: 1903.

Gilbert, Max. *Le bailliage de Caux et les autres bailliages de Normandie.* Rouen: Bibliothèque Municipale de Rouen, 1952.

Glassey, Lionel K. J. *Politics and the Appointment of the Justices of the Peace 1675–1720.* New York: Oxford University Press, 1979.

Goody, John, Joan Thirsk, and E. P. Thompson. *Family and Inheritance: Rural Society in Western Europe, 1200–1800.* Cambridge: Cambridge University Press, 1976.

Goubert, Pierre. "Les officiers royaux des presidiaux, bailliages et élections dans la société française du XVIIe siècle." *Dix-septième Siècle* 42–43 (1959): 54–75.

Greenshields, Malcolm R. "Women, Violence, and Criminal Justice Records in Early Modern Haute Auvergne." *Canadian Journal of History/Annales Canadiennes d'Histoire* 22 (August 1987): 175–94.

——. *An Economy of Violence in Early Modern France: Crime and Justice in the Haute Auvergne, 1587–1664*. University Park: Pennsylvania State University, 1994.

Gresset, Maurice. *Gens de justice à Besançon, de la conquête par Louis XIV à la révolution française (1674–1789)*. Paris: Bibliothèque Nationale, 1978.

——. *L'introduction de la vénalité des offices en Franche-Comté: 1692–1704*. Paris: Belles Lettres, 1989.

Guenée, Bernard. *Tribunaux et gens de justice dans le bailliage de Senlis à la fin du Moyen Age (vers 1380–vers 1550)*. Paris: Belles Lettres, 1963.

Guerout, Jean. "La question des territoires des bailliages royaux: L'exemple de la prévôté et vicomté de Paris (XIIIe–XVIIIe siècles)." Actes du 100e Congrès Natinal des Sociétés Savantes 2, Paris: Comité des Travaux Historiques et Scientifiques, 1978, 7–18.

Guilleminot, S. "La justice de l'ancien régime au XVIIe siècle: 11000 cas dans le présidial de Caen." *Revue d'Histoire Économique et Sociale* 2 (1988): 187–208.

Hamscher, Albert N. "Les réformes judiciaires des grands jours d'Auvergne, 1665–1666." *Cahiers d'Histoire* 1, no. 4 (1976): 425–32.

——. *The Parlement of Paris after the Fronde, 1653–1673*. Pittsburgh: University of Pittsburgh Press, 1976.

——. *The Conseil Privé and the Parliaments in the Age of Louis XIV: A Study in French Absolutism*. Pittsburgh: American Philosophical Society, 1987.

Hanley, Sarah. "Engendering the State: Family Formation and State Building in Early Modern France." *French Historical Studies* 16, no. 1 (Spring 1989): 4–27.

——. "The Family, the State and the Law in Seventeenth- and Eighteenth-Century France: The Political Ideology of Male Right versus and Early Theory of Natural Rights." *Journal of Modern History* 78, no. 2 (2006).

——. "The Jurisprudence of the Arrêts: Marital Union, Civil Society, and State Formation in France, 1550–1650." *Law and History Review* 21, no. 1 (2003): 1–40.

——. *The Lit de Justice of the Kings of France: Constitutional Ideology in Legend, Ritual, and Discourses*. Princeton, NJ: Princeton University Press, 1983.

——. "The Monarchic State in Early Modern France: Marital Regime Government and Male Right." In *Politics, Ideology, and Law in Early Modern Europe,* edited by Adrianna E. Bakos. Rochester, NY: University of Rochester Press, 1994.

Hanson, Paul R. *Provincial Politics in the French Revolution: Caen and Limoges, 1789–1794*. Baton Rouge: Louisiana State University Press, 1989.

Hart, James S. *The Rule of Law, 1603–1660: Crowns, Courts, and Judges*. Harlow: Pearson/Longman, 2003.

Haskins, Charles Homer. *Norman Institutions*. Cambridge, MA: Harvard University Press, 1960.

Hautebert, Joël. *La justice pénale à Nantes au grand siècle: Jurisprudence de la sénéchaussée présidiale*. Paris: Michel de Maule, 2001.

Hay, Douglas, Peter Linebaugh, John G. Rule, E. P. Thompson, and Cal Winslow. *Albion's Fatal Tree: Crime and Society in Eighteenth-Century England*. New York: Pantheon, 1975.

Hayhoe, Jeremy. *Enlightened Feudalism: Seigneurial Justice and Village Society in Eighteenth-Century Northern Burgundy*. Rochester, NY: University of Rochester Press, 2008.

——. "Neighbors Before the Court: Crime, Village Communities and Seigneurial Justice in Northern Burgundy, 1750–1790." *French History* 17, no. 2 (2003): 127–48

——. "'Judge in Their Own Cause': Seigneurial Justice in Northern Burgundy, 1750–1790."

PhD diss., University of Maryland at College Park, 2001.

Helot, Amedée. *Essai sur les baillis de Caux de 1204 à 1789.* Paris: 1895.

Hippeau, Celestin. *Le gouvernment de Normandie au XVIIe et au XVIIIe siècle, apres le correspondence de marquis de Beuvron et des ducs d'Harcout.* . . . Caen: 1863–70.

Holmes, Catherine E. *L'éloquence judiciaire de 1620 à 1660: Réflet des problemes sociaux, religieux et politiques de l'epoque.* Paris: Librairie Nizet, 1967.

Holmes, Geoffrey. *Augustan England: Professions, State and Society 1680–1730.* London: G. Allen and Unwin, 1982.

Hufton, Olwen. "Attitudes Towards Authority in Eighteenth Century Languedoc." *Social History* 3 (1978): 281–302.

——. "Begging, Vagrancy, Vagabondage and the Law: An Aspect of the Problem of Poverty in Eighteenth-Century France." *European Studies Review* 2 (1972): 97–123.

——. "Le paysan et la loi en France au XVIIIe siècle." *Annales d'Histoire Économique et Sociale* 3 (1983): 679–701.

Hurpin, Gerard. "L'administration de la Normandie au temps de Louis XIV." *Bulletin de la Société Libre d'Emulation de la Seine Maritime* (1986): 28–40.

Hurt, John J. *Louis XIV and the Parlements: The Assertion of Royal Authority.* Manchester: Manchester University Press, 2002.

——. "Les offices au parlement de Bretagne sous le regne de Louis XIV: Aspects financiers." *Revue d'Histoire Moderne et Contemporaine* 23 (1976): 3–31.

Imbert, Jean. "Quelque procès criminels des XVIIe et XVIIIe siècles." *Sciences Historiques,* no. 2. Paris: Presses universitaires de France, 1964.

Institute National Études Démographiques. *Boisguilbert parmi nous: Actes du colloque international de Rouen, 22–23 mai 1975.* Paris: 1989.

Isambert, Dieussy, Jourdan, et al. *Recueil générale des anciens lois françaises, depuis l'an 420 jusqu'a la Revolution de 1789.* 29 vols. Paris: Belin-le-Prieur, 1821–33.

Jacob, Robert. *Images de la justice.* Paris: Léopard d'or, 1994.

Kagan, Richard L. "Law Students and Legal Careers in Eighteenth-Century France." *Past and Present* 68 (1975): 38–72.

——. *Lawsuits and Litigants in Early Modern Castile, 1500–1700.* Chapel Hill: University of North Carolina Press, 1981.

Kaiser, Colin. "The Deflation in the Volume of Litigation at Paris in the Eighteenth Century and the Waning of the Old Judicial Order." *European Studies Review* 10 (1980): 309–36.

Keohane, Nannerl. *Philosophy and the State in France: The Renaissance to the Enlightenment.* Princeton, NJ: Princeton University Press, 1980.

Kettering, Sharon. *Judicial Politics and Urban Revolt in Seventeenth-Century France: The Parlement of Aix, 1629–1659.* Princeton, NJ: Princeton University Press, 1978.

——. *Patrons, Brokers, and Clients in Seventeenth-Century France.* New York: Oxford University Press, 1986.

——. *Patronage in Sixteenth-and Seventeenth-Century France.* Aldershot: Ashgate/Veriorum, 2002.

Kim, Seong-Hak. *Michel de L'Hôpital: The Vision of a Reformist Chancellor during the French Religious Wars.* Sixteenth-Century Essays and Studies, v. 36. Kirksville: Truman State University Press, 1997.

Kuehn, Thomas. *Law, Family and Women: Toward a Legal Anthropology of Renaissance Italy.* Chicago: University of Chicago Press, 1991.

La Bussière, P. de. *Le bailliage de Maçon: Étude sur l'organization judiciaire du maçonnais sous l'ancien régime.* Dijon: J. Nourry, 1914.

Laingui, Andre. *La résponsabilité penal dans l'ancien droit, XVIe–XVIIIe siècle.* Paris: Librairie Générale de Droit et de Jurisprudence, 1970.

Landau, Norma. *The Justices of the Peace, 1679–1760.* Berkeley: University of California Press, 1984.

Langbein, John H. *Prosecuting Crime in the Renaissance: England, Germany, France.* Cambridge, MA: Harvard University Press, 1974.

———. *Torture and the Law of Proof: Europe and England in the Ancien Régime.* Chicago: University of Chicago Press, 1977.

Lavergnee, J. Brejon de. "Économie et société dans la *Très Ancienne Coutume de Bretagne* au XIV siècle." *Mémoires de la Société Historique et Archéologique de Bretagne* 60, no. 183 (1983): 35–49.

———. "Les vicissitudes de l'enregistrement des usances locales de Bretagne lors de la redaction officielle de la Coutume de 1580." *Revue Historique de Droit Français et Étrangèr,* extrait du vol. 55 (1977): 559–78.

Le Pesant, Michel. *Le personnel d'un cour souveraine sous la règne de Louis XIV: Extrait de la bibliothèque de l'École des Chartes.* Paris: 1972.

Le Roy Ladurie, Emmanuel. *L'ancien régime: De Louis XIII à Louis XV, 1610–1770.* Paris: Hachette, 1991.

———. *L'état Royal, 1460–1610.* Histoire de France, vol. 2. Paris: Hachette, 1977.

———. "Système de la coutume: Structures familiales et coutumes d'héritage en France au XVIe siècle." *Annales d'Histoire Économique et Sociale* 27 (1972): 825–46.

Lebigre, Arlette. *L'affaire des poisons, 1679–1682.* Bruxelles: 1989.

———. *La duchesse de Longueville.* Paris: Perrin, 2004.

———. *Les grands jours d'Auvergne: Désordres et répression au XVIIe siècle.* Paris: Hachette, 1976.

———. *La justice du roi: La vie judiciaire dans l'ancienne France.* Paris: Albin Michel, 1988.

Linebaugh, Peter. *The London Hanged: Crime and Civil Society in the Eighteenth Century.* Penguin: London, 1991.

Lécole, André. "La haute justice et vicomté de Grainville-la-Teinturière aux XVIIe et XVIIIe siècle." Mémoire de maitrise, U. E. R. des Lettres de Rouen, 1978.

Lemercier, Pierre. *Les justices seigneuriales de la region parisienne de 1580 à 1789.* Paris: Éditions Domat-Montchrestien, 1933.

Lemmings, David. *Gentlemen and Barristers: The Inns of Court and the English Bar, 1680–1730.* Oxford: Clarendon, 1990.

Lemmonier-Lesage, Virginie. *Les arrêts de règlement du parlement de Rouen, fin de XVIe–XVIIe siècles.* Paris: Éditions Panthéons-Assas, 1999.

MacFarlane, Alan. *Justice and the Mare's Ale: Law and Disorder in Seventeenth-Century England.* New York: Cambridge University Press, 1981.

Mandrou, Robert. *Magistrats et sorciers en France au XVIIe siècle: Une analysé de psychologie historique.* Paris: Plon, 1968.

Margot, Alain. "La criminalité dans le bailliage de Mamers (1695–1750)." *Annales de Normandie* 22 (1972): 185–224.

Marion, Marcel. "À propos de la géographie judiciaire de la France sous l'ancien régime: La question de ressort des presidiaux." *Revue Historique* 89 (1905): 80–88.

——. *Dictionnaire des institutions de la France aux XVIIe et XVIIIe siècles.* Paris: A. & J. Picard, 1968.

Martines, Lauro. *Lawyers and Statecraft in Renaissance Florence.* Princeton, NJ: Princeton University Press, 1968.

Maza, Sara. "Le tribunal de la nation: Les mémoires judiciaires et l'opinion publique à la fin de l'ancien régime." *Annales d'Histoire Économique et Sociale* 42, no. 1 (1987): 73–90.

McIntosh, Marjorie Keniston. *Controlling Misbehavior in England, 1370–1600.* Cambridge: Cambridge University Press, 1998.

McLynn, Frank. *Crime and Punishment in Eighteenth-Century England.* Oxford: Oxford University Press, 1991.

Mer, Louis-Bernard. "La procédure criminelle au XVIIIe siècle: L'enseignement des archives bretonnes." *Revue Historique* 274 (1985): 9–42.

Mettam, Roger. *Power and Faction in Louis XIV's France.* Oxford: Basil Blackwell, 1988.

Moote, Lloyd. *The Revolt of the Judges: The Parlement of Paris and The Fronde, 1643–1652.* Princeton, NJ: Princeton University Press, 1971.

Mousnier, Roland. *La conseil du roi, de Louis XII à la Révolution.* Paris: Presses Universitaires de France, 1970.

——. *La vénalité des offices sous Henri IV et Louis XIII.* Rouen: Éditions Maugard, 1945.

——. *The Institutions of France Under the Absolute Monarchy, 1598–1789.* 2 vols., vol. 1, 1979; vol. 2, 1984. Translated by Arthur Goldhammer. Chicago: University of Chicago Press, 1979–84.

Musset, J. "La tentative manquée de la redaction d'un Coutume à Eu à la fin du XVIe siècle." *Annales de Normandie* 4 (1986): 346–47.

Mutel, A. "Note sur les usages locaux du bailliage de Caux dans la coutume reformée de 1583." *Annales de Normandie* 21, no. 3 (1971): 187–205.

Noel, J.-F. "Une justice seigneuriale en Haute Bretagne à la fin de l'ancien régime: La châtellenie de la Motte-de-Gennes." *Annales de Bretagne* 83 (1976): 127–63.

Neveux, Hughes. "La justice, norme ambigué de la paysannerie européenne, XVe à XVIIe siècles." *Cahiers des Annales de Normandie* 24 (1974): 109–21.

Oreilly. *Mémoires sur la vie publique et privé de Claude Pellot.* 2 vols. Rouen and Paris: 1881–82.

Papillard, A. "L'ancien bailliage d'Eu: La justice royale, ducale, seigneuriale et municipale à Eu sous l'ancien régime." *Amys du Vieil Eu* (1987): 106–51.

Parker, David. *Class and State in Ancien Régime France: The Road to Modernity?* London: Routledge, 1996.

——. *The Making of French Absolutism.* New York: St. Martin's, 1983.

——. "Sovereignty, Absolutism and the Function of the Law in Seventeenth Century France." *Past and Present* 122 (February 1989): 36–74.

Parker, Geoffrey, and Leslie M. Smith, eds. *The General Crisis of the Seventeenth Century.* London: Routledge and Kegan Paul, 1978.

Pissard, H. *Le clameur de haro dans le droit Normand.* Caen: Bibliothèque d'Histoire du Droit Normand, 1911.

Plessix-Buisset, Christiane. "À propos des tutelles et curatelles en Bretagne au XVIIIe siècle." *Mémoires de la Société Historique et Archéologique de Bretagne* 60 (1993): 240–61.

———. *Le criminel devant ses juges en Bretagne aux 16e et 17e siècles.* Paris: Maloine, 1988.

Poitrineau, Abel. "Aspects de la crise des justices seigneuriales dans l'Auvergne du XVIIIe siècle." *Revue Historique de Droit Français et Étrangèr* 39 (December 1961): 552–70.

Portemer, Jean. "Un essai de la methode du Chancellier d'Auguesseau (le Édit d'aout 1729)." *Extrait des mémoires de la Société pour l'Histoire du Droit et des Institutions des Anciens Pays Bourguignons, Comtois et Romands, fasc. 19 (1957).* Dijon: Imp. Bernigauc et Privat, 1959.

Potter, David. "'Rigueur de Justice': Crime, Murder and the Law in Picardy, Fifteenth to Sixteenth Centuries." *French History* 11, no. 3 (1997): 265–309.

Potter, Mark. *Corps and Clienteles: Public Finance and Political Change in France, 1688–1715.* Aldershot: Ashgate, 2003.

———. "The Institutions of Absolutism: Politics and Finance in France, 1680–1715." PhD diss., University of California at Los Angeles, 1997.

Prax-Falcou, Hélène. *Le sénéschal et siège présidial de Lauragais: Les magistrats, la procédure criminelle (1670–1790).* Position des thèses, École des Chartes, 1971.

Prentout, Henri. *Les états provinciaux de Normandie.* 3 vols. Rouen: 1915–17.

———. *La Normandie.* Paris: Cerf, 1910.

Pullan, Brian. *The Jews of Europe and the Inquisition of Venice, 1550–1670.* Totowa, NJ: Barnes and Noble, 1983.

Raadschelders, J. C. N. *Government, A Public Administration Perspective.* London: M. E. Sharpe, 2003.

Raeff, Marc. *The Well-Ordered Police State: Social and Institutional Change Through Law in the Germanies and Russia, 1600–1800.* New Haven, CT: Yale University Press, 1983.

Ranum. Orest. *The Fronde: A French Revolution 1648–1652.* New York: Norton, 1993.

Rateau, Marguerite. "Les peines capitales et corporelles en France sous l'ancien régime." *Annales Internationales de Criminologie* (1963): 276–308.

Reinhardt, Stephen G. "Crime and Royal Justice in Ancien Régime France: Modes of Analysis." *Journal of Interdisciplinary History* 13, no. 3 (Winter 1983): 437–60.

———. *Justice in the Sarladais, 1770–1790.* Baton Rouge: Louisiana State University Press, 1991.

Richet, Denis. *La France moderne: L'ésprit des institutions.* Paris: Flammarion, 1973.

Ridard, Abel. *Essai sur le douaire en Bourgogne.* Dijon: 1906.

Riollot, Jean. *Le droit de prévention des juges royaux sur les juges seigneuriaux: Origines et développement de ce droit dans l'ancienne France en matière purement judiciaire.* Paris: 1931.

Robbine, P. E. "Les magistrats du Parlement de Normandie à la fin du XVIII siècle. Thèse de l'École de Chartes." 2 vols. Rouen: 1967.

Romain, C., ed. *Les cahiers de doléances des paroisses du bailliage de Cany.* Rouen: 1909.

Root, Hilton L. *Peasants and King in Burgundy: Agrarian Foundations of French Absolutism.* Berkeley: University of California Press, 1987.

Rosenheim, James M. County Governance and Elite Withdrawel in Norfolk, 1660–1720." In *The First Modern Society: Essays in English History in Honor of Lawrence Stone,* edited by A. L. Beir, David Cannadine, and James M. Rosenheim. Cambridge: Cambridge University Press, 1989.

——The Emergence of a Ruling Order: English Landed Society 1650–1750. London: Long-man, 1998.

——. "Landownership, the Aristocracy and the County Gentry." In *The Reigns of Charles II and James VII and II,* edited by Lionel K. J. Glasssey, 152–70. New York: St. Martin's Press, 1997.

Rosenthal, Jean-Laurent. *The Fruits of Revolution: Property Rights, Litigation, and French Agriculture, 1700–1860.* Cambridge: Cambridge University Press, 1992.

Rothwell, W. "The Problem of Law French." *French Studies* 46 (July 1992): 257–71.

Rouyer, Henri. *De la déclaration de grossesse des filles et des femmes veuves enceintes sous l'ancien régime.* Vitteaux: 1963.

Royer, Jean-Pierre. *Histoire de la justice en France: De la monarchie absolue à la république.* Paris: Presses Universitaires de France, 1995.

Ruff, Julius R. *Crime, Justice and Public Order in Old Régime France: The Sénéchaussées of Libourne and Bazas, 1696–1789.* London: Croom Helm, 1984.

——. *Violence in Early Modern Europe, 1500–1800.* Cambridge: Cambridge University Press, 2001.

Salmon, J. H. M. "Venal office and Popular Sedition in Seventeenth-Century France: A Review of a Controversy." *Past and Present* 37 (July 1967): 21–43.

Schneider, Zoë A. "The Village in the State: Justice and the Local Courts in Nor-mandy, 1670–1740." PhD diss., Georgetown University, 1997.

——. "Women before the Bench: Female Litigants in Early Modern Normandy." *French Historical Studies* 23, no. 1 (Winter 2000): 1–32.

Sharpe, James A. "The History of Crime in Late Medieval and Early Modern England." *Social History* 7 (1982): 187–203.

——. *Crime in Early Modern England 1550–1750.* London: Longman, 1999.

Soleil, Sylvain. "Le mantien des justices seigneuriales à la fin de l'ancien régime: Fail-lité des institutions royales ou récuperation? L'exemple angevin." *Revue Historique de Droit Français et Étranger* 74 (1996): 83–100.

——. *Le siège royale de la sénéchaussée et du présidial d'Angers (1551–1790).* Rennes: Presses Universitaires de Rennes, 1997.

Soman, Alfred. "Deviance and Criminal Justice in Western Europe, 1300–1800: An Essay in Structure." *Criminal Justice History* I (1980): 3–28.

——. "The Parlement of Paris and the Great Witch Hunt." *Sixteenth Century Journal* 9 (1978): 30–44.

——. "Les procès de sorcellerie au Parlement de Paris (1565–1640)." *Annales d'Histoire Économique et Sociale* 32, no. 4 (1977): 790–814.

Soublin, Leopold. *Les grandes bailliages de Haute-Normandie en 1789.* Rouen: 1972.

——. *Le premier vote des Normands, 1789.* Fécamp: E.M.T.N., 1981.

Staves, Susan. *Married Women's Separate Property in England, 1660–1833.* Cambridge, MA: Harvard University Press, 1990.

Stein, Peter. *Roman Law in European History.* Cambridge: Cambridge University Press, 1999.

Stone, Bailey. *The Parlement of Paris, 1771–1789.* Chapel Hill: University of North Carolina Press, 1981.

Strayer, J. R. *The Royal Domaine in the Bailliage of Rouen.* Princeton, NJ: Princeton University Press, 1936.

Tackett, Timothy. *Becoming a Revolutionary: The Deputies of the French National Assembly and the Emergence of a Revolutionary Culture, 1789–1790.* Princeton, NJ: Princeton University Press, 1996.

Tabuteau, Emily Zack. *Transfers of Property in Eleventh-Century Norman Law.* Chapel Hill: University of North Carolina Press, 1988.

Tapié, Victor-L. "Les officiers seigneuriaux dans la société provinciale du XVIIe siècle." *Dix-septième Siècle* 42–43 (1959): 118–40.

Thompson, E. P. *Whigs and Hunters: The Origin of the Black Act.* London: Allen and Unwin, 1975.

Tournerie, Jean-André. "Le présidial de Tours de 1740 à 1790: Recherches sur la crise judiciaire en province à la fin de la ancien régime." Études et travaux de la faculté de sciences juridiques et économiques de l'université de Tours. Tours: Université de Tours, 1975.

Underdown, David. *A Freeborn People: Politics and the Nation in Seventeenth-Century England.* Oxford: Oxford University Press, 1996.

Vardi, Liana. "Peasants and the Law: A Village Appeals to the French Royal Council, 1768–1791." *Social History* 13, no. 3 (1988): 295–313.

Veyrat, Maurice. *Essai chronologique et biographique sur les baillis de Rouen, de 1171 à 1790, avec documents et portraits inédits.* Rouen: Éditions Maugard, 1953.

———. *La haute-justice des archévêques de Rouen, comptes des Louviers 1197–1790.* Rouen: Éditions Margard, 1948.

———. "Les gouvernors de Normandie du XVIe siècle à la Revolution." *Études Normandes,* 27 (4ème trimestre, 1953).

Vivien, Robert. *De l'usage des contrats de mariage en Normandie.* Paris: 1909.

Weisser, Michael R. *Crime and Punishment in Early Modern Europe.* Atlantic Highlands, NJ: Humanities Press, 1979.

Wrightson, Keith. "Two Concepts of Order: Justices, Constables and Jurymen in Seventeenth-Century England." In *"An Ungovernable People: The English and Their Law in the Seventeenth and Eighteenth Centuries,* edited by John Brewer. New Brunswick, NJ: Rutgers University Press, 1980.

Yver, Jean. "Caractères originaux de la Coutume de Normandie." *Mémoires de l'Academie des Sciences et Arts de Caen* 12 (1952).

———. *Le droit romain en Normandie (avant 1500).* Mediolani: Giuffre, 1976.

———. "La rédaction officielle de la Coutume de Normandie (Rouen, 15:. Son ésprit." *Annales de Normandie* 1 (1986): 3–36.

Zorzi, Andrea. *L'aministratione della giustizia penale nella republica fiorentina: Aspette e problemi.* Firenze: Olschki, 1988.

II. Society, Economy and Culture

Arundel de Condé, G. *Dictionnaire des anoblis normands: 1600–1790.* Rouen: Affiches de Normandie, 1976.

Bardet, Jean-Paul. "Mourir à Rouen au temps de Boisguilbert: Les faux-semblants de la crise de 1693–1694." In *Boisguilbert parmi nous: Actes du Colloque International de Rouen, 22–23 mai 1975,* 201–17. Paris: INED, 1989.

———. *Rouen aux XVIIe et XVIIIe siècles: Les mutations d'un espace social.* Paris: Société d'Édition d'Enseignement Supérieur, 1983.

Beaucousin, A. *Registre des fiefs et arrière fiefs du bailliage de Caux en 1503*. Rouen: 1891.

Berenger, Jean, Jean Meyer, et al. *La Bretagne de la fin du XVIIeme siècle d'après la mémoire de Béchameil de Nointel*. Paris: Klinksieck, 1976.

Bloch, Marc. *Les caractères originaux de l'histoire rurale française*. 2ième ed. (1931). Reprint: Paris: Armand Colin, 1952.

Boisguilbert, Pierre Le Pesant de. *Factum de France*. Reprint: Paris: I.N.E.D., 1966.

——. *Mémoire sur l'assiette de la taille*. Reprint: Paris: I.N.E.D., 1966.

Bolleme, Geneviève. "Les Almanachs populaires aux XVIIe et XVIIIe siècles." École Pratique des Hautes Études, Paris, 1969.

Bottin, Jacques. "La production des toiles en Normandie, milieu XVIe siècle: Approche des voies de développement." *L'Homme et l'Industrie en Normandie* (Alencon: Sociétés Historiques et Archéologiques de Normandie, 1990): 77–86.

——. *Seigneurs et paysans dans l'ouest du pays de Caux: 1540–1650*. Paris: Sycomore, 1983.

Bouvet, Michel, and Pierre Marie Bourdin. "À travers la Normandie des XVIIe et XVIIIe siècles." *Annales de Normandie*, Cahiers, No. 6 (1968). Caen: 1968.

Brunelle, Gayle. *New World Merchants of Rouen 1559–1630*. Kirksville, MO: Truman State, 1991.

Cailliard, Michel et al. "À travers la Normandie en les XVIIe et XVIIIe siècles." *Annales de Normandie, Cahiers* No. 3 (1963). Caen: 1963.

Castan, Yves. *Honnêteté et rélations sociales en Languedoc (1715–1780)*. Paris: Plon, 1974.

Chartier, Roger. *The Cultural Uses of Print in Early Modern Europe*. Princeton, NJ: Princeton University Press, 1988.

——. *L'ordre des livres: Lecteurs, auteurs, bibliothèques en Europe entre XIVe et XVIIIe siècles*. Aix-en-Provence: Alinea, 1992.

Chauvet, Stephen. *La Normandie ancestrale: Ethnologie, vie, coutumes, meubles, utensiles, costumes, patois*. Paris: Boivin et cie, 1921.

Clement, Pierre, ed. *Lettres, instructions, et mémoires de Colbert*. 6 vols. Paris: 1861–69.

Collins, James B. "The Economic Role of Women in Seventeenth-Century France." *French Historical Studies* 16, no. 2 (Fall 1989): 436–70.

Collins, James B., and Karen L. Taylor. *Early Modern Europe: Issues and Interpretations*. Malden, MA: Blackwell, 2006.

Coulmin, Pierre. *Luttes pour la terre: La société paysanne en bocage normand*. Coutances: 1979.

Cowan, Alexander. *Urban Europe 1500–1700*. London: Arnold, 1998.

Davis, Natalie Zemon. *Fiction in the Archives: Pardon Tales and Their Tellers in Sixteenth-Century France*. Stanford: Stanford University Press, 1987.

Debu-Bridel, Jacques. *Anne-Geneviève de Bourbon, duchesse de Longueville*. Paris: Gallimard, 1938.

Dewald, Jonathan. *Aristocratic Experience and the Origins of Modern Culture: France, 1570–1715*. Berkeley: University of California Press, 1993.

——. *The European Nobility 1400–1800*. Cambridge: Cambridge University Press, 1996.

——. *Pont-Saint-Pierre, 1389–1789: Lordship, Community, and Capitalism in Early Modern France*. Berkeley: University of California Press, 1987.

Dion, Joseph. *La Fossé-en-Bray de la Fronde à la Revolution*. Rouen: Mémoire de maitrise, Faculté des Lettres et Sciences de Rouen, 2 decembre 1970.

Duchemin, P. *Le canton de Matteville et les districts de Caudebec et Cany pendent la révolution (1789–1800).* Yvetot: 1897.

Erickson, Amy Louise. *Women and Property in Early Modern England.* London: Routledge, 1993.

Esmonin, Edmond. *La taille en Normandie au temps de Colbert, 1661–1683.* Paris: Hachette, 1913.

Fairchilds, Cissie. *Poverty and Charity in Aix-en-Provence, 1640–1789.* Baltimore: Johns Hopkins University Press, 1976.

Foisil, Madeleine. *Femmes de caractères au XVIIe siècle, 1600–1650.* Paris: Fallois, 2000.

———. "Un mort modèle: Le duc de Longueville, 1663." *Recueil des études offert en homage au doyen Michel de Boüard.* Caen: 1982.

———. "Parentelés et fidelités autour du duc de Longueville pendant la Fronde." In *Clientèles et fidelités à l'époque moderne en Europe: Hommage à R. Mousnier,* edited by Y. Durand. Paris: Presses Universitaires de France, 1981.

Follain, Antoine. *Le village sous l'ancien régime.* Paris: Fayard, 2008.

Forster, Robert, and Orest Ranum, eds. *Rural Society in France: Selections from the Annales.* Baltimore: Johns Hopkins University Press, 1977.

Frère, Édouard Benjamin. *Rechereches sur les premiers temps de l'imprimerie en Normandie.* Rouen: 1829.

Furet, François, Jacques Ozouf, et al. *Lire et ecrire: L'alphabétisation des français de Calvin à Jules Ferry.* 2 vols. Paris: Éditions de Minuit, 1977.

Gallet, Jean. "Recherches sur la seigneurie: Foires et marches dans le vannetais, du 16ième–18ième." *Mémoires de la Société Historique et Archéologique de Bretagne* (1974), 133–166.

———. *La seigneurie bretonne (1450–1680): L'exemple du Vannetais.* Paris: Publications de la Sorbonne, 1983.

Goubert, Pierre, and Daniel Roche. *Les français et l'ancien régime.* 2 vols. Paris: Armand Colin, 1984.

———. *La vie quotidienne des paysans français au XVIIe siècle.* Paris: 1982.

Gouhier, Pierre, Anne Vallez, and J. M. Vallez. *Atlas historique de la Normandie: Cartes de communautés d'habitants pour les généralités de Rouen, Caen, Alençon.* Caen: Centre de Recherche d'Histoire Quantitative, 1967–72.

Gricourt, Marie-Claude. "Étude d'histoire démographique, sociale et religieuse de 5 paroisses de archdiaconé du Petit-Caux: Doudeville, Canville, Bacqueville, Brachy et Luneray du milieu du XVIIe siècle à la fin de l'ancien régime." In *À travers la Normandie des XVIIe et XVIIIe siècles,* vol. 3, *Cahiers des Annales de Normandie,* 445–553. Caen: Annales de Normandie, 1963.

Gullickson, Gay. *Spinners and Weavers of Auffay: Rural Industry and the Sexual Division of Labor in a French Village, 1750–1850.* Cambridge: Cambridge University Press, 1986.

Gutton, Jean-Pierre. *La sociabilité villageois dans l'ancienne France: Solidarités et voisinages du XVIe au XVIIIe siècles.* Paris: Pluriel, 1979.

Hainsworth, David Roger. *Stewards, Lords, and People: The Estate Steward and His World in Late Stuart England.* Cambridge: Cambridge University Press, 1992.

Helot, René. *Le bibliothèque bleue en Normandie.* Rouen: A. Laine, 1928.

Hervel, René. *Longueville et la vallée de la Scie.* Rouen: 1958.

Holt, Mack P. *The French Wars of Religion, 1562–1629*. Cambridge: Cambridge University Press, 1995.

——, ed. *Society and Institutions in Early Modern France*. Athens: University of Georgia Press, 1991.

Hufton, Olwen. "Women and the Family Economy in 18th c. France." *French Historical Studies*, 9, no. 1 (Spring 1975): 1–22.

Jéorger, Muriel. "L'alphabetisation dans l'ancien diocèse de Rouen au XVIIe et au XVIIIe siècles." In *Lire et écrire: L'alphabetisation des français de Calvin à Jules Ferry*, edited by François Furet, Jacques Ozouf, et al. Paris: Éditions de Minuit, 1977.

——. "Histoire socio-demographique de la Normandie." Centre de Recherches d'Histoire Quantitative, UA 1013, Rapport d'Activité juin 1985 (Caen: 1985), 41–52.

Jourdain, E. *Recits dieppois: La duchesse de Longueville à Dieppe, 1650*. Dieppe: 1864.

Kaplan, Steven L. *Bread, Politics and the Political Economy in the Reign of Louis XV*, vol. 1. The Hague: Martinus Nijhoff, 1976.

Kaplow, Jeffrey, ed. *Elbeuf During the Revolutionary Period: History and Social Structure*. Baltimore: Johns Hopkins University, 1964.

Kettering, Sharon. *French Society 1589–1715*. Harlow: Longman, 2001.

La Chesnaye Desbois, Aubert. *Dictionnaire de la noblesse*. 19 vols. Paris: 1863.

La Galissonnière, Jacques. *Recherche sur la noblesse de Normandie*. 2 vols. 1667.

Lami, J.-Fr. *L'abolition de la feodalité dans le district de Cany-Barville*. Mémoire de maitrise, Université de Rouen, 1975.

Le Roy Ladurie, Emmanuel. *L'age classique des paysans, 1340–1789*. Histoire de la France rurale, vol. 2. Edited by Georges Duby and Armand Wallon. Paris: Sevil, 1975.

Le Tenneur, Rene. *Magie, sorcellerie et fantastique en Normandie: Dès premier hommes à nos jours*. Coutances: OCEP, 1979.

Le Goff, T. G. A., *Vannes and Its Region: A Study of Town and Country in 18th-Century France*. Oxford: Clarendon, 1981.

Lemarchand, Guy. "La fin de féodalisme dans le pays de Caux." Thèse d'état, Université de Paris, 1989.

Leprevost, A. *Anciennes divisions territoriales de la Normandie*. Paris: 1837.

Leroy, Charles. *Notes sur la seigneurie et paroisse de Venesville au Pays de Caux*. Rouen: Imprimerie Albert Lainé, 1930.

——. *Paysans normands au XVIIIe siècle*. 2 vols. Rouen: A. Lestringant, 1929.

——. *La seigneurie d'Auberville la Manuel au pays de Caux*. Rouen: Librairie Lestringant, 1929.

Mandrou, Robert. *De la culture populaire aux 17e et 18e siècles: La Bibliothèque bleue de Troyes*. Paris: Imago, 1985.

Manning, Roger B. *Hunters and Poachers: A Social and Cultural History of Unlawful Hunting in England, 1485–1640*. Oxford: Oxford University Press, 1993.

Moissy, Henri. *Dictionnaire de patois normand*. Caen: H. Delesques, 1887.

Muchembled, Robert. *La violence au village: Sociabilité et comportements populaires en Artois du XVe au XVIIIe siècle*. Turnhour, Éditions Brépols: 1989.

——. *Popular Culture and Elite Culture in France*. Translated by Lydia Cochrane. Baton Rouge: Louisiana State University Press, 1985.

Norberg, Kathryn. *Rich and Poor in Grenoble, 1600–1814.* Berkeley: University of California Press, 1985.

Porter, Roy. *English Society in the Eighteenth Century.* Harmondsworth: Penguin, 1982.

Sabean, David Warren. *Power in the Blood: Popular Culture and Village Discourse in Early Modern Germany.* Cambridge: Cambridge University Press, 1984.

———. *Property, Production and Family in Neckarhausen, 1700–1870.* Cambridge: Cambridge University Press, 1991.

Sandret, Louis. *La seigneurie et les seigneurs de Cany, en Normandie.* Paris: 1880.

Schwartz, Robert M. *Policing the Poor in Eighteenth-Century France.* Chapel Hill: University of North Carolina Press, 1988.

Sharp, James A. *Modern England: A Social History, 1550–1760.* 2nd ed. London: Arnold, 1997.

Sion, Jules. *Les paysans de la Normandie orientale: Pays de Bray, Caux, Vexin Normand, Vallée de la Seine.* Paris: Armand Colin, 1909.

Underdown, David. *Fire from Heaven: Life in an English Town in the Seventeenth Century.* New Haven, CT: Yale University Press, 1992

———. *Revel, Riot and Rebellion: Popular Politics and Culture in England 1603–1660.* Oxford: Oxford University Press, 1985.

Vardi, Liane. "Construing the Harvest: Gleaners, Farmers, and Officials in Early Modern France." *American Historical Review* 98 (December 1993): 1424–47.

———. *The Land and the Loom: Peasants and Profit in Northern France, 1680–1800.* Durham: Duke University Press, 1993.

Venard, Marc. *Bourgeois et paysans au XVIIe siècle.* Paris: S.E.V.P.E.N., 1957.

———. "Les Femmes dans les confrèries Normands du XIV aux XVIII siècles." *La Femme en Normandie, Actes du XIXe congrès des sociétés historiques et archéologiques de Normandie,* 297–303. Caen: Archives Départmentales du Calvados, 1986.

Villand, R. F. Lamotte et. al. "Notes sur les foires et marchés en Normandie: Circuits commerciaux, foires et marchés en Normandie." IXe Congrès des Sociétés Historiques Archéologiques, et Ethnologiques de Normandie, Rouen, 1975.

Wegert, Karl. *Popular Culture, Crime, and Social Control in 18th-Century Würtemberg.* Stuttgart: F. Steiner, 1994.

Wheaton, Robert. "Afinity and Descent in Seventeenth-Century Bordeaux." In *Family and Sexuality in French History,* edited by R. Wheaton and Tamara K. Harevan, 111–34. Philadelphia: University of Pennsylvania Press, 1980.

Wood, James B. *The Nobility of the Election of Bayeux, 1463–1666.* Princeton, NJ: Princeton University Press, 1980.

Wrightson, Keith, and David Levine. *Poverty and Piety in an English Village: Terling, 1525–1700.* Oxford: Clarendon Press, 1995.

INDEX

absolutism, 26, 27, 143, 184, 202
admiralty courts (*admirautés*), 31, 129, 229, 260n22
Aguesseau, Henri François d,' 20, 24, 107, 126–27, 136, 156–57
Alexander, Pierre, 59, 190, 207, 208, 211
appeals, to Parlement. *See* Normandy, Parlement of, appeals to
arbitration, community, 4, 159, 181–84, 188, 199, 219; and equity, 104; by judges, 181–82, 184; by women, 182, 183
Aristotle, 76, 222; *Nicomachean Ethics,* 19, 104, 175; *Politics,* 2, 16
arrêts (administrative laws), 14, 24, 51, 75, 95, 96, 107, 108–10, 125; on fees, 79–81, 85, 91, 108, 109, 142, 149; and seigneurial judges, 149–50; specific examples of, 53, 106, 109, 110, 152, 155, 159, 204; types of, 108, 109
assizes (court sessions): and broadcasting of news, 188; and cumulative offices, 71, 73; in England, 160, 216, 217–18; grand, 8, 56, 69, 172, 225; and guild issues, 8, 171–72; litigation limits of, 7; on market days, 34–35, 54; mercurial, 51, 71, 73; petty, 6, 29, 54, 162, 165, 175, 198, 202, 210–11, 214, 225, 227; summer, 185; at taverns, 37, 159, 161, 198, 208–9; and towns of the Caux, 30–38

bailiwick courts (*bailliages*), 2, 7, 24, 30–31, 48, 229; *arrêts* granted to, 109; autonomy/power of, 1–2, 10–15; and *cahiers,* 13, 14; and consolidation of power, 125–27, 140–41; and elections to Estates General, 13, 14, 49, 223;

and equity, 91, 97, 104–5, 160; and intendants, 153–57, 203; isolation of, 124–25, 141; jurisdiction of, 61–62, 125–27; and legislative sovereignty, 3–5, 15–18; and military mobilization, 6, 13, 51, 216; Parlement's support of, 14, 125, 140–41, 149; and presidial courts, 151–53; of Rouen, 31, 70, 128, 152–53; and royal law, 106; and seigneurial high justices, 12, 157–58; and sovereign courts, 127–29; as unit of local governance, 13–14. See also common courts; *sénéchaussées*
bailiwick judges. *See* judges, local
bailiwicks, 24, 25, 30–31; and Custom of Normandy, 98, 101, 110–11, 124; governance and administration of, 50–61, 68–69; isolation of, 124–25, 141; and order of community/state, 130, 213, 225–26
baillis (seneschals), 6, 13, 51, 67, 71, 110, 141, 148, 150–51
banishment, 144, 153, 183, 191, 201, 205, 212
barristers, 39, 47, 73, 76, 98, 112, 181
Beauchamel, Michel Alphonse Subtil de, 139–40
Becdelièvre, Pierre de (marquis of Cany), and family of, 35, 37, 43, 207
Beuzebosc, Adrien and François, 72–73
Beza, Theodore, 20
Blois, Ordinance of (1579), 13, 51, 66, 76, 100, 109, 112
Bodin, Jean, 20, 75, 175, 204, 227; on legislative sovereignty, 5, 6, 16–19, 20, 204; on public/private dividing line, 2, 18–19, 20, 221, 222
Bontemps, Jacob, 66

315

Bossuet, Jacques-Bénigne, 15–16
Bourbon, Anne-Geneviève de
(duchess of Longueville), 37, 42,
68, 126
Brienne edicts, 46, 141, 222
Brittany, 6, 26, 220; and *clameur de haro*,
177; and common courts' autonomy/
defiance of king, 11, 26, 46, 125;
and court officers' finances, 133,
135; courts of, 129; and cumulative
offices, 70–71, 80; death penalty in,
203; extraordinary courts of, 129;
and grain/bread issues, 54, 207;
inheritance law in, 115, 116; litigants
in, 165; noble judges in, 63; and
Roman law, 105
Brittany, Custom of, 10, 95, 102, 105,
107–8, 112, 115
Brittany, Estates of, 100, 125
Bureaus of Finance, 125, 128, 139–40,
149, 229, 248n119
Burgundy, 26, 53, 69, 95, 99, 103, 154,
165, 182, 203, 220

cahiers (lists of grievances): and *bailliages*,
13, 14; and calls for judicial reform,
220, 222–23
canon law, 75, 96, 100, 173, 253n39
Cany, 21, 30, 31–35, 36; *bailliage* of, 24,
30, 32, 33, 38, 41, 46, 52, 55, 72, 141,
145, 163, 230; *cahiers* of, 222; courts/
officers of, 32–34; jail of, 33; and
market day assizes, 34–35, 54; nobility of, 35, 37, 38, 42–44, 207
Cany-Caniel, high justice of, 24, 34, 41,
42, 65, 68, 121, 150, 167, 196, 197,
230; and appeals to Parlement, 33,
38, 147, 197; and fees/income, 67, 79;
and judges' powers, 54, 57; litigants
before, 51, 59, 162, 163, 164, 165,
197; market day assizes of, 54
capital punishment. *See* death penalty
cas royaux, 90, 106, 160, 174–75, 199,
251n189; and seigneurial courts, 25,
142, 143, 144, 154
Caudebec-en-Caux: presidial court
of, 21, 24, 30, 33, 119, 120, 129,

144, 145, 151–52, 155, 156, 241n36,
260n23, 272n8; tax court of, 47, 58
Caux, pays de, 23, 29–30; assize towns
of, 30–38; *cahiers* of, 220, 222–23;
common courts of, 21–22, 23; court
jurisdictions of, 230; court officers
of, 29–30, 38–40, 41; and elections
to Estates General, 223; industries
of, 29, 32, 34–35, 40; inheritance/
succession law of, 117, 119; king's
commissioners in, 45–46; literacy
in, 186–87; local usages of, 119–23;
maps of, xiv, v; nobility of, 34, 35,
36, 37, 42–43; population density
of, 241n36; society of, 40, 42–45. *See
also specific towns*
Caux, pays de, Custom of, 53, 96, 118–
19; and local usages, 119–23; and
women's property, 120–22
Chamber of Accounts (*Chambre des
Comptes*), 22, 31, 43, 126, 128, 137–
38, 229; and merger with Court of
Aids, 127, 128, 137–38
Charles IX, 13, 99, 100
châtellenies, 24, 30, 111, 120, 191. See also
prévôtés; vicomtés
children, litigation involving. *See* curatorship; inheritance/succession law;
tutorship; wardship
churches: accounts of, 52–53, 106, 164,
174; benefices of, 106, 174, 188; and
clergy, 7, 52, 173–74; as corporations,
56; and cumulative offices, 2, 48, 52;
judges' place in, 67, 199; lands of, 8,
47, 51, 52, 56, 164; poor rates of, 52,
217
Cicero, *De officiis*, 19–20, 75–76
civil cases: appeals of, 144–46, 147–49;
and business/trade issues, 171–73;
and community life, 164; and customary laws, 162, 166, 174; examples
of, 161–66; as majority before courts,
3–4, 26, 160–61, 161–62, 163, 219–
20; and moral issues, 51–52, 164,
173–74; and property/family issues,
9–10, 162, 165–73; and seigneurial
privileges, 162, 164; and small

triumphs of disadvantaged, 161, 165, 166, 170–71. *See also* property and family litigation

Civil Code (1667), 23, 107, 108, 176

civil law (*droit privé*): local defense of, 96–97, 99; and majority of court cases, 3–4, 26, 160–61, 161–62, 163, 219–20; and public law, 96–97, 100; and royal intervention attempts, 99–100; and royal omnibus ordinances, 99–100; teaching of, 76, 98. *See also* customary laws; public law

clameur de haro (hue and cry), 4, 101, 114, 159, 176–80, 191, 219; and commercial disputes, 179–80; as crossing class/authority lines, 180, 210; and family/property issues, 177, 179; and Grandcourt case, 176–77, 178, 179, 210–12; as Norman tradition, 177; as tax protest, 177, 178–79

clergy, 7, 52, 62, 77, 173–74

Colbert, Jean-Baptiste, 18, 24, 50, 59, 85, 110, 135, 148; law codes of, 23, 107, 109, 182

colonial code (*Code Noir,* 1685), 23

commercial code (1673), 23, 109, 182

common courts, 21–28; autonomy/ power of, 1–2, 10–15, 20–21, 26, 28, 96–97, 110–14; and business of citizens, 3–4, 6, 9–10, 26, 30, 45; and consolidation of power, 125–27, 140–41; dysfunctions of, 218–23; functions of, 213–18; and language/ literacy, 186–87; laws/customs followed by, 1, 3, 10, 16–17, 20, 26; and legislative sovereignty, 3–5, 15–18; and moral/religious transgressions, 8–9, 51–52, 164, 173–74, 216–17; and need for reform of, 220–23; and public/private dividing line, 2–3, 7, 18–21, 28, 96–97, 221, 225–28. *See also* court officers; judges, local; litigants; order, as goal of judicial system; *see also specific courts*

common courts, and state, 124–58; and appeals to Parlement, 140, 144–49; and intendants, 153–57, 203; and

jurisdictional issues, 125–27, 157–58; and oversight by Parlement, 149–51; and presidial courts, 151–53; and relationship with Parlement, 141–51; and seigneurial courts, 141–51, 157–58; and sovereign courts, 127–41; and support of Parlement, 14, 125, 140–41, 146–47, 149

common law, English, 217

commonwealth (*république*), 2–3, 8–10, 18–21

composition, 4, 159, 160, 175, 191, 199, 200, 211, 212

constabulary courts (*maréchaussées*), 6, 31, 58, 129, 229, 250n169, 260n23, 272n8; and criminal cases, 191, 197, 198, 203; and presidial court, 151, 152; and royal law, 106

consular courts (*juridictions consulaires*), 25, 31, 56, 129, 171, 229

Corneille, Pierre, 20, 77

corporal punishment, 144, 153, 160, 183, 191, 199, 200, 202, 211

councillors, 35, 39, 49, 133, 137, 139, 149; cumulative offices of, 69, 70, 74, 93, 152

Council of Justice, 23, 24, 107

Court of Aids (*Cour des Aides*), 22, 31, 43, 65, 128, 137–38, 229, 259n18; and merger with Chamber of Accounts, 127, 128, 137–38

court officers, 5–7, 29–30, 38–40, 41; autonomy/power of, 1–2, 10–15, 20–21, 26, 28, 96–97, 110–14; and business of citizens, 3–4, 6, 9–10, 26, 30, 45; and calls for judicial reform, 222–23; *clameur de haro* against, 180; cumulative offices of, 2, 12, 48, 69–74, 83–85, 93, 130, 215, 216; fee/emolument regulations for, 150; financial stresses on, 130–36; as governed by royal law, 106; and governing class/networks, 68–69; and heredity, 63, 66, 130–32, 223; income of, 49–50; and intendants, 14, 46, 125, 135–36, 140–41, 153–57, 219, 263n75; laws/customs followed

court officers–*(cont'd)*
by, 1, 3, 10, 16–17, 20, 26; and legal reforms, 13; and legislative sovereignty, 3–5, 15–21; as protectors of private realm/property, 2–3, 8–10, 18–21; and public/private dividing line, 2–3, 7, 18–21, 28, 96–97, 221, 225–28; and shifts in provincial governance, 11–13; social status of, 42–44, 61–67; as unable to move up to Parlement, 14, 124, 125, 130, 138, 227; venality of, 10–11, 27, 66–67, 69–70, 84, 87, 90, 91–93, 130–36, 222. *See also* judges, local; litigants; Pont-Audemer, corruption scandal of; *see also specific officers*
Court of Monies (*Cour de la Monnaye*), 31, 127, 128–29, 229
crime: and alcohol, 196, 198; and law, 193–96; and moral/religious transgressions, 8–9, 51–52, 164, 173–74, 216–17; as property/family-related, 9, 192, 196–98; sorcery as, 148–49
criminal cases, 190–212; appeals of, 144–46, 153, 183; and equity, 175; as initiated by commoners, 191–92; as minority in court system, 3–4, 174–75, 192, 225; as plaintiff-driven, 191, 198; as property/family-related, 9, 192, 196–98, 225; and rarity of convictions, 195; sentencing of, 160, 193, 198–205; statistics on, 153–54, 156–57, 203; as transferred to royal courts, 143; trial procedure of, 231–32; witnessing in, 4, 159, 191, 202, 205–9
Criminal Code (1670), 23, 107, 108, 142–43, 144, 156, 183, 195, 205
criminal justice: and appeals, 144–46, 153, 183; community intervention in, 202; and corruption, 198; and judicial discretion, 194, 196, 198–205; and order, 190–96, 199, 201–2, 207–9, 225; punitive and restitutive, 200–201; and punishment, 160, 193, 198–205; and rarity of convictions, 195; and repeat offenders, 196,

201–2; severity of, 194–95; and sovereign authority, 193–94, 204; and witnessing, 4, 159, 191, 202, 205–9. *See also* composition; corporal punishment; death penalty; incarceration; judicial discretion; restitution
criminal statistics (*statistique criminelle*), 153–54, 156–57, 203
cumulative offices (*cumuls*), 2, 12, 35, 48, 69–74, 83–85, 93, 130, 215, 216; and churches, 2, 48, 52; as "collapsed," 73–74; individual/family examples of, 71–73; and intendancies, 70–71; and municipal offices, 58, 69, 70, 71, 84–85, 93, 138, 243n4; in royal and seigneurial courts, 70, 71; and sergeantries, 73; and tax courts, 70, 71, 84, 217
curatorship (*curatelle*), 50, 65, 79, 81, 89, 90, 122, 132, 162, 166, 167–68, 185–86
custom, local usage, and equity, 1, 3, 10, 16–17, 20, 26, 91–92, 159, 175, 194. *See also* customary laws; equity; local usage; *see also specific customary laws*
customary laws, 8, 13, 20–21, 26, 28, 96; attempted codification of, 107–8; and civil cases, 162, 166, 174; creation of, 110–14; criticisms/praise of, 101–2; early acknowledgment of, 103; and legislative sovereignty, 16–18; and national legal culture, 217–18; and property/family litigation, 17, 166, 167–68, 170, 171; teaching of, 76, 98; royal reformation of, 100–101. *See also* civil law; equity; local usage
Customs. *See specific Customs under their geographic names*
customs administration (*traites foraines*), 31, 128, 129, 229

death penalty, 144, 153, 193, 201–5; alternatives to, 144, 153, 183, 201, 204–5; and LeRouge case, 203, 209–12; and ostracism of executioner, 203–4; as rarely imposed, 203–5, 226; Richelieu on, 190 direct-tax courts (*élections*), 2, 25, 31, 44, 47, 185, 229; and cumulative offices, 70, 71, 84, 217; establishment of, 125; and royal law, 106

Doré, Pierre, 47, 48, 52, 62, 68–69, 216

droit français. *See* royal law

ecclesiastical courts (*officialités*), 2, 9, 13, 51–52, 129, 164, 173, 229

edicts, 34, 100, 108, 140, 161, 175, 185, 226; Brienne, 46, 141, 222; on *clameur de haro,* 178; on cumulative offices, 35; on fees, 85–86, 108, 141; on fiscal courts, 127; on legal education, 76, 98; on municipal offices, 84, 85; on presidial court, 150, 152; religious, 60–61, 108, 164, 209; specific examples of, 13, 51, 52, 99, 159, 181–82, 188; on venality, 66, 69, 130, 136. *See also specific edicts*

élections. See direct-tax courts

England and France, compared, 8, 9, 27, 82, 161; arbitration, 181; citizen litigants, 219–20; equity law, 104; inheritance/succession law, 116, 165; need for legal reform, 221; rural society, 44–45; suppression of canon law, 173; women's legal issues, 169

English and French judges, compared, 213–19; and absence of nobility, 12, 42, 43; and arbitration, 181; and citizen litigants, 219–20; as community leaders, 50; and corruption, 219; and criminal cases, 195, 216; cumulative offices of, 215–16, 217; education of, 77; and endogamy, 132; as gentry, 2, 43–44, 62, 213, 215; and interaction with crown, 217, 218–19; jurisdiction/responsibilities of, 2, 48, 215–17; and moral/religious transgressions, 51–52, 216–17; and national legal culture, 217–18; and policing, 57, 216; and political power, 28, 49, 217–18, 223–28; and pauperism/vagrancy, 171–72, 201, 202; and poor rates/relief, 52, 215, 217; as property owners, 62–63, 66–67, 213–15; public/

private power of, 7; records left by, 222; and rural inhabitants, 44–45; social status of, 2, 27, 48, 62–63, 213–15; taxation, 216; and volunteerism vs. venality, 27, 213, 214. *See also* judges, local; justices of the peace

épices (litigants' fees), 11, 49, 79–80, 85, 87, 108, 142, 149, 222, 223

equity, 91, 221; classical derivation of, 104–5; and criminal cases, 175; and judicial discretion, 97, 160, 174, 175–76; and king, 104; two levels of, 104. *See also* custom, local usage, and equity; customary laws; local usage

Estates. *See specific Estates under their geographic names*

Estates General of France, 46, 77, 78, 124, 215; and *cahiers* of local officers, 220, 222–23; and civil law, 99–100; as closed to local officers/judges, 82, 218, 227; and customary laws, 112–13; elections to, 13, 14, 49, 223; and ordinances, 99–100, 108–9; and role of *bailliages,* 13, 14

Estouteville, duchy of, 32, 38, 42, 143

Eu (high justice), 24, 32, 38, 41, 120, 187, 230

Evelyn, John, 74

exceptional tribunals (*tribunaux d'exception*), 24

executioners (*bourreaux*), 203–4, 211–12

extraordinary courts, 129, 229

family/household: commonwealth protection of, 2–3, 8–10, 18–21; and customary law, 17, 166, 167–68; and inheritance/succession law, 115–18, 119, 120–21, 166–68, 256n99. *See also* curatorship; property; property and family litigation; tutorship

famine, 58–59, 93–94, 200, 207–8

fiscal courts. *See* Chamber of Accounts; Court of Aids

fiscal prosecutors, 39, 66, 68, 71

Fontainebleu, Edict of, 60, 108

forest code (1669), 23, 109

Formeville, Pierre de, 84, 91

Fronde, 12, 22, 37, 42, 140

gages (interest on court office), 49, 79, 80, 132, 133–36; *augmentations* of, 87, 130, 131, 135

galley service, 144, 148, 153, 201, 204–5, 211

grain, 171, 173; as controlled by judges, 54, 58–59; executioner's right to, 203–4; and famine, 58–59, 93–94, 200, 207–8; jailer's duty to provide, 88; prices of, 54, 160, 220; riots over, 6, 27, 58, 93–94, 200, 207–8; theft of, 200–201; and use of lord's mill, 54–55, 56, 161, 162, 209, 220

Grainville-la-Teinturière, 36–37, 43, 69, 70; *bailliage* of, 24, 32, 36, 37, 38, 41, 47, 52, 57, 59, 60, 62, 73, 95, 163, 164, 190, 200, 208–9, 230; and death of LeRouge, 209–12; and duchy of Longueville, 36, 37; high justice of, 36–37, 73, 145, 163, 207, 230, 238n93; sergeantry of, 73; tavern assizes at, 159

Grandcourt, Pierre and Anne, 176–77, 178, 179, 210–12

greniers à sel. See salt tax courts

guilds, 8, 24, 29, 35, 36, 53, 54, 56, 85, 93–94, 226

high justices. *See* seigneurial high justices (*hautes justices*)

hue and cry. See *clameur de haro*

Huezé, Jean, 73, 210–12

Hunt, William, 181, 214, 215–16

hunting law transgressions, 205–8

incarceration: escape from, 195, 219; expenses of, 88, 153, 154; facilities for, 33, 191, 201, 212; as sentence, 51, 148, 201, 212

income, of judges and lawyers, 79–82; and cumulative offices, 80; and curatorship, 79, 81, 89, 90; and fees for service, 80–81, 85–88; and land acquisition, 81, 89–90; and loans to insolvent nobles, 82; and tutorship,

79–80. See also *épices; gages;* Pont-Audemer, corruption scandal of

inheritance/succession law, 115–17, 118, 166–68, 170; and arbitration, 181; and *preciput,* 115–16, 117, 119, 168, 256n99; and women, 117, 119, 120–21, 168–69

intendants, 22, 45–46, 50, 88, 110, 124, 133; and *bailliages,* 153–57, 203; and collection of criminal statistics, 153–54, 156–57, 203; and court officers' expenses, 135–36, 153, 154–56; court officers' independence from, 14, 46, 125, 140–41, 153–54, 156–57, 219, 263n75; and cumulative offices, 70–71; and executioners, 204; and foreign exchange, 55; frequent turnover of, 70, 153; and judges' professionalism/integrity, 150–51, 157–58; and problems of famine/war, 58, 59; of Rouen, 24, 45–46, 55, 59, 60, 70, 115, 153–54, 177, 204; subdelegates of, 2, 48, 70–71, 154. *See also* Vaubourg, Jean-Baptiste Desmarets de

judges, local, 5–7, 10–15, 39, 47–94; autonomy/power of, 1–2, 10–15, 20–21, 26, 28, 96–97, 110–14; and bread/alcohol control, 54, 58; careers of, 136–38; culture of, 74, 77–78; corruption of, 82–94, 219; cumulative offices of, 2, 12, 48, 69–74, 83–85, 93, 130, 215, 216; as depicted in literature, 77–78, 188; education of, 67, 75–78; and equity, 91, 104–5; examination of, 57; fee/emolument regulations for, 149–50; as gentry, 2, 12, 35, 43–44, 58, 62, 213, 215; and governing class/networks, 68–69; and heredity, 63, 66, 130–32, 223; income/land acquisition of, 49–50, 79–82; and interaction with crown, 217, 218; kinship relations of, 65; laws/customs followed by, 1, 3, 10, 16–17, 20, 26, 91–92, 95–123; and legislative sovereignty, 3–5, 15–21;

and military mobilization, 6, 13, 51, 216; and moral/religious transgressions, 8–9, 51–52, 164, 173–74, 216–17; as nobility, 11, 36, 57, 63, 65–66, 67, 68–69, 71, 79, 82, 129–30, 138, 214; political power of, 217, 223, 224–28; as property owners, 56–57, 59, 62–63, 66–67, 130, 213–15; as protectors of private realm/property, 2–3, 8–10, 18–21, 75; and public/private dividing line, 2–3, 7, 18–21, 28, 96–97, 221, 225–28; public/private power of, 7, 225–28; and recruitment to Parlement, 14, 138–40; responsibilities of, 50–61; and shifts in provincial governance, 11–13; and size of judiciary, 5–6; social status of, 42–44, 56–57, 59, 61–67, 213–15; and sovereign judges, 129–41; as unable to move up to Parlement, 14, 124, 125, 130, 138, 227; venality of, 10–11, 27, 63, 66, 84, 87, 90, 91–93, 130–36, 213, 214, 222, 223. *See also* English and French judges, compared; justices of the peace

judges, local, responsibilities of, 50–61; alcohol control, 54; at bailiwick level, 53–57; church administration/finances, 52–53; at community level, 53; corporations, 56; court officers, 57; economic issues, 55, 58–59; enforcement of royal policies/edicts, 53, 60–61; grain and bread prices, 54; grain mills, 54–55; grain riots and famine, 58–59; infrastructure, 54; international issues, 61; land/property issues, 56–57, 59, 61; mercantile issues, 56; military mobilization, 6, 13, 51, 216; moral/religious transgressions, 8–9, 51–52, 164, 173–74, 216–17; at national level, 57–58; at parish level, 51–53; policing, 50–51, 53, 57, 216; poor relief, 52, 58, 59, 215; public safety, 54, 58; religious conformity, 60–61; taxation, 60; unwed mothers/paternity issues, 52; war issues, 59–60

judicial discretion, 160, 194, 195–96, 198–205; and equity, 97, 160, 174, 175–76; and lesser charges, 195, 199; and need to strike balance, 190–91, 199; and sentencing, 199. *See also* composition; restitution

justices of the peace (J. P.s), 74, 171–72, 214–17, 224; and arbitration, 181; as clergy, 216; as community leaders, 50; corruption of, 219; and criminal cases, 195, 216; cumulative offices of, 215–16; education of, 77; and famine prevention, 207; as gentry, 2, 43–44, 213, 215; and heredity, 132; and interaction with crown, 217, 218–19; jurisdiction/responsibilities of, 2, 48, 215–17; and moral/religious transgressions, 51–52, 216–17; and national legal culture, 217; notebooks of, 214, 222; and policing, 57, 216; political power of, 28, 49, 217–18, 223–24; and poor rates/relief, 52, 215, 217; as property owners, 62–63, 66–67, 213–15; public/private power of, 7; and rural inhabitants, 44–45; social status of, 2, 27, 48, 213–15; taxation powers of, 52, 215, 217; as volunteers, 27, 214. *See also* English and French judges, compared; judges, local

Justinian, and *Corpus iuris civilis,* 102, 103, 105–6

king's advocates (*avocats du roi*), 24, 39, 49; and costs of offices, 135–36; cumulative offices of, 74, 83, 86; fees/income of, 80, 133

king's commissioners, 45–46

king's prosecutors (*procureurs du roi*), 10, 24–25, 31, 35, 39, 53, 54, 133, 149, 153–54, 172, 190, 209, 224, 226; and costs of offices, 135–36; and criminal cases, 191, 199, 200; cumulative offices of, 68, 69, 73–74, 83; and elections to Estates General, 223

La Fontaine, Jean de, 77, 188

La Marinière, Balthasar (baron of Cany), 35, 42–43
landlords and tenants, 169–70; and rent collection, 161, 219
law, 10, 13, 95–123; as background of authors/dramatists, 20, 77–78; citizens' knowledge of, 185–88, 208–11; and crime, 193–96; and "empire of custom," 97–102; oral/written access to, 185–89; public and private, 96–97, 100; Roman, 102–6; royal, 106–10. *See also specific laws, customs, and codes*
law, citizens' experience with, 185–89; and access to, 185, 187–88; and knowledge of, 185–88, 208–11; and LeRouge case, 209–11
Law, John, 55, 175
lawyers, 95–97; corruption of, 82–94; cumulative offices of, 69–74; education of, 75–78, 97, 98; fraternity of, 97; Maribrasse family of, 68–69, 79, 190, 200–201, 211–12. *See also* barristers; councillors; fiscal prosecutors; king's advocates; king's prosecutors; solicitors
Le Blanc, Louis (intendant of Rouen), 55, 59, 70
legislative sovereignty, 15–21, 26, 103, 107–8; of bailiwicks, 3–5, 15–18; Bodin on, 5, 6, 16–19, 20, 204; and public/private dividing line, 2–3, 18–21, 221, 225–28
Le Grix, Jean, 83–84, 87, 90–91, 92
LeRouge, Marin, 203, 209–12
lesser charges, conviction on, 195, 199
L'Hôpital, Michel de, 10, 19, 92, 131
literacy, 185–88
literature, and depictions of courts/judges, 77–78, 188
litigants, 3–4, 6, 26, 30, 45, 159–89, 219–20; and arbitration, 181–84; and *clameur de haro,* 176–80, 191; commoners as, 160, 163, 164, 191–92; and criminal cases, 190–212; fees paid by, 11, 49, 79–80, 85, 87, 108, 142, 149, 222, 223; literacy/legal

knowledge of, 185–89, 208–11; nobility as, 51, 54–55, 56, 62, 144, 145, 147, 163, 164, 180; occupations of, 164–65; and order of community/state, 9, 160–61, 188–89, 208–9, 220; as poor, 161, 165; power of, 159–60; and property/family issues, 9–10, 162, 165–73; and witnesses, 205–9; women as, 52, 161, 162, 165–66, 209
local usage: in Normandy, 110–14; in pays de Caux, 119–23; as unwritten, 121. *See also* custom, local usage, and equity; customary laws; equity
Locke, John, 8, 47, 48, 204
Longueville, 37–38; *bailliage* of, 24, 32, 37–38, 41, 54, 56, 61, 70, 168, 172, 209, 226, 230, 238n93; high justice of, 37–38, 41, 66, 143, 145, 163, 165, 230, 238n93
Longueville, duchy of, 32, 36, 37–38, 42, 56, 66, 110–11, 120, 126, 203. *See also* Bourbon, Anne-Geneviève de
Louis XIV, 6, 12, 18, 23, 24, 51, 73, 177; and Edict of Fontainebleu, 60; on equity, 176; and lawyers' education, 76; on mercy, 193; and need for legal reform, 221; and Parlements, 21, 221; and royal municipal offices, 69, 84, 85
low and middling (*basses et moyennes*) justices, 25, 30, 33, 142, 229

magistrates. *See* judges, local
maréchaussées. See constabulary courts
Maribrasse family of lawyers: Nicolas, 68–69, 79; Robert, 68, 190, 200–201, 211–12
marine code (1681), 23
merchants' courts (*juridictions consulaires*), 25, 31, 56, 129, 171, 229
military mobilization (*ban/arrière-ban*), 6, 13, 51, 216
Molière, 77, 78
Montesquieu, Charles Louis de Secondat de, 1, 78, 102, 106
mort civile (civil death), 190, 201, 205, 212

Moulins, Ordinance of (1567), 13, 100
municipal offices: as created by royal
edict, 69, 84, 85; as cumulatively
held, 58, 69, 70, 71, 84–85, 93, 138,
243n4

Nantes, Edict of, 60, 108
nobility: as absentee landlords/gover-
nors, 12, 27, 35, 42–43, 58, 67, 215;
of the Caux, 34, 35, 36, 37, 42–43;
changing role of, 11–12, 42–44,
158; crimes involving, 196–97; and
inheritance/succession, 115–16, 119,
168; insolvencies among, 81–82;
judges as, 11, 36, 57, 63, 65–66, 67,
68–69, 71, 79, 82, 129–30, 138, 214;
and judicial reform, 13; as litigants,
51, 54–55, 56, 62, 144, 145, 147, 163,
164, 180; as parlementaires, 125; and
sovereign courts, 14; as supplanted
by gentry, 2, 12, 35, 42–44, 58, 62,
213, 215; women of, 117. *See also*
Longueville, duchy of
Norman Charter, 10, 17–18, 23, 99, 101,
177, 235n35
Normandy, 22–23; common courts of,
21–28; and community of inhabitants, 53; map of, xiii; taxation in,
125, 128; tax uprising in, 22–23. *See
also* Caux, pays de; *see also specific
towns*
Normandy, Custom of, 10, 13, 17, 26,
53, 95, 97–102, 112, 114–18; and
bailiwicks, 98, 101, 110–11, 124; and
business law, 172; and *clameur de
haro,* 176–80; conservatism of, 112;
creation of, 110–14; and definition
of property, 221; efficiency/neces-
sity of, 100–101; and equity, 175; and
inheritance/succession law, 115–17,
118, 170; and local usage, 110–14;
and matrimonial law, 115, 117–18;
printed copies of, 185, 187; and property issues, 113–18, 147; and royal
intervention attempts, 101
Normandy, Estates of, 13–14, 17; dissolution of, 14, 124–25, 128, 153, 227

Normandy, Parlement of, 23–24, 25, 31,
34; and Brienne edicts, 46, 141; and
chambre de l'édit, 60; as closed elite, 14,
124, 125, 130, 138, 227; and common
courts, 141–51; court system of, 127–
29, 229; and Custom of Normandy,
110–11; and fiscal courts, 128, 149;
and *gages* to court officers, 133, 136;
judges of, 130; and other royal courts,
24–25, 127–29, 137–38, 229; and
oversight of seigneurial courts, 149–
51; rebellion/revolt by, 22–23; and
recruitment of judges, 14, 138–40; and
relationship with seigneurial courts,
141–44; and removal of judges, 93;
and support of common courts, 14,
125, 140–41, 146–47, 149
Normandy, Parlement of, appeals to:
from arbitration, 183; of civil cases,
144–46, 147–49; from common
courts, 140, 144–46; of criminal
cases, 144–46, 153; by fiscal courts,
149; increased penalties awarded in,
146; judgments allowed in, 147–49;
judgments upheld in, 140, 144, 146;
of property cases, 147; from seigneurial courts, 33, 38, 144–49, 197; and
social rank of appellants, 145; of sorcery cases, 148–49

officers, court. *See* court officers; judges,
local; lawyers; *see also specific officers*
officialités. See ecclesiastical courts
order, as goal of judicial system, 4, 5, 6,
9, 15, 19, 21, 25, 34, 35, 38, 44, 91;
and arbitration, 183; and citizen litigants, 9, 160–61, 188–89, 208–9, 220;
and common courts' relationship
with crown, 146–48, 154, 156, 158,
227; and competing court jurisdictions, 157–58; and control of grain/
bread, 54, 58–59, 93–94; and criminal cases, 190–96, 199, 201–202,
207–9, 225; and criminal statistics,
156; and defense of customary laws,
112–13; and equity, 175–76; and role
of bailiwick, 130, 213, 225–26

ordinances (omnibus law codes), 13, 23, 99–100, 108–9. *See also* Civil Code; Criminal Code

ordinary courts (*tribunaux ordinaires*). *See* common courts

Ordonnance civile (Civil Code, 1667), 23, 107, 108, 176

Ordonnance criminelle (Criminal Code, 1670), 23, 107, 108, 142–43, 144, 156, 183, 195, 205

Orléans, Ordinance of (1561), 13, 66

Paris: Custom of, 101, 112; Parlement of, 20, 26, 34, 109, 120, 137, 271n120

Parlements, 21, 28, 221. *See also* Normandy, Parlement of, *and entry following*

paulette (fee for hereditary office), 66, 125, 130, 133, 135, 261n31

Phélypeaux, Louis, comte de Pontchartrain, 24

Plessis-Mornay, Philippe du, 20

poaching, 205–208

Pont-Audemer, 131, 156–57

Pont-Audemer, corruption scandal of, 81, 82–94, 178; aftermath of, 92–93; and bribery/extortion, 85–88, 198; and cumulative offices, 83–85, 93; custom, usage, and equity in, 91–92; and dueling, 91; inhabitants' view of, 88–89; and invention/sale of royal office, 90; judges'/officers' view of, 91–92; and poor, 88–89; and property schemes, 89–90; and threat of grain riot, 93–94; and venality, 84, 87, 90, 91–93

preciput (inheritance law concept), 115–16, 117, 119, 168, 256n99

presidial courts (*présidiaux*), 4, 5, 22, 24, 30, 63, 229; and *bailliages,* 151–53; of Rouen, 31. *See also* Caudebec-en-Caux

prévotés, 24, 30. See also *châtellenies; vicomtés*

private/civil law. *See* civil law

private realm: commonwealth protection of, 2–3, 8–10, 18–21; and customary law, 17; and public/private dividing line, 2–3, 7, 18–21, 28, 96–97, 221, 225–28

property, 2, 8–9; commonwealth protection of, 2–3, 8–9, 18; and corruption/abuse by court officers, 89–90; and criminal cases, 9, 192, 196–98, 225; and customary law, 17, 113–14, 166, 171; king's inability to control, 17, 19, 21, 226; as owned by judges, 56–57, 59, 62–63, 66–67, 130, 213–15; of women, 117–18, 120–22, 168–69

property and family litigation, 9–10, 162, 165–73; as appealed to Parlement, 147; and arbitration, 181; and curatorship/tutorship, 166, 167–68; and customary laws, 17, 166, 167–68, 170, 171; and inheritance/succession, 166–68, 170; landlord-tenant cases, 169–70; and women, 168–69. *See also* curatorship; inheritance/succession law; tutorship

public law (*droit public*), 3, 96; and minority of court cases, 3–4, 10, 106, 174–75; and private (civil) law, 96–97, 100. *See also* royal law

public realm (commonwealth), 2–3, 8–10, 18–21

punishment, 190–212; banishment, 144, 153, 183, 191, 201, 205, 212; galley service, 144, 148, 153, 201, 204–205, 211; *mort civile,* 190, 201, 205, 212; and sentencing, 160, 199. *See also* composition; corporal punishment; death penalty; incarceration; judicial discretion; restitution

Pussort, Henri, 23, 24, 107, 109, 184

Rabelais, François, 77–78

Racine, Jean, 77; *Les Plaideurs,* 29, 46, 77, 190

restitution, 160, 174, 175, 181, 191, 199, 200–201, 211

Richelieu, Armand du Plessis, Cardinal de, 10, 18, 63, 92–93, 139, 190

Roman law (*droit écrit*), 96, 101, 102–6, 107, 108, 117; as adapted in southern

France, 99, 100, 102, 103, 254n40; and equity, 104–5, 175; and idea of universal law code, 101, 106; and imperium, 103; in northern France, 103, 105–6; and property issues, 105; as *raison écrit*, 105–6; teaching of, 75, 76

Rouen, 12, 21, 30, 31, 32, 35, 40, 43, 55, 118, 119; and *clameur de haro*, 177, 179; and effects of war, 60; and grain shortages/riots, 58, 93–94, 207; intendants of, 24, 45–46, 55, 59, 60, 70, 115, 153–54, 177, 204; judges of, 130, 132, 137, 138, 140, 144; as judicial/administrative center, 31, 33, 107, 127–29; printers of, 185

Rouen, courts of, 22, 31, 127–29, 229; *bailliages,* 31, 70, 128, 152–53; consular, 31, 56, 129; financial, 31, 43, 65, 84, 127–29, 137–38; presidial, 31, 83, 128, 144, 152; and Parlement, 110–11, 127–29; tax and customs, 31, 129; *vicomtés,* 128; waters and forests, 126, 129. *See also* Normandy, Parlement of

Rousselet, Jean, 37, 52, 159, 161, 165, 166, 208

royal cases (*cas royaux*), 90, 106, 160, 174–75, 199, 251n189; and seigneurial courts, 25, 142, 143, 144, 154

royal law (*droit public*), 3, 15, 52, 95, 96, 106–10; attempted codification of, 107–8; and church issues, 106; and court officers, 106; creation of, 108–10; local acceptance of, 106–7; local reinterpretation of, 17, 79, 92, 97; and minority of court cases, 3–4, 10, 106, 174–75; and private (civil) law, 96–97, 100; types of, 108–9

Saint-Ouen, Tallebot, 62, 63, 65, 81

salt tax courts (*greniers à sel*), 2, 25, 31, 47, 106, 127, 128, 129, 229

seigneurial high justices (*hautes justices*), 2, 4, 12, 25–26, 229; and appeals to Parliament, 33, 38, 144–49; autonomy of, 141; and *bailliages,* 12, 157–58; and *cas royaux,* 25, 142, 143,

144, 154; education/age of, 150; fee/emolument regulations for, 149; jurisdictions of, 230; and low/middling justices, 142; Parlement's oversight of, 149–51; Parlement's support of, 140–41, 146–47, 149; and relationship with Parlement, 141–44

seigneurial low and middling justices (*basses et moyennes justices*), 25, 30, 33, 142, 229

sénéchaussées, 2, 4, 11, 24, 26, 30, 71; and appellate cases, 151; and bread/grain prices, 54; and endogamy, 132; and private criminal prosecution, 191; revenue from, 133; and royal court offices, 135–36; and sovereign courts, 141; as unit of justice/governance, 13

sentencing, 160, 193, 198–205

sergeants and sergeantries, 73, 82, 85, 90, 92

solicitors, 22, 39–40, 68, 72, 73, 74, 83, 112, 136, 181, 185, 186

sorcery cases, 148–49

sovereign courts, 10, 12, 30; and *bailliages,* 127–29. *See also* Chamber of Accounts; Court of Aids; Normandy, Parlement of; Table de Marbre

subdelegates (*subdélégués*), 2, 48, 70–71, 154

Table de Marbre, 127, 129, 229, 260n22, 260n23

taxation, 17, 44, 96, 216; exemptions from, 132; by intendants, 153; judges and, 60, 132; justices of the peace and, 52, 215, 217; and litigation threshold, 45; in Normandy, 125, 128; Norman uprising over, 22–23; royal courts overseeing, 128. *See also* salt tax courts

tax courts (*élections*), 2, 25, 31, 44, 47, 185, 229; and cumulative offices, 70, 71, 84, 217; establishment of, 125; and royal law, 106

Tocqueville, Alexis de, 28

Tournelle (criminal chamber of Parlement), 144–46, 204

tutorship (*tutelle*), 65, 79–80, 105, 145, 162, 166, 167, 181, 183

Valmont, 38; high justice of, 24, 32, 38, 41, 42, 65, 77, 150, 163, 173, 230
Vaubourg, Jean-Baptiste Desmarets de (intendant of Rouen), 45–46, 55, 60, 115, 177
venality, of court officers/judges, 10–11, 27, 130–36, 213, 214; and heredity, 66, 130–32, 223; officers' opposition to, 222–23; in Pont-Audemer, 84, 87, 90, 91–93; Richelieu on, 63, 92–93
vicomtés, 2, 24, 30, 128, 157. See also *châtellenies; prévotés*
Villecoq, Louis de, 86, 87, 89, 92

Villers-Cotterêts, Ordinance of (1539), 195
Vittefleur, 36; high justice of, 24, 32, 38, 41, 163, 230

wardship, 9, 11, 58, 59, 61, 167, 185–86, 225
waters and forests courts (*eaux et forêts*), 25, 125–26, 129, 229, 250n169, 260n24
witnessing, 4, 159, 191, 202, 205–209
women: arbitration by, 182, 183; crimes against, 197–98; and inheritance/ succession laws, 117, 119, 120–21, 168–69; literacy of, 186; as litigants, 52, 161, 162, 165–66, 209; property of, 117–18, 120–22, 168–69